MAKING MONEY

Emerging Frontiers in the Global Economy

Editor

J.P. Singh

Series Board

Arjun Appadurai
Manuel Castells
Tyler Cowen
Christina Davis
Judith Goldstein
Deirdre McCloskey

Series Titles

Sweet Talk: Paternalism and Collective Action in North-South Trade Relations
J.P. Singh
2016

Breaking the WTO: How Emerging Powers Disrupted the Neoliberal Project
Kristen Hopewell
2016

Intra-Industry Trade: Cooperation and Conflict in the Global Political Economy
Cameron G. Thies and Timothy M. Peterson
2015

MAKING MONEY

How Taiwanese Industrialists Embraced
the Global Economy

Gary G. Hamilton and Cheng-shu Kao

Stanford University Press   •   Stanford, California

Stanford University Press
Stanford, California

© 2018 by the Board of Trustees of the Leland Stanford Junior University. All rights reserved.

No part of this book may be reproduced or transmitted in any form or by any means, electronic or mechanical, including photocopying and recording, or in any information storage or retrieval system without the prior written permission of Stanford University Press.

Printed in the United States of America on acid-free, archival-quality paper

Library of Congress Cataloging-in-Publication Data

Names: Hamilton, Gary G., author. | Kao, Cheng-shu, author.
Title: Making money : how Taiwanese industrialists embraced the global economy / Gary G. Hamilton and Cheng-shu Kao.
Description: Stanford, California : Stanford University Press, 2017. | Series: Emerging frontiers in the global economy | Includes bibliographical references and index.
Identifiers: LCCN 2017015910 (print) | LCCN 2017020081 (ebook) | ISBN 9781503604452 | ISBN 9780804792196 (cloth : alk. paper) | ISBN 9781503604278 (pbk. : alk. paper)
Subjects: LCSH: Industries—Taiwan. | Industrialization—Taiwan. | Businesspeople—Taiwan. | Taiwan—Commerce. | Globalization—Economic aspects—Taiwan. | Taiwan—Economic conditions—1945– Classification: LCC HC430.5 (ebook) | LCC HC430.5 .H35 2017 (print) | DDC 338.8/8951249—dc23
LC record available at https://lccn.loc.gov/2017015910

*For our parents, who loved and supported us
and encouraged our collaboration
Glen and Ethel Hamilton
Kao Hsin and Zhong Pei-hua*

CONTENTS

Preface	ix
Acknowledgments	xiii
Introduction: Making Money	1

Part One   The Formation of a Demand-Responsive Economy, 1965–1985   21

1	The Sprouts of Capitalism: Bamboo in Springtime	25
2	America's Retail Revolution: The Hidden Dragon	41
3	Demand-Led Industrialization: Big Buyers in Taiwan	58
4	An Economic Way of Life: The Round Table	84
5	Big Business, Small Firm: Meat and Soup	100

Part Two   Toward a New Asian Economy, 1985–2016   127

6	The Search for a New Asian Economy: The Tipping Point	131
7	High Technology Industries in Taiwan: Turning on a Dime	153
8	Consolidation in China: A New Age of Mass Production	180
9	Consolidation in China: Computers and Smartphones	212
10	Greater Taiwan, Circa 2016: The End of an Era?	233
	Epilogue: The Future of Demand-Led Capitalism	247
	Notes	253
	Index	287

PREFACE

When the two of us first began our collaboration in the 1984–1985 academic year, we thought the secret of Taiwan's industrialization was there in front of us, waiting to be discovered. Hamilton, a sociologist then located at the University of California, Davis, had gone to Taiwan on a Fulbright fellowship to teach and do research at Tunghai University, located in Taichung City, the third largest urban area in Taiwan. A member of the sociology faculty at Tunghai University, Kao was then Chair of the Graduate Institute of Sociology. A PhD graduate from Ohio State University, Kao was a specialist in sociological theory. He had spent a year in the mid-1970s in Germany working on a book about Jürgen Habermas and Max Weber. Hamilton also specialized in sociological theory, had taught it for many years, and thought of himself as working in the Weberian tradition.

Our initial friendship was founded on a common appreciation of Max Weber. Weber came to early fame with his book *The Protestant Ethic and the "Spirit" of Capitalism* (1904–1905), whose core thesis linked the sectarian ethic of Protestantism to the so-called spirit of capitalism. Weber spent the last fifteen years of his life trying to provide a compelling, comparative framework that would assess the veracity of this early work. The approach and many of the concepts that Weber used to build this conceptual framework remain important even today, and the two of us recognized the significance of Weber's work in explaining Asian capitalism, even though we recognized that Weber made errors in his interpretation of China.[1]

By midyear of 1985, we had begun to meet every Friday afternoon for coffee to talk about how we might use Weber's approach to advance an understanding of the rapid capitalist expansion then occurring in Asia and particularly in Taiwan. Gradually, the focus of our discussion shifted from theory to the reality of Taiwan's situation and to the recognition that we needed more empirical knowledge about Taiwan before we could make pronouncements about Taiwan's economic transformation. As the academic year came to a close, we vowed to begin a collaborative study of Asian capitalism, and to do so, we worked out a division of labor. Kao and his students would investigate Taiwan's economy firsthand by means of interviews and fieldwork with businesspeople. Hamilton and his colleagues and students would add the comparative and historical framework that could be used to spell out the distinctive features of Taiwan's economy in the context of other Asian economies. Little did we realize at the time that we would be starting a collaboration that would still be going strong over thirty years later.

In the past thirty years, the research center that Kao started, the Institute of East Asian Societies and Economies, has conducted in-depth interviews with owners and managers of more than 800 firms; most of these interviews have been transcribed. Kao and his students have visited some of these owners and managers numerous times, usually at intervals of several years.[2] Every time Hamilton visited Taiwan, usually once or twice a year, it would be the occasion for additional interviews with some of the most revealing businesses. For his part, Hamilton and his colleagues at University of California, Davis, also started a research program, in the Institute of Government Affairs, to study the comparative and institutional features of Asian economies.[3]

Although this division of labor led to considerable research and many publications, we discovered that capitalism is an elusive topic. We learned that it is impossible to get capitalism to sit still long enough to locate a singular essence, its inner logic, or even to establish a set of fixed characteristics beyond the most general ones. Nonetheless, the results of this capitalist transformation are seen everywhere. The results are a part of most people's everyday lives. Because this transformation is so elusive and yet so pervasive, we have come to think about capitalism in light of the Chinese saying "Rising winds, surging clouds" (*feng qi yun yong*). These four characters in combination signify turbulent times, an age of transformation. A way to interpret this phrase is that we see the wind by watching the clouds; we know a forceful movement is at hand by watching its turbulent effects.

The spread of capitalism has transformed Asia, and this transformation is very much like the rising winds and the surging clouds. Like the rising winds, capitalism is an invisible force; it is everywhere and at the same time it is very difficult to see and to grasp. We all only know capitalism by watching the swirling clouds, by recognizing its effects on people and their daily lives, on nations and their social and political institutions, on the globe and its changing climate. These effects of capitalism, the swirling clouds, are not the same as capitalism itself. To equate the two would be a mistake, but not to see the wind as the source of the swirl is equally a mistake. We know they are related, the wind and the clouds, but how they are related is unclear and changeable; a great many factors combine, in different ways and at different times, to create what we observe as the weather. It is equally so with capitalist currents in the global economy.

ACKNOWLEDGMENTS

After working together and separately on this topic for over thirty years, we have many people to thank.

Kao is extremely grateful for the funding from the National Science Council of the Executive Yuan, now the Ministry of Science and Technology (MOST), after being reorganized in 2014. Over eight hundred interviews with industrialists could not have been carried out without the long-term grant from the council. Also, working with an excellent team consisting of more than a dozen doctoral and master's degree students was such a blessing. Among the industrialists interviewed, Kao is deeply indebted to Mr. Lai Chuan-lin, the founder of Thunder Tiger Corporation, Mr. Lin Chun-shan, Chairman of A-PRO Tech Co., Ltd., and Robert Tsai, CEO of The General Shoes Corporation. The repeated interviews with them have been not only informative but also inspiring, facilitating stronger links between the academic research and industrial developments. Kao also wants to thank the many anonymous interviewees, especially those from multiple industries, for their precious time and collaboration.

For Hamilton, this book is the fifth in a series that examines the economic organization of capitalism in East Asia. Because each book builds on the previous ones, Hamilton gratefully acknowledges research funding at various times from the National Science Foundation, the President's Office of the University of California through its funding of Pacific Rim grants, the Ford Foundation, and the Alfred P. Sloan Foundation, and further support in the form of two professorships from the Jackson School of International Studies at the University of Washington and a Visiting Research Professorship from the University of Hong Kong. During these years, he was also the recipient of a Guggenheim Fellowship and a fellowship from the Center for Advanced Study in the Behavioral Sciences. He wants to recognize and thank several colleagues at the University of California, Davis, with whom he worked closely, especially Nicole Woolsey Biggart, the late Marco Orrù, Jean Strafford, and Robert C. Feenstra.

Most importantly, the research collaboration with Feenstra provided both an underpinning in economic theory and an understanding of the link between the retail revolution in the United States and the industrialization of East Asia. At the University of Washington, his collaborations with Misha Petrovic and Solee Shin have proved invaluable. Hamilton also wishes to thank the many graduate student research assistants who contributed to the databases he used to contrast the ways East Asian economies are organized. These research assistants have been individually acknowledged in earlier books.

Collectively, we want to thank the Chiang Ching-Kuo Foundation for awarding us their organization's very first grant, which got our joint research under way, and also for a later grant that helped us complete this book. We are especially indebted to the Rockefeller Foundation for awarding us fellowships at the Bellagio Study Center in Bellagio, Italy, in 2000, where we first began working on this book. Little did we know then that it would take us this long to complete. We also want to thank the Whiteley Center at the University of Washington's Friday Harbor Laboratories for awards that allowed us to work together for two weeks during three different summers. As we entered the final years of this project, we were extremely grateful for the research assistance of Cindy Hsueh, without whose hard work this project might never have been completed. In Taiwan, we want to recognize the assistance of Day Chung-bor and Chou Hsin-yi, both on the staff at Feng Chia University, and the work and enthusiastic support of former graduate students at Tunghai University Chang Wei-an, Jai Ben-ray, Liu Wei-hsing, Ma Yen-bin, Tu I-ching, Wang Ming-hui, Lin Pao-an, Chang Chia-ming, Ho Tsai-man, Wu Tsung-shen, Chen Chieh-hsuan, Chen Chieh-ying, Chao Huei-ling, and Chen Min-lang and many of their fellow students. In the United States, we wish to thank SUP series editor J.P. Singh, who arranged for faculty and students at George Mason University to read an early draft of the manuscript, and Ming Wan, who was our chief discussant. In addition, we want to thank Timothy Sturgeon, Eric Thun, and Mark P. Dallas for reading and commenting on an earlier draft. We owe a particular debt of gratitude to Stephan Haggard, Ho-fung Hung, and an anonymous reviewer, all of whom gave us extremely helpful guidance that led to the finished book. Finally, we thank our in-house SUP editor, Margo Beth Fleming, who saw the promise in our project and encouraged us along the way to completion.

During the thirty-plus years of our collaboration and friendship, our families have given us much love and encouragement and have shared our work in so many ways. We thank them deeply. Kao especially wants to thank his sisters and Cheng Ying for their long-term support. For many years, Cheng Ying has taken care of Kao's students like their "mother." Hamilton thanks his wife, Eleanor Hamilton, for her love and insistence that the book be finished. Finally, we thank our parents. Kao expresses his deepest gratitude to his parents who gave him intellectual curiosity and a passion for life. Hamilton, too, is profoundly grateful to his parents for encouraging him to pursue a life far beyond the Kansas farm where he was raised. From the very moment that we began working together, both sets of parents cheered us on with their own enthusiasm about what we would eventually produce. It is to them that we have dedicated this book.

MAKING MONEY

INTRODUCTION

Making Money

It is difficult, when they are a world away from each other, to understand the connection between American consumers and Asian manufacturers. What most Americans hear is the unfortunate rhetoric about how some named Asian country is undermining the US economy, how that country is using its cheap labor, low-priced products, and manipulated exchange rates to capture if not destroy American jobs. That named country is currently China. Thirty years ago it was Japan. What Americans do not learn are the actual details of events and policies leading to the decline of American manufacturing jobs and to the huge and growing trade deficit that the United States has maintained with a series of Asian countries since the 1980s. Despite so much information being available in the internet age, Asia, to most Americans, remains a fog. Asian manufacturers are usually nameless and faceless, and Asian states are mysterious, portrayed as monolithic, often authoritarian, regimes that somehow conspire against the best interests of the United States.

Caricatures aside, the decline in American manufacturing is real enough, but the causes of that decline are less than obvious. As we will show in this book, the changes in both the US and Asian economies are parts of larger changes in the global economy. We push the beginnings of these changes to 1954, when in order to encourage investment in manufacturing, the US Congress passed tax-reform legislation allowing for accelerated depreciation on the construction of "property used in . . . trade or business," for "buildings as well as machines."[4] On the books for the next thirty years, this new tax law produced an unintended boom in the construction of shopping centers. When the legislation was passed, there were fewer than 500 shopping centers of all sizes in the entire United States, of which no more than two dozen qualified as major malls.[5] By 1970, after just fifteen years, the United States had over 10,000 shopping centers and hundreds of major malls. By that date, a revolution in retailing was well under way. This tax-reform bill yielded a result opposite to what Congress intended. It not only produced a precipitous and permanent decline in the contribution of manufacturing to the US economy but also kicked off the late twentieth-century transformation of the global economy. This transformation centered more on selling products than on manufacturing them, an approach to making money that we identify as *demand-led capitalism*. This book is about that transformation, a capitalist transformation that has engulfed the world since the end of World War II and that has left no part of the globe untouched.

We tell the story of this transformation from the perspective of one of the most important groups of capitalists leading the change: Taiwanese businessmen and businesswomen. Starting in the late 1960s, Taiwanese businesspeople developed enduring relationships with large American (and later European) retailers, such as Walmart and Target, and factory-less merchandisers, such as Nike and Apple. By the 1980s, the Taiwanese had become the most prominent contract manufacturers in Asia, and they remain so today, nearly forty years later.

Most writers explaining East Asian industrialization do not differentiate Taiwan from the four other Asian countries (Japan, South Korea, Hong Kong, and Singapore) that, by adopting an "export orientation," experienced rapid economic growth in the 1970s and 1980s. From afar, these economies may look similar, but up close, they are quite different.

Equally important, most of these writers confuse economic development and capitalism. *Economic development* is a term that applies to countries; theories of economic development put forward accepted wisdom about how specific national economies grow or fail to grow and by how much. *Capitalism* is a term that applies to the activities of firms methodically interacting in markets for the purpose of making money. Most writers give much of the credit for the success of post–World War II East Asian economies to the economic policies crafted by state planners, that is, to theories of economic development. Although national governments and national policies are important, what these writers miss are the connections among firms that rationalize, on a global scale, the methodical pursuit of making and selling products for a profit. This dimension incorporates a story about the growth of, and tremendous changes in, post–World War II capitalism.

During the past thirty years, we have interviewed over 800 owners and managers of Taiwanese firms in both Taiwan and China, and followed some of them as they, successfully or unsuccessfully, rode the waves of the global economy for the last three decades. We interviewed some of them as many as ten times during that period. These Taiwanese businessmen and businesswomen are among the unheralded leaders of the new global economy. One of the most important characteristics of the global economy today is the centrality of retailers and merchandisers that contract most or all of their manufacturing from firms they do not own. We use the term *big buyers* to identify these retailers and merchandisers,[6] and we call the firms where they place their orders *contract manufacturers*. For most of the last fifty years, Taiwanese businesspeople have been responsible for a sizable percentage of contract manufacturing worldwide. Just how large this percentage is varies over time, but we can get some sense of it by knowing that, in 2012, ten of the top twenty exporters from China were Taiwanese companies, all contract manufacturers.[7] Another indication of Taiwanese companies' global prominence is the 2013 *Manufacturing Market Insider*'s list of the world's top contract manufacturers, showing that Taiwanese businesspeople own three of the top five and four of the top ten companies on that list.[8] By contrast, Mainland Chinese own only one of the top ten firms on the list, Americans three firms, Canadians one, and Singaporeans one. Even the most prominent Taiwanese companies on these lists are little known outside Taiwan because they do not sell products under their own names, but rather are the main manufacturers for major US merchandisers of consumer electronics, such as Apple and Dell. Other major contract manufacturers in Taiwan produce a huge array of products, including most of the world's footwear and many of the private label goods sold by major American retailers, such as Walmart, Target, Costco, and Home Depot.

The "Made in China" label that identifies China as these products' country of origin does not tell us who owns the firms making those products, and many of those firms are Taiwanese owned. The largest Taiwanese contract manufacturers in China are only the tip of a huge iceberg. There are around one million Taiwanese living in China,[9] most of whom are associated with the 90,000 plus Taiwanese firms currently registered in China.[10] Most of these firms are engaged in contract manufacturing, either assembling the final product or making some component that will go into a final product or providing a service to firms making those products. If we add all the exports produced by Taiwanese firms in China to the exports from firms in Taiwan, then Taiwanese businesses make up the largest single group of contract manufacturers in the world.

Taiwan's entry into contract manufacturing began in the late 1960s. From the outset of industrialization in Taiwan until around 2000, the value of Taiwan's exports to the United States exceeded the value of South Korea's exports, even though South Korea has more than twice the population, geographical size, and gross national product (GNP).[11] By 2000, however, most of the largest Taiwanese exporters had moved some or all of their manufacturing operations to China, which allowed South Korean exporters, most of whom maintained their primary manufacturing plants in South Korea, to surpass Taiwan's level of exports. After the 1980s, however, the largest business groups in South Korea, namely Samsung, Hyundai, and Lucky-Goldstar (LG), moved away from contract manufacturing and began to build their own brand names, with products they designed, manufactured, and merchandised. Still, were we to total all the exports of Taiwanese-owned firms, regardless of their location, this sum would certainly exceed the total exports of Korean-owned firms, which include cars from Hyundai and smartphones from Samsung and LG.

Taiwan is a small and rather odd location for businesspeople who are so globally prominent. It is a mountainous island located off the southeastern coast of China. Its population is slightly over 23 million, smaller than New York State's, somewhat larger than Texas's, and a dwarf beside Mainland China's 1.3 billion. Since the 1970s, the global community of nations has not recognized Taiwan as an independent country. That was when nations around the world, including the United States, normalized their diplomatic relations with Mainland China. Because China claims Taiwan as one of its provinces, and because China requires all nations with which it has diplomatic relations not to recognize Taiwan as an independent state, Taiwan became a political isolate. Unlike the Vatican and Palestine, Taiwan has not been granted even the status of an observer state by the United Nations. Nonetheless, in all other respects, Taiwan is an independent country, and among the most economically advanced and politically progressive countries in Asia.

How did people from this small country become so integral to the global economy in the second half of the twentieth century? That is the question we answer in this book. An essential part of that answer is the story of global capitalism itself in the last sixty years, but another, no less important part of the answer includes some special characteristics that allowed Taiwanese businesspeople to create their own, very successful forms of contract manufacturing. These characteristics, mostly social in nature, shaped their fortuitous beginnings and gave them enough organizational flexibility to make money in a constantly changing global economy.

In the following pages, we introduce these characteristics with accounts of two businessmen who met very different fates in their quest to make money.

The Commanding General of Low-Flying Planes

The first time we met Lai Chuan-lin, in 1990, he told us, "I am the Commanding General of everything that flies in the United States under two hundred feet." He laughed when he said this, but he was also serious. We stood in the showroom of his company, Thunder Tiger, located in an industrial park near Taichung, in central Taiwan. Examining model after model of remote-controlled, propeller-driven airplanes, Mr. Lai explained, "With the exception of one Japanese company, I supply all of the major toy companies in the US with almost all of the remote-control planes they sell. The Japanese-made planes may be better built and more expensive than mine, but my company commands the market."

Since that first visit, we have returned to Thunder Tiger many times, and each time it seems like a new company. By the time of our second visit, in 1993, Lai had moved major portions of his manufacturing to Ningbo, in Mainland China, and in his factory in Taiwan, he had begun experimenting with new types of model airplanes. When we returned in 1994, he told us that the Mainland factory was turning out model airplanes at full capacity, and at his factory in Taiwan, he had developed a jet engine for his model planes and had begun making planes with these engines for specialized model airplane enthusiasts. By the 1996 visit, he had found the Mainland manufacturing site to be so well located, in terms of labor and resources, that he had established an industrial park and a property company so that he could attract other Taiwanese manufacturers to the same location.

When we returned to Thunder Tiger in 1997, Lai Chuan-lin was in China promoting the industrial park, but his wife, Hsieh Tsai-yun, showed us around. Hsieh, the general manager of Thunder Tiger, takes care of the books, supervises the labor, and is in full charge of the family firm when her husband is away, as he often was in those days when he was getting the Mainland businesses established. Showing us around the factory and introducing the new workers from Thailand to us by name, Hsieh told us that the jet engines did not have a ready market among hobbyists, and so they had stopped production of the jet engine targeted at that market. But, Hsieh explained, "The military is interested in our jet engines now." "The military?" we said. Quietly, she told us that it was not only the Taiwanese military, but also a foreign air force that had contacted the company, and that they wanted the engines and the remote-control devices for drones that could confuse heat-seeking missiles in times of military combat. To satisfy the military interest, they had upgraded the engine from a five-pound version to one weighing up to fifty pounds. These bigger engines carried sufficient thrust to power much larger aircraft than just toy airplanes. In the end, Lai signed an exclusive, well-compensated contract with Taiwan's military, but as we later learned, nothing substantial emerged from this contract, except the company's promise not to manufacture jet engines and control devices commercially until 2015.

When we returned to Thunder Tiger in 1999, Lai had started making component parts for full-sized airplanes. The composite material that he had used to make the jet engines turned out to be well suited for high-stress areas on many kinds of commercial and military airplanes. He had the manufacturing experience and the research and development skills to win bids for very lucrative orders. In passing, he also told us that he had been elected president of Taiwan's toy manufacturers' association. Smiling, he said, "I still make toys, but I am not sure my business should be classified that way. I am in the airplane business. I always have been."

By the time of our visit in the fall of 2005, Thunder Tiger had changed again. No longer was Lai just in the airplane business. His remote toy automobile operation had greatly expanded. He had gotten the contract to manufacture about 50 percent of all radio-controlled race cars sold by Associated Electrics, which at that time was the world's top brand in this niche market. Also a leading brand name in its own right, Thunder Tiger made radio-controlled cars not only under its own brand name but also for its chief competitor. In 2005, when the President of Associated Electrics retired, Lai and his wife bought Associated Electrics, to become the world's leading producer in both remote-controlled airplanes and remote-controlled cars. Also in 2005, Lai and his wife listed Thunder Tiger on Taiwan's stock exchange. The initial public offering was very well accepted, with the share price doubling in less than a year.

When we talked with Lai Chuan-lin in 2009, he was less upbeat. The United

States, like the rest of the world, was in a major recession. The market for remote-controlled planes and cars had bottomed, and so Thunder Tiger had cut its production. Lai was not sure what was going to happen to his toy business, but he told us, with a smile on his face, that he was developing a new product. About a year before this visit, Lai had had some dental work done, and in quizzing the dentist about the procedure, he had discovered not only that the dentist's drill operated at a relatively low RPM (revolutions per minute), but that the drill used air compression to run a small turbine that housed the drill bit. "That's my technology," he said. "My jet engines are little turbines and they can run at a higher RPM than those drills." And so, seeing an opportunity, Lai explored the market for dental drills, and discovered that the new German-made, high RPM drills were very expensive and that most dentists in Asia were still using slower drills. He believed he had the technology to make a better drill at a less expensive price than the German drill, and that there was a market for that drill in Asia. Lai took us to his R&D rooms and showed us his prototypes for the new drill. They met all his specifications. Lai told us he was going to start marketing the new dental drills in Mainland China sometime in the following year.

In a more recent interview, in 2014, Lai told us that the outdoor toy business was in serious decline. The recession was bad enough, he explained, but the real reason for the decline was that young people do not play outside anymore. "They have the Internet now. They play inside. The worldwide toy business has gone indoors." Although this business was down, there were still buyers for Thunder Tiger's line of remote-controlled vehicles, which now included trucks, helicopters, and boats in addition to planes and cars. The best market right now was not for toys, but for helicopter drones, with mounted remote-controlled cameras, that public agencies and private businesses could use to see, in real time, what was happening on the ground.

In the same interview, Mr. Lai told us that for some time Thunder Tiger had used small electric motors to power its remote-controlled vehicles; now he had perfected an automated process to make those motors in many different sizes. Low-cost and highly efficient consumers of battery power, these motors, he explained, were one of his core technologies. Holding one of the motors vertically in his hand, he said this is a helicopter. Turning it horizontally he said it is a car or a plane. And then turning it upside down, he smiled saying now it is a hedge trimmer. "A hedge trimmer?" we asked. "Yes," he replied, "we are in the final stages of developing a line of garden tools": hedge trimmers, leaf blowers, grass cutters, chain saws, and pole-mounted branch cutters. Touring the factory, we saw the R&D center where the garden tools were being developed, and saw a demonstration video comparing Thunder Tiger's chain saw with a Black and Decker gas-powered model. Thunder Tiger's chain saw cut the log in a fraction of the time required by the Black and Decker model. "Our chain saw," he explained, "turns at a much higher RPM than any other model on the market, and is more energy efficient too."

On the same factory tour, we saw that the entire first floor and part of the second was now given over to manufacturing high-speed dental drills. The previous time we had toured the Taiwan factory, in 2009, Lai's unbelievably immaculate factory was manufacturing engines for the remote-controlled vehicles. That production line had now moved to Lai's new one-million-square-foot factory in China, and his new company in Taiwan, TT Bio, was making dental equipment, specializing in the drills. The Asian market for these drills was good and growing, but the most important market for the drills was now in Europe, where they were selling well against the German competition. The drills nearly matched the quality of the German-made drills, but sold for a third of the cost. Watching the production process, we marveled at how this factory was making the minuscule components of the drill, most less than a quarter of an inch in size, with the delicate holes and curved shapes of a turbine. All these processes Lai had learned from making the engines for his remote-controlled toys, but now they were employed in making much smaller, almost microscopic machines, with much greater precision than the factory had achieved ever before. Lai told us that he plans to spin off TT Bio as a separately listed company on the Taiwan Stock Exchange, and maybe someday, he told us, he would spin off his electrical equipment business, too.

Building on his success year after year, Lai has become one of the best known and richest entrepreneurs of Taiwan's small and middle-sized firms. The circumstances of Lai's initial interest in airplanes did not portend the future he would have. Graduating only from primary school, Lai abandoned his education to make money to supplement his family's income. At that time, in the late 1960s, many Taiwanese children did likewise. He went to work for his older sister, who owned a small toy store. He liked the toy airplanes there, and he remembers this moment as the time when his interest in building toy planes began. Toys were then an important part of Taiwan's economy. In the early 1970s, small and medium-sized firms in Taiwan had just begun contract manufacturing, or OEM (original equipment manufacturing) as it is often called, and one of Taiwan's first major exports was toys, along with plastic flowers, shoes, garments, bicycles, and sporting goods. Using OEM contract manufacturing, foreign firms, overwhelmingly American at first, ordered products from Taiwanese firms, and then sold the finished products under their own brand names. After serving two years in Taiwan's army, as was then required of all Taiwanese males, Lai Chuan-lin began work in a factory manufacturing OEM toys. Ambitious and eager to be his own boss, Lai and his new wife decided to open their own manufacturing business. He had good relations with his former boss, who loaned him money to start his factory, and he obtained additional money from his family, including his sister. At first, he got most of his orders from other toy manufacturers, including his former employer, for whom he made parts of toys that his former employer's factory later assembled. But after attending trade fairs in Taipei, Lai decided to specialize in remote-controlled toys. He would be the main assembler and make some of the key parts himself, like the all-important engines, but he would also rely on a network of suppliers who could quickly supply his own factories with the needed and often changing parts required for the range of products he made.

Lai Chuan-lin's story is not unusual, although his degree of continuing success is exceptional. Many people have worked hard and worked smart for many years, and have reached a level of success and wealth not dreamed of during the generation in which they came of age. However, for every story of success, there are many stories of those who did not succeed, who almost succeeded, or who succeeded but then lost everything. Chairman T is an example of the latter group.

The Great King of Outdoor Furniture

Our first meeting with Chairman T, in 1988, was arranged by the father of one of Kao's students, who knew him well and was willing to act as a go-between. At the time, Chairman T was one of the wealthiest and most influential businessmen in the southern Taiwan. Although he was famous for his flamboyance, we were not prepared for what we would find when we drove into his factory and headquarters compound, nestled in a canyon ringed with giant bamboo and backed by Alishan, one of Taiwan's highest mountains. There, as we parked our very modest, locally made cars, we found ourselves surrounded by seven or eight luxury cars: a Rolls-Royce and several Mercedes-Benzes and BMWs. These cars were extremely rare in Taiwan at the time because the import duties on foreign cars made even modest imports prohibitively expensive. We soon found out that Mr. T collected expensive cars and loaned them out to local politicians, who would use them when they campaigned during Taiwan's relatively new democratic elections.

Chairman T was known locally as *Liangyi Dawang*, the great king of outdoor furniture. Indeed, he made a striking presence. Physically he was very large; his voice boomed, and there was no doubt about who was in charge. Socially, however, he was very warm, displaying what Chinese call *ren-ching* (human emotion, sincerity, or kindness). Chairman T was rich, made wealthy by supplying Walmart, Kmart, and J. C. Penney with most of their plastic outdoor furniture. Mr. T was, truly, the lawn chair king. At that first meeting, Chairman T told us of his self-made success. He began very poor, had only the equivalent of a junior high education, and told us that he had succeeded by the sheer force of his will. He was immensely proud of his automobile collection and regarded those cars as trophies of his success.

His wife, Mrs. T, joined the interview and actively participated throughout. We immediately saw that they were an entrepreneurial team. He had developed the manufacturing processes, ran the factory, and hobnobbed with local officials and the leading businessmen in the region. His wife, who had a BA degree in foreign languages, knew English, and was the person who negotiated with foreign buyers. She also controlled the account books and knew the business inside out. Soft-spoken and charming, she was the one who told us why their lawn chair furniture was the best there was. We left that first interview somewhat bewildered, unsure of exactly what we just witnessed, and with many questions still unanswered.

In less than a year, we had another chance to interview Chairman T. This time he took us through his factory. He explained step by step how he had been able to get the big contracts from Walmart and Kmart. Many other Taiwanese firms had the same general capabilities as Chairman T. His supplier for the raw plastics, Formosa Plastics, Taiwan's largest enterprise group in the 1980s and 1990s, would supply plastic at a reasonable cost to any business that could buy it. The big retailers would often provide samples of the products they wanted the Taiwanese to manufacture. Therefore, most businesspeople devoted few resources to research and development. Most of the design specifications were set by the buyers and not by the producers. Chairman T said his biggest advantage over his Taiwanese competitors was his ability to develop a one-step production process that gave him greater manufacturing efficiencies than other small and medium-sized firms working in plastics. With the support of a sizable number of firms that supplied him with many of the component parts, he was able, he explained, to manufacture, in his medium-sized factory with 300 workers, high-quality products for some of the world's largest retailers, and at the same time, he was able to "cost down" the per unit value for his buyers and still make a profit.

The subsequent interview with Chairman T, this time in 1990, found that he had expanded his ambitions. Next to his own home and factory, he had built a five-story showroom that doubled as a guesthouse for his customers, the big buyers coming from the United States. The bottom two floors displayed his collections of lawn furniture, attractively arranged for his buyers to see. The third floor was devoted to a giant dining room, with a round table that could seat twenty-four people, and an entertainment center complete with a karaoke bar. The top floors provided luxury accommodations for his buyers, king-sized beds, gold-plated fixtures in the bathrooms, and panoramic views of Chairman T's domain and the forest beyond.

This time, moreover, Chairman T had more on his mind than plastics. In 1990, Taiwan was in the midst of a speculative boom, soon to become a bust. The Taiwanese stock market had reached historic highs, over 14,000. The property market was just as hot, with some property values doubling and even tripling in a year's time. This speculative boom had been set off by the Plaza Accord, which had raised the value of Taiwan's currency in relation to the US dollar by about 40 percent in the five-year period after 1985. Although the cost of labor had gone up, the value of Taiwanese money and investments had gone up even more. The Taiwanese felt rich, and many had dreams of getting richer, including Chairman T. At this interview, Chairman T talked mostly about his investments in the stock market, in property, and in several businesses in Cambodia and other Southeast Asian countries. He was also deeply involved in local politics, even contemplating running for office himself. He felt he was on the verge of even greater wealth and success.

In the following few years, Kao and his team saw Chairman T occasionally. Chairman T did run for office and was narrowly elected, but his investments began to fail, one after another. After the revaluation, the relative rise in local wages pushed up the per unit cost of his products. But Chairman T elected not to move his factory to China, as others in the area had started to do, and as his big buyers had requested. That move would have taken him out of local politics, and besides, he had a lot of other promising investments. Losing his cost advantage, Chairman T gradually lost his lawn furniture contracts with his big buyers, first one leaving, then another, and soon he had no orders and no reason to run his factory. The contracts had gone to Chairman T's uncle and nephew, who were his local competitors in the region and who had moved their factory to China. In the same period, the property market bottomed, the stock market crashed, and Chairman T's overseas investments failed. Chairman T left politics under a cloud of corruption charges, lost his factory and buildings to debt collectors, and eventually left Taiwan. A few years later, we heard rumors that he was living in Mainland China, where he had invested in aquaculture, but we had no proof of that. Then in 2011, we read in the local Taiwanese papers that he had fallen from a boat and drowned in Tonlé Sap, the huge lake near Siem Reap in Cambodia, where he ran fish and shrimp farming businesses.

Explaining Asia's Great Transformation

In the nearly thirty years that we have been talking to Taiwan's businesspeople, we have heard many stories like the ones we heard from Lai Chuan-lin and Chairman T. Telling each person's story individually and chronologically, as we have just done here for two businessmen, we have reached the conclusion that these narratives share many common themes— establishing a family firm, receiving help from relatives and friends and even former bosses, searching for marketable products, getting contracts, developing a network of suppliers, expanding, upgrading, diversifying, and most of all, having the desire to make money and the rapidly changing means to do so. Although all the stories have similar features, each person's account of what he or she has done is also unique. Each account tells of fortuitous beginnings, of lucky and not so lucky breaks, and of distinctive personal styles. We have been listening to these accounts for many years now, but taking them as a whole, we realize that these stories do not reveal the secrets of Taiwan's remarkable economic transformation.

Though interesting, these narratives miss the global context in which Mr. Lai's and Chairman T's decisions were embedded. This context provides the frame that sheds light on the transformation that, in the course of a generation, changed Taiwan from a poor, agriculturally rooted society to one of the most advanced industrial economies in the world today. This transformation was not the one time only occurrence often referred to as a *take-off* transition from a traditional to an industrial economy. Instead, as has happened with all economies in today's world, Taiwan's integration into a global capitalist economy has created a continuing transformation, a constant process of changing and adjusting to economic and social forces that both emanate from within and come from outside the country. Each time we interview the owners of these firms, some for the first time and some repeatedly over the years, we encounter a new Taiwan, a new Asia, even a new global economy. These visits do not give clues about a singular explanation for Taiwan's remarkable changes. Rather, each interview provides a glimpse into a dynamic, ever-changing global capitalism, in which Taiwan and Taiwanese industrialists are now forever entrenched.

Between 1986 and 2016, as we have conducted hundreds of interviews with Taiwanese businesspeople and developed databases to systematically compare Taiwan's economy with the other capitalist economies of East Asia, we have become less and less confident that the prevailing interpretations of Asian capitalism are even remotely adequate to explain the complexity of the changes that have occurred just in the last three decades.[12] The principal explanation for Asian capitalism for much of this period has been the *developmental state theory*, which contends that a state's economic policy and an efficient bureaucratic corps of officials promoted and virtually created the Asian economies that we see today. At its base, developmental state theory is a political economy perspective on how economies develop country by country. As we show in this book, however, developmental state theories are not theories about capitalism, global or otherwise. They are theories of national development, country narratives stripped of their global context. Many economists have also offered somewhat different interpretations of economic development, stressing that macroeconomic incentives (e.g., financial institutions that promote open markets for capital and labor; transparent, profit-oriented firms; no unnatural barriers to trade; and so forth) created the conditions that led to rising levels of GNP or some other such indices. Some other scholars have emphasized the importance of Confucian culture in Asia—the importance of education, family, and obedience—in providing the human foundations for national development. And we ourselves, along with others, have offered sociological explanations that highlight the role of social institutions and business networks in Asia. To some extent, all these explanations for a country's economic development are correct and complementary, even though they represent alternative points of view that are rooted in different disciplinary perspectives.

The more interviews we did, the more we tried to make sense of what businesspeople told us, the more skeptical we grew about how useful any of the alternatives were in actually interpreting what was happening in Asia. During these years, we saw the conditions of Asian economies change, sometimes gradually and at other times suddenly and with great drama, as they did after the Plaza Accord, during the Asian financial crisis of 1997, and during China's extraordinary growth since the year 2000. Most of the standard explanations take the high road, the one that goes in the direction of parsimonious abstractions. Lofty sounding explanations that elevate messy governments to a singular entity called "the state," or that discover in all social relationships an essential cultural core, called *guanxi*, seemed to us to lack grounding in the lives of those who actually experienced the changes and by their actions created them.

Lai Chuan-lin did not talk much about the importance of the state, even though he did receive some support from Taiwan's government to continue his work on jet engines. But he had no help from any government official for years and years when he was first getting his company going. He could not even get a bank loan. Far from helping him, the government was in fact his biggest obstacle when he transferred his factory for remote-controlled airplanes to China, and like other Taiwanese businesspeople, he ended up evading government regulations to accomplish what he felt he needed to do. Equally, like all the other businesspeople we interviewed, Mr. Lai did not talk about Confucianism or *guanxi*, conceived abstractly, or macroeconomic incentives.

By contrast, Chairman T talked about the state all the time, but not in terms of incentives offered to him by government officials or even in terms of proposals for economic policy that the government might develop. Chairman T's business was well established and entirely export oriented, and separate from his interests in the state. Chairman T was himself a politician, caught up in the drama of local factions and the ins and outs of party elections. He was not concerned with bureaucratic policies directed toward business as much as he was concerned with the process of getting others and later himself elected to office. This concern was with raucous, rough-and-tumble politics, and with his role as a local boss. There was nothing efficient or rational or even bureaucratic about his engagement with the state.

Listening to the people we interviewed, we found it difficult to pull their words into the explanations offered by those scholars who had never talked to a Mr. Lai or a Chairman T, or any other businessperson for that matter. Most of these standard interpretations were removed from the people who actually ran the economy, made the decisions, propelled the continuing transformation, and got their hands dirty in the details of business. Lofty explanations require lofty heights, not necessarily ivory towers, but at least comfortable locations in capital cities and congenial conversations with key officials who are willing to take the credit for making crucial decisions that businesspeople like Mr. Lai and Chairman T have never heard of or that have any measurable influence on the decisions they make. These explanations are basically static, the unmoved causes that push development forward—the state, social institutions, such as the family, even global economic incentives.

The cause of our skepticism with the contending alternatives, including some of our own previous work, was the continual process of economic change that we witnessed. It became apparent, throughout the period of our collaboration, that there is nothing static about Asian economies. From the perspective of businesspeople, nothing stands still, no decision is final, everything is in flux, no one can rest. Trade statistics confirm what businesspeople tell us. Taiwan's economy has gone through tremendous changes in the past four decades, and not just Taiwan's. All the economies of Asia have changed, as have the economies of most countries in the world, and the past four decades have been the most extraordinary. Mainland China is today's best example of such a rapid transformation, but China's export economy is merely a continuation of a pattern that other East Asian countries started in previous decades.

On the surface, these Asian economies appear remarkably successful, but if we dig deeper, for every firm that is successful and profitable, we find many other firms that fail. During the years of its most rapid growth, Taiwan had tremendously high rates of firm failure, especially if one counts those firms that simply closed their doors without any of the legal formalities that accompany bankruptcies in the United States or Europe.[13] Taiwanese businesspeople recognize that success and failure are constant companions, that any firm, large or small, can be forced to close its doors. This awareness seems to be a primary motivation to keep moving forward, to keep just in front of the curve of advancing markets. None of the contending explanations does justice to the dynamism that pervades all the economies of Asia and the rest of the world as well.

Although we are skeptical about finding a single satisfactory explanation for Asian economic development, we have not abandoned the search for a way to account for what has happened and is continuing to happen in Asian economies. We realize that it is impossible to tell the story of Taiwan's growth without also incorporating the lives, the work, and the perspectives of those who make up these economies: the businesspeople who own and manage the firms that constitute the aggregated entity that we call the economy. On examination, many theories of Asian development are not interpretive explanations in the sense that Max Weber recommended, namely explanations that involve adopting the subjective understanding of the people who are economically engaged and who have a stake in what happens, which would include government officials as well as businesspeople. Many theories merely posit great forces that move societies and economies, without acknowledging that social and economic changes result from people's conscious decisions, although not always with the consequences that these people intended their actions to have. These are theories that have no hands or feet, or heads for that matter.

The Sociological Foundations of Making Money

Reflecting on years of research and interviews, we have found one constant in the midst of continuous change. Strange as it may seem, this constant helps to explain the change. Businesspeople have told us repeatedly that, in reference to their firms, they do what they have done in order to make money. As obvious and as trivial as it may seem, to the people we interviewed, making money is the single most important criterion by which they measure the success of their firms. Rational calculation in pursuit of making money is the central tenet of capitalism, and this tenet is the core principle of Taiwanese businesspeople. They have embraced capitalism.

In listening to their words, we have come to understand that this concern for making money is not a sign of greed. Most people talked, in a personal way, about the need to provide for their parents or their children, about their social responsibilities to friends and communities, and about the desire to achieve social status and a good reputation. But however practical or well-meaning their personal goals, they all see that the way to realize these goals, in the context of their businesses, is by making money. The measure of their firms, indeed the measure of their success in the business world, is whether they make money or not, and how much.

Making money is an important topic in Taiwan because everyone knows that making money is not an easy thing. Business failures are very common, part of a continuous cycle of opening and closing businesses in pursuit of finding a product that big buyers will purchase or of making a component or delivering a service needed by those making products. Whenever businesspeople meet, their conversation inevitably turns to where the profits are, to what products are hot, to who is doing what, and to how much they are making. Even in Chinese families, over the dinner table, there are ongoing and surprisingly sophisticated discussions on wealth and well-being and how to achieve them. It is no coincidence that the standard greeting at the time of the lunar New Year is *gungxifatsai*, "wishing you wealth."

In reflecting on what people tell us and on the decisions they make, it is clear that making money is a collective process fundamental to capitalist economic activities, and as a collective process, it is also a sociological phenomenon. At first glance, it would seem that making money is highly individualized, merely an outcome of individual calculation and execution. But however individualized the calculation, it is immediately obvious that all such calculations incorporate a social world, a world of many actors sharing the same social conventions and understandings. Howard Becker has shown that, even for such seemingly private tasks as composing and performing music, one must enter an established world of conventions about musical notations, set instruments on which to play the music, and existing venues where music can be publicly performed, ranging from local bars to concert halls, MTV, and now YouTube.[14] To step outside this established world of music means that one must reinvent much of what one normally takes for granted. Relatively simple tasks become onerously difficult. Inventing a new system of musical notation or creating new instruments becomes an obstacle and not a help to the goal of writing music for people to hear. Conformity and acceptance of the established world is so much easier and less risky, and leads to much greater success than any other course of action. Becker calls this acceptance of established conventions, the "power of inertia."

Even more than performing music, making money requires acquiescence to known worlds, worlds of products and worlds of business that allow few exceptions, that are relatively unbending, and that rest squarely on codes and conventions and often tacit knowledge that insiders share. These worlds of making money are the worlds of capitalism, worlds in which, as Weber put it, "capitalist acquisition is rationally pursued . . . [and] is oriented toward the *calculation of capital*."[15] As we will describe more fully in the following chapters, these worlds of making money have several dimensions that are worth outlining at the outset.

First, there is always the dimension of individual calculation. Our interviews show that businesspeople must necessarily and continuously strategize on how to position themselves and their firms relative to other people and other firms. Calculations never occur in an economic or social void, but rather always occur in a world that is already fully occupied, filled with previous calculations brought to fruition. That is what makes careful planning so important, and it is through calculation that one objectifies the known world and strategically enters into it as a known and knowledgeable actor.

Second, insofar as businesspeople incorporate others into their calculations, they must enter a world of common understandings, in regard to the roles people play, the rules they may (or may not) follow, and the relationships they establish and maintain. When businesspeople enter into such a shared universe of meaning, then making money becomes a collective endeavor. All tasks, from simple to complex ones, call on shared understandings of how to proceed.

Third, when people act on the basis of shared understandings, they objectify themselves in relation to others. They take on roles that others will recognize and act in ways that others can immediately grasp, and they expect others will relate to them in a similar manner: employer to employee, debtor to creditor, business colleague to business colleague. In submitting to the known world, the world in which they are known and knowledgeable, they also enter into a self-reinforcing reality, a constructed reality that is shared and is made real by consensual meanings and correctly interpreted actions. Such a reality is reflexive, because in the course of making money, one's own actions and those of others become objects on which calculations are based. Such a world is a constantly interpreted world, evaluated for its possibilities, assessed for its opportunities, manipulated for better control, and made the foundation for predictions. Individual calculation is only possible in a world where actions exist within a range of predictability and where risks can be assessed with some confidence that they can be avoided or reduced most of the time. The more businesspeople do business in a reflexive world the better they are at calculating, in relation to others, the chances of their own success in making money.

Fourth, in the business world, such a reflexive reality can be thought of as an economic way of life. Such a way of life is not closed, and in fact can be extraordinarily dynamic. But it is a consensual world, a world with considerable continuity. Like language, where communication is only possible with a common medium, business is accomplished only when common rules exist. Again like language, the medium of business cannot be switched at anyone's whim, but over time, and sometimes quickly so, the vocabulary of business changes. New practices come in at one end, and old practices die out at the other—all without centralized planning and intervention. Such a way of life is constantly being made and remade through people's actions, and is therefore constantly in motion, forever subject to change.

Drawing on our thirty years of study and reflection on this topic, we believe that in order to understand and interpret Taiwan's spectacular economic growth and its integration into the global economy, one needs to understand the intersubjective framework within which Taiwanese businesspeople exist, their economic ways of life. The economic ways of life that exist in Taiwan today were not there in their present forms even in the 1970s at the start of Taiwan's economic growth, but grew gradually as businesspeople and interested actors, including government officials, began collectively to draw out of a rich cultural repertoire the understandings and conventions that have allowed the Taiwanese to have the good fortune to be in the right place, at the right time, and with sufficient flexibility to propel themselves forward into the league of industrial economies through their ability to make money.

At the onset of industrialization, this economic way of life in Taiwan included some special characteristics that helped would-be entrepreneurs develop an approach to manufacturing that relied on cooperation among networks of independent businesspeople. As we describe more fully in Chapter 4, these cooperative networks drew directly on patterns of etiquette common among the Chinese, patterns experienced repeatedly in daily life and incorporated into, and systematized as, conventional ways of doing business in Taiwan. These are the patterns that led to Taiwan's great success in contract manufacturing.

These patterns, however, did not develop in isolation; they matured in the context of Taiwan's economic successes in the global economy. Taiwan's economic way of life, initially based on reciprocity among small firms, had an affinity with making certain types of products assembled from standardized components. This mode of manufacturing, known as *modularization*, has become a standard feature in the process of making most products that consumers buy today, everything from shoes and clothes to smartphones and automobiles. This book, therefore, is about how the global capitalist economy and Taiwanese industrialists, mutually influencing one another, grew up together.

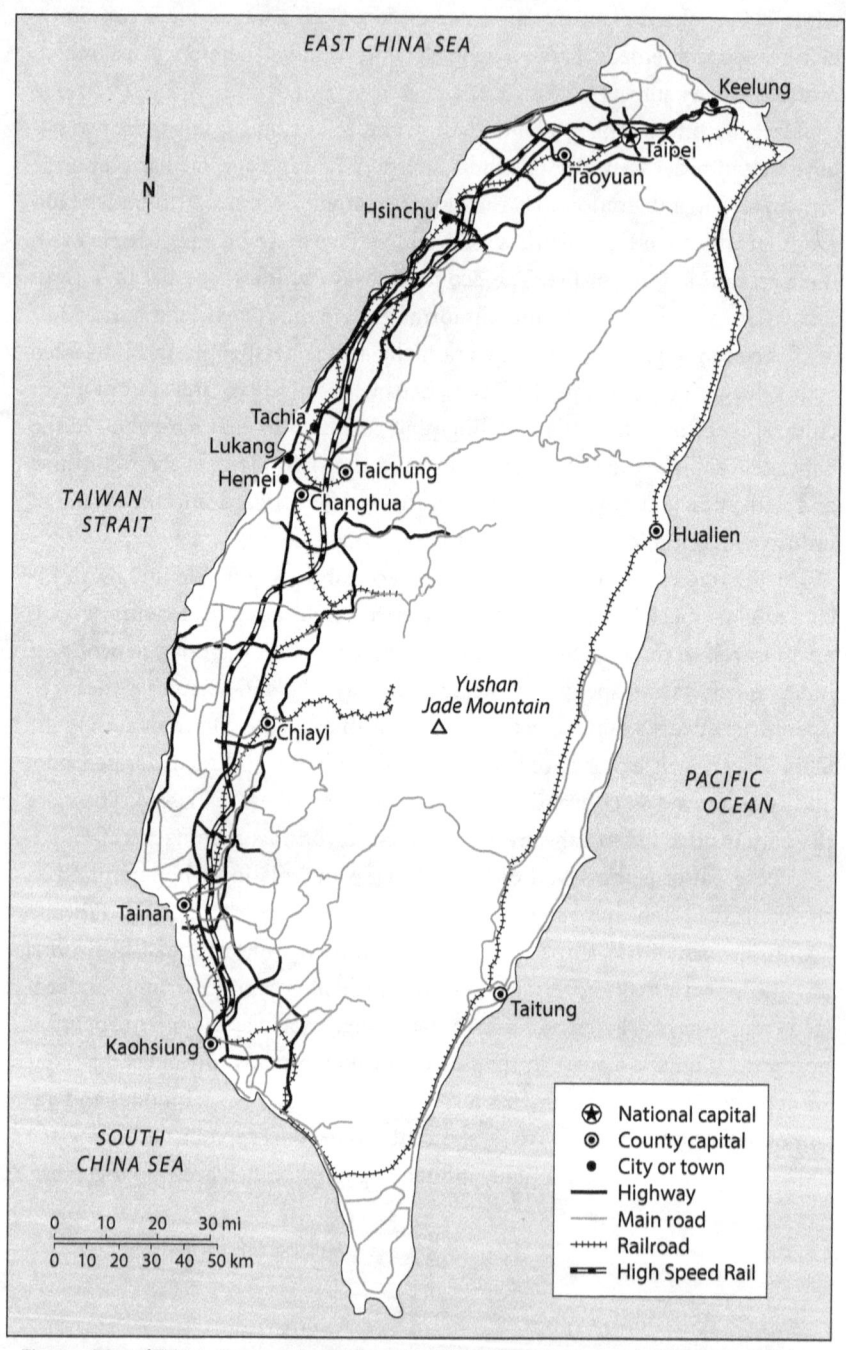

Figure 1. Map of Taiwan. Source: Adapted from the Political Map of Taiwan © Nations Online Project.

Part One
The Formation of a Demand-Responsive Economy, 1965–1985

This book is divided into two parts: Taiwan's economy and businesses before and after 1985. Why 1985? Before 1985, Taiwan's businesspeople were confined to Taiwan. Martial law was still in force, passports were hard to get, and capital could not readily move out of the country. By 1990, Taiwanese could move themselves and their capital around the world with relative ease. The period from 1985 to 1990 was a difficult transitional period for East Asian businesses in general, and for Taiwanese businesses in particular. This was the time when these inward-looking businesses, as well as the economies in which they were located, were forced to adjust to the consequences of the 1985 Plaza Accord.

Signed in the Plaza Hotel in New York City in September 1985, the Plaza Accord raised, over a five-year period, the value of East Asian currencies against the US dollar by around 40 percent. The increased wealth in global terms led in the short term to a speculative bubble that burst abruptly in the early 1990s, plunging Japan into a long recession and periods of deflation and stagnation that continue to this day, creating industrial empires in South Korea, and shifting many Taiwanese businesses to China. For us, 1985 marks the pivotal shift in East Asian economies from which, looking backward, we can trace the organization and dynamism of Asian economies today.

Thus 1985 is the watershed year with which we begin Part Two of this book. Before 1985, specializing in light, labor-intensive industries, Taiwan had already developed a complex but largely self-contained export-oriented industrial economy. This economy was certainly linked to global buyers, who ordered goods from Taiwan's factories, and to global (mainly Japanese) suppliers, who sold to the Taiwanese some of the components that went into the products they made. But it was between these opposite ends of the supply chain that Taiwan's economy realized its industrial potential internally and in historically significant ways. Taiwanese businesspeople led the development of contract manufacturing in Asia. They took the inspiration for this type of manufacturing from the Japanese, but drawing on their own patterns of social relationships, they extended and adapted it to Taiwan's small-firm economy—all before 1985. By that date, Taiwanese businesses had already become the leading suppliers of a vast range of goods ordered by American retailers and brand-name merchandisers. After 1985, Taiwanese contract manufacturers helped to accelerate the global retail revolution that has substantially changed the global economy in the twenty-first century.

As we will explain in Part One, 1965 is the year when the fortunes of East Asia in general and of Taiwan in particular turned toward rapid, export-oriented industrialization. Looking at Taiwan's economy in that year, however, one can find little evidence of a decisive shift. Agricultural production had been growing steadily from the late 1950s, and exports of agricultural products to Japan were substantial. The Taiwanese government had encouraged exports as a way to obtain foreign exchange revenues and thus to sustain the hope that Chiang Kai-shek and his one-party government, the Kuomintang, would once again become the legitimate government for all of China. Some nonagricultural exports had begun, but their numbers were limited. So in 1965 itself, there was no sign that within just a few years the Taiwanese economy, along with the economies of Japan, South Korea, and Hong Kong, would move into hypergrowth.

Part One of this book gives the background to the 1985 pivot point in Taiwan's economic history. Beginning with 1965, it describes Taiwan's transformation over the subsequent twenty years. Its chapters identify the varied threads that have been woven into the fabric of Taiwan's emergent economy, the shape and texture of which becomes clear only in the late 1970s and early 1980s. In Chapter 1, we give an overview of Taiwan's economy as it existed in this first watershed period. In Chapter 2, we switch to what was happening in the American economy in same period, and then we join what was happening on both sides of the Pacific Ocean together. In Chapter 3, using various examples from our interviews, we describe the process by which Taiwan's small-firm economy reorganized as a demand-responsive economy. In Chapter 4, we show how Taiwan's small and medium-sized firms cooperated with each other to form a socially meaningful approach to manufacturing products. Then in Chapter 5, we analyze the economy as a whole, as a going concern that incorporated large business groups and small and medium-sized firms in an increasingly integrated demand-responsive economy. To further illustrate the distinctive path collectively taken by Taiwanese industrialists, we contrast Taiwan's export economy with that of its East Asian neighbors, Japan and South Korea. Through this comparison, we show how Taiwanese manufacturers were the ones most able to form collaborations with American retailers and merchandisers, collaborations that progressively transformed the global economy.

1

THE SPROUTS OF CAPITALISM

Bamboo in Springtime

In 1965, Tah Hsin Plastics was the only factory that Kao remembers seeing between Taichung City and Tunghai University, a distance of about fifteen kilometers requiring a bus ride of about forty-five minutes. Swaths of sugar cane and rice filled the slopes of the basin in which Taichung City lies, a landscape broken then only by streams, dirt roads, and a few small villages. In that year, Kao started his freshman year at Tunghai University, a small liberal arts college of about 800 students at the time. The United Board for Christian Higher Education in China had founded Tunghai University in 1955, after having had to close all the Christian-sponsored universities in China. The board had located this new university on Dadu Shan, a substantial hill halfway between Taichung City and Wuchi, a small fishing village on the Taiwan Strait, directly across from Fujian Province on the Mainland, a hundred miles away. Wuchi would later become the site of the Port of Taichung Harbor, and between 1965 and the end of the century, almost all the land between Taichung City and Wuchi would be switched from agricultural to industrial and commercial use.

In 1965, getting to Tunghai University involved a journey. Kao had to take a train trip of nearly four hours from his home in Taipei to Taichung City. It would have taken much longer had he gone by bus on the two-lane paved road that linked Taichung City with Taipei to the north and Kaohsiung to the south. From the train station, he took a bus to the university. Along the two-lane road that he traveled, he would see many people on bicycles and numerous three-wheeled pedicabs, but very few cars. The familiar sights, apart from the lone plastics factory, were ponds filled with ducks being raised by local farmers, water buffalo pulling plows, and peddlers selling their wares along the side of the road.

Located midway between Taichung City and Tunghai University, Tah Hsin Plastics stood out like a sore thumb. The factory made rain gear: plastic boots and plastic coats. But by the time Tah Hsin Plastics sold the land on which its factory was located and moved its operation to China, almost no vacant land was left along the road between Taichung City and Tunghai University. In 1984, when Hamilton arrived in Taiwan, a few scattered plots remained, but by the end of the century they had all disappeared. Taichung Harbor Road, a broad avenue of six lanes lined by trees and with a chaotic mix of motorcycles, cars, trucks, and buses, had replaced the two-lane road.[1] The North-South Freeway now intersects the avenue just down the hill from the university. Taichung Harbor is the third largest container port in Taiwan. Although still well behind Taiwan's largest port, the Port of Kaohsiung, in size, Taichung Harbor is becoming increasingly important. For several decades, Taichung Harbor had been preparing for direct trade with the Mainland, which did not start until 2008. Before that time, it was a principal port for imports of grain and automobiles into Taiwan, but little else. Now Taichung Harbor is a principal port for exporting intermediate plastic and metal goods to China.[2] Along both sides of Taichung Harbor Road, from Taichung City to Tunghai University and beyond, high-rise buildings have sprung up—Japanese department stores, American banks, multistory apartment buildings, and many hotels.

Behind this high-rise facade are the factories that have made this area of Taiwan famous. As of 2011, the greater Taichung area contained 31,890 registered firms, employing over 400,000 employees. Most of these firms are small, with an average of 13 employees per firm.[3] The area is best known for metal working, machine tools, and electronics. In the early 1980s, the area was known as the "footwear kingdom" (*tzuhsieh wangguo*), so-called for being the center of athletic shoe production. The area was also known for making garments, furniture, and bicycles. The factory owners producing these latter products have mostly moved their facilities to China, but other factories producing other products have filled the void.

Somewhat down the hill from Tunghai University, but curving up behind it, like half a horseshoe, is Taichung Industrial Park. In this park, there are currently 1,037 registered enterprises, including Thunder Tiger. In 1984, the time when we started our collaboration, the industrial park was a recent creation, and there were few firms there, mostly just sugar cane fields. Thirty some years later, the fields are gone and the park is filled to capacity. A second industrial park, the Central Taiwan Science Park, was established in 2003 on the other side of Taichung Harbor Road from Tunghai University and the first industrial park. This park, too, is now full, with 210 registered enterprises. The local government has just opened two more parks. One is the Chungkang Export Processing Zone, located south of the first industrial park, in the area where the footwear and garment factories were once located. This park now has 71 registered enterprises. The second, the Taichung Precision Machinery Park, also adjacent to the first industrial park, now contains 138 registered firms. Both of these parks are still growing.

These four parks are filled with an amalgamation of different kinds of factories, producing such products as flat screen panels to be used in everything from TV sets and laptop monitors to cell phones; optical lenses for digital cameras; audio systems, plastic cases, and other devices for smartphones; and made-to-order semiconductor chips for locally made products. Although its factories are in Vietnam, Thailand, and mainly, China, Pou Chen, the world's leading manufacturer of footwear and one of Nike's chief supplier, has its world headquarters nearby. In the surrounding area, there are also networks of firms specializing in digitalized machine tools, the very machines that will make the products for the next wave of exports from Taiwan, China, and Vietnam.

Looking at the greater Taichung area today, it is hard, even for those who have lived their entire lives there, to remember what this area looked like in the 1960s. And it would have been impossible for those living in 1960s to have foreseen the transformation that would occur over the next fifty years.

The Watershed Year

The initial turning point in Taiwan's export-oriented industrialization occurs in 1965. The watershed event of that year occurred a thousand miles to the south of Taiwan, in the Gulf of Tonkin, where in May the US government accused a North Vietnamese ship of firing on an American ship, prompting then US President Lyndon Johnson to proclaim that the spread of communism had to be stopped lest all of Asia succumb, one country after other, in a so-called domino effect. This moment was the height of the Cold War, a struggle between the democratic imperialism of the United States, on the one hand, and the communist imperialism of the Soviet Union, on the other hand. Asia was the battleground, the hot war zone where the struggle between these two political systems broke into long open conflict.

Immediately after World War II, in 1948 and 1949, Chiang Kai-shek and his nationalist armies had been defeated by Chinese Communist forces, with little or no assistance from the Soviet Union. Chiang's army, leaders and members of the nationalist party (the Kuomintang, also known as the KMT), and government officials fled the Mainland for Taiwan. More than 2 million people landed in Taiwan in 1949, including Kao, at the age of one, along with his parents and siblings. Within one year after that, combat started in Korea, the location of another civil war that was captured by the currents of the Cold War; United Nations' forces intervened, squaring off against North Korean and Chinese Communist armies. The Korean armistice was signed in 1953. But armed conflict in East Asia began again in 1959, with the shelling of Kinmen Island, located only several thousand meters from the Mainland. Held by the nationalist army, Kinmen was Chiang Kai-shek's closest outpost to China, and in 1959, the object of constant bombardment from the Mainland.

Farther south, the Vietnamese Communist armies had defeated the French in 1953, and the country had been partitioned, like Korea, into a northern communist and a southern democratic government. Skirmishes and intrigue between North and South Vietnam had continued to occur, and by the early 1960s, the United States had begun to supply military assistance to the South Vietnamese. The Gulf of Tonkin incident was a continuation of the Cold War confrontation that had started immediately after World War II and, by the 1950s, seemed almost like a normal progression of events.

Responding to Lyndon Johnson's call to arms in 1965, US armed forces were mobilized, and local draft boards accelerated and widened the conscription of young men. Hamilton was among those drafted and among those who eventually went to Vietnam. In the same period, Kao, then a student at Tunghai University, remembers seeing flotillas of B-52s and C-130s flying in and out of Ching Chuan Kang Air Force Base, then the biggest base in Taiwan, and located just a few miles from Tunghai University. One of Kao's college friends was the son of the commanding general of the base, and gaining entrance when many could not, he watched the planes come and go at close hand, and occasionally saw the body bags of soldiers being carried from their deaths in Vietnam to their burial in the United States. He remembers seeing the C-130 transport airplanes loaded high with agricultural goods to feed the American forces in Vietnam. That was the first time he ever saw lettuce, a crop grown widely in Taiwan in the war years by local farmers, but not consumed there.

Although, in the midst of war and conflict, it is difficult to recognize transforming trends, it is now possible to look back and see the beginnings of a new era. The majority of Taiwan's farmers had only a few years earlier been peasants, tenant farmers plowing the fields of absentee landowners and living near subsistence, surrounded by poverty. Shortly after Chiang Kai-shek and the "Mainlanders" arrived in Taiwan, the Kuomintang government embarked on an ambitious land reform program. The two primary goals of land reform were to break up the power base of the big landowners and to return the soil to those who tilled it. These goals had both political and economic ends. On the political side, the forces of the Kuomintang would be unopposed by any other group. On the economic side, the Kuomintang wanted to enhance agricultural production, not so much to help the farmers as to ensure Taiwan's self-sufficiency in rice and other stables. The government needed agricultural self-sufficiency in order to outlast a blockade, should the Mainland forces attack, and they needed ample supplies of foodstuffs should they have the chance to *fangung dalu*, retake the Mainland. Through the 1950s and 1960s, Taiwan maintained one of the largest standing armies in Asia. Around 600,000 troops, one person out of every twenty, stood ready to attack or defend.

Fifteen years of waiting is a long time, but for the Mainland immigrants in Taiwan, the 1950s and early 1960s were essentially a hiatus, a period when many, including Kao's parents, kept their suitcases close at hand, ready for the return trip home. Taiwan was merely considered to be what Chiang Kai-shek called *fuxing jidi*, a base for launching a new attack, a base for regaining the Mainland, but not a place to build up in its own right.

Many scholars look back at this era and see the beginnings of government economic policies that will lead to industrialization. But in truth, government officials intended no such outcome. No one could foresee the future that came, and because no one could foresee it, they could not intentionally plan for it. Such retrospective explanations involve the presentist fallacy of hewing down all the forests of the past and leaving only those trees that remain standing today.[4] The presentist interpretation of Taiwan is like that, selecting only those elements from the past that verify the observer's understanding of the present, and ignoring everything else. But such interpretations miss the subjective understanding people had of their own lives and their own times, with the result that they make what are in reality unintended outcomes the purposeful goals of a select group of primary movers, who in retrospect are able to single out their important contributions.

The past is always intelligible in the present; the future never is. What is clear in Taiwan is that, at least up until 1965, the Kuomintang government was consciously preparing itself for a momentous confrontation that never came. An examination of government expenditures in 1965 shows that 57.5 percent (12,998 million New Taiwan dollars [NT$] out of 22,633 million NT$) of the total budget went to "administration and defense" and another 11.8 percent (2,681 million NT$) went to "education and culture." The budget for economic development in 1965 grew sharply from the previous year and accounted for 18.5 percent (4,194 million NT$) of the total budget, most of which went for building infrastructure, such as roads and railways. The government reported that most of the economic growth in that year came from "the boom in the construction industry."[5]

In 1965, the budget was still very much under the control of the KMT, and Chiang Kai-shek was still very much in charge. The government's legislative arm, the Legislative Yuan, containing ersatz representatives from every province in China, including Taiwan, was strictly a one-party affair. American aid, which had been important to Taiwan in the 1950s, stopped forever in July 1965. The budget itself was not particularly transparent, but it was self-evident that Taiwan's standing army of 600,000 troops received the lion's share because the government's first priority was national defense and, especially in the early 1960s, national offense. Only two years before, in September of 1963, Chiang Kai-shek had sent his son, and later successor, Chiang Ching-kuo, on his first visit to the United States, to meet with US President John F. Kennedy. Recent documents show that the major purpose of this visit was to ask for military assistance to retake Mainland China.[6] In the early 1960s, the Mainland was in the throes of a major drought, and the communist government's disastrous miscalculations during the Great Leap Forward, a period in which tens of millions of people died, resulted in a serious power struggle among contending factions in the Chinese Communist Party. Chiang Kai-shek thought that this moment presented a critical juncture at which to retake China, but President Kennedy rejected the plan, and without US support, Chiang Kai-shek could not go forward on his own. He had neither the offensive weapons nor enough fuel for such a venture. Nonetheless, the Taiwanese military stood ready to invade Mainland China should the opportunity arise, which it never did.

The focus on government control of the economy for noneconomic purposes is also evident in other government policies as well. Many restrictions were placed on both people and money. Imposed shortly after the infamous massacre of Taiwanese citizens by KMT forces on February 28, 1947, martial law remained in force throughout the island until 1987. Political opposition was forbidden and virtually nonexistent. The military was omnipresent. People's daily lives, particularly as they touched on the education of the young, were subject to many subtle and not-so-subtle restrictions and fabrications, including censorship of most information concerning the Mainland. The government also made foreign travel difficult. Passports were nearly impossible to obtain, and were a citizen lucky enough to obtain permission to travel abroad, then he or she had to get not only an exit permit but also a reentry permit.

Shortly after fleeing to Taiwan, the KMT government, mindful of the rampant inflation in China immediately after World War II, tightened its hold on Taiwan's money supply. The government controlled all aspects of foreign exchange, making it impossible for average Taiwanese to obtain foreign dollars in Taiwan or to take Taiwanese dollars out. Banking was completely nationalized. It was exceeding difficult for any private citizen to obtain any kind of loan, including investment capital, without explicit government permission. Because the banks would only consider collateral loans, most people in Taiwan were cut off from any way to raise money, except through their own private networks of family and friends. It is, therefore, clear that in 1965 the priority of the government was not industrial development or even the Taiwanese economy per se.

The Government's Need for More Money

Only in retrospect can we locate a development policy that dates from the late 1950s and early 1960s. A good example of the presentist fallacy at work is developmental state theorists' emphasis on export incentives.[7] Looking at South Korea, analysts have repeatedly stressed President Park Chung Hee's exhortations that Korean companies must export or be penalized.[8] In Taiwan, such exhortations came in the form of two directives: *The 19-point Economic and Financial Reform* of 1959 and *The Statute for Encouragement of Investment* of 1960. Both measures do, indeed, encourage exports, but they do so in the context of trying to limit imports, to control inflation, to stabilize domestic currency, and especially to address "the urgent need for foreign exchange."[9] In the 1960s, Taiwan needed to import many types of goods to support its military, as well as its civilian government. The outflow of domestic capital encouraged inflation and threatened the stability of the local economy. As a consequence, the KMT government promoted measures to systemize the procedures for exporting and developed tax reforms that created incentives for private businesses to export.[10]

The new directives did not, however, lead to a substantial jump in exports.[11] By 1965, aware that US aid was going to be cut off, and still in great need of foreign exchange, Chiang Kai-shek appointed Li Kuo-ting, a nonpartisan technocrat better known as K. T. Li, as Minister of Economic Affairs. K. T. Li, along with a group of fellow technocrats, was charged with finding ways to increase government revenues and foreign exchange. Li headed an effort to initiate export processing zones (EPZs). EPZs had been discussed for some time, but in 1965, with Li in charge, the idea was finally approved, and the first EPZ, on reclaimed land in Kaohsiung Harbor, opened for business in 1966.[12] The idea behind these zones was to establish for foreign firms a duty-free zone where capital, machinery, intermediate goods, and raw materials could come into Taiwan and where finished products would be exported, and to assemble these finished products with Taiwan's low-cost labor. Domestic sales of these same products, however, were forbidden. The first EPZ, planned for 120 firms, was filled to capacity in two years, and two additional zones were opened in 1971, but these two did not fill up right away because, by that time, the firms in the EPZs were no longer the key drivers of the Taiwanese economy.[13] By the early 1970s, domestic firms, many of which were quite modest in size and located outside the EPZs, had taken the driver's seat.

In their first few years, however, the EPZs provided both foreign exchange for Taiwan's government and, more importantly, a physical location where foreign businesspeople began to meet Taiwanese workers, some of whom would soon turn into entrepreneurs themselves. Many of the foreign firms that established factories in those early years remained significant forces in Taiwan's economy for many years to come, not because their own factories became so extensive, but rather because these firms began increasingly to source goods made in Taiwanese factories. Among these firms were RCA, Philips, Hitachi, and Sanyo.

The EPZs themselves, however, were never large contributors to government revenues and, outside of their initial years, never very important in Taiwan's industrialization. Most non-tax revenues that the KMT government received came from the Japanese enterprises that the government had taken over at the end of World War II. In 1965, government monopolies on liquor and tobacco, on sugar production, on electrical power, and on petroleum and gasoline refining and distribution, as well as on a handful of other enterprises, provided the government with over a quarter of its total revenues.[14] One of these additional enterprises was the government monopoly on manufacturing fertilizer. The government set the price for rice, as well as for many other basic commodities. The government then sold fertilizer to the rice farmers, or exchanged fertilizer for rice, for a profit, thereby generating revenues as well as building agricultural self-sufficiency. Without any natural resources, however, Taiwan had to purchase petroleum, as well as other basic chemicals, on the world market, and needed foreign exchange for that purpose, as well as for many others.

The major contributor to Taiwan's foreign exchange was foreign trade, and the main contributors to foreign trade before 1965 were Taiwan's farmers. After the land reforms that began in 1949, Taiwan's peasant tenants became landowning farmers. The government promoted growing rice and other staples in order to ensure adequate food supplies for its military and in case of a communist blockade. Therefore, the government required farmers in the prime rice-producing areas to grow rice, but they also allowed them to devote a portion of their holdings to whatever other crops they wanted to grow. Outside the rice growing areas, farmers had relatively freer choice about what they could grow. During the period of Japanese colonialism (1895–1945), Taiwan had served as a primary supplier of agricultural goods for Japan. Sugar production was especially important. In the 1950s, Japanese trading companies reestablished their merchant networks in Taiwan in order to resume agricultural exports to Japan. Over the course of the 1950s and early 1960s, Taiwan grew into one of the world's leading exporters of a range of agricultural goods, including canned mushrooms, canned asparagus, canned pineapple, processed sugar, and fresh bananas and other fruits and vegetables. Before 1965, most of these agricultural products were sent to Japan. After 1965, these foodstuffs began increasingly to be sent to Vietnam, this in addition to machinery, building materials, and cement.

The government encouraged Taiwan's farmers to become efficient producers. The government sold farmers their fertilizer, supplied farmers with improved strains of seeds that government scientists had helped develop, promoted agricultural cooperatives, and established agricultural experiment stations to teach farmers how best to grow a range of crops. The agricultural cooperatives (*nonghui*) doubled as savings banks from which farmers could borrow small amounts of money and into which they could put their savings. The government's avowed aim with these programs was to make Taiwan agriculturally self-sufficient, as well as to create a source of foreign exchange.

These government efforts invigorated an already economically active countryside. One aspect of the government's agricultural policy was to squeeze revenues out of agriculture by distorting the prices the government set for both fertilizer (artificially high) and rice (artificially low). This policy, however, encouraged farmers to grow other crops with higher returns.[15] Between 1952 and 1968, the value of Taiwan's agriculture grew at over 5 percent per year as farmers gradually shifted their production to cash crops for export.[16] In 1948, nearly 70 percent of the agricultural output consisted of rice and sweet potatoes; ten years later these two crops totaled 55 percent; by 1975, they were only 40 percent. From the mid-1950s to as late as 1965, agricultural products continued to provide well over 50 percent of Taiwan's exports.[17]

As agricultural exports grew, so, too, did the income of farmers. Yearly studies of farmers undertaken by Taiwan's provincial governments show that, in the 1960s, farmers' disposable income grew steadily, with cash and bank savings each up over 200 percent in the decade.[18] Also in the 1960s, loans to farmers through their credit associations and saving banks grew by over 400 percent.[19] In addition, surveys of farmers found that over 40 percent of all loans came through informal channels, such as rotating credit associations organized among family and friends, and these loans, too, showed a rapid increase in late 1960s and early 1970s.[20] A number of other studies also reveal that this rural income was evenly distributed throughout Taiwan's freeholding rural economy.[21] Everyone had more money, not a lot perhaps, but enough to invest in small ways. In retrospect, it is clear that the availability of this money in the countryside led directly into the next phase of Taiwan's economic growth, a phase that we describe in Chapter 3. Before this phase actually began, however, there was no way to have forecast the tremendous growth and economic transformation in rural society that was just around the corner. This transformation in the countryside was an unintentional consequence of government programs, an occurrence that largely happened out of sight of government officials and without their planning. In 1965, the changes that were occurring were nearly invisible, as if they were happening underground, spreading like bamboo in springtime, waiting to shoot forth at the right time. In 1965, there was simply no way for anyone to have predicted that the rural sector would serve as Taiwan's "foundation for development."[22]

State-Owned and State-Subsidized Businesses

In examining the foundations of Taiwan's industrialization, most developmental state theorists pay no attention to the importance of Taiwan's farmers. Instead, they exalt the role of the state-sponsored, private sector enterprises founded in the 1950s that would later play important roles in the 1970s, 1980s, and later. Most of these industries had their origins in the period of land reform in the early 1950s. In exchange for giving up any claim to their land, large landlords received shares of state-owned businesses that were going to be privatized: for instance, the state-owned cement industries. One of the largest landowning families before World War II, the Gu (Koo) lineage gained controlling shares in one of the two licensed cement companies, and used that company, Taiwan Cement Corporation, as a foundation for creating a business empire. This business group, the China Trust Group, emerged later in the 1970s and 1980s as one of the most important in Taiwan. The cement industry was carefully controlled through government licenses, and so the Gu family reaped huge profits throughout the period of industrialization, when almost all the cement used in Taiwan came from local sources. Using their profits, the Gu family started a range of other businesses, mainly financial and service firms. However, the Gu family is the exception and not the rule, because most of the landlord families were less successful in business and largely disappeared from public view.

Another, better known example is that of Wang Yung-ching, the founder of Formosa Plastics Group, which until the 1990s was the largest business group in Taiwan. Wang made a fortune in the lumber business immediately after World War II. Then, at the urging of a friend highly placed in the KMT government, Wang decided in 1954 to invest his own money to establish a factory to make plastics. For this endeavor, he received government permission as well as substantial funds from the United States Agency for International Development (USAID). Using these resources, he opened a factory that started by producing 100 tons of PVC per month. According to his biographer, Kuo Tai, Wang estimated PVC demand based on the ratio of Japanese PVC production to the total Japanese population. Because Taiwan's population was 10 percent of Japan's population, Wang calculated that the Taiwanese demand would be 10 percent of Japanese output, a figure in the neighborhood of 300 tons. Once the factory was completed in 1957, however, the actual demand turned out to be around 15 tons. According to Taniura's excellent study of Formosa Plastics, there was "absolutely no market [for PVC]." Most of the output "wound up in large piles sitting in the company's warehouses."[23]

Recognizing his miscalculation, Wang started a second firm, Nan Ya Plastics Corporation, to manufacture intermediate goods such as plastic film, plastic sheets, vinyl leather, and a cotton-like synthetic material used in weaving synthetic fibers, all products that other firms could make into finished consumer goods. When the demand picked up for these intermediate goods in the late 1960s, Wang Yung-ching expanded his production of these products. Still having excess inventory, Wang decided to establish two additional firms to manufacture such final products as plastic raingear, shower curtains, and diapers, all designed for the export market. By the early 1970s, however, Wang had closed these two factories. By this time, in the final goods sector, "the level of competition [had become] fiercer and fiercer and profit margins [had become] thinner and thinner."[24] The small firms had driven the big firms upstream to an economic location where they were unassailable by the fiercely competing downstream firms.

In Chapter 5, we will revisit these and other large business groups and explore the symbiotic relationship between them and the small and medium-sized firms that began to spring up everywhere in the 1970s. Regardless of how important some of these large business groups became later, in 1965, they were struggling, some unsuccessfully, to find a money-making niche in the Taiwanese economy.

Developmental state theorists also point to the importance of state-owned enterprises. Supposedly, the state owned the "commanding heights" and from there could control the rest of the economy.[25] By commanding heights, these theorists mean the upstream industries, such as China Steel. Most of these state-owned enterprises came into being as one of the Ten Great Construction Projects (*shi da jianshe*). These projects were mostly developed between 1972 and 1978, when Chiang Kai-shek's eldest son, Chiang Ching-kuo, was serving as Deputy Prime Minister, a position that everyone knew was one rung on a ladder that would reach to the presidency after his father died. As a part of his portfolio, Chiang Ching-kuo headed the Committee on Fiscal, Economic, and Financial Affairs in the executive branch of the government, and it was this committee that developed the plan for the Ten Great Construction Projects. The plan included major infrastructure projects, such as the North-South Freeway, a nuclear power plant, a world-class airport, and a high-speed railway, as well as several major state-owned import-substitution enterprises, such as a steel plant, a petrochemical refinery making intermediate products, and a major shipyard. Many of these projects had military implications. For instance, the plan allowed for portions of the North-South Freeway to be converted into airstrips, should war break out. However, most of the projects were responses to what was perceived as a growing demand for services and a modernized infrastructure. Moreover, most of these projects were not started until the mid-1970s, after industrialization in Taiwan was well under way and most were not finished until the late 1970s. (The freeways and airport were finished in 1978, the railway in 1979, Taichung Harbor in 1976, the China Steel facility in 1977, the China Shipyard in 1976, the petrochemical industrial zone in 1976, and the nuclear power plant in 1979.) Far from being the commanding heights, the state-owned enterprises obtained a reputation for being unprofitable, inefficient, and overly bureaucratic.

Hemei and the Rural Foundations of Taiwan's Industrialization

The Taiwanese economy in the 1960s was deceptively quiet. The most important occurrences went unobserved. Government officials did not see them, economists and developmental state theorists did not write about them, and so when it came time to account for Taiwan's sudden and spectacular economic growth, it seemed reasonable to all concerned to talk and write about those things that they did see. How else was one to explain Taiwan's extraordinary transformation? Largely because they were unplanned and were located well outside of Taiwan's few large cities, these important occurrences remain largely unknown even today. Such is the case for Hemei, a small township tucked in the northwest corner of Changhwa County, well away from the main north-south railways and roadways and about fifteen miles inland from the coast. For a twenty-year period, from 1965 to 1985, Hemei was the center of Taiwan's cotton textile industry.

In the early years of Taiwan's industrialization, the manufacture of textiles and garments was a leading industry. The writers mentioning textiles in those years typically emphasize the Shanghai manufacturers who moved to Taiwan in the early 1950s to escape the Communist Revolution, and who founded business groups that later became well known, such as the Chung-shin and Taiyuan groups, and the famous Tainan group (the Tainan *Bang*) that produced yarn and cloth made of synthetic fibers.[26] These groups received some government support in the 1950s and produced textiles for the domestic market, but very little of this production was exported until the 1960s. These same writers, however, missed the textile manufacturers in Hemei, manufacturers who never received government support, even though they produced more cotton textiles by the 1970s than all the government-supported firms combined.[27]

Manufacturers in the Hemei region began making cotton cloth earlier than any of the other textile manufacturers in Taiwan, during the Japanese colonial period. The Japanese colonial government prohibited any Taiwanese-owned industry that would compete with Japanese firms, and so no local textile industry emerged during the Japanese period except in the region of Hemei. Handicraft producers in Hemei obtained an exception from Japanese colonial officials because they specialized in producing very narrow width cotton cloth designed for women with bound feet. Using this exception, handicraft workers, mainly women using non-automated looms, produced a considerable quantity of cotton cloth even during the Japanese period. This cloth was ordered and distributed by Taiwanese merchants located in Taipei's old commercial and financial distinct, Di Hua Street.

After World War II, handicraft production in the area around Hemei grew slowly. Taipei merchants continued to order Hemei cotton cloth, but no longer in the narrow widths. According to our interviews from 1990, to respond to new orders in the 1950s, several Hemei family firms obtained simple weaving machines that could produce better quality and larger quantities of cotton cloth. These firms were run by households in which the male head of household doubled as a rice farmer. The owners, along with their wives, would employ a handful of local girls and a few skilled workers to supplement their own work. One such firm, Heshen Textile Company, was built behind the main house and was surrounded by rice fields.

The main difficulty Hemei factories had in the 1950s was obtaining raw cotton. Cotton cultivation requires a hot dry climate. Being wet and tropical, Taiwan is unsuited for growing cotton, and so all raw cotton had to be imported. In the 1950s, the KMT government restricted imports in order to preserve foreign exchange. Along with other textile factories in Taiwan, Hemei factory owners could obtain some raw cotton at a low cost from the government only when cotton had been received as part of aid packages of surplus agricultural products from the United States. Cotton production remained steady but at low levels throughout the 1950s.

All this changed in the late 1960s. Rather suddenly, the Taipei merchants began to place large orders, and Hemei manufacturers began to produce larger quantities of cotton fabrics, which in turn led to yet larger orders, which in turn led to yet more production. The organization of this process is crucial. The cotton merchants in Taipei were well connected with important buyers, particularly Japanese trading companies, which began to place larger orders of goods in the late 1960s. (We will discuss these intermediate buyers more fully in the next two chapters.) Already well known among Taipei merchants for their cotton fabrics, Hemei producers were not only the first in line when the new orders began to come in but they also received direct assistance from the Japanese. The Japanese trading companies supplied Hemei firms with newer textile machines and raw cotton, and according to one long-time Hemei resident, and general manager of Tayao, a mid-sized textile firm, "Since the Japanese sold these machines to us, they also had to teach us how to use them."

In Hemei, when the first firms receiving these orders could no longer fill them, they began organizing subcontracting networks among their extended families and friends. Using their savings, as well as modest investments from family and friends, most of which were generated from agriculture, the farmers/subcontractors would buy the necessary machinery and use family labor to start their own factories. "Soon," said Tayao's general manager, "one out of three housewives in Hemei had learned to run the machines." Also, workers in the early factories who were not members of the bosses' nuclear families would serve as apprentices for a couple of years and then set up their own small firms and join the networks of their former bosses. Therefore, as more orders came in, the networks continued to expand. Clusters of firms formed production networks that could quickly respond to whatever orders came in. These clusters were so successful in expanding their production capabilities that by the early 1970s, firms in the northern Taiwan area of Taiyuan were subcontracting some of their work to Hemei factories. By the 1980s, according to our interviews, there were about ten major clusters of firms, encompassing over 200 registered firms and many dozens of additional, unregistered small firms. The 1981 manufacturing census showed that about 50 percent of Taiwan's total production of cotton textiles came from the Hemei region at that time.[28] In the early 1960s, the cotton fabric being produced was mainly white cotton cloth, but by the late 1960s, as American buyers started to arrive in Taiwan, Hemei factories became Taiwan's leading producers of denim cloth for jeans.

Conclusion

Flying in a small plane over Hemei in the late 1960s, one would have seen a landscape that was to become commonplace throughout Taiwan in the next decade. Hemei was a precocious township, a forerunner in Taiwan's industrialization. The land reforms across Taiwan in the 1950s had returned the land to the tillers in units of about two to three acres for each household. From the air, these plots are easy to pick out because they are framed with the small canals essential for irrigating rice. By the late 1960s, the plots around Hemei were also dotted with small factories, often crude two- or three-story concrete blocks that seemed to spring out of the soil in the middle of rice fields. One here, one there, in field after field, some linked to a house, some a part of the house itself, some set off to the side of the property, strewn in random patterns that would make little sense from the air—these concrete bamboo shoots marked the springtime of Taiwan's industrialization.

The only way to understand these factories is to know that the peasants who turned into farmers who turned into factory owners, all in the same generation, had built these factories in the only place where they could afford to do so, on their own land, on the land they had obtained for free from the government. They had risked their own money and their own land on ventures that seemed almost too good to be true: a way to make money, a lot of money compared to what they could make farming. Families and friends pooled their resources, they pooled their labor, they shared the risks, and each success seemed to feed further successes.

The mid-1960s were the peak years of agricultural production in Taiwan. From then on, agricultural production began to decline in absolute terms as land and labor turned to manufacturing. In 1969, the manufacturing sector's total contribution to the economy exceeded that of the agricultural sector for the first time.[29] Also in 1969, as it grew into a major supplier to small and medium-sized firms, Wang Yung-ching's Formosa Plastics became the largest privately owned firm in Taiwan. The year before, in 1968, Chang Yung-fa, who was to become the founder and board chairman of the Evergreen Group and the owner of the largest container ship company in the world in 1985, had started his business with one fifteen-year-old bulkhead freighter, the *Ever Trust*. As the 1960s ended, nothing had quite come together yet. The Ten Great Construction Projects had not yet begun; the large firms were still trying to find their niches; most farmers had no other occupation; and the rice fields were devoted only to growing rice. But in a few places, like Hemei, the sprouts of capitalism had already begun to appear.

2

AMERICA'S RETAIL REVOLUTION

The Hidden Dragon

The changes that occurred in Hemei, as well as elsewhere in Taiwan, between 1965 and 1985 are directly linked to changes that occurred in the United States during the same period. With few exceptions, the many writers attempting to account for the industrialization that spread across Asia in these years completely miss the relevance of this connection. Instead, political economists explain the process of industrialization in Japan and in the Four Little Dragons (South Korea, Taiwan, Hong Kong, and Singapore) by concentrating on forces inside these countries, and mainly on state officials, state policy, state-business relationships, and more generally, a state-created environment that permitted firms to grow and compete internationally. Similarly, economists stress the factors of production and the incentives encouraging free trade: the reduction of tariff barriers, the openness of the financial system, and the rates for interest and exchange. They all emphasize that Asian industrialization was *export-led*, but then look inside the country to locate the reasons for the sudden explosion of products going abroad. They are biased toward the production end of the continuum between supply and demand, and accordingly, they develop supply-side narratives to account for industrialization. None of these writers, however, has gone outside Asia to explore exactly what export-led means. Our research clearly shows that export-led means *demand-led*.

The demand we are referring to here is not that generated by final consumers, but rather by the big buyers, by retailers and by factory-less brand-name merchandisers, such as Nike and Apple. These companies may design the products they sell, but they do not manufacture them. Instead, they "buy" the products from their suppliers, in anticipation of selling those products to their consumers. Big buyers create what we call *intermediate demand*, which is the sort of demand seldom considered when we think of the terms *supply* and *demand*. Instead, when we hear these terms, what we invariably think of are two abstract, amorphously oscillating aggregations—supply on the one side and demand on the other side—that somehow seek a stable middle ground, that point of equilibrium where they match.[1]

Supply and demand are, however, neither abstract nor amorphous terms to businesspeople who need to calculate, if they are factory owners, how much of any one product they should manufacture or, if they are retailers, how much of any one product they should stock. Here the equilibrium point between supply and demand is an actual target, made real by the calculations of both manufacturers and retailers. The goal of these businesspeople is to reduce, if not eliminate, the gap between what is manufactured and sold at a certain price (including profit) and what is bought by final consumers at that same price.

Here is where the big buyers come into the picture. They are willing to be *market makers*.[2] They are willing to assume the risk of, and pocket the profits from, closing the gap between the manufacturers and the final consumers of products. But these intermediaries—the retailers and merchandisers—are only willing fully to assume this risk when they can predict with some accuracy that they can actually close the gap. Historically, this ability to predict what final consumers would buy was an elusive goal, more of an art than a science, but in the second half of the twentieth century, the science overcame the art of selling. Or at least the big buyers believed it so, for they, using all available technologies, embarked on a campaign that made them the leaders of the new global economy. It is in this "spirit of capitalism" that the connection between the retail revolution in the United States and the industrialization of East Asia should be understood.

The First Phase of the Post–World War II Retail Revolution, 1955–1985

The transformation in post–World War II retailing started innocuously enough and with no Asian connection. As we noted in the introduction, in 1954, the US government unintentionally jump-started the boom in shopping center construction with legislation to reform taxes. One section of that bill allowed business owners to take accelerated depreciation on buildings and machines. Intended to encourage manufacturing, the legislation instead gave builders the added incentive they needed to construct shopping centers on the comparatively cheap land around the perimeters of cities.

At the time of the shopping center boom, retailing in the United States was already in the process of change, moving from independently owned and locally operated retailers to large chains and consolidated holdings.[3] In the 1950s and 1960s, large department stores, usually located in the downtown core of most cities of any size, dominated general retailing. The largest of these were chain stores. Targeting middle-class households, Sears and J. C. Penney were the two leading general retailers in the United States for most of the first three decades after World War II. Other downtown stores with famous names, such as Macy's, Bloomingdale's, Filene's, and I. Magnin, were in the largest cities; these were centrally owned by holding companies (Federated Department Stores was the owner of these four) but locally managed. These stores targeted customers more affluent than those targeted by Sears and J. C. Penney. Supermarket chains, such as Safeway and Kroger, expanded quickly in the post-war era and controlled the lion's share of food retailing. Therefore, when the shopping center boom started in the 1950s, it was merely an add-on to what was already a full and dynamic assortment of retail stores.[4]

The new shopping centers, however, soon became the leading edge of the changing retail landscape. Their numbers in the United States jumped quickly: 500 in 1955, 7600 in 1964, 10,000 in 1970, over 50,000 in 2006. After the 1980s, their numbers outside the United States grew even faster. The world's largest shopping malls are now in Asia and the Middle East. They have become a sign of modernity even in the most underdeveloped countries.[5]

The Feedback Loop Between Retailers and Their Customers

The United States, however, pioneered the shopping center movement. Two factors pushed this change in the first two decades after 1955. We think of these two factors as two spheres of activity, inhabited by two respective sets of actors performing those activities: America's middle-class population and the retailers who served that population's social needs. These sets of actors mutually influenced each other, forming a feedback loop. One level of activity consisted of America's broad, amorphous middle class changing in ways that produced an array of new identities, and the other level of activity occurred in the world of business, where the other set of actors, the retail entrepreneurs, responded to those new identities with goods and services that helped, when they were successful, to reinforce and enlarge those new identities with consumable markers of their customers' status, signifiers that in turn encouraged more people to adopt these identities as their own—a feedback loop.

First, on the societal level, post-war urban life was reshuffled in the late 1940s and 1950s. In the decade after the war, migrants from rural areas began to flood urban cores, which increased class and ethnic tensions.[6] In the same decade and for a variety of reasons, middle-class families began to move to the suburbs, where they bought homes of their own on large lots. With the Great Depression and the war now behind them, the broad middle class became more affluent and more willing to spend its money than ever before. Private ownership of automobiles jumped, and a new consumerism began to blossom, spurred in part by the introduction and widening popularity of television and other forms of entertainment. City and country roads were being widened and paved, and in 1956, the Eisenhower administration passed the National Interstate and Defense Highways Act, which quickly led to the construction of 41,000 miles of high-speed freeways. The availability of new cars and new roads led many to move to the new suburbs. There, the new shopping centers with plentiful free parking complemented the other changes and quickly attracted an ever-larger number of affluent customers. And as more customers came to shop at these centers, more and larger shopping centers were built, which attracted still more people to shop there.

These trends first began to accelerate in the 1960s. It was a decade of social movements. The civil rights movement that started in the 1950s peaked in the first half of the 1960s. It continued to push rural blacks into northern, southern, and western cities. The student movement, fed in part by greater government funding for higher education in response to Cold War competition with the Soviet Union, started in the early 1960s, but grew to an all-encompassing movement after the Vietnam War began, when the student movement and the antiwar movement became indistinguishable from one another. By the late 1960s, the feminist movement gained coherence and momentum, as many young and middle-aged women joined the labor force and called for equal rights and equal pay.

All these movements spawned a significant shift in lifestyles. What might be thought of as middle-class lifestyles grew increasingly differentiated into consuming subcultures. Children up to a certain age required products of a certain kind. Adolescents and young adults, especially, found themselves at the center of their own world, with music, dress, drink, and entertainment designed just for them. Ethnicity and race became markers for distinct ways of life. Sports enthusiasts began to band together around their selected activities. And working women learned about the clothes they needed; the labor-saving devices they should have for their households; and the quickly prepared, mostly pre-processed, and often frozen foods they should buy to feed themselves and their families.

The second level of changes driving the success of the new shopping centers occurred within the world of business, namely the new types of chain stores lining the malls: the discounters and the specialty retailers. These new stores were entrepreneurial responses to the changes in society, and by supplying goods and services to various subgroups, they helped in turn to define and further promote the ongoing social changes that were occurring.

In the 1930s, during the Great Depression, forty-four states, starting with California, passed fair trade laws that required retailers to sell products at prices no lower than those set by the manufacturers. In effect, these laws outlawed discount retailing. States passed these *price maintenance* laws to protect small, independent retailers from the chain stores (such as Sears and Montgomery Ward) that had begun to gain acceptance in the 1920s.[7] However, after World War II, the large retail chains began to undermine the intent of these laws by selling store brands of the most popular goods (e.g., J. C. Penny's underwear, Macy's shirts, and Sears's Kenmore washers and Craftsman tools) at lower prices than those offered by other retailers for comparable products. By the early 1960s, enforcement of fair trade laws had become increasingly cumbersome and ineffective. The courts in a number of states found fair trades laws unconstitutional; legislatures in other states simply repealed the laws. In 1975, with the Consumer Goods Pricing Act, the US Congress declared all fair trade laws invalid.[8]

These legal changes opened the way for discount retailers. Kmart, Walmart, Target, and Kohl's all began discount operations in the same year, 1962.[9] Like a succession of waves coming ashore, a progression of other discount chains soon followed.[10] These were mostly "category killers," chain stores that specialized in one sector of retailing and drove most of the locally owned competitors in that sector out of business. The first waves included the drug stores (CVS started discount retailing in 1963 and Rite Aid in 1968) and the apparel stores (The Limited in 1963, The Gap in 1969, and TJX in 1977). These were followed by the consumer electronics stores (Circuit City in 1968 and Best Buy in 1983), and then the hardware stores (Home Depot in 1978 and Lowes in 1992), the warehouse stores (Costco in 1983 and Sam's Club, which Walmart owns, in 1983), and the office supply stores (Staples in 1986 and Office Depot in 1986). By the late 1980s, nearly every consumer good had been put into one *product world* or another, worlds that retailers had defined by establishing large chain stores to specialize in those products. Besides the stores listed above, there were chains selling books (Borders, Barnes and Noble), lifestyle goods (Crate and Barrel; Pottery Barn; Bed, Bath, and Beyond), kitchenware (William Sonoma), and ever more finely differentiated apparel (Victoria's Secret, Forever 21). The main competition for all these specialty retailers was not the locally owned retailer, but rather the rapidly expanding general merchandise discount chains: Kmart, Walmart, and Target.

Ironically, the first discount stores initially relied on brand-name products that could then be discounted. The upmarket department stores already sold brand-name goods, but now the mix of different kinds of retailers, all ensconced in shopping centers and all requiring branded products of one kind or another, created an opportunity for entrepreneurs who could develop distinctive lines of goods. The most successful of those entrepreneurs who grasped this opportunity in the late 1960s and 1970s specialized in designing and merchandising products without owning factories to make those goods. Some companies, such as Mattel in toys, Eddie Bauer in clothes, and Schwinn in bicycles, switched from manufacturing to merchandising, but most companies never owned factories and relied on contract manufacturing from the first. Moreover, many of the products they sold were redesigned or were totally new products never manufactured in the United States.

The list of factory-less brand-name merchandisers is exceedingly long and illustrious. Nike is one of the best known examples of a company that relies exclusively on contract manufacturing, but most athletic shoes were made by contract manufacturers from the first. The list of apparel and accessory companies that began mass merchandising in the 1960s or later includes Calvin Klein, Christian Dior, Gucci, Guess, Hugo Boss, Laura Ashley, Liz Claiborne, Pierre Cardin, and Yves Saint Laurent, to name only a few of the best known. A few of these apparel merchandisers also started exclusive retail chains, including Ralph Lauren, Anne Klein, Coach, Eileen Fisher, and Benetton.

Consumer electronics is the most technologically advanced, complexly organized, and finely differentiated area of merchandising and contract manufacturing. We will describe the world of consumer electronics in Part Two, but it is worth noting that even before 1985, consumer electronics products were divided between those made and distributed by manufacturers under their own brand names and those designed and marketed by merchandisers but made by contract manufacturers.[11] Although brand-name manufacturers, such as Sony, often appeared more successful at the outset of a new product introduction, alliances between merchandisers, such as Apple, and contract manufacturers typically became more successful in the long run.[12]

The changes in American society and the changes in American retailing formed a mutually reinforcing cycle that drove the retail revolution forward. However, in the first decade of this cycle (1955–1965), Asia was not involved in these changes. Almost all of the consumer goods sold in the United States then, regardless of location, were manufactured in the United States. In 1965, imports accounted for less than 10 percent of total US consumption in all categories of consumer goods, and usually less than 5 percent.[13] The only category of imports above 10 percent of domestic consumption was steel, a primary product, mostly coming from Japan. But after 1965, US consumers began to buy imported goods, in all categories, at an ever increasing pace. At first, imports of consumer electronics led the way, with exports accounting for over 25 percent of total US consumption by 1970, but rising imports of shoes, toys, and an array of other categories of goods soon followed. By 1985, for many categories of goods, imports exceeded 50 percent of total consumption, with consumer electronics approaching 70 percent. Only heavy household appliances, like washers, dryers, and refrigerators, lagged behind.

Chain Store Logistics

The rapid spread of new shopping centers, with their array of anchor department stores, specialty retail chains, and supermarkets, created logistical nightmares for companies attempting to stock their shelves and to keep track of their inventories. The technological innovations that began to deal with these nightmares involved logistics, computerization, and product standardization.

Logistics

From the 1960s on, the new interstate highway system allowed trucking companies to supplant railroads as the primary distributors of goods. Before the 1960s, without access to high-speed roads, trucks were an expensive way to deliver goods over long distances. Trains were much more efficient and less expensive, but trucks were still needed for the short hauls to resupply individual stores. Chain stores relied on railways to deliver goods to regional centers where products could be offloaded and warehoused until individual stores ordered the items needed for their warehouses. However, after the freeways were built, it became possible to use large trucks as the main form of distribution.

The gradual shift from rail to truck was greatly enhanced by Malcom McLean, then the owner of a large trucking company, who conceived of and founded a containerized shipping company, Sea-Land, which made its first run from Newark, New Jersey, to Houston, Texas, on April 26, 1956. McLean's "fundamental insight" was his recognition that "the shipping industry's business was moving cargo, not sailing ships." With this insight, he "understood that reducing the cost of shipping goods required not just a metal box but an entire new way of handling freight. Every part of the system—ports, ships, cranes, storage facilities, trucks, trains, and the operations of the shippers themselves—would have to change."[14]

Within just a few years after his first run, several more US companies entered the business, most of them trying to adapt inexpensive, surplus World War II ships to carry containers. However, all the container shipping companies struggled financially because investors were reluctant to put their money on any one company in a business that appeared to be marginal to the US economy. Moreover, standardization was completely lacking. Each company had a different size and shape of container; the railways were uninterested in hauling the various types of containers, truck companies did not have the capital to outfit their trucks to haul containers, and ports did not have the necessary cranes and docks to load and unload containers to and from the ships.

All this changed in the years immediately after 1965, for two reasons. First, the involved parties became committed to standardization so that large capital investments in containerized shipping could begin. By 1966, "truckers, ship lines, railroads, container manufacturers, and governments reached compromises on issue after issue."[15] The standardized measure for container size came to rest on a measure called the *twenty-foot equivalent unit*, or TEU, but the actual sizes of the containers continued to vary in height and width, depending on the cargo.[16] Investments quickly poured in, and a second generation of much larger ships dedicated to containerized shipping was ordered and soon built.

Second, one of the reasons the different players were willing to compromise was that, starting in 1965, the Vietnam War had initiated a huge buildup of supplies needed to conduct a war in a faraway, undeveloped country, with few roads and no ports other than the one in downtown Saigon. A full-scale mobilization of US resources began, including the construction of a major deep water port at Cam Ranh Bay. The initial number of US soldiers that President Johnson ordered to Vietnam in 1965 was 65,000 (bringing the US troop level in that country to 184,000), but that number soon ballooned to over 536,000 US troops on the ground in 1968, not including the large numbers of civilian contractors and government personnel. At first the US military resisted standardized containerized shipping, but by the end of 1968, "the military... became its greatest advocate."[17] From that time forward, container ports quickly became the most important hubs for international shipping. The West Coast container ports in Los Angeles, Oakland, and Seattle became the most advanced container ports in the United States, and many countries around the world scrambled to construct their own container port facilities, including Japan, Korea, Hong Kong, Singapore, and also Taiwan, all of which started receiving containerized shipping by 1970, even before their own container ports were completed.

In 1968, Malcom McLean's Sea-Land was one of the successful bidders for military contracts to ship goods to Vietnam.[18] The containers going to Vietnam were packed full of supplies needed for the war, but they were empty on the return trip. The US military had paid the fare for the round trip, and so anything that Sea-Land could load into the containers and sell after the return trip to the United States represented pure profit for Sea-Land. The buildup in Vietnam included establishing post exchanges (known as PXs), where anyone with access, which included US soldiers and most US civilians, could buy cigarettes, alcohol, and an assortment of quasi-luxury goods. Among these goods were a large variety of items from Japan that the US troops could buy and then mail as gifts to family and friends back home. Hamilton remembers buying, in 1968, seven Seiko watches, two Akai tape decks, and a set of Noritake china. He also remembers that, at the time, the consensus among the US troops was that these goods from Japan were not only relatively inexpensive but also well designed and well made.

Along with the several million Americans serving in Vietnam at some point between 1965 and the war's end in 1975, Malcom McLean must have thought so too, because, as one Sea-Land executive recalled, "We've got these empty ships coming back from Vietnam.... So we have a meeting, and Malcom says, 'Anybody know anybody at Mitsui?'" In the 1960s and 1970s, Mitsui, the general trading company of the huge Mitsui business group, was the largest trading company in Japan. Two weeks after that meeting, a large delegation from

Mitsui arrived at Sea-Land's facilities in New Jersey and negotiated contracts to build a container terminal for Sea-Land in Japan, to handle trucking inside Japan, and to act as Sea-Land's in-country agent. That was in 1968. "Before September 1967," notes Marc Levinson, in *The Box*, his history of containerized shipping, there was "no commercial container service at all . . . on the Japan–West Coast route."[19] In 1968, seven different companies, including Sea-Land, were competing to ship containers of Japanese goods to the United States. For a year or so business was slow, but "the cargo would soon come, in a flood that no one could imagine."[20]

Computerization

In 1963, Sea-Land, with nearly 3000 employees, kept track of its incoming and outgoing containers on large magnetic boards; employees with long poles pushed numbered metal pieces around to show where the containers were located at any given time. Then, "at the end of each day, photos were taken of the board to provide a permanent record." That system of keeping track of Sea-Land's inventory ended in 1965, when computers arrived to do the job.[21]

Computers arrived in the headquarters of the major retailers at about the same time. These computers, however, were too primitive to keep track of the hundreds of thousands of individual stock items, called *stock keeping units* (SKUs), that most department stores carried. Macy's flagship store in Manhattan carried over 2 million separate SKUs.[22] The most computers could do in 1965 was to carry out relatively simple tasks, such as keeping track of personnel records and payrolls. In 1964, IBM had just introduced its 360 mainframe series, and in 1965, Digital Equipment Corporation sold the first commercially successful minicomputer for $18,000, which was one fifth the price of IBM's cheapest 360 mainframe. In 1968, Data General released its Nova computer, with 32 kilobytes of memory, for only $8,000; but it was only in the 1970s that computers became cheap enough and powerful enough for companies to begin routinely computerizing their inventories.[23] That was about the same time that Steve Wozniak and Steve Jobs founded Apple Computer (1976), and only slightly before IBM started selling personal computers (1981). From the mid-1970s on, as generation after generation of mainframe and minicomputers quickly gained computing and storage capacity, computerization began to reshape the way business was done, and perhaps no area of business was more transformed than retailing.

Product Standardization

The key to using computers to track inventories was to devise a simple way to identify products and then to enter that information into a computer. The first step in this direction occurred in 1969, when representatives from supermarket chains and food manufacturers met to work out a system of inventory codes that could be used to identify and keep track of distinct SKUs.[24] The large supermarket chains had a huge number of items they needed to stock, but very few ways to keep track of those items other than counting what was left on the shelf at the end of the day and restocking from the warehouse that they had to maintain. Prompted by IBM, the committee anticipated that computers would soon be powerful and cheap enough to allow some type of computerized inventory system to be established in each store. To develop this system, the supermarket chains and the food manufacturers established a nonprofit organization to register standardized identifications for all items being sold.[25] This identification system was to use what became known as universal product codes (UPCs). Food manufacturers agreed to place a UPC on each product they sold to supermarkets so that the stores could then keep track of the products they sold by means of a computerized cash register at the checkout counter. The next step was to figure out what the mark on the product should look like and how that mark should be read by a computer. By the time the first product, a pack of Wrigley's gum, was scanned in a supermarket near Columbus, Ohio, in 1974, IBM had solved these two problems with the invention of barcodes and scanning devices.

The originators of the UPC system thought that their innovation would be confined to food retailing, but with the rapid expansion in the use of ever more powerful computers, the *point-of-sales* (POS) inventory system quickly expanded beyond food retailing and beyond in-store inventories to become a way to keep track of inventories for entire firms. Executives from Walmart and Kmart were among the first to recognize that standardized product identification, logistics, and computerization could be tightly integrated at the corporate level to provide a foundation for cost reduction and store expansion. In 1981, Walmart required all its suppliers to use barcodes on all products shipped to Walmart. When some resisted Walmart's directive, Walmart communicated to all its suppliers: "If you don't draw the line, we do."[26]

Logistics, computerization, and product standardization provide the technological foundation for demand-led industrialization in East Asia. Without continuing innovations in each of these spheres, retailers could not have developed such a systematic, global approach to locating and buying goods that they would then sell to their customers. Also, until these three elements were sufficiently integrated, there were real limits to what and when retailers and brand-name merchandisers could profitably order from overseas factories. Initially, the transportation and coordination costs were simply too high and the quality too questionable for Asian-made goods to be sold to middle-class customers in the shopping centers spreading across the United States and, by the 1970s, across Western Europe, too.

The Rise of Global Orders

Only after 1965, only after the beginning of the huge supply buildup during the Vietnam War, do we see US retailers beginning to look to Asia as a place to source goods for their stores. That was the time when international containerized shipping reduced the costs of shipping goods enough to make low-cost Asian-made goods competitive with those made in the United States. From 1965 to 1975 is the crucial decade when the flood of goods would begin.

In the 1950s, trying to circumvent fair trade laws, Sears and J. C. Penney had already found contract manufacturers to make their private label products. Among these contract manufacturers were the "Big Five," the so-called founding fathers of apparel manufacturing: "Regal Accessories (Irving Alpert), Republic Cellini (Hy Katz), Marlene, Spartan Mayro, and CBS (Jack Clark)."[27] These manufacturers were all located in the southeastern part of the United States, where the wages were cheaper and the unions weaker than in the apparel manufacturing districts in the Northeast. By the 1960s, however, the wages in the South had risen enough that the Big Five had trouble supplying sufficient quantities of private label goods at the low prices that Sears and J. C. Penney required to undercut the brand-name manufacturers. The Big Five began to look for manufacturers that could fill their orders.

Sometime in the last half of the 1960s, the Big Five began to work "almost exclusively with the Japanese trading companies, especially Mitsui," to fill their orders.[28] As we will describe in Chapter 3, the Japanese trading companies found that labor costs were too high in Japan to make low-cost apparel there, but these companies began to develop suppliers for their orders in Hong Kong, Taiwan, and South Korea.

Hong Kong was the first location to develop high-volume textile and apparel exports to the United States and Europe. As the Chinese Communists' forces were nearing their victory in 1949, a number of Shanghainese textile factories owners moved their factories from the Mainland to nearby countries. The British colony of Hong Kong was the place where many of the most prominent textile industrialists settled;[29] a few also moved their factories to Taiwan. In the early 1950s, when China ended almost all cross-border trade, Hong Kong was set adrift, no longer the entrepôt connecting China with Southeast Asia and struggling to accommodate over a million refugees who had fled the Mainland after the Chinese Revolution. The Shanghai industrialists in Hong Kong preserved their factories, but lost their markets in China, and had to create new markets elsewhere, either that or go out of business. They survived by traveling to all their potential markets and showing samples of their cotton yarn and inexpensive cloth to potential customers.

With the assistance of Japanese trading companies, they gradually found their markets, initially in South Korea and Southeast Asia, but then increasingly in Great Britain and in the United States.[30] Hong Kong exported a substantial volume of goods before containerized shipping began, but these goods were overwhelmingly break-bulk items that could be shipped easily in the holds of large freighters.[31] The trade statistics tell the story. During the 1950s, exports remained low and steady; then in 1960, suddenly, the exports to the United States began to grow, nearly doubling by 1965, and then more than doubling again by 1970. By that time, less than 13 percent of Hong Kong's exports were going to Great Britain, and about 50 percent to the United States. In the late 1950s and early 1960s, the main exports were bulk items, yarn and woven cloth, but by the mid-1960s, a few of the larger textile mills and many small factories, using Hong Kong's cheap refugee labor, had started to turn the textiles into clothes. The main vertically integrated mills also began to diversify into weaving woolen and synthetic fabrics and making knit sweaters.

This was the time when American and British buyers who represented low-cost retail firms (e.g., five-and-dime stores, such as W. T. Grant) began to place their first orders in Hong Kong, and one of the earliest buyers to do so represented J. C. Nichols, the real estate developer of the first suburban mall in the United States, the Country Club Plaza in Kansas City.[32] In 1960, textiles and clothing accounted for 55 percent of Hong Kong's exports and, in 1966, 52 percent, but after that time, the share of textiles and clothing in the total exports began to decline as the share of toys, plastic flowers, wigs, and an array of other relatively inexpensive consumer items began to climb.

The same trajectory of US-bound exports occurs in Japan during the same years and in Taiwan and South Korea a few years later. Although the trajectories of export growth were the same, there were major differences among these countries in the exports themselves. Whereas Hong Kong manufacturers continued to specialize in clothing, among other goods, Japan by the late 1960s had begun exporting more expensive items, including many kinds of consumer electronics and automobiles. Taiwan's exports to the United States grew quickly after 1968, and South Korea's after 1970. At first, these exports were similar, but they soon began to diverge. Taiwan's small and medium-sized factories began to make limited amounts (i.e., batch orders) of an exceedingly large number of different kinds of consumer goods. By contrast, South Korea factories making export goods were much larger and were vertically integrated into Korea's largest business groups, called *chaebol*. These factories specialized in making large amounts of a limited number of mass-produced goods.

The Diversification of Intermediate Demand

In 1969, in its annual report, Kresge, whose flagship chain was Kmart, then the largest discount chain in the United States, reported that only 5 percent of the company's sales came from imported items, but the report went on to say that company would expand "imported merchandise from the Orient" in the "near future."[33] Kmart opened its buying office in Taiwan in 1971. By 1992, Kmart had placed over 500 million US$ worth of orders for goods from Taiwan alone, which accounted for 40 percent of all its imports.[34]

Kmart's pivot to East Asia was the same turn taken by most retailers and merchandisers in the same years. As transportation costs came down, retailers and brand-name merchandisers began to see countries in East Asia as places where they could cultivate suppliers for the goods they wanted to sell. At first, sourcing goods in Asia was a hit-or-miss proposition. There was a lot of confusion about where to go and from whom to order what was needed, but by the late 1970s, the landscape for suppliers was gradually becoming clear. The factories in different countries had different capabilities, and retailers and merchandisers began to know in which places to cultivate which kinds of supplier and what procedures to follow in each location. For instance, before 1990, Nike split its orders between South Korea and Taiwan. For the very large runs of the least expensive running shoes for men and boys, which were sold in such stores as Kmart and Walmart, Nike went to footwear manufacturers in Korea. For more limited runs of specialty athletic shoes and for more fashionable athletic shoes sold to women and girls, which were sold in stores specializing in sport shoes and in department stores, Nike went to footwear manufacturers in Taiwan.[35]

We do not need to rely on anecdotal evidence to see this divergence of orders. In 1972, the US customs began to itemize imports and exports down to a product-by-product level, using a 7-digit system of classification, the Tariff Schedule of the United States Annotated, known as the TSUSA classification. This system lasted until 1988, when it was replaced by the 10-digit Harmonized Tariff Schedule. Both systems of classification are "fine enough to distinguish between four-wheeled and three-wheeled baby carriages, or between bicycles having wheel sizes between 55 and 63.5 centimeters and those having wheel sizes 63.5 centimeters or larger, or between parts of almost any export product and the whole product itself."[36] Using the year-by-year customs reports that Robert Feenstra has compiled into a comprehensive database,[37] we can follow the diversification of Asian exports coming into the United States from 1972 to 2006.

This diversification does not show up in a more general classification at the three-digit level. For instance, in 1988, South Korea exported close to 450 million US$ worth of household appliances to the United States and Taiwan exported 180 million US$ worth of household appliances to the United States, but if we break this category down to a seven-digit level, we see that nearly 90 percent of Korea's exports in this category consisted of one set of items, microwave ovens in different sizes and shapes. Taiwan's exports in this category are extremely diverse, including vacuum cleaners, irons, hair dryers, curlers, coffee machines, and so forth. In the same year, in the general category of rubber and plastic products, Taiwan's exports totaled over 650 million US$ and Korea's over 250 million US$, but if we look inside that category, we find that Taiwan's exports were divided into toys, Christmas tree ornaments, religions articles, handles, knobs, lids, pipes, hoses, tubing, tableware, trays, cases, bags, and a whole array of household furnishing, including Chairman T's plastic outdoor furniture. By contrast, nearly 80 percent of South Korea's exports in this category are various types of automobile tires. For every major category of export, including shoes, we find the same result.[38] Different Asian countries began to specialize not just in different products, but also in different modes of production.

We can see the pattern emerge: big buyers gradually learned to go to those factories in those locations where they could obtain the best results. Because they selectively went to those locations to get those results, the factories there began to deliver them more efficiently and with greater quality; otherwise they would risk losing the next round of orders. As the efficiency and quality went up, differentially in each location, more buyers came to specific places to order specific goods. Economists call this escalating cycle of rationalized development *increasing returns*. One economist, W. Brian Arthur, who studies how to model increasing returns, stated: "The increasing-returns world in economics is a world where dynamics, not statics, are natural; a world of evolution rather than equilibrium; a world of probability and chance events. Above all it is a world of process and pattern change."[39]

Conclusion

Before 1985, Asian industrialization is best understood as a story of increasing returns that grew from intermediate demand, from the cultivation of suppliers in Taiwan, South Korea, Hong Kong, and Singapore. Most of us studying these East Asian economies in the 1980s failed to see the "hidden dragon," failed to see the direct connection between what was happening in Asia and the retail revolution that was happening in the United States at the same time. Looking only at Asia, we viewed this sudden, dramatic export-oriented growth as an unprecedented economic event, as an occurrence that had to be explained in terms of some equally extraordinary aspects of these developing Asian societies. Had we been able to link the developments in the United States with those in Asia, we would have been less inclined toward seeing local miracles and more inclined toward recognizing significant global changes in the organization of capitalism. But significant changes in large-scale phenomena can only be recognized in hindsight. Too much is happening at any one moment for analysts to distinguish those events that lead to decisive changes from those events that, although seemingly important at the moment, lead nowhere. With hindsight, however, we can make the connections that were obscure to most previous researchers.

Rather than a supply-side narrative, our account is more accurately seen as a narrative of how the Taiwanese economy became one of the first *demand-responsive economies*. Over the past forty years, the world's most globally engaged economies have become increasingly demand responsive. By demand-responsive economies, we mean that such economies are organized "backward," from demand to production, instead of "forward," from production to demand. In making this claim, we are arguing that global retailers and merchandisers, generating *intermediary demand* in anticipation of final demand, have superseded manufacturers as the driving force that organizes, directly through supply chain contracts and indirectly through their vast market power, whole sectors of the global economy.

The big buyers are not benign intermediaries. A few of the largest are big enough to influence the internal organization of entire economies, and collectively, they drive the global economy today. Big buyers not only create demand among final consumers but they also organize suppliers and develop supplier markets to fill that demand. Through using advanced consumer research, point-of-sales information, supply chain management, and sophisticated information technology, retailers and merchandisers have restructured the relationship between buyers and suppliers, making the latter a price-sensitive organizational extension of the former. These forged links between market-focused big buyers, on the one hand, and globally dispersed and largely faceless manufacturers, on the other hand, have had direct repercussions on economies around the world. In general, the more globally involved the capitalist economy, the more demand-responsive that economy has become.

That is the lesson we learn by looking at the global economy today, but equally we want to know how economies became demand responsive in the first place, and what, empirically and theoretically, does that mean? The following three chapters give an answer to these questions by showing how the Taiwanese economy developed in response to orders given by global retailers and brand-name merchandisers. The establishment of suppliers for these retailers in East Asia created what is known as the "Asian miracle," the extraordinarily rapid and ongoing industrialization that began in the late 1960s and that continues today, albeit in constantly changing configurations.

3

DEMAND-LED INDUSTRIALIZATION

Big Buyers in Taiwan

Sometimes, when riding the crest of an era, it seems as though the present wave will never end. Then, suddenly, one encounters an unexpected current that changes everything. Looking back at the Vietnam War, it is obvious to us that this period marked a turning point for the people of Taiwan, a turning point that was not just economic but rather was, in the first instance, political.

At the beginning of the Vietnam conflict in 1965, Taiwan's political future seemed tied to that of the United States. Taiwan, the island fortress holding communism at bay, was America's true friend, and its government was the only acknowledged government of China. The Vietnam War seemed to be merely a continuation of the conflicts that had sprung up on the periphery of the Cold War. Only six years later, however, this political illusion shattered. On October 25, 1971, as a consequence of a shift in power within the General Assembly, the United Nations stripped Taiwan's government of its "permanent" seat in the Security Council and removed it from the General Assembly. The People's Republic of China was, all of a sudden, the only government with a legitimate claim on China. Then in February of 1972, trying to outflank the North Vietnamese, Richard Nixon, then the President of the United States, traveled to China, shook hands with Mao Zedong, the archrival of Chiang Kai-shek, and initiated diplomatic relations with the Mainland. With that handshake, Taiwan forever lost its claim on China. The People's Republic of China proclaimed Taiwan to be merely a renegade province, and quickly, nation after nation terminated diplomatic relations with Taiwan in favor of the People's Republic of

China. Finally, in 1978, the United States broke off diplomatic relations with Taiwan as well. In a world of independent nations, Taiwan became an isolate, neither independent nor subject to another country's authority. The government struggled mightily against the tide, and the Taiwanese people felt stung by the rejection of the world community, but to no avail.

While Taiwan experienced one diplomatic setback after another, the economy had begun to change. Imperceptible at first, by the early 1970s economic growth was nonetheless apparent to those close to the action. When Kao returned for a year in 1973, to teach at Tunghai University, the Taichung area seemed little changed from his undergraduate years there. The same two-lane road, and the same rice and sugar cane fields, lay undisturbed. State policies were also largely unaltered from the previous decades, held intact by the Chiang Kai-shek's fading dream of reuniting with the Mainland. That dream officially ended in 1975, when, at the age of eighty-seven, Chiang Kai-shek died. After a short interregnum, Chiang Kai-shek's son, Chiang Ching-kuo, assumed the presidency in 1978, and began to promote pragmatic economic and political policies.[1] These policies turned the government's focus from a reengagement with the Mainland toward building Taiwan internally.

When Kao, PhD degree in hand, once again returned to Tunghai University in 1978, the changes in Taiwan were pronounced. The government's Ten Great Construction Projects had been started and some even completed. The airplane on his return flight landed in the new international airport located in Taoyuan, about forty-five kilometers outside Taipei. The expressway between Kaohsiung and Taipei was under construction, and the link between Taipei and Taichung had recently opened. Not owning a car, he traveled to Taichung by train, but more quickly this time, for new and faster electric trains had replaced the old coal-fired locomotives from the past.

Kao remembers, however, that the biggest change was the road to Tunghai University. Taichung Harbor had been built, and the new road connecting Taichung to the harbor was under construction. In place of the two-lane road, there was now a six-lane highway, and although rice and sugar cane fields still lined both sides of the road, there were also many new buildings. Strategically located near the expressway, a new hotel had been built, the National Hotel. Eating in the hotel restaurant for the first time, then one of the best restaurants in the Taichung area, Kao was struck by the fact that almost every table in the restaurant was occupied by foreign buyers and local businesspeople examining boxes of shoes and garments and sporting equipment. He was also surprised in that same year by learning that one of his college classmates, Chen Hsian-chen, owned a total of six shoe factories. Other classmates were also businessmen, although none quite so successful as Chen. Clearly, in the politically disastrous decade between 1965 and 1975, the economy had quietly but decisively changed directions in ways that no one had foreseen and that, in 1975, almost no one understood.

Our interviews did not begin until after 1986, and even in the first year of our work, we began by interviewing the larger firms, thinking that they were driving Taiwan's economy. But we quickly realized that the small and medium-sized firms were where the economic action was. Other researchers discovered the importance of this sector about the same time, and several researchers did so somewhat sooner, in the early 1980s.[2] However, no researcher saw the importance of small and medium-sized firms during the crucial decade itself, when the economic momentum and basic organization of Taiwan's economy took shape.

These were the decisive years, roughly from 1970 to 1985, when Taiwan's economy first became organized as a sophisticated, globally oriented supplier market for Western retailers and brand-name merchandisers. In the late 1980s, we did not immediately recognize that we were observing the outcome of an organizing process that had begun in the previous decade. Interviews capture a moment in time. Even for experienced researchers it is easy to stretch that singular moment back into the past and forward into the future, and thereby to render stationary what is, in fact, a passing train. However, as the interviews accumulated, revealing a succession of moments, we began to see through the eyes of Taiwan's businesspeople that the global economy is a whirl, an ever-changing, ever risky, ever surprising confluence of people and products and money, a whirl in which opportunity and disaster, wealth and bankruptcy travel in the same coach.

In 1970, the transformation was just beginning. Most exports, but especially consumer electronics, were produced in just-built factories in export processing zones that were partially or wholly owned by foreigners.[3] Japanese and Americans owned many of the largest factories producing consumer goods produced for export. By 1985, the great majority of the manufacturing in Taiwan, including consumer electronics, was taking place in Taiwanese-owned factories. The Taiwanese had taken over not only the manufacturing but also most other aspects of export trade, such as trucking, packaging, shipping, insuring, and financing. In these fifteen years, the Taiwanese became the world's leading demand-responsive manufacturers.

In this and the next two chapters, we give an account of the organizing process by which this transformation occurred. We have reconstructed this decade through a series of interviews, observations by anthropologists, and an assortment of other material, including trade statistics, Taiwan's manufacturing census, and articles in the popular press. The picture that emerges is one of sudden engagement with Japanese and Western buyers, a rapid expansion in the types and quantities of products being manufactured, increasing sophistication of manufacturing processes, hot competition among manufacturers for OEM contracts, and declining profits for factory owners, all in a little over a decade. By the time of the Plaza Accord in 1985, Taiwan's economy was intricately organized and dynamically changing in response to the intermediary demand generated by Western and Japanese big buyers.

Taiwan's Demand-Led Industrialization

It is hard to date the exact moment when Taiwan's demand-led industrialization began, but it is certain that the new economic trend in Taiwan began when the first big buyers arrived. We do not know who these buyers were, because no one noticed them sufficiently to record their arrival. It is also certain that the initial intermediaries were not the Taiwanese themselves. In those early years, as far as the Taiwanese were concerned, Taiwan was a closed island, and they and their resources were locked inside. Martial law was enforced. The government strictly controlled both people and money. The Taiwanese, therefore, simply did not know the foreign markets for which they would soon be making products. And, of course, very few locals spoke any English at all, this even though the United States would soon become Taiwan's major export market. The historical context makes it clear that the foreign buyers came to Taiwan before the Taiwanese went to the buyers in the United States, Europe, and Japan, as they would do with increasing frequency after martial law was lifted in 1987.

Japanese Trading Companies

It is very likely that the first buyers of Taiwan's manufactured products were Japanese trading companies, very likely the same trading companies that handled Taiwan's agricultural exports to Japan. In our interviews from the late 1980s, factory owners across a wide range of industries recalled getting their start working with Japanese firms in one way or another. In the late 1960s, as American retailers began to use Japanese trading companies to fill orders for garments and footwear, these trading companies encouraged a range of Japanese firms to relocate to areas outside of Japan where cheaper labor could be found.[4] Drawing on their expertise in marketing, financing, and information gathering, the Japanese general trading companies "turned into overseas project organizers ... and [played] a key role in helping Japanese manufacturers, and particularly small and medium-sized enterprises, set up shop in labor-abundant developing countries to produce technologically mature, labor-intensive products by investing jointly and providing needed infrastructural services."[5] Two former Japanese colonies, Taiwan and South Korea, were the two places where Japanese firms placed sizable investments, in Taiwan in the late 1960s and in South Korea in the early 1970s.[6]

Aside from our interviews and a few scattered references, however, it is difficult to find much on the role played by the Japanese trading companies in Taiwan's first period of rapid growth, from about 1965 to 1975. If they mention Japanese companies at all, most analysts refer only to those notable cases of large Japanese manufacturing companies establishing joint ventures in consumer electronics, such as Tatung's 1964 joint venture with Toshiba for producing television sets.[7] Our interviews, however, suggest that these trading companies served as the brokers that got Taiwan's industrialization under way, a crucial but unheralded role.

Several reasons further support this conclusion. The first reason is the language. In the 1960s, many ethnic Taiwanese older than thirty-five or so could speak some Japanese. They had learned Japanese during their compulsory primary school education in the colonial period. Moreover, Japanese was not only the language of instruction but also the language of international business, as well as the language of government. In the earliest years of growth, therefore, Japanese businesspeople and ethnic Taiwanese could speak to one another with some level of understanding and cultural familiarity.[8]

The second reason is that, in the late 1960s, Japanese trading companies began to diversify their role in the Japanese business groups by expanding their operations outside Japan. In the immediate post-war period, Japanese trading companies played an important role in rebuilding Japan's domestic economy. They coordinated and brokered exchanges among Japanese firms, especially firms in the groups of firms that had constituted the pre-war *zaibatsu*. Having formed around family-owned holding companies, the *zaibatsu* were disbanded by the US occupation government on the grounds of being illegitimate monopolists. After the American occupation ended, the firms constituting the former *zaibatsu* regrouped, but without the family-owned holding company at the top. In these reconstituted business groups, now called *keiretsu*, the general trading company, along with the main banks, served as one of the core firms that maintained the interrelatedness of group firms. By the 1960s, the general trading companies, called *sogoshosha*, served as the main import-export agents for firms in their respective business groups, and in addition began increasingly to serve as independent agents in establishing sources for goods for which they had received orders, but that were not supplied by member firms in the quantity, quality, or price desired by the ordering firm.

It was their role as independent agents that was especially important for Taiwan. In the early 1960s, after over a decade of rapid economic growth, Japanese labor costs began to climb. During the years from 1964 to 1966, the average monthly cost of labor in Japanese textile factories was three times higher than in Taiwan's, at 69 US$ per month, as opposed to Taiwan's 23 US$ per month.[9] In the same period, the average wage in US textile factories was 333 US$ per month. The rising wages in Japan encouraged the general trading companies to begin to look at locations outside Japan as more profitable places to perform the skills they had perfected in Japan, skills in making a market, creating infrastructure, and arranging financial backing. In the same deal, the general trading companies would make money in multiple ways. They would receive orders from American and Japanese retailers, and then would arrange production for the orders. In the early years, they had to create competent suppliers: they would broker deals leading to joint ventures between a Japanese company and a local company and, if needed, would supply or otherwise arrange for financing. Then, they would import and sell the machine tools needed to establish the factory, train the Taiwanese in how to use the machinery, supply the intermediate goods needed to make a product, and coordinate the delivery of the goods to retail markets in Japan or, more frequently, in the United States.

The third reason we make this connection is that, during the late 1960s, Taiwan became the largest recipient of Japanese foreign investment.[10] Records on foreign direct investments in Taiwan show that the absolute total of US investments exceeded investments from Japan, but Japanese investments involved over three times as many individual investments as those from the United States did.[11] These figures point to the different investment strategies being carried out by US and Japanese businesses. On the US side, a few large US multinationals (e.g., RCA) set up stand-alone manufacturing plants in Kaohsiung's export processing zone to produce televisions and other consumer electronics, and on average these investments were much larger than foreign direct investments from Japan. In fact, in 1975, nine of the ten largest foreign companies in Taiwan, by revenues, were American companies; the other one, Philips Electronics Industries, was a Dutch company.[12] By contrast, guided by the general trading companies, Japanese companies usually established joint ventures with Taiwanese firms. Some of these Japanese companies were themselves modestly sized companies; others were subsidiaries of the large Japanese business groups. In both cases, however, the firms established with Japanese direct foreign investments were smaller and economically more diverse than American firms. Typically, the Japanese firm controlled the technology and supervised the manufacturing process, and a Japanese trading company secured the order and then marketed the final product. In the 1960s, Hitachi, Matsushita (Panasonic), Sanyo Electric, Ricoh, Mitsubishi Electric, and Casio, among many other Japanese firms, started operations in Taiwan.

Fourth, although the figures seem more like rough estimates than accurate assessments, a number of analysts state that Japanese general trading companies served as the broker for over half of Taiwan's exports from the late 1960s through most of the 1970s.[13] If this figure is nearly correct, then we must conclude that the general trading companies were not just mere merchants, but rather were active agents in financing, supervising, and supplying the Taiwanese manufacturers. In effect, the Japanese trading companies initiated Taiwan's supplier markets.

This seminal role did not last long, however, for very soon Western buyers and Taiwanese trading companies began to play active roles in establishing Taiwanese suppliers of goods ordered by Western retailers and brand-name merchandisers. In the resulting mix, Japanese trading companies increasingly began to specialize in a narrow, but still important segment of the overall market economy, namely in supplying Taiwanese manufacturers with capital goods and intermediate inputs required in the manufacturing process, such as machine tools, gear boxes for bicycles, and specialty metals and chemicals needed in a wide range of products. Starting in the 1950s, Japanese exports to Taiwan increased almost every year until the late 1990s.[14] If our interviews provide a sample of what was happening in the entire economy, then most of these Japanese exports were the result of orders placed by Taiwanese businesspeople through Japanese trading companies for intermediate goods needed to manufacture Taiwanese exports.

In those initial years of economic growth, however, Japanese trading companies played all the crucial roles that got the Taiwanese businesspeople started. Moreover, they provided the Taiwanese more than just access to distant markets, advanced technologies, and manufacturing know-how. Most importantly, they showed the Taiwanese how to make money within the global economy. They showed them how to participate as suppliers, how to be reliable and trustworthy partners to firms that ordered goods from them and about which they had little knowledge.

American Buyers and Local Trading Companies

The success that Japanese trading companies had with sourcing goods in Asia soon did them out of the business they came to set up. American buyers quickly established buying offices in Taipei, Seoul, and Hong Kong. Sears opened its Taiwan buying office in 1967, Kmart and J. C. Penney did so in 1971, and the Associated Merchandising Corporation (buyers for Dayton Hudson, which founded Target and later took that name for itself, and Federated Department Stores) and Mast Industries (buyers for The Limited) followed in 1973.[15] By eliminating the middleman, American buyers could reduce their costs, but more importantly, they could begin to work with the Taiwanese manufacturers and could help them be better suppliers. As they became better suppliers, the Western buyers began to order greater quantities of a much wider range of goods.

Here the US trade statistics are revealing. In the very first year they were collected, 1972, the seven-digit US Customs data show that Taiwan was already exporting products to the United States in over 2100 categories.[16] By 1985, that number had risen to over 8400 categories. This increase represents an extraordinary growth in the variety of products Taiwan made for export to the United States.

Most of the value of these exports, however, was quite concentrated, with nearly 30 percent of the total value coming from only the top ten product categories and nearly 80 percent of the total value coming from the top hundred categories. The top twenty exports in 1972 were dominated by consumer electronics and items of clothing, most of which were likely produced through multinational manufacturing and joint ventures.[17] However, once outside the top twenty or so items, one begins to find a wide variety of products that were almost certainly ordered by US retailers and made in Taiwanese-owned factories. Among the second set of twenty exports are types of umbrellas, luggage, bicycles, toys, household utensils, handbags, Christmas tree lights, and curtains. Going further down the list, the array of products is dazzling: types of handbags, sewing machines, loudspeakers, religious articles made of plastic, inflatable rubber toys, guitars, belt buckles, gloves, clocks, headwear, badminton sets, baseballs, bicycle tires, tennis rackets—all these along with many kinds of garments and shoes.[18]

The customs records show that, from 1972 to 1985, these second-tier products were shipped in greater and greater quantities and accounted for more and more of the total value of exports. This shift occurred at the same time as Taiwanese manufacturers were taking increasing shares of the export production in consumer electronics made in Taiwan.[19] By the time our interviews started in 1987, Taiwanese businesses, rather than foreign-owned firms, dominated every sector of Taiwan's export economy.

As we interviewed factory owners from the late 1980s on, the question we always had in the back of our minds was, How did this particular factory come to be making that particular product? And, every time, the answer to that question was that they had the order from a buyer. Without the order, the factory owners said, they would not make whatever they were making. They explained that the capital invested in the factory and in the inputs used to make the goods had come out of their own pockets, or out of the pockets of a small group of family and friends who were the primary investors; therefore, they would not risk making something that had not already been ordered. When we probed where the orders came from, the owners typically told us that American buyers had ordered the products, and as proof, they would show us the US brand names on the products they were shipping.

But at this point, the obscurity would start. How were the orders actually arranged? Part of the obscurity was due to our failure to ask the crucial questions. In the 1980s and early 1990s, we, along with most other observers, focused more on how Taiwan businesspeople put together their production networks than on how they obtained their orders. We knew they had the orders, we knew they depended on having the orders, and so we did not query them on the intricacies of how the ordering system worked. However, part of the obscurity also came from the fact that the orders had come from a variety of sources. Some came directly from the retailers or brand-name merchandisers, others were handled by Japanese trading companies, and yet others were arranged by local trading groups.

Knowing the importance of local trading companies, we interviewed the owners of several dozen local trading companies. We learned that in the years of our interviews, mostly in the early 1990s, the owners of these trading companies had to work hard to get the orders. They would take a case of samples to the United States or Europe, and go from retailer to retailer looking for orders. These trading companies were colloquially referred to as "suitcase companies" (*pibao gongsi*). But suitcase companies became commonplace only after the Taiwanese were able to travel overseas freely and after the foreign exchange markets were open, and neither of these events occurred until after 1987.

The important next question, then, was how had the ordering system worked during the crucial decade between 1965 and 1975. We knew that during that decade, the government did not provide much, if any, assistance. In the early 1990s, a lot of export manufacturers obtained contracts by showing their wares at trade fairs and in fixed stalls at the Taipei World Trade Center. But the Taipei World Trade Center did not open until 1988. Before that, the China External Trade Development Council handled most of the official matters involving trade. This council was established in 1970, but was continually short staffed and underfunded. Allowed only thirteen employees, the first general secretary of the council, Wu Kuan-hsiung, recalled being so frustrated with the lack of government support that he quit after a few years and went to Singapore. As early as 1973, he had recommended that the government build a trade center, but the plan was put off year after year. The government, he complained, liked industry, but not commerce or trade.

Putting together bits and pieces of information from our interviews and from other sources, we think it is likely that the American buyers and the local trading companies began to collaborate in the early 1970s and built a momentum that continued through the 1980s. One fact stands out for this period: local trading companies grew in number at a pace even faster than the Taiwanese economy grew in the same period. In 1973, official records show that there were 2,777 trading companies in operation in Taiwan,[20] but by 1985, that number had risen to 55,000. One out of every ten registered companies was a trading company. The trading companies were uniformly small, averaging less than ten employees each. Knowing the trading companies from our interviews in the early 1990s, we surmise that nearly every category of export products was represented by many local trading companies competing for orders.

Although small, the local trading companies took on a multitude of roles, chief among which was to work both sides of the demand-supply equation. Their offices were usually in Taipei, near the buying offices established by American retailers. They worked to identify products that were salable to the big buyers and then worked to obtain orders for those products, thereby generating demand. Then the owners of the trading companies would help to arrange production networks to fill the order, thereby generating supply. They were more than simply matchmakers; they were instrumental in creating competent suppliers for American buyers. Local trading companies helped to create a market of suppliers willing to bid on and to make nearly any product imaginable.

Imitation and Innovation

Although we did not ask many questions about the process of obtaining orders, we did ask again and again how factory owners were able to make the products for which they had the orders. Many of the products were extraordinarily intricate or required very complex manufacturing procedures. It always seemed remarkable to us that the Taiwanese manufacturers, often with very limited education, would be able to figure out how to make the products that they were, in fact, making. For instance, the founder of Thunder Tiger, Lai Chuan-lin, had only an elementary school education, and yet, among his many accomplishments, he figured out how to manufacture miniature drone jet airplanes. Chairman T, the Great King of Outdoor Furniture, who at the time of our interviews had huge contracts from both Walmart and Kmart, had only the equivalent of a junior high education, and yet he invented a one-step manufacturing process to change raw plastic granules into finished products. And their stories are not unusual. In fact, most factory owners in Taiwan's first wave of industrialization not only did not have advanced degrees but also had no training in manufacturing or in making their specific product.

The question that we asked repeatedly was how they learned to make the products. The answer that we received was always that they used some form of imitation and innovation based on an existing product. To imitate and innovate well is surprisingly difficult. The term often given to this process is *reverse engineering*, which makes the process sound simple, but there is nothing easy or automatic about copying someone else's design. In the case of OEM production, the big buyers would often bring samples, sometimes amounting to nothing more than just an idea sketched out on a piece of paper, with them to Taiwan, and ask the manufacturers, or more likely the owners of trading companies, Can you make it for such and such a price? Then, before manufacturers could obtain the order, they would have to deliver a prototype, just to show that they could do it. The turnaround time on such queries was often very short, because frequently the buyers would just sit in their hotel rooms waiting for the prototype to appear. With a very short lead time, the Taiwanese manufacturers would have to produce a sample.

This process of innovating based on an existing product design is a skill that Taiwanese manufacturers learned how to perfect. In the first decade of rapid growth, many of the OEM products were comparatively simple and were ordered in fairly small batches. Taiwanese manufacturers learned how to produce these products in a variety of ways, some from their experience in working in other factories, some from instruction provided by Japanese trading companies and suppliers of machine tools, and some from the big buyers themselves. However, once in business, they learned quickly from others in their production network. In this context, learning was both singular and collaborative.

It was singular in the sense that one firm typically took the lead to produce the prototype. The owner and key employees of this firm would design and make a prototype. At this stage, very few people might be involved, but those people would have to have a lot of knowledge about the product, and would have to go to some lengths to acquire this knowledge. Factory owners frequently told us that they would obtain this knowledge by going to trade shows, by finding samples of similar products and taking them apart, by closely reading trade journals where new developments are announced, and by pursuing others who had knowledge about the product or the materials the product was made of. Wherever they obtained this knowledge, they would then actively try to innovate on the design to come up with something special that would give their product a distinctive feel.

Learning was also collaborative in the sense that the process of production was a function of the network and not simply the firm. Learning how to produce a given prototype required considerable cooperation among a group of independent manufacturers. These manufacturers would have to work together very closely on coordinating all aspects of production. During this collaboration, the division of labor among manufacturers had to be cost effective, because any inefficiency would cut into their collective profits. The network of producers, therefore, would constantly learn how to produce products with higher quality while achieving lower costs, and how to work together seamlessly. This process of manufacturing led not only to improvements in product design but also to a new process of production particularly well suited to contract manufacturing.

As a result of these everyday practices, Taiwanese businesspeople could quickly take advantage of money-making opportunities that began to appear in the 1970s. The constant interaction between the product and the process of production, as well as between the firm and the networks of which the firms are a part, created in Taiwan's first wave of industrialization a particularly dynamic approach to manufacturing that worked in close coordination with the demands of big buyers. This period marks the beginning of contract manufacturing in Taiwan.

Here are some examples from our interviews that illustrate these various levels of interaction.

Ta Yang: Making Baseballs

We heard about the factory called Ta Yang in 1988 from a student at Tunghai University, who also arranged though family connections for us to interview the owner, Mr. Yang. Although we knew the factory, which produced baseballs, was located in Nyausung Xiang (Pinebird Village) in Kaohsiung County in southern Taiwan, it still took us hours to find it. We finally located it in the middle of a rice field off a road without a name. The setting made the factory seem large, but with only 100 employees, all of whom were local residents, Ta Yang would be listed in the government's statistics at the time as a medium-sized firm. Obviously proud of his accomplishments, Chairman Yang told us that making baseballs was not an easy matter; he referred to it as "high technology." It took him and his close friend and co-owner a long time to perfect the manufacturing process to produce high-quality baseballs. And Ta Yang's baseballs were of the very highest quality because, as Mr. Yang, informed us, the factory supplied the major league baseball teams in the United States with about 10 percent of all the baseballs they used in a season.

Chairman Yang established his factory in 1974. He and his friend had previously worked for several years in the Kaohsiung Export Processing Zone in a Japanese company, called Sakura, which made baseballs for the major league teams in Japan. They learned the technology of making baseballs in the Japanese factory, and then decided to open their own firm on his family's plot of land in the rural hinterland of Kaohsiung. Once they established their factory, they found, however, that the high performance standards for baseballs were difficult to meet. Baseballs have to be perfectly round, precisely balanced, and well constructed to withstand the crushing blows of a baseball bat. Moreover, most of the components needed to make such a baseball had to be imported, such as the leather coverings and the cork interiors. Recognizing their shortcomings, they approached Sakura again, this time asking for technological assistance in obtaining the intermediate supplies to make the component parts. Sakura agreed in exchange for Ta Yang's becoming a contract manufacturer for Sakura. Based on this technology transfer, Ta Yang was able to meet Sakura's high standards and was able to put together a production network, with different independent firms in the area making the different component parts of the baseball. These parts were then transported, as they were needed, to Ta Yang for final assembly. Ta Yang began to produce baseballs not only for Sakura but also for any firm that would make an order.

The relationship with Sakura did not last very long. An American buyer heard about Ta Yang and contacted the owners. After the buyer thoroughly tested Ta Yang's baseballs, Chairman Yang received an OEM contract. After that, contracts with other brand-name distributors in the United States soon followed. Ta Yang's volume of business grew, and the owners had to expand their production network several times. When we interviewed Chairman Yang in 1988, he quietly told us that the production process was very labor intensive and that he was considering a move to Mainland China. We later learned that he had made the move.

Kai Hsiang: Making Jacks

The first time we interviewed Ling Wen-chuen, the general manager of Kai Hsiang, a hydraulic jack manufacturing firm in Chiayi, was in 1990. Although we would revisit him many times during the next fifteen years, that first visit left a lasting impression. At the time, he was a youthful thirty-four years old and was completely at ease with having us in his factory. A very jovial man, he kept us there for the better part of a day, which ended with a banquet that he hosted for us and the entire research team, a total of twelve people.

In 1990, Kai Hsiang was the second largest of the six major jack factories in Chiayi, a modestly sized city in southern Taiwan of a little over 300,000 people. It employed about 200 people in the main factory and worked with a large subcontractor network consisting of over one hundred small firms. Kai Hsiang was one of a number of businesses owned by Ling Wen-chuen's parents, and his role as general manager was given added weight by the fact that it was a family business, nominally owned by his father, but in reality owned by the entire family collectively.

These family businesses began with Ling Wen-chuen's grandfather, who owned a pharmacy in Chiayi. Having a taste for business, but not wanting to take over the family store, Ling's father, Ling Suen-yi, looked around for other opportunities. In the early 1960s, responding to the growing export markets in Japan for agricultural products, farmers in southern Taiwan had begun to invest heavily in growing a range of animals commercially, including pigs, chickens, fish, and shrimp. Sensing an opening, Ling Suen-yi started a factory producing feed for chickens and fish. As a part of this business, he had to import corn and other grains to make the feed, and he had to go around the island of Taiwan to market his product to feed shops. Through his contacts in the feed business, Ling Suen-yi heard, in the early 1970s, about a Japanese luggage company that wanted to locate a contract manufacturer to make some low-end suitcases. The Japanese were willing to invest some capital in such a company. Ling Suen-yi quickly took them up on the offer, and investing some of his own money in the factory as well, he started making luggage. While Ling Suen-yi worked full-time to establish his luggage factory, his wife took over the agribusiness. Through working with the Japanese company, he upgraded the quality of his luggage and then landed some additional OEM contracts.

In 1980, running a successful luggage export business, Ling Suen-yi was approached by a friend of a friend. This person owned the jack factory Kai Hsiang, which he wanted to sell. The factory was not doing well, and the person was willing to sell the factory to the Ling family at an attractive price. A few years earlier another jack factory, called Hsinfu, had opened in Chiayi. The owner of Hsinfu and Ling Suen-yi were friends, and sensing an opportunity, Ling Suen-yi hoped that if he bought Kai Hsiang he could collaborate with Hsinfu to produce a wider range and larger quantity of hydraulic jacks. The year before all this, Ling Suen-yi's son, Ling Wen-chuen (the person we interviewed), had graduated from National Taiwan University in Taipei, with a BS degree in forestry. In the year after his graduation, he worked for his father in the luggage company, learning sales and marketing and making use of the English he had learned in college. When Ling Suen-yi bought Kai Hsiang in 1981 for 20 million NT$, his son immediately became the general manager.

In the late 1970s, in addition to Kai Hsiang and Hsinfu, four other jack assembly factories had started operation in Chiayi. Although each one was independent and in competition with the other firms and although each had a network of dedicated subcontractors, they also shared some subcontractors who made specialized parts. As a function of being part of an extensive network of assembly factories and overlapping parts suppliers, the entire agglomeration of firms, although internally competitive, shared substantial knowledge about how to manufacture products with hydraulic components. As general manager of Kai Hsiang, Ling Wen-chuen made good use of this information to improve the production facilities in his factory.

The agglomeration of jack factories in Chiayi created a large demand for steel of a certain size and quality. Not far from Chiayi, near Kaohsiung, is the state-owned steel mill, China Steel, as well as several large, privately owned steel mills. At first, the jack factories ordered steel from some of these mills, but they soon switched their orders to a newly established local steel mill. This firm has been established in the late 1970s by a local man who had worked as an apprentice in one of the Kaohsiung mills. As the jack factories began to receive substantial orders, this person was encouraged to open a mini-mill dedicated to serving the specific needs of the jack manufacturers in Chiayi.

In its first years of operation after it was bought, Kai Hsiang was a subcontract manufacturer for Hsinfu, which was then on its way to becoming the world's largest producer of hydraulic jacks. Ling Wen-chuen told us that in that first year of operation, the firm made 200 million NT$ in total revenues, with profit margins running about 6 percent. After two years, it turned a profit. Because Kai Hsiang was a subcontract assembly firm for Hsinfu, however, its production depended on Hsinfu's ability to get OEM orders. Although the firm was quite successful, Ling Wen-chuen wanted to expand his business. Using his English language skills, he went to Taipei, and eventually to the United States, to meet American buyers. When we asked him how he knew what firms to go to, he said that that was no problem. What he had done was to go to the subcontract firm in Chiayi that was making the brand-name-labeled cardboard boxes used to package the finished jacks to see what American companies were ordering jacks. He then went to those companies, and as a result, he was able to get substantial OEM orders on his own behalf. These orders allowed him to expand his network of subcontractors. By 1987, within six years of Ling Suen-yi's buying the jack factory, Kai Hsiang became the second largest jack assembly firm in Chiayi.

Our first interview with Ling Wen-chuen was in 1990. Within five years of that first interview, most of the jack assembly firms in Chiayi, including Kai Hsiang, had moved operations to Mainland China. The Ling family luggage business continued in full operation, with one large factory in Mainland China and the small factory in Chiayi, where the high-end luggage continued to be made. The factory making animal feed ended operations at about the time that the farmers in southern Taiwan began to quit raising animals and seafood so extensively, due to pollution and other causes. No longer running their agribusiness, Ling Suen-yi's wife opened a stock brokerage firm. The Ling family jokingly called their businesses "nomadic" (*youmu*), because they never stopped searching for new opportunities to make money.

Yeh-Bao: Making Bicycles

Located about forty kilometers northwest of Taichung City, Ta Chia is one of many small villages lining the coast and skirting the river flood plains along Highway 1. Well removed from the main north-south freeways, Ta Chia before the 1970s was noted only for making small products woven from grass: hats, floor and bed mats, and slippers. Only eleven years later, by 1981, Ta Chia had become the center of Taiwan's export bicycle industry, and by that time Taiwan had become the world's largest bicycle exporter.[21] At the peak of the bicycle industry in Taiwan, in 1986, the number of bicycles exported reached more than 10 million.[22] Giant, Taiwan's best known bicycle company, is located in Ta Chia. It is the largest of many bicycle assembly firms in the region. Yeh-Bao is another firm in Ta Chia, but its owner, Lin Chun-shan, built his business by specializing only in the manufacture of bicycle frames.

Chairman Lin started his first business in 1975. At the time, he had recently graduated from a nearby technical school with a specialty in telecommunications and had received the equivalent of a high school degree. Not knowing what to do, he returned to his hometown, Ta Chia, to look for opportunities. In the early 1970s, as Ta Chia was becoming a center of bicycle production, there were many opportunities in the region to enter the industry in one capacity or another. With very little capital and acting on the advice of a friend, Lin and his wife decided to start a company making the plastic saddle bags that attach to the rear fenders of low-end bicycles. They called their company Jun-ye (successful enterprise), and, depending on the workload, employed between ten and twenty people, all from the local village. Their orders for the saddle bags came from other firms in Ta Chia. These bags would be attached to the bicycles in the final stages of assembly, just before the bicycles were packaged and shipped to the OEM buyers.

In 1978, building on his personal connections within the local community of bicycle assemblers and part suppliers, Chairman Lin got an opportunity to establish a new firm to make one of the technologically most difficult parts to manufacture, the frame. He called this firm Yeh-Bao (wild treasure) in Chinese and A-PRO in English. He initially used low-end metals, mainly aluminum and stainless steel, to construct the frame. The first couple of years, he recalled, were extremely difficult because he had to work out the production technique for making the frame solid and unbreakable. Precision welding is crucial to the process, because so much pressure is placed on critical points on a bicycle, particularly the metal fork holding the front wheel. "You know an automobile has four wheels, but a bicycle only has two. Can you imagine," he said, "a 200-pound American guy riding on a ten-pound bicycle at a speed of thirty miles an hour. Oh boy, the frame has to hold together!"

Because competition at the low end was so tough, Chairman Lin decided he had to upgrade his position in the network of firms around Ta Chia. He borrowed money from his friends and bought new equipment to improve the quality of his frames. He also began to use new metals, including titanium, as well as higher grades of aluminum and steel, and new welding techniques. Then he hired the best welders he could find, paying them double and sometimes triple the going local wage for welders. When he first bought the specialty metals from a Japanese company, the Japanese company sent representatives to teach him and his welders the best techniques to cut and weld the frames. But Chairman Lin complained to us that Japanese companies never explain everything. They always keep some of the core technology to themselves. Therefore, as Lin and his employees began to work with the new metals and the new welding techniques, they had to work out many of the problems on their own, and they had to test and retest the durability of their frames. Chairman Lin, however, continued to buy the high-end materials from Japan (e.g., titanium and later carbon graphite) and to rely on Japanese manufacturers for key components, such as Shimano derailleurs.

Once they had perfected the manufacturing process, Chairman Lin began to participate in international bicycle fairs, usually held in Cologne, Germany, and in New York City, and he started to obtain OEM orders, especially from Europe. Quickly his business improved. He had successfully upgraded his firm's position in the manufacturing network, just as the entire network had also upgraded itself as an OEM producer for major European and American retailers of bicycles.[23] As Yeh-Bao grew in size, the firm was able to handle yet larger and more differentiated orders. Chairman Lin's strategy matched the strategy of the entire network of firms, namely to make differentiated products: mass-produced low-end and middle-range bicycles and batch-produced high-end models, this along with a lot of bicycle accessories.

By 1992, when we interviewed Chairman Lin for the first time, he had established six independent factories in Taiwan, each making different component parts. The very first firm, Jun-ye, was still in operation, then managed by Lin's wife, and was making sophisticated bicycle accessories. Yeh-Bao was the largest of the six firms. Chairman Lin was the owner and boss (*laoban*) of each of these factories. We asked him, since he was making so many different bicycle parts, why not vertically integrate and make the entire bicycle himself, or at least become a downstream assembler. He answered decisively that that would not be a wise move. "If you try to vertically integrate in Ta Chia," he said, "then everyone will be your competitor. If you keep your firms separate, then you will be everyone's supplier." He said there were other reasons not to integrate as well. If you make a small number of products, you do not have to make a huge capital investment in any one of them. Modest investments, he said, get better returns with lower risks. Finally, he noted that Taiwan's tax code also favors having multiple companies rather than one big firm. Continually starting small firms means that you can deduct startup costs, a savings that would not be available if one began a new operation within an existing firm. Also, multiple firms create multiple lines of credit. One big company has only one credit line. And finally, different sizes of firms are subject to different tax rates. Although all these reasons are important, he reflected, the main reason not to vertically integrate is the risk of going it alone, of trying to make money without help from others.

Chairman Lin thought it was much better for him to make himself indispensable within the overall network of firms. The bicycle industry is continually changing, he said; it is a "fashion industry." A network of firms is much more flexible in changing with the trends than is one big vertically integrated firm. "It used to be that the big firms in South Korea would make huge quantities of bicycles," but the Taiwanese producers were able to follow the trends so much faster that the "Koreans got out of the bicycle business."

Pou Chen: Making Shoes

Among Taiwanese firms, Pou Chen is a legend. In the late 1990s, Pou Chen, along with its subsidiary, Yue Yuen, became the largest shoe manufacturer in the world, making nearly a quarter of all athletic shoes sold in the world. Also, among private sector Taiwanese firms, Pou Chen is one of the largest employers, with over 500,000 employees worldwide and with over 80,000 employees in one of its Mainland Chinese factories alone. Like other Taiwanese firms, however, Pou Chen started small.

When we first interviewed Pou Chen's owner, Tsai Chi-jui, in 1988, it was a considerably smaller firm of about 500 employees, operating five assembly lines producing shoes,[24] but by Taiwan's standards of the day, even then it was relatively large. In 1969, Tsai Chi-jui, along with his three younger brothers, had started Pou Chen in their hometown of Yuanlin, in those years a modestly sized town in Changhwa County, south of Changhwa City. Reasonably prosperous in the 1960s, Yuanlin was noted for its agricultural products, particularly mushrooms, asparagus, and preserved fruits, as well as its food-processing plants that canned and bottled and otherwise prepared these food products for export as well as for domestic consumption. A graduate of a local teacher's college and then a teacher in the local junior high school, Tsai Chi-jui wanted to take advantage of the new economic opportunities that he saw appearing in his hometown in the late 1960s. He borrowed 500,000 NT$ (equivalent to 12,500 US$) from close family members, so that he and his three younger brothers could start a factory.

With ten employees in addition to the four brothers, Pou Chen began making the kind of plastic slippers known colloquially in the United States as *flip-flops*. At the time the Tsai brothers opened their firm, several other factories in the area had also started making the same style of plastic shoes. Some of Tsai family members had had previous experience making slippers out of woven grass, which they obtained from Ta Chia. Now they began to use that experience to make these new kinds of shoes. The flip-flop had been designed by an American firm in imitation of a style of Italian-made leather shoes for women. The flip-flops initially sold well in the American market, but the price per unit was very low. American buyers for the main retail outlets, especially Kmart, Sears, and Walmart, the latter then only a regional discounter, began to place orders in Taiwan. The raw plastic material used to make the flip-flops was readily available in Taiwan from Nan Ya Plastics, a subsidiary of Formosa Plastics. Working through a local trading company, the Tsai brothers landed a contract for a quantity of these plastic shoes. At the same time this was occurring, the US demand for flip-flops surged, which led in turn to much bigger orders. The US buyers for the retail chains then began to come directly to the suppliers, Pou Chen included, and began to work closely with them to increase both the quantity and the quality of the products. Tsai Chi-jui recalled being especially impressed with buyers from Walmart, with whom his firm gradually developed a close relationship.

In the early 1970s, when Pou Chen began to receive direct orders from the main retail buyers, it increased the size of its factory and began to develop its own subcontracting network. At this time, the market for non-leather shoes in the United States began to diversify. Pou Chen's breakthrough came when the company got some large orders for a new type of shoe, canvas-covered plastic shoes, variously called *sneakers* or *tennis shoes*. The construction was fairly easy and the unit price was very low. Working with its production network, however, Pou Chen was able to keep production costs down, produce these shoes in large quantities, and still make everyone a profit.

As orders for sneakers began to come in to Pou Chen, two related developments pushed Taiwan shoe manufacturers in new directions. First, the technology used in making shoes changed dramatically when Mitsubishi's general trading company, CITC, transferred Japanese technologies for making shoes to Taiwanese suppliers. CITC was one of the primary intermediaries between specialized sporting goods retailers and Taiwanese shoe manufacturers. In Japan, a new type of shoe was then being developed, a highly functional and durable shoe that would become known as the *athletic shoe*. These shoes required new machinery, advanced plastic materials, and high-quality sewing and lamination techniques. Making these shoes was also very labor intensive. Taking advantage of Taiwan's cheaper labor costs and batch production techniques, CITC taught Taiwanese suppliers the new shoemaking technologies and sold them the machines and the materials to make the shoes.

The German shoe manufacturer Adidas had been trying to develop a similar type of shoe, with technologies similar to those developed by the Japanese. Keeping in step with their Japanese competitors, Adidas decided in 1971 to try contract manufacturing in Taiwan as well, and signed an agreement with Hwagang, a shoe company located in northern Taiwan. In the following year, 1972, Reebok came to Taiwan, as did the Japanese company Mizuno. These companies signed contracts with several shoe manufacturers, among them Chinglu, a firm located in the same county as Pou Chen. Although they had been in business for only about five years, all these contracts for athletic shoes made Taiwanese shoe manufacturers one of the main global suppliers for this new type of shoe.

The extraordinarily rapid growth of the Taiwan's shoe manufacturers created huge demand for specialized inputs and for the machines to make shoes;

many of these needs were initially supplied by the Japanese trading companies. By the mid-1970s, local firms began to emerge that supplied both the inputs and the machinery. This follows the general rule in demand-responsive economies: orders for final products come first; markets for intermediate inputs for those products come later. This progression encourages niche suppliers for intermediate inputs to emerge.

The second important development in Taiwan's shoe industry was the arrival of Nike and a surging global demand for athletic shoes that was, in part, created by Nike. In the early 1970s, Kihachiro Onitsuka, the owner of Asics Tiger, cooperated with the American company Blue Ribbon Sports, which later became Nike, to manufacture a shoe designed by Philip Knight. Knight's story is well known: he saw that there was no shoe designed for running and other athletic endeavors. He designed the shoe and contracted with Asics Tiger to make it. In only a few years after the shoe's introduction, Nike captured a huge share of the newly developed US market in athletic shoes. At first, this market seemed to be a niche market that filled, as well as created, demand arising from the new popularity of jogging and aerobics. But the niche expanded, as more and more athletic type shoes were worn for all occasions. At the beginning, Asics Tiger made the Nike shoes, but faced with competition from Adidas and Reebok, Knight decided to move his contract manufacturing out of Japan. He split his orders between footwear manufacturers in South Korea and Taiwan, with Korean companies making mass-produced shoes for low-end markets, and Taiwanese companies making the batch-produced specialty shoes. In Taiwan, Nike's lead firm was Fung-Tai, also located in Taichung County, about thirty minutes north of Yuanlin.

From 1966 to 1985, the global export of sport shoes from Asia grew 1200-fold. Most of these shoes were produced in only two countries, Taiwan and South Korea. By 1985, Taiwan and South Korea produced 50 percent of all shoes imported into the United States. By this time, American shoes manufacturers had gone into a decline from which they would never recover. Because of the sudden demand in the United States for these new types of shoes, the large retailers and brand-name merchandisers did a lot of research on how to put the shoes together to get maximum performance. In the early years, recalled Tsai Chi-jui, when Pou Chen made flip-flops and sneakers for the big-box retailers, price was the most important issue. Later, when Pou Chen began to cooperate with the brand-name merchandisers, the ability to use advanced technology was more important than price. What all these brand-name companies most needed were manufacturers who could transform their R&D models into a manufactured commodity that yielded a good profit for all concerned. The secret of the Taiwanese manufacturers was having the know-how to do this.

As Pou Chen continued to make sneakers for the big-box retailers, the company started to invest heavily in new equipment needed to produce athletic shoes, equipment sold to the company by CITC. By 1977, Pou Chen had also set up its own internal research division (*neibu yanjiu xiaozu*) to further develop materials to make shoes. They began to do some subcontracting work for other Taiwanese firms that had primary orders for athletic shoes. Then in 1979, they received their first order from Adidas, through a local trading company arm of Hwagang. At the time, Hwagang handled all of Adidas's local sales (as the sales agent), did a large portion of Adidas's contract manufacturing, and arranged for subcontractors to do the remainder. This arrangement was very successful for Pou Chen. Then in 1982, Pou Chen became the primary OEM manufacturer for New Balance, and gained a good reputation for the quality of its shoes. The quality of its production attracted Reebok, which signed an agreement with Pou Chen in 1988. Then in 1989, Nike signed on as well.[25]

By the time Pou Chen received its first big contract from Nike in 1989, Pou Chen was transferring much of its manufacturing capacity to China. The golden period for shoe production in Taiwan was just ending, and the great rush to China was just beginning. In retrospect, we can see that the golden period for Pou Chen was just about to begin as well.

Demand-Responsive Manufacturing

Between the late 1960s and 1985, Taiwanese manufacturers developed into sophisticated suppliers of consumer goods for global markets. In the beginning of that period, they had very little experience in any kind of manufacturing and very limited knowledge of the consumer goods that they would soon be making for overseas markets. At the end of that period, they had developed advanced expertise in the process of manufacturing for OEM buyers and equally advanced knowledge of the products that they were making. In slightly over fifteen years, Taiwanese manufacturers, the Taiwanese economy, and the global economy had become tightly interconnected and transformed.

The modular organization designed for flexible production grew out of the demand-responsive production systems that developed in Taiwan during the first fifteen years of rapid growth, from 1970 to 1985. Each of the case studies in this chapter has illustrated this manufacturing process.

- The manufacturing of each product came to rely on production networks that broke the production process down into distinct steps that standardized the product, the component parts, and the roles of the participants.
- All varieties of contract manufacturing (e.g., OEM and ODM, original design manufacturing) grew out of a progressively reorganizing economy in which individual firms were parts of larger economic units. As the orders for products increased, this form of manufacturing became increasingly sophisticated and highly responsive to buyer demand. This form of manufacturing was not a second-class or substandard form of production, which some analysts make it out to be.[26] The literature often describes the goal of OEM producers as needing to upgrade, but our interviews show that even in this first wave of industrialization, demand-responsive manufacturing, as a definable process, began to take shape and was progressively rationalized over time.
- Demand-responsive manufacturing was the result of conscious organizing on the part of Taiwanese manufacturers. It was done intentionally, in part because of the limited resources they possessed and because of the social organization that they were accustomed to.
- As our interviews show, from the outset, Taiwanese manufacturers operated on three principles. The first principle of contract manufacturing is to make money for your buyers. If they don't make money, they will not be back. This understanding led Taiwanese manufacturers to organize by taking the big-buyer's perspective into account and, in fact, by making it their own perspective. The second principle of OEM production is to work for the return contract. Meet the buyer's expectations in quality, quantity, and price point the first time. If the buyers come back, then they will have made money and will be feeling they could make more. The third principle of OEM is to make money for yourself. How you achieve these three principles is through taking calculated risks. However, if you don't make money for yourself, you will not be able to survive. Maybe you will not make money with the first few contracts, but if you make yourself indispensable to your buyers, you will make lots of money over the long haul.
- Organizing to make money for your buyer means organizing from the perspective of the buyer. Organize backward from the product itself and from

the order for that product. The big buyer has given you the specifications for the product, and you know how many that buyer wants. Do not try to develop a totally new product. Simply try to reproduce an existing product with high quality, at low cost, and in the desired quantity. The production unit you organize is in direct response to the product and the orders. Different ways to organize production evolve over time, but in the early years, it was always a production network.

Organizing to make money for yourself means doing three things:

- First, establish a foothold in the production networks, learn by doing, make incremental changes to improve what you are doing, cost down the production process, and accept low margins in the short run in hopes of receiving larger margins going forward. Be a network player. And accept network agreements about the profit margin. When the opportunity arises, fill the niches that appear in the production process or develop new niches that others will find useful.
- Second, try to get multiple orders for the same product from different sources. Multiple orders will allow you to develop a strategy of product differentiation, based on standardized parts for all models.
- Third, modularize the production across the producing units. Standardize each step in the production to make the manufacturing process transparent to all those engaged in making the product. Adopt external standards for the products, as specified by the buyer, and adopt internal standards for the process of production, as developed and specified by the network of independent manufacturers.

Taiwanese entrepreneurs developed and perfected a model of how to manufacture for foreign buyers, demand-responsive manufacturing. The model they developed led to a comprehensive reorganization of the Taiwanese economy. This economy was organized around products that big buyers ordered and services related to those products. For each product, sets of competing core firms emerged. These core, modestly sized firms assembled products and, sometimes, made key parts and also subcontracted components to other firms. This production strategy led to the development of clusters of firms and to internal markets for intermediate goods and services. These flexible networks supplying final and intermediate goods and services would expand when demand was high and would contract when demand was low. Typically, the product concentration led to a geographical concentration as well, because the production system relied on just-in-time delivery of parts to the assembly location. The Taiwanese learned these techniques from the Japanese, but they perfected them in Taiwan.

As overseas demand for products increased, product differentiation also increased. This proliferation of similar products created concentric rings of manufacturing networks, networks that intersected across numbers of core manufacturers. These intersecting rings contained many niches for expansion and development of additional products and for supporting services. Buyer demand also led to rigid cost controls that fed back across all supporting sectors, which in turn created the continuing need to rationalize production and upgrade products relative to big-buyer orders.

Conclusion

In the two decades after 1965, the leap into industrialization made by Taiwan's networks of small and medium-sized firms looks miraculous. These firms started their rise to their current position by producing products that they had no previous experience making. If we were looking only at one firm or even one industry, then we might explain the jump—say, from fish food to hydraulic jacks or from plastic saddle bags to titanium bicycle frames or from straw sandals to the world's most sophisticated running shoes—in terms of some peculiarity of the founders or some special characteristic of the industry. But this jump from one product to another, and from one price point to a lesser one, occurred across Taiwan's economic landscape in the same two decades.

The American retail revolution explains part of the reason that this sudden transformation occurred. Taiwan's production networks had help. Japanese trading companies and other firms from Japan helped develop, cooperated with, and profited from these networks; American buyers provided specifications and technical assistance and supervised the quality and price of products they would buy from them. But why were Taiwan's small and medium-sized firms the principal drivers and primary beneficiaries of this leap into industrialization, and not the large firms in Taiwan, which certainly profited as well, though indirectly? And why was this contract manufacturing centered in Taiwan and not somewhere else, in places like Japan, South Korea, Hong Kong, or even China?

These are the questions we will answer in the next two chapters.

4

AN ECONOMIC WAY OF LIFE

The Round Table

The question that we tried to answer in the early years of our research was how farmers, farmers' sons and daughters, and other people from many walks of life could organize themselves so seamlessly into a web of independent small and medium-sized firms that they could then produce very complicated products. We believed that the answer to this question would give us a clue to explain Taiwan's rapid industrialization. As the years passed and as we witnessed the changing role of Taiwanese manufacturers in a transforming global economy, we also realized that the answer to this question helped to explain their success as contract manufacturers.

In 1987, when we began to write about the organization of Taiwanese businesses, we used the term *network* to describe the web-like patterns that linked people and firms together in a complex mix of personal and business relationships. As the previous chapters show, we still use the term, but now with a fuller sense of what that term implies in the context of Taiwanese society. Initially, we described these networks case by case, but we could not put our finger on why this organizational strategy was so common across all cases and so readily understood by businesspeople, regardless of where they came from and what they were making. Finally, we recognized the obvious: people conducted their business activities as an extension of the way they organized their everyday activities, and for the Taiwanese such activities center around their families and around consuming food and drink. That recognition had been obscured by the very term, the social science concept of *network*, that we used to describe the activity we were observing.

When we first used it, the term *network* was just coming into vogue in several disciplines, including sociology, and it seemed entirely appropriate for us to use that term to describe how small and medium-sized firms banded together to make products that no one firm or no one firm owner could handle. Network has since become a ubiquitous concept that people from many disciplines, ranging from engineering to sociology, use to signify the linkages among independent entities, and a developed methodology has emerged to systematically analyze specific structural relationships within networks. When we used the term in 1987, it seemed intuitively correct, but as the word became more widely used, and as its meaning in the social sciences became associated with static structural forms created by groups of actors, then the term needed more and more qualifications if we were to use it to depict Chinese business organization.

Social scientists came to define networks as a thing, in a world of other things, such as firms and markets.[1] Networks became reified as particular types of configurations representing stable forms of arranging interfirm and interpersonal relationships. As more or less stable structural forms, networks could be analyzed with the appropriate methodology, and the conclusions could be generalized across all societies.[2]

It was in this context that an interest in Chinese business networks emerged. These networks were seen as archetypical networks, the best examples of trust-bearing networks found anywhere in the world. The elevation of Chinese business networks to this exalted status came with the "discovery" of *guanxi*, not only as a Chinese term for a type of close interpersonal relationship but, more importantly, as evidence for the empirical reality of a theoretically predicted condition: something that was neither a firm nor a market and that was embedded in social institutions.[3] Chinese business networks, however, are neither alternatives to firms and markets nor archetypical examples of how networks are depicted in Western social science. They are dynamic and not static forms of organizing.[4] They are processes more than things, a way of organizing more than the organization itself. Above all, Chinese business networks are more expressions of relational ties than institutional structures and more a matter of social etiquette than an indication of organizational boundaries.

Recognizing the fluidity of Chinese society, we realized that we needed to conceptualize networks in a way that captured the everyday life experience of Taiwanese businesspeople, a way of life that centered on family and on eating and drinking, as we illustrate in the following example.

The *Weiya* Banquet

It was on our second visit to Xingfu, the world's leading manufacturer of hydraulic jacks at the time, that we joined the banquet. The day of our visit was in January of 1992, a couple of weeks before the Chinese Lunar New Year. Mr. Chung, the Vice President of the company, had invited us for a return visit, partly to hear the conversation between the owner of the firm and his 400 subcontractors and partly to eat. The loading dock, where the trucks normally were loaded with crates full of jacks, had been cleared for the day, and in their place were more than a hundred round tables, each large enough to seat ten to twelve people. At the time of our visit, Xingfu employed about 400 persons. By employee numbers, it was the largest of the six major jack companies located in Chiayi. The production of these six companies in 1992, we were told, accounted for over 70 percent of the world market in hydraulic jacks, which, when one considers that nearly every car in the world has at least one in the trunk, amounts to a huge number of jacks.

On this particular day, Chairman Hong, the owner of Xingfu, met with his key employees and subcontractors, mostly owners of small independent firms making component parts for his jacks, as well as the hydraulic exercise machines that Chairman Hong was just beginning to manufacture when we visited. Starting at 4 p.m., the meeting lasted about an hour and contained no hints of negotiation, bargaining, or arm twisting of any kind. Chairman Hong extolled the quality of everyone's work. A few subcontractors spoke up, offering their suggestions. It was abundantly clear, however, that the reason for the gathering was not the meeting itself, but rather the banquet. Promptly at 5 p.m., the meeting adjourned. Everyone gathered in the loading docks for the *weiya*, the yearly banquet occurring just before the New Year, in which the *laoban* (the bosses) throughout Chinese societies express their thanks to all those joining together in common economic endeavors. By everyone in this case, we mean not only all the employees who worked directly for Xingfu, but also all the employees who worked for all the subcontractors as well. On that day, Chairman Hong fed more than a thousand people.

Everyone sat at the round tables. Hong and his top managers went from table to table talking to many people at each table, and downing a glass of Chinese wine as a toast. We joined the procession, listening to the conversation and downing our glasses of wine in unison with the others. After ten or so tables, the two of us sat down while we were still able. But Chairman Hong and his staff continued until every table had been visited and every person had been toasted. We marveled not only at his capacity for Chinese wine but also at the obvious importance of the occasion for bringing all the workers together and making them feel part of one common endeavor, part of one family.

Many of the 400 subcontractors were also part of other family firms, and this *weiya* was only one of the several they would attend this year. In fact, some of the subcontractors worked for all the jack firms in Chiayi. One such person was Mr. Wei, whose firm we visited several times. Mr. Wei was the owner of a twelve-person firm that did high-precision drilling for twelve different companies in Chiayi, including the top six jack manufacturers. Although Mr. Wei did not attend all the *weiya* to which he was invited, he did eat regularly throughout the year at many round tables hosted by the owners of many different firms.

Mr. Wei owned a key firm in the very dense network of independent firms that constitute the manufacturing industries of Chiayi. The work of all the firms rose and fell with the OEM contracts they received. In those years, when the orders were many, the subcontracting networks of each firm expanded to include many other firms, but when the orders fell, the networks shrank. Most of the major manufacturers, however, maintained a core group of subcontractors that mainly, if not solely, worked just for them.

The *weiya* banquets, along with the other banquets that occur throughout the year, symbolize the contingencies of building and maintaining good relationships among people and firms that work closely together, which is, more or less, what we mean by networks in Chinese society. It is because of the relationships and their importance in the activities of daily life that people need to build new, and to maintain existing, relationships. Relational bonds form the underlying grammar of Chinese society, much as organizational affiliations form the underlying grammar of American society.[5] Because relationships are so important in economic life, owners of all such firms, however large or small, devote considerable time, effort, and money to relationships and, therefore, to eating together, to hosting and being hosted by others. And when they eat together, they, like everyone else in Chinese society, eat at a round table.

The round table is both symbolic of Chinese society and a part of daily life. Chinese meals are always shared by those seated around the table. The dishes are placed in the middle and starting with the eldest or the person with the highest prestige or the guest, everyone, using chopsticks, helps themselves to a proportionate share of each dish, a bite or two at a time. It is improper to be aggressive, to take more than your share at any one moment. Everyone around the table trusts that they will get their share of the food, whatever that share may be. In this context, food is not divided equally, each portion being allotted to individual plates, as is often the case in Western meals. Instead, eating at the round table is a way of sharing food, not a way the food is shared. The round table is not a method of allocation, but rather a way of serving others as well as yourself. This pattern also applies to drinking. Alcoholic beverages are not consumed individually, but rather together, as part of toasting. Sharing food and drink, eating from a common bowl, makes commensality in Chinese societies a relation among intimates.

In this sense, the round table is a closed circle. Who eats at the same table and who does not is an important social indicator in Chinese societies. Understanding who can join this circle and when, and who cannot, and under what circumstances, is a key to understanding Chinese social and economic life.

A closed circle, however, does not mean a fixed circle. Rather one should think of intimate circles as a set of concentric rings, each wider and more encompassing than the next.[6] The ring closest to the center, the one represented by the smallest round table is that of the household, consisting of the nuclear family extended to include three generations, children, parents, and grandparents. In Chinese society, the nuclear family is the most exclusive segment of a lineage, and is defined by two hierarchal axes, one based on generation, between father and son, and the other based on gender, between husband and wife. Within this group of intimates, the normative sentiments are ones of duty and respect. From this core, the larger rings extend out, connecting relatives, friends, classmates, colleagues, and on out to anyone with whom one has a bond of similarity. In the rings beyond the nuclear family, however, the relationships become less hierarchical and based more on friendship and affection. Norms of reciprocation and mutual obligation among friends and colleagues replace the obedience that exists between parent and child and between husband and wife. Who is included in each widening ring depends on social circumstances. The arrangement at a wedding banquet would be different from that at a *weiya* banquet, but subtle demarcations are no less present.

The seating arrangements for the *weiya* banquet at Xingfu were carefully thought out. The core managers and exclusive subcontractors sat near the center. Other subcontractors and their employees sat further away. Our own table was close but not too close to the core tables, befitting our rank as visiting but honored guests. Regardless of where one's own round table was placed, everyone symbolically ate together, as if the entire loading dock were one big round table. The food was the same, the drink was the same, the host was the same, and the occasion was shared by all.

On the surface, a wedding party and a *weiya* banquet share the same social logic and many of the same social rules, but in the end, they turn out to be quite different. This difference is essentially the difference between a family and a family firm. A family exists for many purposes, including reproduction, social status, and emotional fulfilment. Whatever other purposes it may fulfill, the family firm exists primarily for making money.

The *Laoban* and the Family Firm

Most firms in Chinese societies are family firms. If we define family firms as those where a family has principal ownership and control of the business, then family firms are certainly one of the most, if not the most, common forms of business organization throughout the world. We do not want to claim that Chinese societies are unusual in this regard. But there are some important features of family firms in Chinese societies that distinguish them from family firms elsewhere. We might think of these differences in the following way: in the United States, for instance, however the ownership and control of a firm is put together, the firm, insofar as it is a formal organization, is incorporated. It is a corporation. That is the law. Insofar as they are part of economic institutions, then, family-owned businesses are corporations as well.

In Chinese societies, the reverse is true. However the firm is formally organized, whether as a partnership, a corporation, or a joint stock company, the firm is integrated into a social framework in which their owners must act in a way that makes them recognizably a family firm. Put more simply, *familization* is a mutually recognized way of organizing business.

Using the organizational principles of families as the principles to run businesses does not, however, make a household and a firm synonymous. Even though the point where the household ends and the firm begins is often ambiguous, no one confuses the two, for the simple reason that at the head of every family is a *chiajang* (family head), but at the head of every firm is a *laoban*.

Laoban is a term identifying the person in charge of a business. No *laoban*, no business. The word is often translated as "boss," but its use is more restricted than that. A farmer raising crops and making money on family-owned land would be called a landowner (*dichu*) but not a *laoban*. Only the person in charge of a business is called a *laoban*. The size of the business is unimportant. A peddler selling "rotten doufu" would be called *laoban*. Likewise Li Ka-shing, one of the richest Chinese businessmen in the world, if not the richest, would be called by the same title. Doing business, on the one hand, and being in charge of the business, on the other, is the crucial distinction.

Laoban, however, is not a formal title. No man or woman on his or her business card would put *laoban* as his or her title. Nor would the wife of a businessman put *laobanniang* (the boss's wife) on hers. And yet every business has a *laoban*, a person in charge, and every business only has one *laoban*. As the Chinese saying goes, there is only one tiger per mountain (*yishan burong liang hu*). Formal titles, such as *dongshihchang* (chairman of the board) and *chongjingli* (general manager), are the titles appearing on business cards, and quite often one or the other would be the *laoban*, but in other firms the *laoban* would have no formal title whatsoever. For instance, in a number of firms we visited, the sons held the titles, but the father, who had no formal position, was the *laoban* and made all the crucial decisions himself. *Laoban* is, therefore, a social term denoting the person who has the acknowledged position of authority in the firm. It is a personalized position, a role that defines all the relationships both within and outside the firm.

The *laoban* role, however, is not merely social but has actual economic substance as well. First and foremost, the term denotes the person who has the "the power of control and disposal."[7] The *laoban* typically, although not universally, has the majority ownership of the firm. As is common in most Chinese-dominated economies, where investment capital is often raised through family and friends, the *laoban* controls the majority of the shares, even if he does not actually own them himself. With this ownership comes the right to make the decisions regarding budget, personnel, and management. In small firms, the *laoban* and often his wife, who typically has the title *laobanniang*, combine all these functions. As firms grow larger, or as they become diversified and sited in different locations, the *laoban* often delegates the management but closely retains control over the allocation of resources and the hiring of key personnel.

We found repeatedly in our interviews in both small and large firms that the *laoban*'s wife assumes extremely important roles.[8] She often takes care of the books. It is customary in Chinese households that the wife takes care of household finances, and in many firms, the wife assumes a similar role, but she also typically manages labor, especially when the workers are female. In quite a few cases, the wife, being the most proficient in English, also handles the primary contacts with buyers. This sort of division of labor makes sense in very small firms where the profits are insufficient to hire others, but it is also very common in the largest business groups as well. Regardless of the type or size of firm, the wife of the *laoban* has a recognized and legitimate role to play, if she wishes to assume it, a role that continues even after her husband dies.

There are many examples showing the crucial roles of the *laobanniang*. Following traditional practices, Wang Yung-ching had multiple wives. His first wife and second wife played no role in his businesses, but his third wife (*sanniang*) was very influential. There are many other examples as well, but perhaps none so clear as the case of Jungxing Textile Group in Taiwan. Late in his life, Bao Chaoyun, the owner and *laoban* of the many firms in his group, worked closely with his mistress, Chou Yinxi, in running the affairs of the business, and while Bao was alive, Chou was acknowledged to be the *laobanniang*. When Mr. Bao died, Ms. Chou continued to run the group, even over the objections of Bao's son by his only wife. Recognizing Ms. Chou as the successor to the owner meant, in effect, not only that she was the legitimate holder of authority within the group but also that she was capable of running the business and thus able to make money.

This example, like so many others we could give, illustrates another feature of the *laoban* role, namely business competence. *Laoban*, as well as *laobanniang*, are recognized by their technical and professional competence. They must earn the respect of those with whom they work, which includes their employees and also independent subcontractors. This competence extends in every direction. The *laoban*, even of a very large firm, knows the technical details of his or her business. Nearly every independent owner must become an expert, albeit in a very narrow field of expertise. Owners obtain this knowledge and expertise through many different channels, including dealing with their networks of colleagues and friends, working with buyers, going to tradeshows, and reading extensively in trade publications. Most owners of small and medium-sized firms do not need the most advanced technology, but they do need a level of technology that can be commercialized, that allows them, in other words, to make money. Therefore, as products go through cycles of boom and bust, as buyers' orders shift, the *laoban* tries to keep one step ahead of the changing markets.

The central role of the *laoban* is what makes firms into family firms. This role is equivalent and structurally very similar to the role of family head. Firms metaphorically become families and family rules apply, even though everyone knows the difference between the two. In Chinese society, fictive kinship is extremely important. People are brought into sets of relationships by identifying their positions through kinship terminology, as brothers, cousins, sisters, and uncles, and acting accordingly. Similarly, the firm is socially constituted as a fictive family—with the *laoban* and the *laobanniang* as real (to some) and fictive (to others) heads of an organization in which the logic and roles of families serve as a model of operation. In this sense, any firm having a *laoban* in charge is a family firm, regardless of its formal constitution.

Bandi: The Inner Core of the Firm

When firms are small, a husband and wife perform all the roles of ownership, management, and accounting themselves. But as the firms grow larger, these roles become more specialized and complex, and move beyond the capability of any one or two persons to do them all. When this expansion occurs, the *laoban* typically develops a core group of people to help him or her run the business. This group of personnel is called the *bandi*. The term means literally manage the foundation (of the firm). Because the role of *laoban* is individualized and personal, being a *bandi* member involves personal relationships with the *laoban*. The *bandi*, in effect, constitutes the *laoban*'s personal staff.

The logic of the *bandi* is precisely the logic of the personal staff. It extends the power of the person in charge. In this sense, the *bandi* is based, in the first instance, on the ties of personal loyalty to the *laoban*. Without trust, there can be no *bandi*, and when businesses are in their infancy, and technology is relatively simple, personal trust between the owner and the employees was often enough. But as industry in Taiwan grew more complex, in terms of both technology and being spread out in numerous geographical locations, the technical and professional competence of the *bandi* became increasingly important. In medium-sized to large businesses, especially the ones with technologically sophisticated operations, the *laoban* nurtures a close relationship with a small number of key people who know the production processes inside and out, the special techniques, and the key financial matters of the firm. With this group, the *laoban* runs the business, no matter what the formal organization.

The group itself is usually informal and contains a range of people. Because the *bandi* are extensions of the *laoban*'s control over the business, the composition of the group typically reflects those aspects inside the firm that most need control: management of labor, production quality, and financial resources. The general manager is usually a member, as is the *laoban*'s personal secretary. Family members, such as a son or brother, may or may not be members depending on the circumstances, the competence of the individual, and the feelings and trust between them and the *laoban*. In one firm, we recall that one brother was included in the *bandi*, but the others were not.

Many owners told us that the *bandi* increased their flexibility whenever serious problems would arise. The *laoban* would call the *bandi* together, and they would collectively and quickly solve the problem. The intimate knowledge that each member of the staff possesses about the firm, as well about each other, allows for frank discussions and rapid decision making, all from the *laoban*'s point of view. Because everyone in the firms knows who is in the inner circle, who is close to the *laoban*, the implementation of these decisions is relatively uncomplicated.

The personal staff organization of Chinese family firms is not without its persistent problems. Some firms are troubled by the personal animosities and petty jealousies among staff members who compete for closeness to the *laoban*. The tension becomes so bad that on occasion some key members of the *bandi* simply leave and start their own firms. Therefore, the most able *laoban* are those who pay close attention to the needs of their *bandi*. The owner of one medium-sized firm told us: "If I drive a Bentley, then I had better make sure my general manager drives a Mercedes," and as a matter of fact he did. Together, the *laoban*, the *laobanniang*, and the *bandi* control the internal aspects of family firms. These internal matters fall under the direct authority of the *laoban*, and require the obedience of all those working in the firm.

The personal nature of this authority is often onerous. People may find the *laoban* less than fully competent; they may not like his personality; they may object to having his son or daughter promoted when they are not. Any matter of conflict or unease may undermine their willingness to continue in the firm. This is particularly true, if they have an opportunity to start their own firms and become *laoban* themselves. This occurred in the early years of industrialization, when Taiwan's economy was booming. In those years, labor turnover was extremely high, and the number of firms in proportion to the total population was also extremely high. It was very difficult to retain workers and very difficult to expand firms beyond a certain size.[9]

Although the social distance between *laoban* and employees have increased with the increasing size of firms, it is not unusual to find that the *laoban* and *laobanniang* eat together with their employees, sharing a common eating location and often the same round table. The *laoban*, his family, the *bandi*, and the employees represent concentric rings. Each ring out from the center requires a distinctive type of relationship to the household in which the father/*laoban* has duties and responsibilities to everyone in the household/firm, and they all have the responsibility to follow the decision of the father/*laoban*. The rules of family life and the rules of family firms, though different, still talk to each other. But without the family firm being able to make money, there is no conversation between family and firm.

The Round-Table Etiquette of *Laoban* Networks

During the initial years of rapid industrialization, the key to making money, however, was not simply the family firm. Rather, the key was the integration of family firms into groups of firms in which each *laoban* was an independent player in the group. Throughout our work, we have called such groups *networks*," and we have viewed each *laoban* as a node in the network. Leaving the question of terminology aside for the moment, most products made in Taiwan during this period—including textiles and garments, shoes, bicycles, sporting gear, computer-related products, and even semiconductor chip sets—were manufactured by groups of independent firms working together to make the products. Such interlinked groups were and still are ubiquitous. Large, medium-sized, and small firms can all participate in the same group. What determined the composition of each group were more the products and the quantity of the products being made than some particularistic feature of the people making the products. All the groups, therefore, differed according to what was being manufactured and how it was being manufactured. All the groups, however, resembled one another in terms of what held them together.

These production networks are, in formal contexts, sometimes referred to in Chinese as *weixing gongchang*, or satellite assembly systems. The term itself connotes roundness, a circle, like a round table. Derived from Japanese methods of production, this term, which refers to the whole production unit, the core firms as well as the peripheral ones, is seldom used by the factory owners themselves. More commonly, businesspeople refer to their activity by denoting their subcontracting roles in relation to the main firms with the term *xieli gongchang*. *Xieli* is often combined with *tongxin* as a set phrase, *tongxin xieli*, which can be roughly translated as "working together with the same spirit." Used in conjunction with production, *xieli gongchang* connotes a type of relationship that independent firms have with the firm that contracts them, namely working together cooperatively. This kind of cooperative subcontracting is similar in spirit to being a guest at a banquet.

We have come to understand that the round table is not merely a metaphor for how these business networks operate but is, more properly, a real aspect of the daily life of Chinese entrepreneurs. The round table is a "lived-in" metaphor, a part of the tacit knowledge that guides how subcontracting networks are organized and operate. In this sense, we can speak of a *round-table etiquette* that informs participants as to how they can cooperate in making money.

This etiquette is, more or less, as follows. Like every round-table meal, every *xieli gongchang* has an implicit hierarchy. This is a hierarchy without command and obedience. There is always a host, someone who calls people to this production circle. The host creates a *functional hierarchy*. In business networks, the host is usually the person receiving the OEM order, the contract from the buyer. The host, as in a round-table meal, is not necessarily the most important person at the table. Instead, he may be a trading company *laoban* who gets the order, and the most prestigious people in the circle may be the skilled craftspeople who know how to execute the order and to put people together. What is the fair share varies with every order, and who is present at the table varies with every order, too. The subcontractors come in as independent guests who work cooperatively with the host. Making money is the most important goal, but individual maximization does not work if the network is to function properly. This is a circle of colleagues who share the fate of the group. The operating norm of the group is "reciprocity" (*huxiang*), and individual performance is judged through this normative lens. The network is crucial for money making, and in the context of the network, individual aggressiveness at the expense of one's colleagues does not work. Nor does any attempt to get more than one's own share. Profit sharing and risk sharing are one and the same thing. Making money and reducing risk are both done through these networks.

Eating and drinking and doing business all draw on the same etiquette. This is the etiquette of polite behavior that acknowledges each participant's equality with the others, while at the same time placing people in a hierarchy that is functional for the activity. If one partakes in the joint activity, one is obligated to abide by the placement of people and rules of reciprocity that apply to everyone. Some act as host, some act as guests, and everyone eats for as long as the meal lasts.

This mixture of permanent fundamental equality and temporary functional inequality is a key characteristic of Chinese business networks. Although such networks may persist for some time, they are temporary. They last only as long as the contract lasts. Taiwanese businesspeople understand this and use the phrase *Tiansha wu bu san de yanxi* (In this world, there are no unending banquets) to signify that good times always come to an end. The mistake made by many analysts of Chinese society, a mistake often attacked by their critics, is to view Chinese business networks—the people, the trust, the specific interrelationships—as being more fixed, stable, and permanent than they really are and then to reduce Chinese societies to the workings of such networks. But the actual networks, in truth, are not long term, and the social relationships underlying these networks have to be constantly built and rebuilt. Although the organizational format that networks represent is an enduring framework of action, any specific network is a creation of people who come and go, of people who use this format for their own special purposes, of people wanting to make money and needing to change with changing circumstances. In Taiwan's production networks, the products change, the manufacturers change, the buyers change, everything changes, except the round-table etiquette. It is the etiquette—the social and cultural package—that provides structure in the midst of rapid change, that serves as a source of continuity and predictability where otherwise there would be little or none.

Conclusion

The remarkable success of contract manufacturing in Taiwan has a sociological foundation. In the late 1960s and early 1970s, when the Japanese trading companies and American buyers first arrived in Taiwan, people from many walks of life pooled their money and started businesses in response to the new opportunities that suddenly appeared. They organized these businesses in the same way as they organized their lives, and this mode of organization had a special affinity to contract manufacturing. They did not have the education or the expertise to make and to brand products on their own. But they had enough ingenuity and enough assistance to figure out how to make products ordered by others. Each small firm would take a piece of the action, would cooperate in producing the final products, and would share in whatever profits came their way. Modularization and low-overhead cost structures were characteristics of Taiwan's production networks from the start, and so was the desire to make money and to do whatever it took to keep the businesses going.

The role played by this sociological foundation, however, should not be overstated. The round-table etiquette that served as an underpinning for Taiwan's economic success is not a characteristic of Taiwan alone; it is shared by other Chinese societies.[10] Moreover, it is not a recent development, but is, instead, one with considerable history. Chinese economies have changed as much as any economies have in the past two centuries. Throughout the Qing dynasty, which ended in 1911, economic activity was institutionally framed by regional associations (*huiguan*), which had linkages into rural areas and which, along with the state, were the organizing force for much of the economy. The normatively framed collegiality within these associations operated in much the same way as that within production networks in Taiwan.[11] Virtually all firms represented in these associations were independently owned either by a single family or by partners. The strong egalitarian rules of etiquette within these associations gave predictability to collective economic activities that were otherwise unregulated.[12]

By the end of the nineteenth century, however, Chinese entrepreneurs working along the China coast came into direct competition with Western firms. Small firms embedded in a framework of regional associations could not compete with Western firms in such areas as banking, insurance, mass distribution, department stores, and manufacturing plants. Chinese entrepreneurs needed larger and more highly capitalized firms to compete in the same sectors as Western firms. Chinese entrepreneurs began to experiment with corporate forms borrowed from the West, especially the limited liability company.[13] Though few Chinese firms so organized were successful initially, by the late 1930s, nearly all the largest Chinese firms in Hong Kong and Shanghai had adopted this corporate form, and had raised considerable amounts of money from shareholders, who acted as silent partners to the person who served as the *laoban*. This organizational format, which often relied on raising money through interpersonal networks of family and friends, removed the Chinese firm from the regionalized institutional framework of the traditional economy, and made it revolve around the personal networks of an entrepreneur who operated in an environment of state-supported legal regulations. The modern Chinese family firm that we described above is a direct descendant from those adopting the shareholding format of limited liability companies. Round-table etiquette persists, even though the institutional format changes.

In the second half of the twentieth century, offshore Chinese economies, such as those in Taiwan and Hong Kong, began rapidly to industrialize. As we described in the previous chapters, the key driver of this industrialization was the retail revolution in the United States that in turn stimulated contract manufacturing in Asia. Japanese trading companies arranged most of the early contracts between American buyers and Taiwanese and Hong Kong manufacturers, but as demand increased, both sets of manufacturers were able to work closely with the buyers, on one hand, and to organize effective production networks, on the other. For this purpose, cooperative production networks proved to be flexible in response to Western orders and to be able steadily to upgrade in terms of quality, speed of delivery, and costs—characteristics that in turn brought in more orders. From 1965 through most of the 1980s, the emergent Taiwanese and Hong Kong economies were the result of the capabilities of would-be businesspeople to organize in response to increasing and rapidly changing demand. The comparative advantage that their form of organization gave them was that it allowed them nearly to monopolize the production of certain types of goods that needed to be produced in limited batches and that had short product cycles, a category of merchandise called nondurable consumer goods.

But there are no unending banquets. This price-sensitive, low-overhead, cost-cutting mode of manufacturing had its limits. Hong Kong entrepreneurs could not maintain their momentum and remain in Hong Kong. Rising wages, increasing property values, and relentless pricing pressure from contract buyers, competing networks, and upstream suppliers of component parts pushed many manufacturing networks out of Hong Kong and made conditions increasingly difficult in Taiwan as well. This bottom-up form of manufacturing was ill suited for mass-producing large, capital intensive products, such as automobiles. It is equally ill-suited for branding, merchandising, and globally distributing products. Also, these production networks could not easily change into some other form of business organization, such as large vertically integrated corporations. As we will explain in Chapter 5, by the mid-1980s, Taiwan's (but not Hong Kong's) economy had become increasingly demand responsive. Firms of all sizes, including state-owned firms as well as firms in Taiwan's large business groups, became integrated around the production of goods made for export. In this economy, export production was controlled by the smaller and not the larger half of Taiwan's industrial structure. And as time went on, it became increasingly difficult for firms to change their location in the organization of Taiwan's economy, at least until the late 1980s, when everything seemed to change.

Before that time, the continuing success of Taiwan's small-firm economy would seem to invalidate the lessons of industrial organization and business history. These lessons conclude that big firms eventually win out and small firms eventually disappear or become marginal to the economy as a whole. Vertically integrated, multidivisional corporations, capturing economies of scope and scale, supposedly are inevitable in expanding industrial economies. But, as we will explain in the next chapter, these lessons did not apply in Taiwan, at least not in the way predicted by economic theory.

5

BIG BUSINESS, SMALL FIRM
Meat and Soup

A strange thing happened to Taiwan's economy in the twenty years between 1965 and 1985. As exports of consumer goods surged and as the entire economy expanded exponentially, the number of small and medium-sized firms grew nearly as fast as the overall economy. According to one calculation, "the number of reported firms increased by 315 percent . . . and the average firm size expanded 15 percent." In the same period, the exact opposite and more predictable outcome occurred in South Korea, where the "average firm size jumped by 300 percent and its firms grew in number by only 10 percent."[1]

The South Korean case follows the typical pattern. In the initial growth phases of an industry, when the startup costs and other barriers to entry are relatively low, many firms jump at the opportunities in a new field, but as growth accelerates, some firms emerge as winners, and others go out of business or are bought out by the more successful firms. For instance, when the automobile and computer industries began in the United States, many small manufacturers entered these fields, but as these industries matured, those firms that offered a better value for the price or that had better advertising and trendier designs captured the lion's share of the markets. These industries, as well as the South Korean economy, follow the general rule that as an industry (or economy) matures, a greater concentration of total sales is captured by fewer and fewer firms at the top.[2]

In Taiwan, before the late 1980s, the process seemed to go in the other direction. As Taiwan's economy industrialized, and as Taiwan's industries mushroomed, the concentration within industries and in Taiwan's economy as a whole, did not increase and, in fact, in many final goods sectors substantially decreased. The organization of Taiwan's economy appeared to spread out among more and more firms instead of being consolidated in a dwindling number of large business groups. With Taiwan's population approaching 20 million in the mid-1980s, there were nearly 700,000 registered businesses in Taiwan, all of which had their *laoban*. This works out to be one *laoban* for every fifteen persons, and if we count only adults, then one *laoban* for every eight persons.³ A joke circulating in Taiwan in 1980s is hardly an exaggeration: "Throw a rock out of a window and the odds are good for hitting the general manager or president of a Taiwan company."⁴ Over 98.5 percent of all registered firms had fewer than 300 employees, and over 90 percent had fewer than 50 employees. This is a deceptive number, however, because most Asian economies have a high percentage of small firms, although not nearly so many firms per capita. What is even more surprising about this number, however, is that, unlike the situation in other Asian economies, a very large percentage of these small firms were involved in export production. The Taiwanese government calculated that firms having fewer than 300 employees accounted for nearly 50 percent of Taiwan's total manufacturing and 65 percent of all exports.⁵ By contrast, large firms of more than 500 employees represented a steady, if not slightly declining, share of total production. Between the mid-1960s and the 1980s, the share of net value added for these large firms went down from 46 percent to 37 percent, a figure that would be much lower if we were counting only firms producing exports.⁶

These figures take on a special significance when we examine Taiwan's largest business groups. These Taiwanese business groups consist of independent firms that are collectively owned by one or more families. From the early 1970s until the late 1980s, Taiwan's top one hundred business groups primarily produced intermediate goods or supplied services for other firms in the domestic economy. So marked was this tendency that one Taiwanese economist argued that Taiwan's private sector had a dichotomous market structure. The large segment of small and medium-sized firms dominated manufacturing and export production, while the much smaller segment of large and very large firms produced goods and services for local use.⁷ This characteristic is particularly true for the top one hundred business groups. Among the top ten groups in 1983, which accounted for nearly 50 percent of total sales and assets for the top one hundred groups, only two business groups made final products, Yulon (known as Yue Loong until a 1992 spelling change) and Tatung Electronics. We will discuss both firms later in this chapter, but for now it is enough to know that, throughout the entire period, Yulon produced automobiles for domestic use. Only Tatung produced goods for export, as well as domestic use. All the other top ten business groups either produced intermediate products or provided services for the local economy.

Another characteristic of these business groups is the relative lack of vertical integration among firms in the groups.[8] If we trace the development of these business groups over time, it is possible to chart a typical trajectory of expansion. The first firms established in a group typically form around a core, money-making business. For example, several of the largest groups started with initial firms in textiles. However, after solidifying the group's position in that particular business, perhaps by adding a closely related firm, the owners then established additional firms in unrelated areas, usually in the financial (e.g., insurance) or service sectors. As a consequence, up until the late 1980s, Taiwan's business groups resembled a loose collection of firms specializing in a range of unrelated enterprises whose targeted customers were people and firms in the local economy.[9]

Among Asian economies in the 1980s, Taiwan's industrial organization was unusual, if not unique. Moreover, Taiwan's unusual qualities help explain why its entrepreneurs became so adept at contract manufacturing.

Export Production in Japan and South Korea: Firm Integration Through Organization

We can understand Taiwan's unusual industrial organization by contrasting its export production in 1985 with that of the other two major export-led economies in East Asia, Japan and South Korea.[10] In these two countries, the largest business groups controlled export production, but in Taiwan, the small and medium-sized firms did. This difference in export production was telling, for it suggests differences in the mode of production, in the types of products the respective groups manufactured, and in the price structures on which the manufacturing processes were based.

In Japan, as we described in Chapter 3, some of the business groups, known collectively as the *keiretsu*, emerged in the 1950s from the former *zaibatsu*, which had dominated the Japanese economy before World War II and which the US occupation forces had outlawed as monopolies. Once the US occupation ended, the former *zaibatsu* regrouped, but without holding companies at the top. Other *keiretsu* developed after the war from the expansion of very successful core businesses. During the heyday of Japanese global success in the 1980s, six horizontal *keiretsu* and ten additional vertical *keiretsu* formed the organizational core of the Japanese economy and controlled much of the Japan's manufacturing capacity and most of its manufactured exports.[11]

The horizontal *keiretsu*, epitomized by the Mitsui and Mitsubishi groups, linked huge corporations in every major industrial sector into a loosely knit group with a main bank and a trading company at the center.[12] For instance, in 1982, the Mitsubishi group consisted of twenty-eight major corporations, including a major steel mill, two companies making nonferrous metals, five chemical companies, two cement and glass companies, two companies making cars and trucks, and a company making electrical and electronic products, among others. These companies were not family-owned businesses, but rather were owned by other firms in the group. Each main firm in the group held shares, usually less than 5 percent, of the other main firms in the group. Centered on the main bank holdings, this elaborate cross-shareholding scheme allowed the group collectively to become the majority shareholder of all the major firms in the group, thus preventing hostile takeovers and providing long-term stability for the group as a whole. The coordination of each group's strategy was accomplished through a monthly meeting of the presidents of all the main firms.

Whereas the horizontal *keiretsu* encompassed the main sectors across Japan's economic landscape, the vertical *keiretsu* provided manufacturing depth in each sector.[13] These sets of vertically integrated firms were linked to, and were largely owned by, a core enterprise at the middle. Japan's leading industrial groups (including Toyota, Nissan, Matsushita, Hitachi, Toshiba, and Sony) are vertical *keiretsu*, and in the early 1980s each had over twenty large corporations in its core production network. For instance, in 1984, Toyota had thirty-four firms in its group, and the lead firm owned an average of over 26 percent of all the other firms in the group. Other firms in the group held smaller percentages of shares, but enough to maintain majority control. These highly successful industrial groups had ties to multiple horizontal *keiretsu* and were, somewhat ironically, referred to as "independent" groups. Besides the ten independent groups, each of the major firms in a horizontal *keiretsu* was also the lead firm of its own vertical *keiretsu*, which turned the top echelon of the Japanese economy into a horizontal and vertical web of interconnected firms. In addition to this web-like network of large corporations, there were also scores of independently owned small and medium-sized firms that were attached to each of the major firms in the vertical *keiretsu* and that produced component parts required by the larger firm to which they were informally attached. All of these interconnected firms represented, collectively, a huge umbrella-like network controlling most of Japan's booming economy in 1985.

Japanese scholars have referred to the business strategy of these *keiretsu* as *one-setism*, meaning that each group, encapsulated by both vertically and horizontally linked firms, was more or less self-sufficient in producing its products.[14] Upstream, downstream, and service firms (including banks, trading companies, and insurance firms) were all in the same group, forming a community of common economic interests. Ideally, firms in a group did not have to rely on other firms outside their own community of firms for anything substantial, including capital. These preferential exchanges within groups meant that the lattice-like networks of firms substituted for a system of market exchanges. These preferential exchanges were important because the horizontal *keiretsu* aggressively competed with one another for a share of domestic and export markets.

The South Korean business groups, called *chaebol*, also dominated export production in South Korea, even more so than did the Japanese business groups. Here, too, preferential pricing for transactions among firms within the *chaebol* substituted for market pricing. But, unlike the Japanese *keiretsu*, the *chaebol* were without a main bank because the Korean government controlled the banking system. Also, unlike the *keiretsu*, *chaebol* were centrally managed, family-owned business groups. A designated individual, usually the founder or the founder's heir, was the person in charge, and a small number of individuals within the *chaebol* typically controlled the business strategy for the group as a whole.

Differences aside, however, in terms of manufacturing and merchandising products, the *chaebol* and the *keiretsu* were similar. Like the *keiretsu*, the largest *chaebol* practiced a strategy of one-setism. The five largest *chaebol* in 1985 (Samsung, Hyundai, Lucky-Goldstar, Daewoo, and Sunkyong) hotly competed with one another for shares of the domestic and export markets. Each *chaebol*'s upstream and downstream firms were vertically integrated in the production of the group's primary products.[15] In 1985, the five largest *chaebol* controlled over 50 percent of all Korean exports, nearly 50 percent of all manufacturing sales, 10 percent of the total labor force, and about 30 percent of the value added in manufacturing for the entire South Korean economy.[16] Although the South Korean economy was at the time less than a tenth the size of the Japanese economy, and although the largest *chaebol* were smaller than any one of the horizontal *keiretsu*, they dominated the Korean economy, and especially the export sector, even more than did the *keiretsu* in the Japanese economy.[17]

Also, like the *keiretsu*, the *chaebol* organization of firms emerged before rapid industrialization began, and once industrialization was under way, the market share of exports controlled by the leading business groups grew at an even faster pace than the overall economy. In South Korea's case, the *chaebol* dominance of the Korean economy began after the Korean War concluded, during the presidency of Syngman Rhee, when United Nations forces (led by the United States) took up long-term residency along the border dividing North and South Korea. After the coup d'état in 1960, led by Park Chung Hee, the *chaebol* organization at the top of the Korean economy became even more prominent, and even more concentrated in the outskirts of Seoul, near the seat of government and the armed forces. In both the Japanese and Korean cases, the largest business groups in the two economies were in the best position to take advantage of the new opportunities created by post-war changes in the global economy. South Korean newspapers recognized this fact when they referred to the *chaebol* as being like an octopus, grabbing everything in sight with all eight legs.

Considering the size and the strategy of vertical integration adopted by Japanese and Korean business groups, it is not surprising that they were well suited for manufacturing certain types of products, but not for others. The Japanese and the Korean groups excelled at mass-producing complex, capital intensive products, such as consumer electronics, large household appliances, and automobiles. The tight integration of large firms within the groups increased their level of manufacturing expertise, which gave them a competitive advantage for making such products, but it also raised the overall cost of production dramatically. Their large size and capital intensity meant that, in order for them to make money, they had to manufacture and sell large quantities of relatively expensive items. And the best way to secure a market for these products was to develop a brand name and a merchandising strategy based on that brand name.

The Japanese *keiretsu* that were successful in pursuing this brand-name strategy typically expanded their production to match the market for their products. They did so by increasing the size and number of firms in the overall group. By 1985, Toyota, Matsushita, and Sony had become huge groups of firms employing hundreds of thousands of people, and the larger they grew, the more they had to top their previous efforts at both manufacturing and merchandising. In the 1970s, the exports from the Korean *chaebol* were mostly based on contract manufacturing, but by the late 1980s, the *chaebol* had reached the limits of what they could do by relying on contract manufacturing alone. In the 1980s, after several earlier sharp downturns caused by sudden increases in the price of oil, known as "oil shocks," the leading *chaebol*—Samsung, Hyundai, Lucky-Goldstar, and Daewoo—began to shift their main strategy to manufacturing products under their own brand names. Globalization became their mantra.

Taiwan's Export Production: Firm Integration Through Markets

On the eve of industrialization, Taiwan's economy had a different starting point and took a different path. As we described in Chapter 1, by the end of the 1960s, the three main sectors of Taiwan's economy—the state-owned, the large, and the small and medium-sized firm sectors—had not yet come together. Supported by their respective governments, the large business groups in Japan and South Korea served as the organizing hubs in those economies even before industrialization began in earnest, but in Taiwan, there was no equivalent center of gravity and no comparable organizing agents that would make the three sectors cohere to form an integrated economy.

Before Integration
State-Owned Firms

The state-owned sector in Taiwan was aloof, set off from the rest of the economy. Before Japan invaded China in 1936, the KMT-led Chinese government was never able to secure its authority over competing powers: the warlords who controlled China's periphery and some of its heartland, the huge landlords in the south and central regions of China who evaded taxes, and the industrialists and financiers in Shanghai and other big cities who controlled the most modern sectors of China's economy. When Chiang Kai-shek and the KMT retreated to Taiwan in 1949, the KMT government vowed not to make the same mistake: as explained in Chapter 1, the government declared martial law after the February 28, 1947, rebellion and eliminated or otherwise curtailed Taiwan's local elite; the government also did away with Taiwan's large landlords through land reforms that redistributed the ownership of farmland to the tillers, giving them a few hectares each; and the government took control of all businesses formerly owned by the Japanese. The KMT state privatized a few of the lesser enterprises to compensate large landowners whose holdings had been redistributed. Everything else, the state kept for itself, including all banks and credit services, all sources of energy (electrical generation and petroleum acquisition, refining and distribution), all transportation facilities (railways, ports, and highway ownership and construction), and the production and sale of fertilizer and certain food and drink (sugar processing facilities, tobacco, and alcoholic beverages). The KMT Party (as opposed to the government itself) claimed ownership of all communications and media (telephone, radio, and television). In 1952, the first year for which economic statistics are available, the government-owned portion of Taiwan's total industrial production (not including party ownership) stood at 56 percent, with 100 percent ownership of electricity, gas, and water facilities. In the remaining years of the 1950s, the government's portion hovered at slightly above 50 percent, and the ownership of utilities remained at 100 percent.[18] The percentage of state ownership and control was far higher and more comprehensive in Taiwan than it was in either Japan or South Korea.

The KMT state and party maintained control over these vital sectors for the next forty-plus years, in part because the government needed the revenues. More importantly, government ownership of these sectors prevented the formation of large, privately owned monopolies that would form competing power centers beyond state control. This position grew out of the KMT's legitimating ideology, the Three Principles of the People (San Min Zhuyi). First formulated by Sun Yat-sen, the founding President of the Republic of China in 1911, the Three Principles served as the cornerstone of Chiang Kai-shek's regime in Taiwan. Repeated ad nauseam in every school and at every public event until the mid-1980s, the Three Principles upheld the ideals of nationhood (*minzu*), of power by the people (*minquan*, sometimes translated as democracy), and of the economic and social welfare of the people (*minsheng*). Translated into action, the Three Principles legitimated KMT policies that allowed no intermediate power centers, including big business, to exist between the people and the state.

This ideology masked, but also reinforced the deep divisions in Taiwanese society after the KMT retreat to Taiwan. The repression and martial law after the February 28 massacre drove a wedge between the incoming Mainland

Chinese and the local Taiwanese Chinese. For nearly three decades, until the 1980s, Mainlanders held tight control over all branches of the central government, including the state-owned enterprises. This control effectively excluded Taiwanese entrepreneurs from expanding their businesses into sectors already dominated by the state. Instead, the government bureaucratized the management of these state-owned firms and ran them, sometimes quite inefficiently, until piecemeal reforms started to privatize some of the state-owned enterprises in the 1990s.

Despite being monopolies, these enterprises did not bring in much money for the state. Revenues from these enterprises, including public utilities, brought in less than 10 percent of the government's total revenues until 1965. Between 50 and 60 percent of government revenues throughout the period came from taxes, including customs duties, which contributed about 20 percent of the total revenues throughout the 1950s. The only lucrative government-controlled enterprise was the monopoly on the sale of tobacco and alcoholic beverages, which netted the government over 20 percent of total revenues until 1968.[19]

That the state-owned enterprises contributed over 50 percent of total industrial production until the 1960s is not an indication of a powerful state-owned sector. Quite the opposite is true. It is simply an indication that the total output of Taiwan's industrial sectors was slight. Starting at an extremely low point after World War II, Taiwan's industrial output (including the contribution by the state-owned businesses) during the 1950s slightly more than doubled, a poor showing by any measure. By 1980, however, it had expanded by over forty times the 1952 level, with most of the growth coming in the twelve years after 1968.

State-Supported Enterprises

In the 1950s, recognizing the absence of local industries, the KMT government helped a number of Mainland and Taiwanese businesspeople gain a foothold in certain selected upstream sectors that the government did not control, mostly chemicals and textiles. The founder of Formosa Plastics, Wang Yung-ching, was one of the businessmen so favored. Through his connections inside the KMT, he was able to get permission to apply for funding from USAID to establish a plant manufacturing polyvinyl chloride (PVC), the basic substance out of which various forms of plastic products are made. Also favored were the former large landowners to whom the government gave the controlling shares of the Taiwan Cement Corporation. This stake in Taiwan's largest cement company launched the Gu (Koo) family-owned business group. Both Wang and the Gu family were Taiwanese locals. Most of the other businesspeople who received some form of state sponsorship were Mainlanders. The most important of these were the former owners of the large textile mills in Shanghai who had relocated their factories to Taiwan. Some of these individuals founded important business groups, including the Far Eastern, Chung-shing, and Yulon groups.

These state-supported enterprises were mostly upstream firms making intermediate products for the domestic market. However, the domestic market was so weak that these businesses, encouraged by a government needing foreign exchange, exported a significant percentage of their relatively meager production in the late 1950s and early 1960s. That is the period when Wang Yung-ching had to export a significant portion of his intermediate plastic products because his estimate for local demand had been far too high. This is also the period when the large textile manufacturing business groups were exporting much of their production of cotton fabrics to the United States and Southeast Asia.[20] There was a limited demand for these fabrics in Taiwan. Even cement was exported. One of Taiwan's largest producers of cement in 1963, the Asia Cement Corporation, produced 37,000 metric tons of cement a month and "sold most of its product abroad."[21] In retrospect, we can see that the earliest exports came from Taiwan's largest firms simply because networks of small and medium-sized firms had not yet been established to make products for export and the KMT state had not yet begun to build up Taiwan's infrastructure.

Other large businesses in the 1950s and early 1960s grew with government support. These firms mainly produced products for the domestic market. Tatung was one of these.[22] Founded in 1918, during the colonial period, as a construction company, Tatung developed into a multi-firm business group by the end of World War II. Among its businesses were a steel mill, a machinery and tool factory, a high school, and a university. After the war, with KMT support, new firms in the group began to produce household appliances: electric fans in 1949, electric rice cookers in 1960, refrigerators in 1961, and black-and-white televisions in 1964. Tatung began producing these products after receiving assistance from Toshiba, a vertical *keiretsu*, and from Westinghouse Electric Corporation, a US company specializing in household appliances, among other things. Although Tatung would later become an important contract manufacturer, in this era it was primarily a producer of goods for the domestic market.

Yulon is another one of these state-supported firms that later grew into one of Taiwan's largest business groups. In 1948, the founder of the group, Yen Tjing-ling moved most of his family's textile business from Shanghai to Taiwan, just ahead of the communist takeover. Once in Taiwan, Yen's wife, Viven Wu Yen, took over management of the textile company, and Yen, in 1953, established the Yulon Engineering Company with a "capitalization of . . . 50,000 US$, a small plant, and a few score of workers."[23] After signing joint ventures with Japan's Nissan Motor Company and America's Willys Motor Company in 1957, Yulon became Taiwan's first and, for some time, its only firm manufacturing automobiles, trucks, and buses.[24] In 1960, "The number of trucks, buses, and sedans produced was 917. In 1964, it was 1,797."[25] By this time, Yulon was making nearly 60 percent of its own parts, with plans to increase this percentage to 75.[26] Chairman Yen also had plans for Yulon to export automobiles, and it did for a short time to a few undeveloped countries in the Middle East and Southeast Asia. But neither set of plans worked out. Sold in Taiwan's protected market, Yulon's sedan could not meet the quality or the price of its Japanese competitors in export markets. And Yen's plans for vertical integration ended in the late 1960s, wiped out by the government's decision to allow other firms to manufacture vehicles.

This growth spurt in manufacturing and in the exports of manufactured goods shows up in government statistics from the early 1960s, but to a large degree it was a false dawn, a glimmer of apparent growth resulting from the state's import substitution policies implemented in the 1950s. In the postcolonial world that emerged after World War II, the dominant development policy for the governments of most new states throughout the world was import substitution. Ideally, governments would establish upstream firms in those sectors that would most reduce the importation of needed goods. The upstream firms, protected by high tariff barriers, would theoretically produce the intermediate products that would lead to the establishment of downstream firms that would, in turn, produce those goods for the local economy. The policies would thus provide an industrial platform for future development and prevent the outflow of national wealth.

Wherever they were tried, these policies were never very successful and led, in most cases, only to short-term growth. Such short-term gains generally did not lead to successful industrialization because local markets were typically too small and the potential consumers too poor to propel industrialization forward. These policies mostly pumped money into domestic industries to start production, but after the initial bump in growth, the economy stagnated because demand could never match supply. Only in geographically large countries or those having ample natural resources, such as India, China, or some countries in Latin America, could such inwardly focused economic policies be sustained for a while. But in other locations, such as those needing to purchase oil, iron ore, and other necessary resources, import substitution policies were untenable even in the short run.

Political economists cite Taiwan as an exception to this rule.[27] They argue that such government visionaries as K. T. Li and Lin Kuo-ying (K. T. Li's predecessor) had the foresight to push those state-owned and state-supported enterprises started under an import substitution regime toward an export orientation. Taiwan's industries, they argue, were able to make the switch and thereby provide the foundation for Taiwan's rapid industrialization.

There is more than a grain of truth in this narrative, but the main parts of the story are missing. The first part is correct: state-supported enterprises did stimulate the local economy, and networks of small and medium-sized firms did form around these businesses. Starting from a very low base in the early 1950s, exports had grown by around 400 percent by 1965. The best export success had come from the government's promotion of raw and processed agricultural products. In 1965, agricultural products accounted for 54 percent of Taiwan's total exports; exports of just three items—bananas, sugar, and canned foods—provided over 34 percent of the total.[28] The only sizable manufactured export in that year was textiles, which made up slightly over 15 percent of the total. Moreover, 61 percent of all exports went to other Asian countries, with Japan leading the way with 31 percent of the total.[29] The United States received only 21 percent of Taiwan's total exports in 1965, mostly a mixture of textiles, plywood, and processed agricultural products. In 1965, the big buyers from the United States were nowhere in sight.

Part of what is missing in the narrative is that the state-supported firms did not organize the smaller firms within a common economic endeavor, as occurred in Japan. Nor did they marginalize the smaller firms, as occurred in South Korea. Instead, networks of smaller firms competed against the larger firms, and often won. The other and most important missing part is that shortly after the first bump up in supply, the economic situation in Taiwan changed, almost overnight: the retail revolution in the United States created rapidly increasing demand for a large and growing mix of consumer goods; the Vietnam War had established the logistical connections between Taiwan and the US market, and the big buyers arrived in Taiwan, with Japanese trading companies arriving first.

Small and Medium-Sized Firms

The jump in the number of small firms in Taiwan started gradually in the late 1950s, and then exploded in the late 1960s and early 1970s. In the 1960s, the small firms making nonagricultural consumer products were located mostly in the larger cities (Taipei, Taichung, and Kaohsiung) and were producing goods for local markets. In 1965, nearly 45 percent of Taiwan's registered firms in the manufacturing sector were in food production. The other 55 percent made clothes, paper products, electric fans, sewing machines, and similar products—all for the domestic market.[30] Indeed, as we pointed out earlier, there was no indication in 1965 that an export explosion was just a few years away.

The small firms, however, were active. By 1963, Tatung had a lot of local competition from them. Fourteen years after Tatung began manufacturing electric fans, seventy other factories were producing them as well; only three years after Tatung started making electric rice cookers, thirty other factories were making the same product; and after only one year of producing refrigerators, Tatung had eight competitors making refrigerators.[31] Yulon also faced the same problem. After the government ended Yulon's monopoly on manufacturing vehicles, a wave of competition from foreign firms paired with local networks of small and medium-sized parts suppliers set Yulon on the path to developing its own subcontracting network of suppliers, ending Yulon's plans for vertical integration, as well as for exporting automobiles. By the mid-1980s, there were five additional firms making vehicles, none of them very large and all of them producing only for the domestic market. In addition, over 2000 small and medium-sized firms were making automobile parts for export, mostly for the aftermarket automobile supply stores in the United States and Europe.[32]

The same thing happened to Wang Yung-ching's Formosa Plastics. After establishing Formosa Plastics and then finding very little local demand for his plastic goods, Wang Yung-ching started several factories making final consumer products. But he folded those factories when large numbers of small and medium-sized firms began to compete with his companies making consumer products. Formosa Plastics also faced competition in the upstream market as well, when other, smaller chemical firms started making PVC and other more specialized plastic components.

A similar scenario occurred in the Kaohsiung Export Processing Zone in the late 1960s and early 1970s. Once foreign corporations set up factories to manufacture consumer products that would then be exported, networks of small firms sprang up to make components for those products and then, after a short time, began to make products in competition with the foreign-owned factories. During the first years after it opened in 1966, this EPZ employed nearly 20,000 people and by 1973 over 50,000. Most of these workers were female, but many men were also employed, and most came from rural areas in southern and central Taiwan. Some of these employees went on to start their own firms in competition with their former employers, and many of these firms were located in the countryside. In Chapter 3, we described how the two owners of Ta Yang obtained the experience necessary for making baseballs while working in an export processing zone for a Japanese firm making the same product. Scores of other firms began making electrical components and other inputs that went first into products made by foreign firms and then into products made by Taiwanese firms. One by one the foreign corporations withdrew from Taiwan, driven out by low-cost Taiwanese manufacturers.

These examples have a common feature. Networks of small, medium-sized, and modestly large firms developed production networks that competed with the much larger state-supported firms, and in each case, the larger firms had to fight off the competition posed by the networks of smaller firms. Consequently, most of the larger firms moved upstream or changed their business strategy as a result of this competition.

The Taiwanese businesspeople called this pattern of converging competition posed by these networks "a swarm of bees" (*i wo feng*).[33] Perhaps a better analogy would be to think of this swarming competition as a *gold rush effect*. In a gold rush, a great many people get caught up in the stampede to find gold. The startup costs to join the rush are relatively low, and so many can join the search in hopes of being among the lucky few who strike it rich. However, those individuals who make the most money are those who supply the miners with the goods and services they need to search for gold—the shovels and sluice boxes, the food and other supplies, and transportation to and from the goldfields for the miners and for whatever booty they discovered.

Something similar to a gold rush happened in Taiwan. As opportunities for making money began to appear, people throughout the country, but especially in rural areas, began to join the rush to make money. This rush was collective in nature. The startup costs for individual firms were typically raised through personal networks of family and friends. By parceling out the manufacturing process among many firms, each firm doing a set of tasks that contributed to the final product, the cost to individual firms as well as the general cost of administrative overhead was kept to a minimum. Moreover, the costs for the overall network were even lower when the firms were located in the countryside, where factories could be sited on land that farmers had obtained at no cost from the government's land reforms.

The outcome of this conjunction of sudden economic opportunities, modest capital accumulation, and Taiwanese social organization was dramatic. Anthropologists doing fieldwork in rural villages during the 1960s and 1970s were themselves surprised at the sudden change and somewhat at a loss for explanations. Hu Tai-li, studying a small village, Liu Ts'o, in the greater Taichung Basin, reported that there were no factories established in the1960s, but suddenly, after 1970, "approximately twenty, small-scale factories have emerged in the village. Thirteen of them are machinery-processing plants. The remaining ones are dedicated to wood-product manufacturing, electro-plating, vacuum-modeling and sealing, electronics, and hat and bag manufacturing. In addition, four families have established similar kinds of small-scale factories outside the village." Hu illustrated the change with an account of one man, A-I, who dropped out of junior high school to go to Taichung to learn how to operate machines. He found a job operating a precision drilling machine for metal. He saved his money and borrowed additional money from his family to buy a used boring machine. He then moved back to Liu Ts'o and installed the machine in a room he built attached to the side of his family home.

> For the first three years, A-I's factory had only one boring machines doing the work delivered to him by four "center" factories in Taichung city and county. These center factories accept orders from foreign countries directly or through Taiwan's export merchants, and then distribute the work to "auxiliary" plants. The center factories and auxiliary factories usually don't sign contracts. The former give the latter instructions on quality and pattern, and some provide equipment and raw material. After founding, boring, milling, etc., the finished parts were collected and assembled in the center factories.[34]

Stevan Harrell found a similar pattern of change in the village he studied in a rural area in northern Taiwan, near Taipei City, in the 1970s. Before the middle 1960s, this village was poor, with few sources of income for anyone except for farming, coal mining, and growing tea. Then, in the late 1960s, factories "had begun to appear.... [B]y 1970 there were several tens of registered factories in the ... area. Most of these were of the light-industry sort, producing textiles, toys, plastic shoes, electronic circuits, or a myriad of other consumer goods, some for export and some for domestic consumption."[35]

In periodic field research that spanned over twenty years, from 1955 to 1979, in the village of Xin Xing near the coastal city of Lugang in west central Taiwan, Bernard and Rita Gallin also discovered the same pattern. Although agricultural land around Xin Xing was well suited for growing rice, farming after the land reforms occurred on such small plots that it was difficult to provide for a large family on agricultural income alone. Therefore, in the early 1960s, many young, single men temporarily migrated to urban areas to find work. Then, suddenly, the economy changed, and the migrants began to return with skills and connections to start their own factories.

> The early 1970s represented the major turning point for the fortunes of the local area. It was then that the villagers' economic system was transformed....
> In 1956 the bus ride from Lugang to Xin Xing was made on a dirt road flanked by clusters of village houses, farmland, and one brickworks. In 1978–79 the ride was made on a cement road flanked by clusters of village houses, farmland, and over 30 factories. These were labor-intensive and ranged from large establishments that manufactured textiles and furniture, to medium-sized enterprises that built bamboo and wood products, to small, satellite factories (or family workshops) that performed piece work for larger firms. In addition to those situated along the road, the area was dotted with other factories that also produced articles for local and foreign consumption. Further, the neighboring township housed [an] ... industrial park that was located six miles from Xin Xing and was the site of the largest export shoe manufacturing concern in the province.[36]

Demand-Responsive Integration

Taiwan's sudden industrialization coincided with the arrival of big buyers from Japan and the United States. These big buyers were the emissaries of the retail revolution that was occurring in the United States and that was just beginning in Europe. Their arrival created an intermediate demand for products that networks of small and medium-sized firms could supply—a huge variety of mostly small products and their component parts: fabrics, clothes, non-leather shoes, toys, bicycles, luggage, consumer electronics. These were the kinds of short-cycle, low-end products that the huge business groups in Japan and South Korea would be unwilling to manufacture because the profits were not high enough per item, the production runs were too short, and the items themselves kept changing. But these are exactly the kind of products that Taiwan's small and medium-sized firms started producing in ever larger and ever changing quantities and with increasing quality and manufacturing sophistication.

All the products made by these production networks required a huge quantity of inputs—cotton and synthetic fabrics for clothes; raw plastics for shoes, toys and lawn furniture; aluminum and steel for hydraulic jacks and bicycles. Some of the inputs initially came from Japanese business groups, whose upstream firms produced very high-quality intermediate products, but quickly the largest Taiwanese firms and business groups began to find their niches. When compared with the Japanese, these Taiwanese suppliers could work more closely with Taiwan's factories and provide them with exactly the input they needed at a price they could afford to pay.

By 1970s, Taiwan's largest and most successful business groups found themselves squeezed between the state-owned sector, where they were forbidden to go, and the small and medium-sized firm sector, where they could not compete. Moreover, these large business groups could not compete with American firms and Japanese business groups that were making high-end goods, such as automobiles and branded consumer electronics. Therefore, the path of least resistance took these business groups into those service and capital intensive industrial sectors where they could establish something close to a monopoly in supplying the intermediate components and business services needed by the rest of the local economy.

Formosa Plastics epitomizes this strategy. For twenty-five years, starting in 1969, Formosa Plastics Group was, by far, the largest business group in Taiwan, though still half as large as any of the top four *chaebol* in South Korea.[37] It was also one of the most vertically integrated groups in Taiwan. However, the group was vertically integrated in the upstream sector and made almost no final products for the consumer market. In 1983, its eighteen firms included three core vertically integrated firms (Formosa Plastics, Nan Ya Plastics, and Formosa Chemical and Fibers) and subsidiary firms that further processed the products of these firms for specialized uses, such as synthetic fibers for weaving in fabrics and powerful resins for laminating plywood and other products. Having consolidated its upstream position, Formosa Plastics also expanded to include a hospital and an Institute of Technology. A few years later it started adding firms making upstream products for consumer electronics, an enterprise sector that grew rapidly in the middle 1980s with the worldwide boom in personal computers.

Formosa Plastics's rise to preeminence was entirely due to the wide range of consumer products that used the upstream products that Formosa Plastics sold. Intermediate export demand became the driving force integrating the three sectors of the Taiwanese economy. For the next fifteen years, as Taiwan's GNP and export growth soared, the contribution of the three sectors to Taiwan's industrial production stabilized. For the entire period, the state-owned sector contributed about 20 percent to Taiwan's total industrial production, and the big firm and the small and medium-sized sectors about 40 percent each. When we convert those percentages to the direct impact on exports, then state-owned firms exported little, large firms around 40 percent, and the small and medium-sized firms about 60 percent of total exports.[38] The demand generated by big buyers, in turn, created the demand for intermediate goods and services, as well as the demand for such primary products as oil, steel and basic utilities.

All three sectors became interdependent and grew at roughly the same rate as the expanding economy. Charting the growth of exports from East Asian countries into the United States, we can see that Taiwan's growth matched or exceeded that of all the other countries in the region. Taiwan's total exports to the United States in the TSUSA categories of exported products and in total dollar value of all exports to the United States exceeded those of South Korea, Hong Kong, and Singapore for the entire period from 1972 until the turn of the century.[39] Japan's exports to the United States remained much larger than Taiwan's because of Japan's huge economy and early dominance in consumer electronics and automobiles. Nonetheless, Taiwan's exports of nondurable consumer goods (clothes, toys, shoes, luggage, furniture, small household goods) exceeded those from Japan throughout the period.

It is no exaggeration to say that the small firm tail of Taiwan's industrial structure wagged the entire economy, but these exporting firms did not set the prices for the goods they sold. Those goods were overwhelmingly manufactured on contract. The big buyers set the prices, order by order. The calculus used by big buyers to set prices was not established, solely or even mainly, by the cost of production. Rather it was based on the selling price of goods at the retail end, in the United States and Europe. These prices, including the profits that big buyers expected to have after the batches of goods were sold, were determined, in large part, by the competition the retailers faced in their consumer niches. The costs of production in Taiwan had to adjust to the reality of consumer markets far from Taiwan. Taiwan's small and medium-sized firm networks had no leverage in these consumer markets; they could negotiate neither prices nor profits with the American consumer. They were forced, in the end, to accept the price demanded by the big buyers, either that or forego the contract.

Economists have a name for this situation. When the imbalance in economic power is characterized by *one* buyer and many sellers, the situation is called *monopsony*; when the imbalance is due to a *few* buyers and many sellers, it is an *oligopsony*. What the Taiwanese manufacturers faced in the 1970s was an economy-wide oligopsony of a particular kind. The big buyers were the funnel through which the exports from Taiwan had to pass in order to reach the consumers in the United States and Europe. Without this intermediary passage, the small and medium-sized firms would have been unable to establish contact with Western consumers. Therefore, by the mid-1970s, a relatively small set of big buyers controlled the economic behavior of a large portion of Taiwan's economy. The price structure established in the export sector spread over the entire economy. All the players in the economy had to become demand responsive, had to adjust to a world market for the goods they produced.

In their negotiations with Taiwanese manufacturers, the big buyers could not, of course, demand just any price for a contracted good. There had to be some reality at the manufacturing end as well. But here is where the gap formed between prices in supplier markets and prices in consumer markets. When retailers and merchandisers first came to Asia, they were unable to calculate the cost of production in Asia. Using the retail prices in the United States, they calculated backward and offered what the Taiwanese manufacturers thought were high contract prices per unit of goods. Taiwanese manufacturers remember the early 1970s as the fat years, when everyone made money. But as the rush to make money accelerated, more and more production networks formed and competed for the same or similar contracts. Meanwhile, Western buyers gained experience in working with Taiwanese manufacturers. They could themselves begin to calculate production costs and could play one group of manufacturers off against another one. Accordingly, the price of goods in the supplier markets began to fall (relative to inflation), and the gap between buying prices in Asia and the selling prices in the United States for the same product became wider, more predictable, and much more lucrative. By the early 1980s, Taiwan had become the location most favored by retailers and merchandisers for contract manufacturing.

Production networks in Taiwan had to respond to falling prices and precarious orders. Increasingly, manufacturers facing uncertainty about the terms of the next contract had an incentive to figure out how to produce better quality goods ever more cheaply. In practical terms, this incentive encouraged the formation of more extensive networks.[40] Everyone was cautious about making additional capital investments in equipment and labor. When there were large orders, core manufacturers in a production network would outsource a significant part of their production; when the orders shrank, the core manufacturers did most or all parts of the manufacturing process themselves. Networks expanded, contracted, overlapped, and intensified. The cost of equipment was spread out among many different family firms, and the cost of labor was absorbed by members of the nuclear family and by their relatives, friends, and neighbors. The result was increasing flexibility in the manufacturing process, but also thinner profit margins all around.

There was also another result. As the production networks spread out into rural areas and decentralized across Taiwan, an economic space opened up between these flexible production networks, on the one hand, and the far upstream suppliers of industrial inputs and business services, on the other hand. Increasingly specialized products needed increasingly specialized inputs and services. A large number of midstream suppliers emerged to fill that space, and some of the more successful suppliers developed into multi-firm business groups. Each industry and each region began to develop its own set of dedicated suppliers.

Our interviews with the owners of the San Wu business group provide one of the best illustrations of the tiered market integration of Taiwan's economy. In 1986, among the top one hundred business groups in Taiwan, the San Wu business group, with four firms, was the eightieth largest in terms of assets and eighty-sixth in terms of sales.[41] When compared with the business groups in Japan and South Korea, the entire group was minuscule, much smaller in total group sales than the sales of any one main firm in a horizontal *keiretsu* in Japan. The group came into being when several families pooled their money to establish, over a decade, the group's four firms: two textile firms, a firm specializing in processing rubber for industrial uses, and a firm making hydraulic motors and pumps. The firms had very little to do with each other. The two textile companies were located in different parts of Taiwan and served different sets of production networks. The firm making the hydraulic equipment was independent of the other three. The only two firms in the group having some cross transactions were San Wu Textiles and San Wu Rubber, and that was only for a portion of the products they made. Each firm was managed by a member of a different family. What held the group together was common ownership; each family owned shares in all the firms.

As a midstream supplier of textiles, San Wu Textiles, the largest firm in the group, provided various types of specialty fabrics to production networks in the Hemei area. Beginning in 1969, the firm wove cotton cloth for the small and medium-sized firms making apparel in the region. In 2014, when we had our last interview with the current owners of San Wu, Chairman Chen Chieh-Hsi, and his son, the Executive Director and heir apparent, Rick Chen, they remembered the twenty years after the founding of the firm as the "golden age" of Hemei textile and apparel industries. "The whole supply chain was in place. Everyone made money." The company even made money when, in the late 1970s and 1980s, the cotton textile business had declined because cotton clothes had lost their cachet with American consumers, who had switched to clothes made predominately of synthetic fibers: polyester, rayon, and nylon. At the time of the first of our three interviews, in December 1987, San Wu Textiles had shifted most of their output to synthetic fabrics. Raw cotton was relatively expensive, because it had to be imported into Taiwan, but the raw material for the synthetic fabrics was local and cheaper than raw cotton.

To manufacture the synthetic textiles, San Wu bought large bales of raw synthetic gossamer-like material from Nan Ya Plastics, a wholly owned subsidiary of Formosa Plastics. Then, through a multistep process, San Wu Textiles converted these bales of synthetic cotton into different kinds of threads, and then wove these threads into different kinds of fabrics. These fabrics had all been pre-ordered by San Wu Textile's customers, the owners of small and medium-sized firms making final products for export. They used these fabrics in dozens of different kinds of products: the tops for athletic shoes, apparel of all kinds, upholstery for furniture, even the fabric that goes into rubberized conveyer belts.

Although San Wu Textiles relied on Formosa Plastics as its main supplier of raw materials, the relation between San Wu and Formosa Plastics was strictly arm's-length and was not based on any kind of personal tie. Chairman Chen told us that San Wu bought its supplies from Formosa Plastics in one of two ways, either directly from its subsidiary, Nan Ya Plastics, or from a Japanese trading company that acted as a consolidator, buying huge lots of the synthetic material from Nan Ya Plastics at a reduced price and then selling that material to the many firms that wanted to buy it. "Whichever is cheaper, that is the way we buy it." The Chairman also told us in that first interview with San Wu that he liked doing business with Wang Yung-ching, the legendary owner of Formosa Plastics. "When he has ten dollars, he'll put two in your pocket." He continued, "He eats meat, we drink soup" (*Ta shih rou, women he tang*).

These words go to the heart of the relationship between the large upstream suppliers of intermediate goods and services and the small and medium-sized downstream manufacturers of products for export: it's unequal, but everyone still has something good to eat. The metaphorical meals of meat and soup that Chairman Chen mentioned also conveyed another and more subtle message: the big upstream producers sat at different round tables and ate different food than did the owners of the small and medium-sized firms downstream. These two groups of owners belonged to different economic spheres and traveled in different social and political circles. When they met, it was mainly through the medium of market transactions, through exchange relationships in which the small and medium-sized firms had to negotiate with the midstream firms, which in turn had to negotiate with the large upstream firms.

The midstream firms, such as San Wu Textiles, remained economically distant from the large upstream suppliers, but stayed close to their export-making customers. At times, they would sit with them at the same round table and share food and drink, but they were not the hosts. Although they were usually the largest firm at the table, they were not the ones receiving the big-buyer contracts. And they, too, had to accept the terms and conditions of the large upstream suppliers, like Formosa Plastics. But both the large upstream and the midstream, firms had to be mindful that the viability of the entire supply chain rested on the downstream firms producing products that met the big-buyers' requirements for quality and price. Even though they belonged to different economic spheres, all the various levels of firms needed one another, and they all needed the products and infrastructure that the government and state-owned enterprises provided—the electricity, the petroleum, the steel, the aluminum, and the entire transportation system of ports, rails, and freeways. All three sectors waxed and waned together.

Conclusion

By the mid-1980s, Taiwan's economy was closely tied to the US economy. Although products made in Taiwan flooded the stores lining American shopping malls, few Americans could name a single Taiwanese firm. The products either had no brand name at all, like most small items in discount stores, or carried an American or European brand name. Most Americans, however, could name a number of Japanese businesses (e.g., Sony, Canon, Nikon, Toyota, Honda, Panasonic, Hitachi), and most Americans owned branded products that they recognized as Japanese. Sony's Walkman had created a worldwide fad in the 1980s, in much the same way as Apple's iPod did in the 2000s. Toyota became America's leading imported automobile in 1975, and by 1986, was selling more than one million vehicles per year in the United States.[42] The 1980s were Japan's heyday; it was the world's second largest economy, the country with the largest trade surplus in history to that point. Ezra Vogel had just published the widely read book *Japan as Number 1, Lessons for America*, and American business schools had started offering courses on Japanese management techniques, just-in-time manufacturing, and quality circles. Japan seemed to be the future.

South Korea, too, was on the horizon. Americans were also starting to recognize South Korean brand names. In 1985, Hyundai had not yet begun to export automobiles to the United States, but it was gearing up to do so and would start before 1990. Samsung products, particularly microwaves and televisions, were selling well, even though America consumers regarded them as low-end competition to Japanese and American brands. Clearly though, South Korea was on the way up, as Alice Amsden's 1989 book, *Asia's Next Giant*, predicted.

While Japan and South Korea were in most consumers' sightlines, Taiwan's enterprises were nearly invisible. They were the unseen, silent partners of many American corporations. A growing awareness of Japanese and Korean competition worried US makers of consumer products. US recessions in the mid-1970s and again in the early 1980s had driven many shoppers to the large discount retailers, such as Kmart and Walmart, and these retailers had responded with larger orders from Taiwanese manufacturers. The same economic downturn had pushed a number of American companies to close their factories in the United States and to buy their branded products from Taiwanese factories. Schwinn Bicycle Company and Eddie Bauer were two US firms that did this, but other merchandising retailers that had never owned factories in the United States, such as The Limited, contracted all of their production in Taiwan.

This shift of contract manufacturing to Taiwan highlighted the differences in export production between Taiwan and its two neighbors to the north. Japanese and South Korean business groups had a difficult time competing with Taiwanese exporters for low-end, nondurable consumer goods, but had a competitive advantage in mass production of capital intensive products and in long runs of standardized items. These business groups had (or could obtain) the capital needed to build on this advantage, and did so by building larger, state-of-the-art factories and pouring millions of dollars into research and development to make products that were well-designed, fully functional, and efficiently manufactured.

These business groups needed to manufacture products whose prices were globally competitive. Unlike the Taiwanese exporters whose prices were determined by big-buyer contracts, Japanese and South Koreans set their prices according to their competitive niche in the United States and then worked backward to make that price achievable. Organizational compliance substituted for market transactions. South Korean *chaebol* used an internal price structure to achieve the targeted price. The upstream firms in the *chaebol* would sell their components and material to the downstream firm at below-market pricing, a fact substantiated by the Korea Fair Trade Commission.[43] Japanese *keiretsu* practiced a form of internal pricing as well, in a system referred to as *two-part pricing*, which for upstream firms consisted of a fixed fee that matched the cost of production and then a variable fee from the profit sharing between the upstream and downstream firms that resulted from the final sale of a product.[44] Occasionally, as part of the group's business strategy, the *keiretsu* and the *chaebol* would even elect to sell exports at prices below the cost of production in order to gain global market share. They could do this by shifting profits from firm to firm within the group. Also, using tariff barriers, Japanese and South Korean governments helped their local business groups maintain profitability by allowing them to sell their products domestically at higher prices than they sold for in overseas markets.

Therefore, by 1985, Taiwan had emerged as Asia's leading location for contract manufacturing. The trajectory of Taiwan's economy was steadily diverging from the paths taken by Japanese and the South Korean economies. Meanwhile, Hong Kong's economy had also changed and was now quite different than it had been previously. Rising wages and high property values were driving Hong Kong's small and medium-sized firms across the Chinese border into the Pearl River Delta. Although many of the leading Hong Kong entrepreneurs had begun in manufacturing, the large business groups they founded had moved into real estate and large infrastructure projects, such as power generation and port construction. A notable exception to this pattern is the Li & Fung group, which grew into the world's leading intermediate sourcing agent for apparel merchandisers. But the factories that Li & Fung contracted with to make the ordered apparel were not in Hong Kong, but rather in China and in South and Southeast Asia. In Singapore, the manufacturing sector in the local economy was mostly owned by American firms, especially Hewlett-Packard (HP), Apple, and Seagate Technology. The large, locally owned business groups controlled privately owned banks, real estate, media, and entertainment. In 1985, Japan and the four Asian Dragons were all prospering, but only Taiwan excelled in contract manufacturing.

Nineteen hundred and eighty-five was the peak of Taiwan's first wave of industrialization. These were the golden years for the large family-owned business groups in Taiwan, the years when Wang Yung-ching was Taiwan's most famous businessman, famously wise and famously successful, and when the business group he owned was the largest in the land. This was when Chang Yung-fa's Evergreen Group became the world's largest container ship company, when two of the world's ten largest container ports (Kaohsiung and Keelung) were located in Taiwan, and when China had no container port among the top twenty-five ports.

Thirty years later, in 2015, the economic landscape has completely changed. None of the industries in Taiwan's first wave of industrialization remain anchored in Taiwan. Formosa Plastics is no longer Taiwan's largest business group; the China Credit Information Service's list of the top one hundred business groups in Taiwan now consists mostly of groups that emerged after 1985; the Port of Kaohsiung is Taiwan's only container port ranked among the world's top fifty, at number thirteen, and seven of the world's ten largest ports are located in China.[45] In the last thirty years, East Asian economies have transformed, but Taiwanese-owned businesses still rank among the world's leading contract manufacturers.

Centered on the role of Taiwanese businesses in the global economy, Part Two is the account of these changes in East Asia between 1985 and 2015.

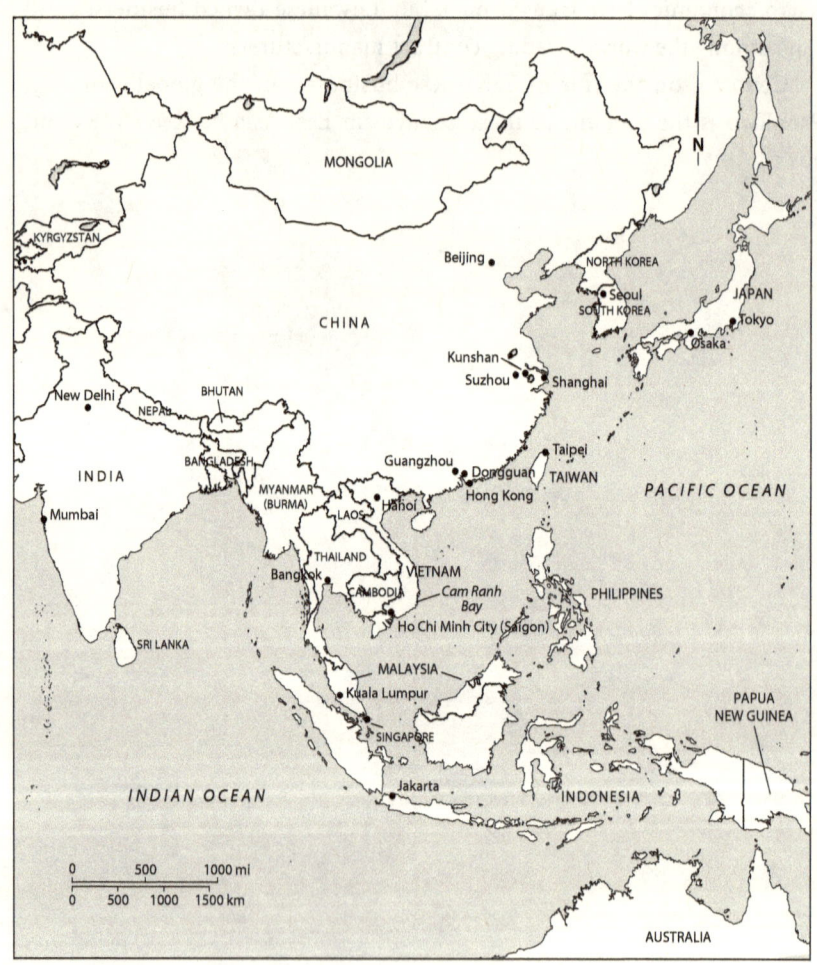

Figure 2. Map of East Asia.

Part Two
Toward a New Asian Economy, 1985–2016

The Plaza Accord was signed on September 22, 1985, in the Plaza Hotel in New York City. The initial impact of this turning point—and this year—played out in a ripple effect over the next decades. Faced by a recession, sharp declines in US exports, even sharper rises in imports, and skyrocketing interest rates at home, the Reagan administration negotiated a currency reform with the leading four major industrial countries, including Germany and Japan. The purpose of the reform was to reduce the value of the US dollar against the other major currencies. During the five years after the agreement, the Japanese yen, the New Taiwan dollar, and the Korean won increased in value by over 40 percent against the US dollar. Set against the backdrop of new technologies in the United States and changing government policies in East Asia, this currency adjustment set in motion a transformation that still reverberates across Asian economies today.

During the previous two decades (1965–1985), Japan, South Korea, and Taiwan had rapidly developed demand-responsive industrial economies. The demand generated by big buyers led quickly, step by step, to the creation of internal supply chains that provided a great many of the components and services that firms needed to manufacture consumer goods for export. Although the three economies were organized in very different ways, we can still think of them as self-organizing. Local entrepreneurs progressively occupied most of the available economic niches required for the export production of consumer goods. South Korea and especially Taiwan continued to rely on Japanese businesses for some intermediate products and services, but as time went on, each economy became industrially more integrated and self-sufficient in producing those products for which it had a competitive advantage.

This advantage was largely determined by the way in which the internal price structures across exporting firms matched the pricing pressures faced by big buyers in distant markets. Operating in a high-overhead environment, Japan's industrial advantage was in producing long runs of relatively expensive, capital intensive, company-branded, and extensively promoted consumer products and in supplying large quantities of specialized intermediate products to other (mostly Asian) economies.[1] Taiwan's very low overhead satellite assembly systems gave Taiwanese firms an advantage in the modularized production of modest batches of relatively inexpensive consumer goods that had been ordered in advance by Western and Japanese buyers. South Korea occupied the middle ground between these two extremes. In the early 1970s, South Korean firms competed in many of the same supplier markets as the Taiwanese did, but as time went on and as the *chaebol* grew larger and more vertically integrated, the *chaebol*'s best strategy veered toward making the same or similar products as those the Japanese *keiretsu* were making. Between 1965 and 1985, as the big buyers and East Asian firms worked out a regional division of labor, East Asian economies became integral parts of global capitalism.

During the years after 1985, a new Asian economy emerged. In the ensuing decade, the internal integration of leading East Asian economies unraveled. Often reluctantly, the owners and managers of East Asian businesses moved their manufacturing plants to different countries or, if they stayed put, had to reinvent themselves by making new products for different markets. No longer did these economies bend toward self-sufficiency. Rather, each economy became a part of a shifting, continually readjusting pan-Asian economy that, after the Asian financial crisis in 1997 and China's accession to the World Trade Organization in 2001, came to rest, at least temporarily, in Mainland China.

The chapters in Part Two account for the emergence of this new pan-Asian economy and for the roles that Taiwanese businesspeople played in its creation. In Chapter 6, we outline the reasons why the Plaza Accord provided the tipping point leading to economic changes across the region. We also look closely at the dilemma faced by Taiwanese businesspeople in deciding whether to move part or all of their factories to China. In Chapter 7, we examine the high technology sectors in the Taiwanese economy that emerged in the 1980s and 1990s and masked the move of light industries to China. Remarkably, even as Taiwan's key exporters in the pre-1985 era left Taiwan, the Taiwanese economy continued to grow, and a new rising set of industrialists making consumer electronics greatly augmented the reputation of the Taiwanese as the world's leading contract manufacturers. In Chapter 8, we follow several waves of Taiwanese industrialists who moved their factories to China, where we observe how different businesses reestablished their manufacturing operations. Once in China, some of these firms vertically integrated their production and greatly enlarged the size of their work force. Other firms tried to recreate their previous production networks in a new location. In Chapter 9, we closely inspect the consumer electronics industry in China, especially the manufacture of laptops and smartphones. Many writers portray this industry as being led by key manufacturers, such as Samsung, or by leading merchandisers, such as Apple. Instead, we examine the manufacturing core of the industry, mostly contract manufacturers who make the components for the entire range of phones, tablets, and laptops, expensive as well as inexpensive ones, and who give this industry its dynamism. In Chapter 10, we return to Taiwan to observe its economy today and the new migrations of Taiwanese industrialists into South and Southeast Asia and beyond, forming a greater Taiwanese economy in which highly diversified contract manufacturing is being challenged by a constantly changing capitalist global economy

6

THE SEARCH FOR A NEW ASIAN ECONOMY

The Tipping Point

In 1985, the six-lane road leading up the hill from Taichung City to Tunghai University crossed the eight-lane toll road that went from Taipei in the north to Kaohsiung in the south, a distance of nearly two hundred and twenty miles. Taichung (in the middle of Taiwan) was about half way between the two cities. Going for a weekend trip in 1985, Hamilton could board a bus in Taichung and arrive in Taipei about three hours later. The duration of the trip, however, depended on the traffic, which was highly variable. The toll road was filled with cars, trucks, motorcycles, even some slow-moving tractors. Most of the cars were assembled in Taiwan, such as the Yulon Sunny and Bluebird or the Ford and Liuhe joint venture Pao Tianxia (literally, "running heaven and earth"). The trucks were mostly imported from Japan. Many were small, but some were huge, such as the trucks hauling scores of hogs squeezed together into racks stacked five and six rows high. However, the locally made and imported Japanese motorcycles ruled, whizzing in and out of lanes, dodging trucks and cars, going where no larger vehicle could maneuver.

Watching the chaos on the road was an education in itself. First-generation drivers adopted the rules of the road that they learned as pedestrians walking down crowded streets: some went fast, some went slow, all of them darted in front of others without bothering to signal their intention to anyone close by. Speed and congestion combined to create a constant drama of drivers attempting to free themselves from slowdowns. The shoulder of the road was viewed as an extra lane, where drivers could speed past the slower vehicles on the left.

Serious accidents were common, and when someone died, the wrecked vehicle remained for a while on the side of the road where the accident occurred. Hamilton thought that these vehicles served as reminders to other drivers that they should be careful, but when the burned-out hull of a bus stayed in the same spot for weeks, he asked the reason and was told that this lingering edifice was there to help the wandering ghosts of those who had died an early death find their way to peace. In those years, the new Taiwan and the old Taiwan combined in ways that only those living there could understand.

Taiwan's Changing Society

In 1985, the chaos on the road replicated Taiwan's hectic, rapidly changing society. During the previous twenty years, the people of Taiwan had grown accustomed to their successes. They believed that hard work guaranteed a better life, like the popular Taiwanese song of the day "Ai-biahnh Jah-eh Eah," whose refrain was "hard work makes you a winner."[1] Working toward a better life, however, was a motto adopted more by families than by single individuals. The family unit, propelled by its two core axes of father and son and of husband and wife, carried over into the family firms. In villages and towns, family houses were frequently turned into small factories, where during the workday the family sat together assembling components that would later go into products that would be exported to the United States. As the workday ended, the factory reverted back into a living space where the family shared dinner. These families had grown rich enough to afford televisions, which seemed never to be turned off, and motorcycles, which seemed to be everywhere. If wealthy enough, the family even owned a small truck or car. The public sidewalks outside these homes were turned into parking lots for the motorcycles and storage areas for the parts being constructed. Outside the towns, the rural countryside filled with two- and three-story concrete structures that served as both homes and factories. The urban and the rural blended together in the chaotic mosaic of a newly developing economy, an economy in which everyone participated and through which everyone thought he or she could obtain a better life in the future.

Optimism in 1985 was palpable and justified. All you had to do was just look around and remember what life had been like twenty years earlier. Per capita income was nearly four times higher in 1985 than it had been in 1965.[2] The same percentage jump in income had occurred in other countries in East

Asia, so that by 1985, the whole region shared a rapidly rising standard of living.[3] For the Taiwanese, life had changed for the better and would, they believed, continue to improve in the future. Hard work would make that belief come true.

The evidence for this continuing improvement came from Taiwan's government. In 1965, Taiwan's government did not see Taiwan as its natural home. Taiwan's government wanted to be the legitimate government for all of China. Taiwan was only its temporary site, and not a place for future investments. Although that illusion faded in the early 1970s when Taiwan lost its seat in the United Nations, it officially ended in 1974 with the death of Chiang Kai-shek. When his son, Chiang Ching-kuo, became President in 1978, government attention turned toward making Taiwan economically strong and prosperous and politically more tolerant and flexible. Chiang Ching-kuo started the slow process of changing an authoritarian state into a constitutional democracy. Before he died in 1988, he had allowed, in 1986, the establishment of a political party (the Democratic Progressive Party) to oppose the KMT; in 1987, the end of martial law; and, also in 1987, return visits to the Mainland for veterans. He also picked his successor, Lee Teng-hui, a native-born Taiwanese who had been his Vice President.

The KMT government during Chiang Ching-kuo's presidency tried to build a better social foundation for future economic development. Among other acts, the legislature passed a new labor law, the Labor Standards Act of 1984. The new law guaranteed a minimum wage, vacation time, and pensions, and set limits on the minimum age for workers and on the maximum hours a day they could be expected to work.

The new law certified trends that were already under way. Earlier, in 1968, the government had made education through junior high compulsory for both boys and girls. After graduating from junior high, these students could take a national examination that would permit them to attend high school, and later they could sit for another set of examinations that would channel the brightest students into college. In the twenty years before 1985, rising expectations led more and more students of both genders to attend high school and then college. The government, too, led the way by establishing more public universities and by subsidizing students who were qualified to attend college. Also, as was happening in other East Asian countries, Taiwan's birth rate began to fall in the 1970s and continued to fall through the first decade of the twenty-first century.[4] By 1985, the combination of a falling birth rate, new child labor laws, and higher rates of students attending college and seeking professional jobs after graduation had reduced the number of workers in the manufacturing sector of the economy. Because the government prohibited the hiring of foreign workers at that time, there was a steady decline in the absolute numbers of workers and a steady increase in their wages.[5]

The Second Phase of the Post–World War II Retail Revolution, 1985–2007

Increasing wages and changing standards of living set the stage for declining profits. The determining factor for declining profits, however, occurred at the retail end of the supply chain, in the United States and Europe. By 1985, large retailers had started to computerize their inventories and to rationalize their supply chains. These moves quickly led to cutthroat competition and an industry-wide reorganization that resulted from implementing what is known as *lean retailing*.[6]

Retailers and merchandisers had a good start on working out their logistical headaches before the mid-1980s, but it was not until then that the retail industry took full advantage of a set of emerging technologies that reinforced one another to form an identifiable lean retailing package.[7] The key elements of the package started with an initiative taken by supermarket chains to develop some way to track in-store inventories. As we discussed in Chapter 2, by the 1970s, supermarket chains dominated food retailing in the United States and were instrumental in establishing, for individual stores, computerized point-of-sales (POS) inventory systems based on barcodes and scanning devices. Other retailers soon adopted the same technology, but on a company-wide platform that allowed corporate management to integrate all aspects of a company's retail businesses. By 1981, as it was moving from a regional to a national discount chain, Walmart required all its suppliers to adopt the UPC system and to add the associated barcodes to their products. Kmart and other larger retailers adopted the same practices, and within a few years, barcodes and scanners became ubiquitous among all the industry leaders.

This method of tracking inventories allowed retailers to adopt other technologies. First, with POS data, retailers knew exactly what needed to be restocked. With this knowledge, they could eliminate the large warehouses in favor of distribution points that relied on just-in-time deliveries of those products in short supply. Already important in retail logistics, trucks, rather than trains, now became central players in the just-in-time deliveries, so much so that large retailers began to establish their own fleets of trucks. Moreover, POS data allowed retailers to fine-tune the products each store in the chain carried relative to a specific set of customers that frequented that store.

Second, this method also reduced the guesswork about what goods to order from the merchandisers promoting particular products and the manufacturers actually making those products. Chain stores could now order more of those items selling well and less of those not selling well. Therefore, the turnaround time from ordering to final delivery of a product needed to be shortened. At this point, roughly in the middle to late 1980s, retailers and merchandisers began to work out a new approach to ordering products. This approach is captured in a new vocabulary that came into use in the late 1980s describing the supply and demand continuum from the point of view of retailers rather than manufacturers.[8] *Supply chain* and *supply chain management* became terms that valorized consumers and consumer demand and validated the importance of retailers, vis-à-vis manufacturers, in assessing that demand. Conceptualized in terms of this new vocabulary, producers of primary goods (such as steel and chemicals), makers of component parts, assemblers, and factory-less merchandisers found themselves lined up in chains of suppliers (now called *vendors*) that ended in, and were managed by, retail firms. The retail end of the chain increasingly gained leverage over the entire chain, creating, in effect, "price-sensitive networks of firms that turned manufacturing into organizational extensions of retailing products."[9]

Third, these networks, especially those stretching across oceans, required a standardized computer language so that ordering products and settling accounts could be handled seamlessly among firms widely separated in space. In the 1970s, big buyers going to Asia to purchase goods from their suppliers typically used letters of credit from their banks. By the 1980s, with the adoption of computer language protocols (first, Voluntary Interindustry Commerce Standards, or VICS, and later Electronic Data Interchange, or EDI), the process of ordering goods and settling accounts could be accomplished electronically with minimum ambiguity.[10] Global communications based on the Internet and global logistics based on containerized shipping by sea and air tied the lean retailing package together, making the package a worldwide going concern that all retailers and merchandisers could use, regardless of size.

These innovations forced retailers to adapt quickly to the new competitive landscape or lose out to their competitors. Not all retail firms could afford these technologies as they were introduced. In fact, most retailers could not. It was very costly for firms to computerize their inventory systems. Scanning devices and electronic checkout registers were expensive. Eliminating the traditional warehouse stockpiles and investing in new distribution centers, as well as in a fleet of trucks, were even more expensive. And most retail firms did not have the staff or the expertise to develop competent, low-cost suppliers for the large number of items that they carried, especially suppliers located in East Asia.

The differential adoption of the lean retailing technologies set off a fierce competition among retailers and merchandisers in the United States and Europe, a competition that led to many mergers, acquisitions, and bankruptcies.[11] By 1985, the shopping center boom had spawned a rapid consolidation of retail chains in both Europe and the United States. A few big discount retailers (Kmart, Walmart, and Target in the United States and Carrefour, Aldi, Tesco, and Metro in Europe) expanded geographically to become national and international chains, and logistically to become general merchandisers selling groceries as well as an ever-widening array of consumer goods.[12] Their expansion decimated locally owned and regionally operated retailers. Specialty retail chains, the category killers described earlier, also expanded. Large, newly established chain stores soon dominated specific retail sectors: drugstores (e.g., Walgreen, CVS, and Rite Aid), hardware (e.g., Home Depot), consumer electronics (e.g., Circuit City and Best Buy).

Going into the 1990s, the successful retailers and merchandisers had deepened their existing supply lines and forged new ones. The most successful American retailers had gone to East Asia, particularly Taiwan, to increase their competitive advantage in the United States.[13] East Asian manufacturers were therefore instrumental in fostering competition among retailers and merchandisers in the United States and were major beneficiaries of it, but it came at a considerable cost to them as well. Fierce competition in the United States squeezed profits in Asia.

The Plaza Accord and Its Reverberations

The Plaza Accord turned out to be a tipping point not only for East Asia but for the United States and the rest of the world as well. In Taiwan, in the period leading up to the signing of the Plaza Accord, rising wages, declining profits, and increasing competition for big-buyer orders made the business environment more difficult but, for most firms, still manageable. However, the step-by-step currency adjustments that started with the Plaza Accord soon made it impossible for many business ventures across East Asia to continue in their original location. As a result, many East Asian firms relocated some or all of their manufacturing to locations where land and labor were less expensive and where governments welcomed them with favorable terms. These movements, in turn, transformed East Asian economies, hollowing out some sectors and forcing others to upgrade production in order to compete in new markets with new products.

In the United States, however, the Plaza Accord turned out to be a very different kind of tipping point. With this agreement, the United States started down a new path. The US government abandoned the policy stance that the US economy was, in theory at least, an independent player in a world of other equally independent players, encumbered only by selective tariff barriers at national borders. With the Plaza Accord, the United States now led the charge for a new world order based on mutual economic interdependencies among nations. Thereafter, coalitions of leaders from developed and developing economies began to coordinate their activities in order to achieve what they saw as optimal outcomes for the global economy. Chief among the tools to accomplish these policy goals was exchange rate manipulation.

The idea behind using exchange rates as a policy tool reflects the belief that, in an ideal world, trade among nations naturally trends toward an equilibrium between the values of imports and exports.[14] Economic theory suggests that, in those countries accumulating a capital surplus from exporting more than they import, the value of their currencies should increase relative to the currencies of those countries with excess imports. The logic behind this assumption is that the one-way transfer of wealth between trading countries increasingly impoverishes the importing countries, reducing the capacity of their currencies to purchase the same goods at the same price as the exporting countries. Economists refer to this fluctuating value of an equivalent batch of goods in each of the trading countries as the *real exchange rate*.

In the real world, however, nations set exchange rates so that fixed units of money in one location equal fixed units of money in another location. Economists call this the *nominal exchange rate*. Most countries allow the nominal exchange rate to float within a defined range. The fluctuations within that range (i.e., the daily market rate) are determined by the buyers and sellers of those currencies. In a few locations, however, the nominal exchange rate is linked, so that two currencies are exchanged at a fixed ratio to each other. For instance,

US and Hong Kong currencies have maintained a ratio of 1 US$/7.8 HK$ for over thirty years. Although linked exchange rates make international business transactions more predictable by eliminating currency fluctuations as a source of risk, linked *nominal* exchange rates do not adjust to changes in *real* exchange rates.

This is the theoretical framework that informed the negotiations that led to the Plaza Accord in 1985. In trying to resolve the trading disputes that had been arising and the US trade deficit that was starting to mushroom by the early 1980s, officials in the Reagan administration interpreted the problems with international trade as being the result of a misalignment of exchange rates. In general terms, the problem had arisen from actions taken by the US Federal Reserve Board, which, in an effort to end an inflationary spiral in the United States, had pushed prime interest rates up to a record high of 21.5 percent in December of 1980. Although the prime rate came down in the following five years, it remained over 10 percent until early in 1985. These high interest rates attracted foreign buyers of the US dollar, which in turn, made the US dollar appreciate against floating foreign currencies. However, as the US dollar rose in value, most of the leading developed and developing nations let their currencies subside in value relative to the US dollar. Therefore, the prevailing interpretation of the US trade deficit was that these floating nominal exchange rates made the prices of US imports too low and the prices of US exports too high for the balance of trade to equal out. This interpretation further implied that this imbalance was causing undue hardships for American manufacturers. The shoe industry was particularly up in arms, and was seeking congressional action to protect the industry from imported shoes. As advocates of free trade, Reagan officials wanted to head off any protectionist legislation that was then in the works. Moreover, they felt that the "footwear case [should] be considered as part of a larger whole—a broad new trade policy."[15]

The Plaza Accord was going to solve America's trade problems. The accord was the result of secret negotiations among five industrial nations—West Germany, France, the United Kingdom, Japan, and the United States. A small group of leading Reagan appointees, headed by Treasury Secretary James A. Baker III, took matters into their own hands.[16] They wanted the five nations to coordinate their domestic economic policies in order to internalize the effects of their growing interdependence.[17] The common means of coordination was the exchange rate.[18] Among the five, Germany and Japan had burgeoning surpluses and the United States an onerous deficit. The Reagan appointees saw that the solution to the various problems was to push the value of the US dollar against the Japanese and German currencies down toward where the real exchange rate might be located.[19] In addition, the United States promised to reduce its national deficit (viewed by many as a sign of growing impoverishment), and Germany and Japan promised to raise domestic demand in their countries for consumer goods. The assumption was that cheaper US exports would be purchased in overseas markets, Americans would buy fewer of the now more expensive imports, and trade would be balanced.

Of course, none of this came to pass. On the surface, everything went according to plan. In the next year, the value of the US dollar was pushed down over 40 percent relative to the German mark and the Japanese yen, but the US trade deficit did not decline right away. Neither did the US budget deficit. Nor did consumer demand in Germany and Japan rise appreciably. In trying to assess the source of these problems, Baker and other Reagan officials in 1987 came up with what they thought were some answers. First, the governments of Germany and Japan, they thought, did not try hard enough to incentivize domestic demand. The two governments needed to further reduce taxes and interest rates so that their citizens would have more money to spend on consumer goods. Second, Baker and the others realized that a larger problem was the US trade deficit in relation to Taiwan and South Korea. Both Taiwan and South Korea had allowed their currencies to float, but in a very narrow range (a so-called managed float), and in an effort to enhance exports, the governments of both countries kept the value of their currencies low relative to the US dollar. Since neither Taiwan nor South Korea signed the Plaza Accord, neither felt obliged to appreciate its currency. As a consequence, in 1987, after their meeting in Venice, the G7 finance ministers issued a communique calling, among other things, on "newly industrialized economies" to comply with the agreement reached with the Plaza Accord and to become responsible players in the new world economic order.[20] Taiwan and South Korea buckled under the pressure to comply. By 1989, the New Taiwan dollar had appreciated by 49 percent and the South Korean won by 34 percent against the US dollar. From then on, the New Taiwan dollar would float against other major world currencies, going up and down, following Taiwan's oscillation in the global economy.[21]

After the Plaza Accord, the leading industrial countries, led by the United States, charted a course toward liberalization of the global economy.[22] In 1989, in its statement to the US Congress, the US Treasury Department reported that "the major industrial countries are continuing their efforts to coordinate their economic policies to achieve shared objectives. The coordination process has now become an accepted feature of the international economic landscape."[23] And so it has remained since that time.

The coordination process, however, did not lead to that perfect equilibrium so abstractly conceived in the pure world of market fundamentalism. After slight adjustments in the value between US exports and imports, the trade deficit started to rise again in the mid-1990s and, over the next ten years, reached heights never dreamed possible in the Reagan years. The manufacturing sector in the US economy continued to decline ever more dramatically for the next two decades, and the US footwear industry collapsed. By the end of the 1990s, over 97 percent of all shoes purchased in the US were imported, overwhelmingly from Taiwanese contract manufacturers located in Mainland China.[24] These shoes bore such brand names as Nike, Reebok, Timberland, Rockport, and Nine West.

Tajia le (Everybody's Happy)

The currency manipulations in Japan, South Korea, and Taiwan produced a paradox: too much money and too little profit. On the one hand, rising Asian currencies brought new wealth. Because Japan was the first in Asia to allow its currency to float, the Japanese were the first to experience this paradox. Suddenly the value of Japanese companies jumped, as their property and stock prices shot up.[25] In the four years between 1986 and 1990, both the Japanese stock market and major urban property markets tripled in value. *Keiretsu* firms quickly found it more profitable to make money from what was known as the *zaitech boom* (i.e., from speculation in their stock portfolios and other financial assets) than from selling their products abroad.[26] Japanese investors also went on a spree, buying real estate around the world. In the United States alone, they bought, among many other properties, the Rockefeller Center in New York City, Columbia Pictures, the Mariners baseball team, and the Pebble Beach golf course. These purchases generated so much notoriety that the American press began to write about a "Japanese conspiracy," which led the Japanese government to warn Japanese businesses not to buy high visibility properties.[27]

However, alongside the new wealth coming from the stronger yen, the costs of doing business in Japan shot up. The *keiretsu* system of production relied on networks of firms providing locally sourced inputs—everything from steel and chemicals to assembled components. Even at constant prices, the costs of producing exports would have jumped up at the same rate as the rising yen. But prices did not remain constant. The flood of new money resulting from the boom in the value of property and stock also pushed up other costs. Very quickly, the managers of Japanese firms realized that, with the rapidly climbing value of the yen, a rise that the Japanese termed *endaka*, their products would no longer be competitive in foreign markets. What followed is known as *kudoka*, the hollowing out of the Japanese domestic economy. "As the yen climbed ever higher, not only parts makers but also suppliers of raw materials and semi-processed goods such as plastics and metals began making the move.... [Even] small Japanese firms moved into Asia in record numbers during the *endaka* mania of the 1980s and early 1990s."[28] According to Hatch and Yamamura:

> As the 1980s wore on, *endaka* made it increasingly difficult for Japanese MNCs [multinational corporations] in Asia to continue to import parts from Japan. The price was simply too high. To remain competitive, they had to begin purchasing locally produced parts.... Most of the big assembly firms managed to persuade their Japanese subcontractors to pack up and move to Asia or sign technology license agreements with domestically owned suppliers in the region.[29]

Although Japanese firms made huge investments in Southeast Asia, the largest *keiretsu* investments were in the United States. Within six years of the signing of the Plaza Accord, the vertical *keiretsu* (the assembly firms and their main suppliers) associated with Japanese vehicle manufacturing had invested over 8 billion dollars to establish plants in the United States to make cars and trucks for US consumers. Fearing the rise of US protectionism, three of the twelve major investments by assembly firms (including the first ones by Toyota and Honda) occurred in the early 1980s, but the huge wave of investments and firm transplants came after 1985. In addition to the main assembly plants, there were "at least 250 Japanese automobile suppliers' production facilities in North America" by 1991.[30] The same *keiretsu* suppliers also built factories in Southeast Asia (mostly in Thailand) to assemble cars and truck for that region, as well as to make component parts that were in turn shipped to Japan and the United States.[31] The Plaza Accord led not only to a hollowing out of the Japanese economy but also to a regional and even global reorganization of Japanese production networks. Much the same outcome occurred in Taiwan only a year or so later.

People in Taiwan experienced the same paradox: too much money, too little profit. Starting in 1986, the Taiwanese experienced an even more dramatic boom in wealth from property and stock prices than did the Japanese. Taiwan's stock market "shot up more than tenfold" and property prices more than quadrupled in less than four years.[32] The excitement generated by the possibility of rising wealth brought tens of thousands of new investors into the stock and property markets. Even Kao's graduate students jumped in. Chairman T, whose story we presented in the introductory chapter, was one of those who got caught up in the boom. He said he was making more money from his investments in stocks and property than from selling his plastic lawn furniture to the big-box retailers. Speculation and luck seemed to fill the air, so much so that in the late 1980s more than 3 million people (about one out of every seven adults) were placing bets on an illegal, island-wide lottery called *dajia le* (everybody's happy), a lottery in which people placed wagers on the last two numbers of Taiwan's legal lottery.[33] A common Taiwanese saying was on everyone's lips: "There was so much money raining down on Taiwan that everyone was up to their ankles in it" (*dai-uan-zi-im-ka-bhak*).

This "era of speculation" was caused, in part, by the fact that loaning money to local businesses (or even investing in your own business) was no longer a good investment.[34] With the increased value in the New Taiwan dollar, Taiwan's contract manufacturers were in trouble. Their contracts with US buyers had been negotiated in US dollars, whose value was falling, but their costs were in the local currency, which was rising. Now the squeeze was on. Profits had dried up. Even worse, losses had begun.

We saw the effects of the losses firsthand. Early one afternoon in 1991, we were in the middle of our second interview with Ling Wen-chuen, the *laoban* of a hydraulic jack company in Chiayi, when the phone rang. The person who staffed his trading company office in Taipei was calling to tell him about a sudden 5 percent appreciation of the New Taiwan dollar relative to the US dollar. He immediately calculated that this level of appreciation would cause him to lose money if the order the company was currently filling were to be completed as agreed. Lin told us he would have to stop the interview for a while so he could call several of his major subcontractors, which he proceeded to do. A short time later, seven or eight subcontractors came to his office. They drank *laoren cha* (old folks' tea) and chewed betel nuts as the talk got under way. We sat in the next room listening to the conversation for more than an hour. We heard them talking, evaluating, and renegotiating. Power in the conversation was not equally distributed: Lin had the factory where the assembly was done and the order. In a most subtle way, he bargained back and forth, inserting personal matters (*ch'ao ching*), mentioning long-term friendships, and emphasizing how manufacturing had to be lubricated with goodwill. It was clear that everyone knew they were going to lose money on the order. The issue was how to distribute the loss. A new agreement was reached. Everyone would share a piece of the loss. Mr. Lin felt he could not absorb the shortfall himself because it was so large. Finally, there was a consensus. In essence, they agreed that if one fails, then they all fail. After the others had left, Lin told us, "You don't like it, but you have to do it."

We're Still Here

By 1990, a crisis point was reached. While property prices had reached bubble proportions in Japan, Taiwan, and South Korea, profits from manufacturing had all but vanished for most products except for those in high technology sectors, which were newly energized by the worldwide introduction of personal computers. In that year, the speculative boom across East Asia came to an abrupt end. The asset bubble burst for stocks in 1990 and for property in 1991. By the end of 1990, the Japanese stock market had fallen by more than 50 percent from its 1989 peak. Taiwan's stock market had hit its peak in 1990, and six months later it had fallen by 70 percent. Property prices across East Asia went down as well, but not nearly so drastically.[35]

Now began the hard years for most of the Taiwanese businesspeople outside the high technology sectors. Earlier, like frogs in a pot of water coming to boil, these Taiwanese entrepreneurs had not known when to jump. With the end of the bubble, they had no choice. It was jump or die. The retailers and merchandisers from the United States were not willing to reduce the price points they were demanding. The footwear and bicycle manufacturers we interviewed told us that their buyers had required them to find other locations where they could make the ordered goods more cheaply. Otherwise, they would lose their contracts. The hubris of the 1980s quickly gave way to desperation and panic in the early 1990s.

The end of martial law in 1987, however, had opened some options for the Taiwanese. Although some opportunities for travel on a Taiwanese, Republic of China (ROC), passport had opened up in 1979, it was not until 1987 that Taiwanese could both travel and freely move money outside of Taiwan. Traveling and moving money to Mainland China, however, were still illegal. For this reason, and perhaps for political reasons as well, many businesspeople were reluctant to invest in the Mainland. Instead, the first wave of business investments went to Southeast Asia, mainly to Malaysia in the area around Penang.[36] The peak year of these investments was 1990, when nearly 75 percent of Taiwan's foreign investments in Asia went to Southeast Asia and only a quarter of the Asian total went to China.[37] But then the journey west to China started in earnest. In 1991, investments in Southeast Asia fell and investments in China quadrupled and remained at a high level for the rest of that decade and into the next; investments in Southeast Asia fell continually throughout the 1990, picking up again only after the 2007 financial crisis.[38]

Some of the first movers, such as Pou Chen, the footwear manufacturer we discussed in Chapter 3, had secretly started moving some of their production to China as early as 1988. Since it was then illegal to travel or to transfer assets to China, these early movers used Hong Kong as an intermediary. After 1987, Taiwanese had free access to Hong Kong, which was only an hour's plane ride from Taiwan. Taking money out of Taiwan at the time was a problem, but Taiwanese businesspeople devised many ways to evade KMT restrictions. Once in Hong Kong, they could park their money in a bank, where it could then be exchanged for US dollars or Chinese *renminbi* (RMB) and wired to China as needed. The Taiwanese themselves could travel to China easily from Hong Kong. The Mainland Chinese border control personnel assisted the subterfuge by stamping a separate sheet of paper so that the ROC passports contained no evidence of their owners' entries and exits from China.

By 1990, it was common knowledge among Taiwan's businesspeople that the move to China had already begun for many firms. This was about the time the stampede to China started. In September of 1992, we called Chairman Tsai, the owner of a medium-sized footwear manufacturing firm in Ta Chia, to arrange for an introduction to another footwear manufacturer whom we wanted to interview. We had interviewed Chairman Tsai once before, in 1990, and had been impressed with his knowledge of footwear manufacturing and with his many contacts within the industry. We wanted this introduction because we were hearing about the exodus and wanted to know more about the reasons for going and the reasons for staying.

As late as 1987, the footwear industry had been concentrated in the Lukang region of Taiwan, which is only a short distance from Taichung. From this base, Taiwan's footwear manufacturers had dominated the world market in upmarket, non-leather shoes. But beginning in the late 1980s, footwear manufacturers, along with other traditional sectors of manufacturing in Taiwan, including makers of garments, sports gear, and toys, had begun to relocate their manufacturing sites to the Pearl River Delta, between Hong Kong and Guangzhou. After a short hesitation in the wake of the Tiananmen Square massacre in 1989, the migration of Taiwanese firms to the Mainland had gone from a trickle to a flood. By the time we made the call to Chairman Tsai, we knew that most footwear manufacturers had already left Taiwan. We were eager to interview the firms remaining in Taiwan to find out what was happening in the industry and to discover their reasons for staying. Answering the phone, Chairman Tsai told us that the person for whom we wanted the introduction was no longer in Taiwan. He had moved his firm to the Mainland. Chairman Tsai quickly added, however, "We're still here."

At that time, as far as we could find out, Chairman Tsai's firm was the last major footwear firm with all its facilities still remaining in Taiwan. In 1993, he reluctantly moved his entire manufacturing operation to Zhongshan, a district located next to Macao in the Pearl River Delta. Mr. Tsai was very proud to be the last to go, for he had held out as long as he could. Having an excellent reputation for high-quality manufacturing, Mr. Tsai's firm was (and still is) the long-term OEM producer of Timberland shoes, as well as shoes bearing other exclusive brand names. In Tachai, he had developed over many years an outstanding set of subcontractors on whom he relied and who relied on him, and so it was with great reluctance that he decided to move. He knew that he could not reestablish the same network of subcontractors in Zhongshan. But he had to move because his main buyers told him that if he did not move they would discontinue their contracts with him. Quality was not the problem. Nor was the capacity to produce shoes in large quantities. Rather, the key issue for the buyers, really the only issue, was the unit price of the shoes; it was too high. In Taiwan, he and his subcontractors had trimmed their profits as far as they could, and some had even begun to lose money. But Tsai's big buyers—the brand-name merchandisers in the United States and Europe—were facing problems of their own. The move to the Mainland by other footwear manufacturers had substantially reduced the unit cost of shoes for their American and European competitors, and thus in order to maintain their profit margins, they had to require their OEM producers to lower their unit costs. Mr. Tsai was caught in the squeeze. The OEM contract counts for everything in Tsai's business, and so to maintain the contract, he moved the location of his manufacturing.

In the five-year period between 1987 and 1992, Taiwan's footwear exports to the United States plummeted from over 30 percent of all US imports of shoes to about 3 percent. The two of us could hardly believe the speed of the exodus, not only of the footwear manufacturers but also of the makers of a whole assortment of goods, everything from apparel and toys to bicycles and any number of plastic products, including plastic lawn furniture. We decided to check out the situation for ourselves. A new six-lane freeway, financed by the Taiwanese government to connect the clusters of manufacturers located along the coast to the Taoyuan airport in the north and to the seagoing ports in Taichung and Kaohsiung, was nearly completed. We drove along the freeway to the Footwear Kingdom, the area around Lukang, and then over to Hemei, which had been the stronghold of apparel manufacturing. Although the freeway was new, there were very few vehicles on the road, and as we descended from the elevated road that passed over the key manufacturing area, we saw what looked like a ghost town. The roads were lined with closed factories. At lunchtime, we went to a restaurant located in the heart of Hemei, which had been a lunchtime gathering place for local entrepreneurs. When we got there, we were the only customers in the restaurant, and no one else came in for lunch while we ate. The owner of the restaurant said that most of the *laoban* had left the region and moved their factories to China. As we returned to Taichung along the same expressway, we talked about the irony of driving along the brand new, government-funded super highway that was intended to link factories no longer there to the airports and seaports that were supposed to receive the goods that were instead being shipped around the world from China.

The Journey West

"Going west" (*xijing*) in Chinese has a connotation similar to what the same phrase once meant to Americans: going toward unknown adventures, a combination of opportunity, risk, and even danger. The Chinese term resonates with the adventures of the band of four in the classic Chinese novel *Hsiyouchi* (*The Journey to the West*). In this epic tale, the Monkey King, the Pig, and two monks travel west from China's heartland to India to locate the sacred scripts that will bring Buddhism to China, and to find enlightenment and immortality for themselves.

In the early 1990s, Taiwanese businesspeople felt they were setting off on a similar, but considerably more secular adventure, a difficult and hazardous journey into the unknown, this time for achieving wealth and longevity in their role in the global economy as contract manufacturers. For them, however, *xijing* meant going west across the Taiwan Strait to the Mainland, a comparatively short trip in geographical terms, but politically and socially a very distant one.

Since the imposition of martial law at the end of World War II, when the Kuomintang government assumed control of Taiwan, Taiwan had been a closed society for everyone except the elite, who could travel on official business, and students, like Kao, who could earn graduate degrees by studying aboard. In 1986, as a direct but unintended consequence of the Plaza Accord, the KMT government opened Taiwan's borders so that its citizens could travel overseas more easily. The government even permitted veterans of Chiang Kai-shek's army to visit their hometowns in the Mainland. Families separated for four decades could now reconnect, even though they could not travel directly to the Mainland but had to go through Hong Kong. The newspapers were soon filled with stories of tearful reunions for the first returnees, but also with accounts of the social gulf that forty years of political separation had made. Once the door to China opened, however, many walked through for other reasons, most of them having to do with business.

The good beginning to this rapprochement soon stalled, when on June 4, 1989, the jubilant student movement in Tiananmen Square ended with the deaths of many people at the hands of the People's Liberation Army. Suddenly everyone hesitated to go to China, and a number of American and European corporations even withdrew their businesses, fearful that instability would undermine their investments. However, for the owners of many of Taiwan's most successful export-oriented businesses, by the end of 1990, the push to get out of Taiwan was greater than the reluctance to go China.

The Taiwanese relocated their businesses to two general locations in China, one in the Pearl River Delta in the hinterlands of Hong Kong and the second in the areas outside Shanghai. By the end of 1991, in just one county in Guangdong Province, Dongguan, Taiwanese businesspeople had already established over 4000 factories, which in turn employed over 2 million people, most of whom were migrant workers from China's interior provinces. Few, if any, of the Taiwanese businesspeople had family ties to people in the area. The Taiwanese had originally migrated to Taiwan from areas in Fuchien Province, and spoke a different language than the Cantonese-speaking people living in Guangdong did. However, Mandarin (the language spoken in northern China, also known as the language of Beijing) was the language of education in both Mainland China and Taiwan, and so the Taiwanese did share a common language with both Guangdong natives and the migrant workers who came from many other parts of China. This common language made the Taiwanese comfortable in their decision to move. Moreover, the infrastructure in the Pearl River Delta for manufacturing products for export was being established, spearheaded by manufacturers from Hong Kong, who had moved into the area in the preceding decade. Therefore, the initial decision to go somewhere in the Pearl River Delta was easy, and was made even easier when, in 1992, China's former supreme leader, Deng Xiaoping, went to the Pearl River Delta on his "southern inspection tour," where he famously proclaimed that "to get rich is glorious."

The first time Kao visited the Pearl River Delta was in 1994, when he accompanied Lin Chun-shan, the Chairman of A-PRO (whom we introduced in Chapter 3), to see the bicycle cluster that was then being set up in Longhua, just outside Shenzhen in the Pearl River Delta. The cluster consisted of twenty-six suppliers and an assembly plant. In 1994, Longhua was just a village. The roads were unpaved, and almost impassable when the rains came. There was only one restaurant that the Taiwanese deemed adequate. Every night, the same transplanted Taiwanese would go to the same KTV karaoke bar to sing the same Taiwanese popular songs. And every morning, migrants queued in long lines, wanting jobs that paid an average of 36 US$ a month. The Taiwanese, as well as the workers, lived in dormitories and during the day ate food in company cafeterias. Later, the owners of the firms in the cluster started a second cluster in Kunshan, outside Shanghai, where the local government gave them many advantages.

However, most firms did not leave Guangdong at that time. In 2004, one analyst estimated that the Taiwanese population of Dongguan was over 120,000. Longhua also changed quickly. The small village turned into a large city of over a million people by 2010, and is now a principal manufacturing site for the world's largest contract manufacturer, the Taiwanese-owned Hong Hai, better known in China as Foxconn.

In the early 1990s, the area around Shanghai did not seem as inviting to Taiwanese as the Pearl River Delta. In those years, Taiwanese investments in Guangdong easily exceeded those made in the Shanghai region, but by 2004, Taiwanese investments in the Shanghai area were nearly double those made in the Pearl River Delta. By 2010, the Taiwanese population in Shanghai exceeded 500,000.

Kao first went to Shanghai in 1991, along with a delegation of forty owners of small and medium-sized businesses. They traveled to northern and east central China to check out the conditions there. Bruised by the global retreat from investing in China after 1989, the Chinese government was eager to restart foreign investment, and began actively to court Taiwanese and Hong Kong businesspeople to restart their investments in China. The Chinese government offered a good deal: tax breaks, cheap land, and an efficient land and sea infrastructure. In Beijing, the vice premier of China, Chou Jai-hua, welcomed the delegation and hosted a banquet. In Shanghai, local government officials showed them possible locations to site their factories. Kao remembers that the officials took them to an undeveloped area called Pudong, across the river from Shanghai city, and suggested that this might be a location where they could invest. The Taiwanese businesspeople hesitated from making any investments at that time, feeling reluctant to move but recognizing at the same time that a move was inevitable.

Pudong has since become Shanghai's financial center, and two years later, in 1993, when the Taiwanese finally invested in the region, it was principally in Kunshan, a city about forty minutes from Shanghai, the same location to which the bicycle cluster moved as well. Also in 1993, Lai Chuan-lin, the owner of Thunder Tiger, whose business career we outlined in the introduction, started manufacturing many of his remote-controlled planes in a location near Ningbo, also in the hinterlands of Shanghai. Recognizing a business opportunity, he also founded a business park especially for other Taiwanese businesspeople who wanted to invest in the Shanghai area.

In Chapter 8, we will analyze how some Taiwanese-owned businesses organized their manufacturing operations in China. Here we will simply note that, although Deng Xiaoping declared that getting rich was glorious, for most Taiwanese there was no glory in moving their factories to China. It was difficult decision. People had to weigh the economic rationale for going there in the first place against the expense and hardships they encountered in setting up their business in a new location and, even more importantly, against the personal unhappiness for their families and for themselves in enduring long, lonely periods of separation.

Taiwanese women, particularly, found the move to China intolerable, both those who went and those who stayed behind. The owners of firms often asked some of their female employees to shift their jobs to China. These women were typically professionals who held key positions in the firm. One woman with whom we talked, Hsueh Jenhwa, had worked for six years as a sales manager for a firm making pedals for both high-end and mass-market bicycles. The firm was doing okay in Taiwan, but when the bicycle suppliers began to move to China, the firm started to decline. After a change of management, the new *laoban* decided he had to move the factory to China. He asked Hsueh to go to China shortly after the firm began to establish its new site of operations near one of the bicycle clusters in the Pearl River Delta. As soon as she arrived in China, the firm started to receive orders, even before the new factory was finished. The *laoban* appointed two managers to handle the operations in China, but he also had to spend much of his time there as well. He found it very difficult to get the construction done, because for everything he needed to do, he had to pay money under the table to make construction go smoothly. Once the factory was completed, the management team worked very hard to fill the open orders, but, to their surprise, the efficiency of the migrant workers was terrible. The factory employed about 100 workers. The management team tried to push the employees to work harder. Eventually, the Taiwanese managers resorted to a military style of control, with very strict discipline. The workers were mostly female migrants from outside the region and in their late teens and early twenties. They ate and slept in dormitories, and spent the rest of the day working in the factory.

Factory work in China was so unlike what it was in Taiwan, Hsueh recalled. There were no personal connections between migrant employees and the Taiwanese staff, and an equally large gap existed between the local Chinese from Guangdong and the Taiwanese newcomers. Conditions were especially bad for the few Taiwanese women in the region. They never took public transportation. Although the firm employed local drivers, the women constantly worried about their safety. Security around the factory was poor, and the Taiwanese in general felt isolated and embattled, but the women even more so. The male staff at night would go to bars, where they would drink, sing, and carouse with the bar girls. The women ate in restaurants either by themselves or with a few other Taiwanese women, and the service was always poor. They did not talk to any of the locals. The loneliness and boredom was intense. Even though she had doubled her salary by going to China, after two months there, Hsueh quit her job and returned to Taiwan. "It just wasn't worth it," she said.

The women most influenced by the exodus were not the women who went to China, but rather those who stayed behind. The owners and managers who felt compelled to take their factories to China were mostly married men, and their firms were family firms. The wives of these men (the *laobanniang*) all realized that the success of their firms was at stake, but the thought of their husbands leaving quickly became a major issue, not just for them and their children but also for Taiwanese society. At first, the *laoban* thought they could appoint competent managers to run the factory in China and that their trips to China would be periodic at best. But then reality set in. The transition was hard. Construction, day-to-day labor management, working with other Taiwanese owners to create a new satellite assembly system, dealing with the local officials—nothing was easy and everything required more time and money and patience than had been foreseen. The result was that owners and managers had to spend long periods away, and while they were away, many cured their loneliness by taking a second wife. By the mid-1990s, articles began to appear in local Taiwanese newspapers about what they called *bao er nai*, literally, "keeping two wives."[39]

Many families broke up as a consequence of the husbands' infidelities in China. Some Taiwanese men even decided to make China their new home. Many more families had to work through these very hard years as best they could. One family about whom we have firsthand knowledge experienced a particularly tragic outcome. When the husband announced that he had been ordered to China, his wife broke down, crying. She said that she could not, by herself, raise her two sons who were about to finish middle school. The husband finally agreed to take the sons with him to China, where he would put them in school. But after a year, he realized that the Chinese schools were so unsatisfactory that he had to send the two boys back home. A short time later, he suffered a heart attack and died in China. He was neither the first Taiwanese *laoban* to die in China nor the last. Their work there was usually hard, long, and lonely, and after work, the men often drank too much and ate too little.

Conclusion

The Plaza Accord proved to be a tipping point for East Asian economies, as well as for global capitalism. Many of the changes that did occur because of the accord might have happened anyway, although over a longer period of time. But the Plaza Accord pushed events forward in unexpected ways, compressing a cycle of economic boom, subsequent collapse of property and stock markets, and the desperate flight of owners and managers to find new factory locations where money could still be made. The outcome of this combination of economic implosion and then explosion was the creation of a new pan-Asian economy.

In the late 1980s, economists and political analysts debated whether the Plaza Accord had been a success or not, and they generally concluded that the agreement accomplished its goals. "In policy terms," wrote Destler and Henning in 1989 in their authoritative book on the accord and its aftermath, "the Plaza strategy was a clear success."[40] In 1989, it seemed like a success, because the dollar's devaluation was followed by a slight decline in the US trade deficit. But, as the following decades would reveal, that judgment about the Plaza Accord and its aftermath was premature. As a maneuver to correct the US trade imbalance, this and later agreements failed miserably, in large part because the economic logic that informed the agreements was simply incorrect. Trade among nations is not well represented by equilibrium models. One of the many problems in imagining that world trade has a natural balance among nations is that there are no capitalists in this picture, no traders, no organizers, just the ebb and flow of goods across national borders guided, perhaps, by some invisible hand. But capitalists do exist, and they are loath to lose their businesses and to stop making money.

The Western and Japanese big buyers and the East Asian manufacturers were not inclined to see the currency adjustments as the end of their business alliance. Instead of being passive observers of changing economic conditions, they became (somewhat reluctantly) aggressive converts to a new global economic order. Internationalization became the order of the day. Having mastered the lean retailing package, the big-box retailers in the United States and Europe led the way. With smaller home markets, the European retailers (e.g., Carrefour, Aldi, Metro, and Tesco) expanded beyond their national borders earlier than the US retailers; but in the 1990s, they also expanded rapidly beyond Europe, especially into Latin America and Asia. Walmart only began its international expansion in 1991, with a joint venture in Mexico, but by 2002, as measured by sales outside its home market, Walmart was the world's most global retailer. During the same period, many other retailers and merchandisers also developed global footprints, both for procuring and for selling their products.

As retailers and merchandisers expanded in the 1990s, East Asian economies turned inside out. Asian firms that had been local became, in a matter of a few years, international firms with global concerns. The owners and managers of these firms could no longer rely on close relationships and tacit knowledge to conduct their business. Making money now relied on many tools, on becoming indispensable suppliers, on making constant innovations, on becoming professional managers of labor and capital. Not everyone was able to make the transition, but many of those who did became more successful than ever.

7

HIGH TECHNOLOGY INDUSTRIES IN TAIWAN

Turning on a Dime

The retail revolution of the late 1950s initiated the swing toward demand-responsive manufacturing, especially for fashion-oriented goods. Nurtured by US and European retailers and merchandisers, firms specializing in contract manufacturing took over the manufacture of a large array of these goods and their constituent components in the period before 1985. This trend diversified and accelerated after 1985, for the reasons we outlined in the previous chapter.

Consumer electronics, however, was a laggard. In the 1960s and 1970s, consumer electronics was a relatively new, capital intensive industry that depended on brand-name manufacturers making technological breakthroughs to develop new products. The key products—radios before World War II and televisions after it—were manufactured in Fordist fashion by the leading firms in the sector. RCA (Radio Corporation of America) emerged as the largest single manufacturer of the products that make up what we now call consumer electronics. RCA was a multidivisional, vertically integrated company that manufactured components parts that went into its radios, photographs, and televisions.[1] It also sold components to other firms, provided integrated service for its products, supported authorized dealers, and supplied credit for consumers buying its goods. In addition, RCA produced records, was a major recording studio, and established the National Broadcasting Company (NBC), the oldest broadcasting network in the United States. Other firms producing electrical and electronic products were also vertically integrated, including General Electric, Westinghouse, and Zenith.

In the first decades after World War II, seven companies (RCA, Philco, Zenith, Motorola, Magnavox, Admiral, and Sylvania) dominated the market for black-and-white televisions in the United States.[2] The fierce competition among these firms drove down prices, which allowed 85 percent of American families to buy one or more televisions by 1959.[3] The dominance of these firms is largely explained by a truism: *Where people buy those products they desire largely determines what they are able to purchase.* In the first two decades after World War II, the distribution channels for electronic products were controlled by manufacturers and not retailers. During these early years, the electronics manufacturers remained embedded in the old industrial order that Alfred Chandler wrote about so eloquently, an order that preceded what we know today as consumer electronics.[4] It was not until 1963 that a former RCA executive, Jack Wayman, then Senior Vice President of the manufacturers' Electronic Industries Association, started the Consumer Electronics Association on a small scale. The association held its first Consumer Electronics Show in 1967, displaying mainly televisions, radios, and phonographs.[5]

These same products were, of course, already widely available to consumers, but they were typically categorized as household appliances, and sold in appliance stores along with refrigerators, stoves, washing machines, dryers, and small assorted items such as toasters and vacuum sweepers. The major manufacturers (e.g., Admiral, General Electric, Westinghouse, and RCA) made a full line of household appliances in addition to radios and televisions, and sold these appliances in designated retail outlets.[6] These were *authorized dealers*, most of whom were limited to selling a very narrow range of brands, sometimes only one brand. For example, Magnavox maintained a franchise system of about 2600 dealers that sold only Magnavox products. General Electric even owned some of its own retail outlets.[7] Furniture stores also sold these products, where they were marketed as items of décor and often sold to customers in large console models that combined a television, radio, and phonograph in one decorative wooden case.

In 1964, Sears, the largest department store chain in the United States, undercut this closed system of retailing.[8] Following its previous strategy of selling private label products, Sears wanted to begin selling color televisions under its in-store brand, Silvertone. After RCA and Zenith both refused Sears's request to produce a private label color television, Sears made a contract with the Japanese manufacturer Toshiba, which soon produced a 16-inch Silvertone television for the American market at a much cheaper price than comparable

American-made models.⁹ Using different Japanese manufacturers (e.g., Matsushita, Sharp, Sanyo, and Hitachi), J. C. Penney and Montgomery Ward, along with other retailers, followed suit with their own small-screen, private label televisions. In quick succession, Motorola, RCA, General Electric, Admiral, and Zenith all offered their own small-screen, black-and-white televisions made on contract by Japanese firms.¹⁰ The color televisions they continued to make themselves—for a short time at least.

In 1965, Sony was the only Japanese manufacturer that sold its televisions under its own brand name, "following an exclusive distribution strategy through a few large and reputable stores."¹¹ But within two years, Matsushita (Panasonic), Toshiba, and Hitachi introduced their own branded televisions as well. By this time, color televisions had captured much of the television market, which spurred a new round of price competition, only this time with US manufacturers competing with Japanese manufacturers as well as with other US firms.¹²

Even before the US market was inundated with Japanese-made televisions, American manufacturers had reached a point of no return. As the industry grew more competitive, American workers had also started to unionize and to demand higher wages.¹³ The increasing cost of labor, the price competition among American firms, the entry of cheaper black-and-white and color televisions from Japan, and the growing success of color televisions prompted the leading US manufacturers to move a portion of their factories out of the country, some across the border to Mexico and many to Asia. In 1965, the Taiwanese government approved opening the world's first export processing zone in Kaohsiung, and among the first firms to sign on when the zone opened in 1966 were the US television producers. In the next five years, RCA, Philco, Admiral, and Zenith established factories in Taiwan. Also present were TRW, General Instruments, Texas Instruments, and IBM, all of which made components for the television industry and for electronic calculators and business machines. In addition, during these five years, Philips, the Dutch electronics firm, built the first of many factories that it would eventually build in Taiwan. By 1971, these firms employed about 50,000 persons, mostly women, who assembled the final products.¹⁴ This transfer of factories and technology marked the beginning of Taiwan's high technology industries.

In this chapter, we analyze the development of high technology industries in Taiwan from the opening of the Kaohsiung Export Processing Zone in 1966 to the beginning of the new century, when most of the high technology firms began to move their assembly plants to China. We will follow the expansion of these industries in China after 2000 in subsequent chapters. Our first interviews with businesspeople in high technology sectors date from the late 1980s. To put these interviews into a historical context, we have reconstructed earlier advances in these sectors with the help of abundant primary and secondary materials.

The Growth of High Technology Industries in Taiwan, 1965–1999

Making Televisions

The high technology industries in Taiwan started in a very different way from the other industrial sectors, the sectors that were so robust before 1985. For apparel, footwear, bicycles, and a huge number of other items, big buyers helped create competent suppliers from whom they could order goods. These buyers mostly represented the factory-less merchandisers and the new retail stores popping up in malls across the United States. By contrast, in 1966, at the dawn of high-tech industries in Taiwan, it was the manufacturers themselves that set up factories in Taiwan.

For the next decade, Taiwan's export processing zone in Kaohsiung became the top location in Asia for multinational electronics firms from the United States to site their overseas factories, and shortly thereafter Kaohsiung Harbor became Taiwan's first container port.[15] These factories initially made various component parts and assembled black-and-white televisions, both of which were then shipped to the United States and Europe.

Besides the American firms and Philips, the one European firm, factories were also established in Kaohsiung's export processing zone by Hong Kong Chinese. These companies made transistor radios, phonographs, and televisions for Asian markets.[16] Initially, they bought some of their components from American firms. A number of Japanese electronics firms, including Hitachi, Fuji, Matsushita, and Sanyo, also built factories in Kaohsiung and elsewhere in Taiwan, and unlike American firms, they began business in Taiwan by establishing a number of joint ventures with Taiwanese companies. The Japanese companies also bought components, entered into licensing agreements with American firms, and exported some of their televisions to the United States.

In addition to these foreign firms, eleven Taiwanese firms also began to assemble televisions, for the Taiwanese market. Using components bought from American and Japanese firms, as well as from a growing number of local component parts manufacturers, these firms made upward of 300,000 black-and-white sets per year in the late 1960s, until the local market was saturated. Some of these firms then turned to producing components and televisions for export.[17]

To those foreign firms agreeing to site factories in the Kaohsiung Export Processing Zone, the Taiwanese government promised abundant cheap labor (daily wages for an assembly line worker averaged 1 US$), few labor disputes, an educated labor force (97 percent of the school-age population had received a minimum of six years of education), and an ample supply of engineers and technicians (graduates from the local colleges and vocational schools). The firms were also promised tax exemptions (no corporate tax for the first five years); inexpensive land, power, and water; duty-free status for all imported raw materials and parts and for all exports; and the ability to repatriate profit and capital.[18]

Within five years, Taiwan's electronic exports were booming and consumer electronics became one of Taiwan's leading export sectors. Most of the exports initially came out of solely owned American factories and out of Japanese-Taiwanese joint ventures, but through the decade Taiwanese firms produced more and more of the final products.[19] At first, these were mostly black-and-white televisions and their components, but as early as 1969, RCA started making a few parts for its color televisions in Taiwan as well, and had begun actively to collaborate with Taiwanese firms to manufacture picture tubes.[20] The other American manufacturers were also actively sourcing some components from Taiwanese firms. In addition, Texas Instruments was producing some hand-held calculators in Taiwan, which included buying components from local firms. By the 1975–76 fiscal year, the total sales figure of RCA Taiwan Ltd. made it the seventh largest company in Taiwan. The Taiwan branches of Zenith, Texas Instruments, Admiral, Philips, General Instruments, and Sylvania-Philco all ranked among the top one hundred companies in Taiwan by sales in the same year.[21] Factories in Taiwan were turning out millions of television sets per year, over 7 million in 1977 alone.[22]

The expansion of American firms in Taiwan did not mean they were successful in the United States. Such are the vagaries of capitalism. In the United States, price maintenance laws had come under attack and were declared unconstitutional in many states. Then, in 1970, the last holdout, Magnavox, was ordered by the Federal Trade Commission to cease its restrictive franchise relationship with appliance stores.[23] This action ended the manufacturers' point-of-sales control over their distribution channels and introduced discount merchandising into consumer electronics. Within the decade, consumer electronics superstores (e.g., Circuit City, Best Buy) emerged to become the appliance stores of the 1980s and beyond. Imports from East Asia came flooding in.

As competition among retailers increased in the United States, competition among Asian manufacturers spread and intensified. South Korean *chaebol*, principally Samsung and Lucky-Goldstar (later known as LG), started to manufacture and export color televisions to be sold in discount stores at price points cheaper than their Japanese and American competitors could offer. On a smaller scale, two Taiwanese companies, Tatung and Sampo, also started to export televisions to the United States. Facing tough competition and loss of sales, Magnavox in 1974 sold out to Philips, which allowed the Dutch firm to enter the US market with a well-known brand name. In 1976, imports from all sources accounted for a third of all televisions purchased in the United States.[24] In that year, 42 percent of American consumers bought their televisions in appliance stores, and about 7 percent bought from furniture stores. Department and catalog stores, both categories in which Sears dominated, accounted for nearly 37 percent of the market. Discount chains, including Kmart, Walmart, and others, sold only slightly over 11 percent of the total market.[25]

This sudden flood of imported televisions prompted action from the US government. In 1970, the US Treasury Department accused Japanese manufacturers of "dumping" televisions in the US market. Over the next six years, as these accusations increased, Sony and Matsushita, along with five other Japanese manufacturers, built assembly factories in the United States. To curtail foreign competition and to limit further declines in US employment in the television industry, the Carter administration in 1977 negotiated an Orderly Market Agreement (OMA) with Japan, and in the following year with Taiwan and South Korea as well. In lieu of the US government imposing tariffs on color televisions, the three countries voluntarily agreed to limit the number of color televisions exported to the United States. Much to the dismay of American manufacturers in Taiwan, the OMA also limited the number of televisions they could ship to the United States.[26] The intense competition, declining market share, and falling profits forced several American manufacturers to stop making televisions during the 1970s, including Motorola, Philco, and Admiral. All the others lost significant shares of the US television market and, over the course of the next decade or so, would cease manufacturing televisions altogether.

This shakeout among US manufacturers directly impacted Taiwan's electronic firms. Admiral sold its Taiwan factory to local businesspeople. Other American manufacturers began to rely increasingly on local Taiwanese firms to make their key components and were willing to transfer technology to do so. More importantly, several American firms began to source their black-and-white televisions, and later their color ones, from Taiwanese firms, principally Tatung and Sampo. Both Taiwanese firms even established assembly factories for color televisions in the United States.[27]

The same shakeout, as well as the increasingly successful competition from Japan, limited the ability of US firms to compete in the new waves of electronic products that began to appear. In the early 1970s, videocassette recorders (VCRs) were developed in the United States, but by 1975, as VCRs became popular consumer items, two Japanese *keiretsu*—Sony and Matsushita (Panasonic and JVC)—captured the US market with their superior technology and widespread marketing through an increasing variety of retail outlets. Taiwanese and South Korean manufacturers joined in at lower price points, and by 1983, imports accounted for 100 percent of the US market.[28] Then, with the introduction of the Sony Walkman in 1980, the world of consumer electronics took off, and from that time forward imports dominated the US market in all categories of mass-marketed consumer electronic products, even for personal computers, which Apple and IBM had just introduced in, respectively, 1976 and 1981.

Television manufacturing laid the industrial foundation for the explosion of Taiwan's high technology industries that would occur in the following decades. Less than fifteen years after the opening of the Kaohsiung Export Processing Zone in 1966, export television production moved from factories owned by multinational corporations to those owned predominately by local Taiwanese. In that period, large clusters of small, medium-sized, and modestly large firms arose to manufacture components and assemble final products.[29] The number of television sets manufactured continued to climb even as the ownership of the firms switched from foreign to local and even as the profit per unit continued to dwindle.[30] However, unlike television production in Japan and South Korea, Taiwanese firms at the time could not establish a global brand name for their televisions, and so continued to make televisions on contract for other companies to brand and sell. The sector contained many clusters of many small to modestly large firms, but there were no conglomerates large and powerful enough to organize these clusters into vertically integrated *keiretsu*-like networks. Instead, like the owners of firms making other products in Taiwan, the owners of these firms were always on the lookout for new opportunities that would allow them to make more money than could be had in the television industry. Those opportunities were on the horizon.

Making Computers

The opportunities to make more money from consumer electronics came from two simultaneous developments: first, from the take-off of computer manufacturing, greatly aided by some misguided decisions made in 1981 by IBM, then the world's leading manufacturer of computers; and second, from a 1973 government-sponsored initiative that established the Industrial Technology and Research Institute (ITRI) to obtain technology transfers from American companies to manufacture integrated circuits. The government initiative was slow to gain traction until the mid-1980s, when it merged with and partially led advances in computer technology. In this section, we will follow the rapid growth of the computer industry that starts in the late 1970s. Then, in the next section, we will pick up the KMT's government initiative to create a semiconductor industry.

In 1983, in its lengthy report to the US Congress on international competitiveness in electronics, the Office of Technology Assessment concluded that, for computers and semiconductors, "IBM is still an order of magnitude ahead of its competitors ... [T]he world computer industry can still be pictured as IBM on the one hand and everyone else on the other."[31] The report to Congress contained short and mildly optimistic sections on the computer industry in Taiwan and South Korea, and, by contrast, extolled the strength and competitiveness of Japanese manufacturers. In retrospect, it is easy to see that the Office of Technology Assessment did not sufficiently understand where this industry was going. Indeed, it would have been difficult for anyone in the early 1980s to have guessed that, within the next thirty years, Taiwanese and South Korean manufacturers would have eclipsed IBM, would have pushed Japanese manufacturers to a second tier, and would lead the world in the production of computers and computer-driven devices, such as mobile phones. Strangely, it was decisions made by IBM that, at least initially, led to this outcome.

In 1980, IBM led the world in the production of computers, mostly the so-called mainframe computers. IBM designed, built, sold, and serviced these very large, complex computers for governments and large businesses, and dominated the US market for these computers, with over a 60 percent share of the total. Even IBM's most compact and least expensive mainframes were the size of a large refrigerator and cost nearly 100,000 US$. Most were room size and cost millions. At the other end of the computer spectrum were microcomputers, "desktops" that Commodore, Apple, and Radio Shack had just introduced in 1977 to a fairly small group of enthusiasts, mostly computer hobbyists. Between the two extremes were minicomputers, which ranged in size and cost and which were used by small businesses. These minicomputers were essentially small mainframes, and sold in a range around 15,000 US$. IBM also designed, built, sold, and serviced these minicomputers, and claimed nearly 20 percent of the US market, nearly twice as much as the share of the next largest manufacturer.[32]

Partly to counter rising sales of the microcomputers, especially the Apple II computer, which by 1980 was beginning to sell well, IBM decided to enter the desktop market with its own personal computer, the IBM PC. However, for the IBM PC, unlike for its other computers, IBM decided to outsource most of the components. This decision to outsource was likely influenced by ongoing antitrust action by the US Department of Justice, but perhaps also by IBM's (mis)calculation that mainframes and minicomputers would continue to dominate the business world, and that the PC sector would remain a relatively small segment of the total computer market.[33] IBM modularized its PC into core components and peripherals (*hardware*), using Intel's microprocessor as the central processing unit (CPU), and into an operating system (*software*), using Microsoft's MSDOS as the binary language used to input, process, and output information.[34] The only part of the PC that IBM did not outsource was its proprietary *basic input/output system* (BIOS), a software interface that allowed the MSDOS operating system to interact with the PC's hardware. The rest of IBM's PC package consisted of thousands of individual parts—including everything that went into making the PC chassis, motherboards, hard-disk drives, printers, monitors, power systems, pointing devices—and many types of software that would work with the MSDOS operating system.

IBM introduced its PC computer in 1981, and enjoyed immediate success, almost matching the sales figure for the Apple II by the following year and then far surpassing it, reaching a 25 percent share of the American PC market by 1985. However, in the same year that IBM introduced its PC, several other American companies, most notably Compaq Computer, began to sell their own computers that would run the same software programs as the IBM PC. These computers were called IBM compatibles or IBM clones. These companies used the same Intel microprocessor and Microsoft software that IBM used, but had developed their own BIOS, by reverse engineering and "clean room design," which prevented IBM from successfully suing its competitors for patent infringements.

Taiwanese manufacturers had a role in IBM's success, as well as a much larger role in its subsequent decline. These manufacturers entered into this competition among US firms along several different paths. At first, some Taiwanese firms entered directly, as suppliers for American computer makers. In 1966, IBM joined the American television manufacturers in the Kaohsiung Export Processing Zone, where the company both produced some parts for its computers and developed a network of suppliers for additional parts. Tatung was the first firm to become an IBM supplier, but many other firms signed on as well. According to interviews conducted by Pan Mei-lin, "Through the process of qualifying as an IBM supplier, countless Taiwanese firms learned how to improve their product quality. IBM [played] a role in providing know-how to its Taiwanese component and parts suppliers."[35] When the IBM PC went into production, the company got many of the components from suppliers in Taiwan, including the PC monitors, for which Tatung, building on its experience in making televisions, was a key supplier.

Other firms entered the computer industry indirectly, through making related electronic products, including televisions, which gave some firms, such as Tatung, enough knowledge to make computers at a later point in time. Several of the firms we interviewed in late 1980s and early 1990s made electronic gaming machines before they made computers. In the late 1970s, video game parlors were being opened throughout Taiwan. Going to these parlors was a fad, something akin to gambling. If you won the game, you were awarded bonus points redeemable for more games or cash. These parlors used electronic gaming machines that had been reverse engineered from Japanese companies such as Nintendo. In March 1982, however, when the KMT government wanted to stop the gambling among adolescents and young adults that was associated with these parlors, the government banned these machines and ordered the gaming parlors closed. These actions left the manufacturers of the gaming machines without a market. Many of these manufacturers subsequently entered the computer business.[36]

Chuan Nao was one of these firms. In 1990, when we interviewed Mr. Yu, the general manager, the company was assembling computers for sale mainly in Northern Europe, which he described as an easy place to market computers because the competition was less intense. At the time of our interview, the company employed around 1000 people in Taiwan and another 100 in various countries around the world. When Chuan Nao was making gaming machines in the early 1980s, however, it was a very small firm making video game machines for the domestic market and for export. Most of the component parts needed for the gaming machines were used in televisions and were readily available in Taiwan, but after the government banned the gaming machines, Chuan Nao decided, in 1983, to enter the computer business, first as a trading company importing electronic components from Hong Kong and, then, after finding that business too competitive, as a manufacturing firm making 16-bit IBM PC clones. Mr. Yu told us the switch was not difficult, because most of the parts needed for IBM PC clones were also available in Taiwan, except for key components such as the Intel microprocessor, which had to be imported. Highly successful at first, Chuan Nao marketed its computer under its own brand name, Compal, but the company gradually moved into contract manufacturing and is now one of the world's leading manufacturers of laptop and notebook computers.

DTK was another firm that, in 1981, began business with twenty employees making video game machines. After the government ban went into effect, DTK started building motherboards for Apple II clones, and then moved on to making the same component for IBM clones. In only six years, DTK's sales surged from 2 million to 5 billion NT$, representing an annual growth rate of over 100 percent. In the same period, the number of employee jumped to 700. By 1987, relying on over forty small firms to supply components, DTK became Taiwan's largest exporter of motherboards.

Another point of entry was the move from making electronic calculators to computers. This was the case with the founder of Quanta, Lin Baili, known by his Cantonese name, Barry Lam. Lam, along with several classmates from the Electrical Engineering Department at National Taiwan University in Taipei, started a small firm, Santron, in the early 1970s. The firm made cheaper versions of the calculator produced by the Japanese company Casio. In reflecting back on his time at Santron, Lam said, "We knew nothing then and we learned little by little. Though I just stayed in Santron for one year, I learned the spirit of being fearless."[37] Lam left Santron to join a team of engineers at Kinpo Electronics, which soon became the world's largest contract manufacturer for calculators. As the computer wave swept over Taiwan, Lam teamed up with C. C. Leung to found Quanta Computers in 1988. Quanta is now the world's largest producer of laptop computers, with over 70,000 employees. However, in 1991, when we interviewed one of the managers at Quanta, it was a modestly sized assembly firm making IBM clones as a contract manufacturer for Dell and Gateway, among many other firms.

Some of the computer-related firms we interviewed, however, started in entirely different businesses and then shifted when their former business was no longer viable. When we interviewed O Cheng-ming, the Chairman of Universal Microelectronic, in 1990, the firm was one of the world's leading manufacturers of transformers and AC to DC converters, which are essential components for many consumer electronic products, including computers. The company, however, had been started in the early 1970s to manufacture shoes. About the time of the Plaza Accord, the profit margin for footwear manufacturing had diminished so much that Chairman O began to look for other opportunities. When an American company offered him a contract to build computer parts and a guarantee of five years of orders, he jumped at the chance. He acknowledged that the move was difficult. "The computer market was flourishing at the time, and computer parts were in high demand. However, there were over 1000 parts manufacturers—so competitive. We succeed, though, thanks to our strong R&D."

Whatever path they took into the computer business, most of the people doing so shared two characteristics. First, they learned their trade through what we might call "self-education by imitation." The early founders of computer firms were all "tinkerers," computer enthusiasts who learned by imitating successful products.[38] Second, the firms they started were mostly partnerships, collaborations among friends and colleagues who pooled their money to establish their business. In the late 1970s and early 1980s, Taiwan's computer enthusiasts numbered in the tens of thousands, mostly young men, who wanted to build their own computers. Several computer malls opened in Taipei, most prominently the Chung-Hua Arcade and Kuang-Hua Public Market, where these computer tinkerers could buy almost any part needed to make any available electronic product, including computers.[39] Lined with small computer shops, mostly trading companies importing components and selling them along with components made in Taiwan, the malls were beehives of activity. Here people learned how to make computers, do-it-yourself computers.[40] Then in the closing months of 1980, a circuit diagram for the Apple II appeared in several electronics magazines, including *Electronics & Radio-TV Technical Monthly*. Within weeks, "parts, kits, and fully assembled Apple II compatibles showed up in the computer malls.... [By] December 1982 ... Taiwan was home to at least 100 companies manufacturing Apple II compatibles."[41] Apple, however, objected to the illegal copies of Apple II, and in 1983, sued eight Taiwanese companies in two separate legal actions. The Taiwanese court upheld Apple's suit, and after appeals were filed, Taiwan's High Court concluded the case in Apple's favor in December 1984, and sentenced the owners of the violating firms to prison.[42] By 1985, most of the makers of the Apple II compatibles had turned their attention to IBM PCs and IBM PC clones.[43]

Perhaps the most famous firm that exemplifies this pattern is Acer, the most internationally well-known brand-name manufacturer among Taiwanese computer firms. In 1991, we interviewed President Wang, the CEO of Acer, who in 1976 helped establish Multitech, Acer's predecessor, with Stanley Shih, Acer's *laoban* and Chairman of the Board. Shih and Wang had been classmates while earning graduate degrees from National Chiao Tung University. Shih had previously worked in a local electronics firm and had been instrumental in developing electronic calculators and watches. But when that firm went out of business, Shih, his wife, and several classmates pooled $25,000 to start Multitech, a firm distributing components and instructions on how to build your own computer. Starting with eleven employees, Multitech did not turn a profit until several years later when it began making several Apple II–compatible computers, marketed under the name Little Professor (Xiao Jiaoshou). After Apple sued several other companies in Taiwan that were also making copies of Apple II, Multitech joined the wave of firms making IBM PC clones, and in 1986, beat IBM in introducing a computer using 32-bit CPU architecture. For success in the computer industry, President Wang told us, "Timing is even more important than quality." Being first to market with a product is crucial.

Multitech changed its name to Acer in 1987, when it was listed on the Taiwan Stock Exchange. By that time, Acer had become Taiwan's thirty-fifth largest business group (by sales) and consisted of thirteen independent firms employing over 5000 persons, still a miniscule business group by Japanese and South Korean standards.[44] Nonetheless, Stanley Shih had ambitions for Acer and tried to vertically integrate his production of computer hardware and peripherals and to build extensive distribution channels. By the mid-1990s, however, it became apparent that Acer's plans to go it alone were going to be limited. The US subsidiary did not succeed in marketing the brand name, and the semiconductor initiative was losing money. The Acer group had to pull back its plans to manufacture semiconductors and other components and had to work with existing networks of suppliers and with an array of big buyers as well. Although Acer had built a global brand name, and was one of the most popular computer brands in Europe, Acer was also a contract manufacturer for many other companies. When we visited the firm, computers for Groupe Bull, the French computer group, were coming off the line.

After 1985, with the misadventure with Apple II clones behind them, computer firms in Taiwan increasingly became contract manufacturers for computer businesses worldwide. The mix of small, medium-sized, and modestly large computer firms in Taiwan had an affinity with the standardized modular architecture of the IBM PCs and its clones and with the American and European firms offering them for sale. Everything was in place. In addition to firms with experience in electronics, there were firms specializing in machine tools, plastics, metals, molding, packaging, fast-freight forwarding, and shipping. Taiwanese contract manufacturers offered a full package service.

Starting in the mid-1980s, the computer industry was analogous to the fast-changing fashion world with which Taiwanese manufacturers were already familiar. The standardized modular architecture of the PC led to low startup costs for American and European manufacturers, who could easily offer PC clones by outsourcing parts or even whole systems from contract manufacturers. This led to a proliferation of American and European companies selling PCs. By 1990, there were over one hundred companies worldwide offering PCs. The same standardized package also led to low startup costs for Taiwanese manufacturers, who could get into the business by producing one part or another. This led to a proliferation of Taiwanese companies entering some sphere of the computer business. The relationship that the two parties established was interdependent. When American manufacturers, in hot competition with each other, needed to turn out new and better models every year (or even quicker), they increasingly turned to Taiwanese firms to make the outer shells, internal components, and peripherals. Constant updates, constant price constraints—everything had to be produced in batches at the lowest cost. Ever flexible, the Taiwanese networks were able to respond quickly to changes in products and costs and to process the orders ever more efficiently. And so more and more orders came in.

The PC industry, however, was unlike the world of fads and fashions in two respects. First, at the beginning of Taiwan's involvement, the industry was driven not by retailers, but rather by manufacturers responding to rapid changes in technology, technology that brought more computing power, more memory for storage, more software packages, and all in a package that became easier and easier to use. In a matter of just a few years, the core market switched from home enthusiasts to office workers. PCs became essential tools for business. Second, despite the expanding number of Western companies offering PCs for sale, the "connection between the PC maker and the final customer was often weak (via advertising and marketing) or nonexistent."[45] The rapid product cycles and the hit-or-miss distribution efforts by Western PC sellers resulted in overproduction and rapid depreciation of products that were constantly going out of date. The sellers' profit margins veered toward zero.

In 1990, even though IBM's PC was still the market leader with 13 percent of the total, it was clear that IBM's competitors had won the competition. First, in the mid-1980s, Microsoft had introduced Windows, a new operating system built on top of the old MSDOS. Microsoft now worked directly with Intel to ensure compatibility between each new generation of Intel's microprocessor and each new version of Windows. The issue of compatibility with the IBM PC was no longer important. The key concern became compatibility with "Wintel," as the two companies came to be known collectively. Interconnectivity within and across businesses was the most important factor in what brand of PC companies purchased. Therefore, most companies signed on to the Wintel combination, with Windows running on over 90 percent of all PCs sold in the early 1990s. With its market share down to 7 percent in 1990, Apple Computer was the only major PC seller that maintained its own proprietary operating system. With Wintel the clear winner, the hardware manufacturers increasingly concentrated on standardized components that would be compatible with the Wintel PC package.

The second factor that doomed IBM's PC was a new retail model that directly connected Taiwan's hardware manufacturers with final consumers in the United States, a direct sales model that eliminated retailers. In 1984, working out of his college dorm room, Michael Dell began to sell IBM-compatible computers customized to the buyer's wishes. He soon dropped out of college, had over $70 million in revenues in his first year of business, and in 1988, went public with his company, Dell Computer Corporation, on the Nasdaq stock exchange. By 1992, Dell Computers joined the Fortune's list of the 500 largest companies in the world, with Michael Dell as the youngest CEO ever to be on that list.

Dell's business model was direct sales. Although listed as a manufacturer, Dell Computers was essentially a merchandising/retailing company that was entirely demand responsive. With standardized parts to choose from, Dell Computers offered its customers a range of choices for getting exactly the Wintel-compatible Dell computer they wanted to buy at the lowest possible cost and then assembled the purchased computer on demand. Because the company targeted businesses, offering them company-wide interconnectivity with the same hardware and software packages on all their computers and an on-call service agreement, it also lowered their cost based on large purchases. The point-of-sales data fed back over the network of component parts makers, most of whom were Taiwanese companies, allowing them to quickly adjust their production schedules to actual demand. Dell Computers also established an online site where individuals and business customers could order directly. Although slow to take off, the online site soon accounted for over a quarter of Dell's revenues. By 1999, Dell became the world's leading seller of computers, forcing many Dell's competitors out of business and causing the many of the remaining competitors to establish direct selling channels themselves.[46]

Dell and other PC sellers using direct sales (e.g., Gateway) counted on Taiwanese manufacturers to source most of the requisite components for their desktop computers. As laptop and notebook computers became more popular among consumers, styles that limited the number of plug-and-play add-ons, Dell began to rely on Taiwanese contract manufacturers to design and even to ship the computers to the final customer. In its online persona, Dell was merely a brand-name intermediary connecting individual consumers to global manufacturers who happened to be in Taiwan.

Part of the reason American PC sellers initially turned to Taiwanese firms was that, as AnnaLee Saxenian brilliantly demonstrated, there were many Taiwanese working in Silicon Valley who had connections in Taiwan.[47] These connections created dense networks of interactions between the two locations. However, another part of the reason Taiwanese manufacturers became so important to both American and European PC sellers was that Japanese and South Korean manufacturers were less flexible and, more importantly, were competitors, instead of collaborators, with American firms.

The affinity of Taiwanese manufacturers for the standardized PC architecture simply did not exist among Taiwan's industrial neighbors.[48] Japanese *keiretsu*, each developing its own proprietary systems, put most of their resources into competing with IBM mainframes and minicomputers, and for the most part missed out on capturing a significant share of the PC market. A latecomer in the computer business, Toshiba was the only *keiretsu* to produce a globally competitive PC.[49] A number of Japanese companies, however, were important high-volume producers of some of the standardized components, such as the DRAM (dynamic random access memory) chips and flat screen panels, but the slow-moving *keiretsu* organizations simply could not keep up with, and make a profit from, the constantly changing PC industry.

South Korean *chaebol* were also unable to manufacture PCs successfully. The *chaebol* suffered from the same liabilities as the *keiretsu*. They were large, vertically integrated companies that were proficient in mass-producing VCRs and microwave ovens, but were largely unsuccessful in producing PCs and, later, laptops and notebook computers. In South Korea, the *chaebol* controlled distribution channels throughout the domestic economy and tried to control them overseas as well. Although they did some contract manufacturing early on, within the *chaebol* system of production, there was "not enough flexibility to manage in a dynamic environment such as the PC industry, and little room for innovation within the system."[50] Also, as Dedrick and Kraemer concluded, "Perhaps the biggest problem [was] the lack of focus. Computers [were] just not important enough to the companies that produce[d] them in Korea. . . . The big conglomerates [were] busy with everything from microwaves and semiconductors to cars, shipbuilding, finance, and real estate. Even within the electronics industry, there [was] a lack of strategic focus on PCs."[51]

Ironically, another factor that was important in the success of Taiwan's PC manufacturers was the lack of government support. The Taiwanese computer industry grew from the bottom up. In the 1970s and through most of the 1980s, Taiwan's PC makers had very little or no government support. Most companies were too small and had too little collateralization to obtain bank loans. Most of the early firms started with funds pooled by colleagues, families, and friends. The Taiwanese government paid little attention to these firms until after the mid-1980s, by which time the whole PC industry was already a going concern. By contrast, the governments of Japan and South Korea pumped money and other resources into their respective largest business groups to promote their computer businesses. However, all this top-down planning, which included low-cost loans, government-led consortiums, and high-priority initiatives, created computer industries whose competitive targets were mainframes and minicomputers—the stronghold of IBM and other East Coast computer manufacturers (e.g., Honeywell, DEC, Data General, and Wang Laboratories). In the early 1980s, this target seemed obvious. However, by the time these governments and business groups realized that PCs were going to be the core of the computer industry, it was like turning a battleship; they were just too slow and it was just too late for the companies of either country to successfully compete with American PC sellers who were backed by networks of Taiwanese companies that could turn on a dime.

Making Semiconductors

Although Taiwan's computer industry initially grew from the bottom up, in response to the burgeoning demand from American and European buyers, the industry did join forces with the government's top-down initiative in the years after 1990. Quite unexpectedly, this merger led to new generations of consumer electronic products—notebooks, tablets, MP3 players (e.g., the iPod), and especially smartphones, so far the most prominent new consumer electronic product in the twenty-first century. The story of how this merger occurred is an account of how personal decisions leading to crucial innovations are shaped by the institutional environments in which they occur. People make decisions that make sense to them given where they are in time and place.

In the early 1970s, the Taiwanese and South Korean governments anticipated that high technology industries would be critically important for the futures of their respective countries. Corporations associated with Japanese *keiretsu* already had huge leads in technology and in marketing products, but it was unthinkable for the two governments to relinquish the high technology arena to the Japanese. The dilemma for policy makers, therefore, was to find an entry point where local firms had a competitive advantage in manufacturing global high technology products. In both cases, the two governments ended up following the path of least resistance, by going along paths already taken.

In South Korea, it was clear early on that whatever strategy the Korean government adopted, it would necessarily revolve around the largest of the large *chaebol*, principally Samsung, Lucky-Goldstar, Hyundai, and Daewoo. In 1973, Park Chung Hee's administration formed an alliance with these top *chaebol* to promote chemical and heavy industries. Known as the Big Push, this program allocated funds and other government resources to the leading *chaebol* so they could start new companies in their groups to provide primary and secondary inputs for the production of consumer products made for export. The manufacture of electrical appliances and electronics was one of the six targeted areas.[52] Following the logic of one-setism, these *chaebol* and their partners in government saw that Korea's competitive advantage was in the capital intensive mass production of necessary components for, and final assembly of, consumer electronic products. After 1973, the top four *chaebol* began building up their production of components for the electronic products they made primarily for export, including radios, televisions, VCRs, audiocassette players and microwaves. In 1983, after the Korean government designated semiconductors as an additional strategic industry, Samsung, Lucky-Goldstar, Daewoo, and Hyundai spent the equivalent of billions of US dollars to build factories to manufacture the DRAM semiconductor chips that were necessary components in all computers and many other electronic devices.

These *chaebol* made DRAM chips in competition with each other, as well as with Japanese and American producers. At the time, there were over a hundred American firms making semiconductors.[53] However, about 60 percent of the total American output came from four companies: IBM, Western Electric, Texas Instruments, and Motorola. IBM and Western Electric only made chips for their own use. Texas Instruments and Motorola sold their chips on the open market.[54] Five Japanese *keiretsu* accounted for three quarters of Japan's production (Nippon Electric, Hitachi, Toshiba, Fujitsu, and Matsushita). These firms both used the chips in their own products and sold them on the open market.[55] South Korea's entry into this crowded field seemed foolhardy, but that country's state-of-the-art technology, cheaper labor, and low defect rates allowed *chaebol* factories not only to compete but also to capture an increasing percentage of the global market for each new generation of memory chips.

The Taiwanese government followed a very different path than the Korean government did. Instead of concentrating resources in a few very large business groups, the Taiwanese policy led to the proliferation of many small and medium-sized firms spread out across a rapidly diversifying sector. In 1973, the same year that the South Korean government initiated the Big Push, Taiwan's Ministry of Economic Affairs established the Industrial Technology Research Institute (ITRI). ITRI was the creation of a group of politicians, technocrats, and business professionals associated with Sun Yun-suan. A trained engineer and highly successful executive at the state-owned Taiwan Power Company, Y. S. Sun joined the KMT government in 1967 as Taiwan's Minister of Communications, and then two years later became the Minister of Economic Affairs. In this role, Sun wanted to find a way for Taiwan to become a genuine participant in high technology industries, rather than just as a source of cheap labor. ITRI was Minister Sun's answer.

The technocrat behind Taiwan's export processing zones, K. T. Li, was the most prominent member of Sun's group of advisors and by then was the Minister of Finance. In our interview with K. T. Li in August of 1989, he explained the government's rationale behind establishing ITRI. He told us that most of Taiwan's businesses were too small to have adequate funding to develop truly innovative products. However, a state-owned firm would be unsatisfactory because it would be too bureaucratic and not attuned to market forces. "If ITRI were state-owned, institutional forces would always interfere. State accounting procedures would surely make things difficult and our [legislative bodies in government] would try to take advantage of the situation." Therefore, he told us, the ideal organization would be some form of publicly funded, privately staffed platform for employing advanced technology to develop successful products. Then the plan was that once these products were developed, they would be spun off into private companies. The result was a modest organization with part government and part private funding, divided into four operating units, one of which was the Electronics Research and Services Organization (ERSO). Set up as an autonomous agency and staffed largely with engineers, one part of the ITRI program would be to negotiate technology transfers with American and European companies, and another part would train private entrepreneurs in using those technologies to make practical products.[56]

A key transfer occurred in 1976. After RCA decided to exit the computer business (and thus not to compete with IBM), officials in ITRI persuaded RCA to enter into a five-year technology transfer agreement with ERSO to design and produce integrated circuits (ICs).[57] Patented in the early 1960s, integrated circuits made it possible for manufacturers to concentrate multiple electronic instructions on small silicon chips, called semiconductors. These chips quickly replaced transistors performing discrete functions, which had earlier replaced vacuum tubes, as the key components in electronic products. IC technology allowed miniaturization, and by 1976, integrated circuits were used in multiple electronic products, including televisions and VCRs. ICs were also core components in computers.

The agreement with RCA permitted a team of thirty-seven ERSO-affiliated engineers to undergo a year of intensive training at an RCA plant in the United States to learn how to design and manufacture ICs. After their training, these engineers returned to Taiwan to build a prototype ERSO-owned facility to manufacture ICs, which would, in turn, be sold to private firms in Taiwan. In exchange for its services, RCA would be able to buy a specific quantity of chips from the Taiwanese factory.[58] ERSO's IC venture was, however, a very modestly funded operation. "The plan," according to AnnaLee Saxenian, 'was to transfer the technology out of the lab to the private sector by soliciting private investments." However, because the investments would be large and the outcomes risky, very few investors came forward.[59] Finally in 1979, with funding from ERSO and five local companies, ERSO spun off United Microelectronics Company (UMC).

Unlike the products from the *chaebol* in South Korea, the targeted products from ERSO and UMC were not the ubiquitous DRAM chips found in many types of products, but rather application-specific integrated circuits (ASICs), chips designed and built for specific purposes. "The identification of a niche market and of an emerging technology," noted Saxenian, "allowed Taiwan to avoid direct competition with established industry leaders in the United States," and "differentiated the Taiwanese from Korean and Japanese producers pursuing high-volume products like DRAM."[60] The ASIC niche market, however, was not well developed at first, and for the first few years, UMC struggled to make money. Then the firm got a break, producing dialer chips for electronic telephones, a product that had just been developed. From there, UMC designed and manufactured a range of chips for special applications in computers and other products.

Another ITRI project that was also slow to take off but was critically important later was the creation of a science park in the outskirts of Hsinchu. Sited near National Tsing Hua and National Chiao Tung Universities and the ITRI headquarters, the Hsinchu Science Park opened for business in 1980. Much like the export processing zones, the science park was supposed to attract foreign firms willing to advance Taiwan's sophistication in producing electronic products, but none came, "not even . . . Chinese-American firms like Wang Laboratories and Silicon Valley-based Wyse."[61] However, because of the numerous tax-breaks and inexpensive property, a number of local firms located themselves in the science park, including UMC and Acer.

The direction of the Hsinchu Science Park changed dramatically after 1984, when Morris Chang arrived on the scene. Chang, the founder and long-serving CEO of Taiwan Semiconductor Manufacturing Company (TSMC), was instrumental in making Taiwan one of the world's leading producers of semiconductors, an outcome no one could have predicted at the time. Morris Chang was not a native of Taiwan, and until 1980, he had set foot in Taiwan only once before, for a short time in 1974. Born in a city near Shanghai, he left China at the start of the Chinese Revolution in 1948, going to the United States to attend Harvard and later the Massachusetts Institute of Technology, where he received BA and MA degrees in mechanical engineering. Then he went to work for Sylvania in its semiconductor division. After three years, he took a position at Texas Instruments (TI), staying there for twenty-five years and rising to become the head of TI's worldwide semiconductor unit. He left TI in 1983 to become the President of General Instruments, but after two years at General Instruments, K. T. Li (then Minister Without Portfolio in the Taiwanese government) and others persuaded him to move to Taiwan to become the President of ITRI.

One of the reasons Morris Chang left General Instruments, he told us in a wide-ranging, three-hour interview in May 1996, was that he wanted a chance to start an entirely new type of semiconductor fabrication plant (*fab* for short). Until this time, all existing semiconductor factories would be designed to make a specific chip, and then expensively retooled to make another specific chip, and so on. By contrast, Chang wanted a semiconductor factory that could quickly and with minimum retooling make almost any type of chip. Chang's vision was that other companies would design and order chips, and his factory would make the chips for them on demand; it would be an OEM factory for semiconductor chips, known in the industry as a *foundry*.

Chang told us that his vision for such a foundry in Taiwan came from two insights. First, in 1984, when he was President of General Instruments, an American friend came to him to solicit an investment. The friend wanted to raise 50 million US$ to build a semiconductor factory and wanted General Instruments to invest in the idea. Chang replied that he needed a detailed business plan. After a month passed without seeing a business plan, Chang called his friend to find out when the plan might be coming. Apologizing for not calling, his friend replied that his plans had changed. His company would just design the chips and then some chip factory would manufacture what he had designed. For that plan, all he needed was 5 million US$, and he already had that. Chang replied,

> "If you just design it, you need some companies to make it for you, right?" "Sure," his friend replied, "some companies like Toshiba and Hitachi can make it.... It will be easier if we just design the chip and let other companies make it for us." And so my friend started a design house, a so-called fabless. After that phone conversation with him, I thought to myself that there must be other people who have the same idea as my friend, design only but not manufacture. Then, some OEM companies must be required. However, it was just a thought. I was busy then, too busy to think of this.

The second source of his vision had come several years earlier, when he was at Texas Instruments in charge of that firm's semiconductor division. Chang noticed that the defect-free rate was twice as high in TI's Japanese factories as in its American factories. If a semiconductor has even the slightest defect, the chip will not function properly and must be discarded. Chang and his team tried to track down the reason that TI factories in Japan had so many fewer defects than TI factories elsewhere in the world. They made one experiment after another, and finally realized that the quality of every level of worker (on the floor, line supervisor, technician, and engineer) was higher in Japan than in the United States. When Chang visited Taiwan in 1980, he realized that Taiwanese workers had levels of education, dedication, and discipline similar to those of Japanese workers, and thus Taiwan would be a good place for a semiconductor factory.

Based on these two insights, Chang came to his conclusion: "The first one is the demand from the market. I anticipated that there would be more and more fabless companies and so OEM factories would be needed. The second one is that the low defect-free rate in Taiwanese factories would be an advantage." As President of ITRI, he argued for the establishment of an OEM semiconductor factory, the first in the world. However, Chang reported that neither the government nor private investors were enthusiastic. "Ninety-nine percent of the people (I talked with) thought that the development of TSMC would be a failure for two reasons. First, in general, the business of semiconductors was too risky. Second, a dedicated OEM manufacturer never existed before; we would be the first one."

Chang told us that the government was a reluctant investor in the project. After some hesitation, Premier Yu Kuo-hua, the second highest ranking person in Taiwan's government at the time, offered 48 percent of the required funds. Yu believed that the firm should not be state-owned; 48 percent was a figure that ensured that. Yu also had another stipulation: Chang would have to raise the rest of the money himself, and at least 20 percent of that amount had to come from foreign firms. The rest could come from local investors. Chang told Yu, "I am quite familiar with some foreign companies . . . but in Taiwan, I know very few people. I have heard about Wang Yung-ching (the CEO of Formosa Plastics), but I don't know him." In that case, Yu said, if Chang could raise the foreign capital, then he would help out with the locals. Deciding that he could not strike a better bargain, Chang began calling all the American and Japanese companies (including Matsushita) with whom he had contacts. He talked for two hours with the CEO of Intel, who, in a second phone call, told

Chang, "Maybe you are not mad, but the business is too risky [for Intel]." Then he talked with his former employer, the CEO at Texas Instruments, who also thought that the proposal was too risky. The TI CEO was very nice though, because "the other companies that I tried to talk to didn't even reply to me." A short time later, however, an executive from Philips, the Dutch electronics company, got hold of him to express Philips's interest in investing. When Chang asked him how he knew about the project, the executive said that they had read about the plans in the newspaper. After hearing the plans were for an OEM foundry, Philips also grew nervous about the investment, because the people at Philips "didn't think that [such a project] would be successful in Taiwan." However, because Philips had already made huge investments in Taiwan, the company decided to take chance, agreeing to 27 percent of the total cost.[62] True to his word, Yu then located a few local investors, including Wang Yung-ching at 5 percent, who would put up the balance of the funds needed to get the foundry started.[63]

Money in hand, Chang started TSMC in the Hsinchu Science Park, with 300 employees. The founding charter stated TSMC's principle of operation: the company was forbidden to make any downstream products and forbidden to be in competition with other firms making final products. In this role, TSMC was to be to the computer industry what Formosa Plastics was to the plastics industries: the core manufacturer of components that other firms used to make consumer products. Therefore, unlike other semiconductor companies, Chang told us, TSMC was "not set up for designing (chips), even though designing is essential to the industry." The company would be strictly OEM, would make only the chips other firms designed. "Design," Chang reasoned, "is closely associated with the market [for chips], which includes the market for PCs, the market for advanced telecommunications, and the market for advanced home electronics." Chang thought that people in Silicon Valley knew these markets because of the heavily networked environment in which they live and work. The word about what products are hot travels quickly through Silicon Valley. But Asia is far from Silicon Valley and far from the final markets for any of these products. "Japan," he said, "is really good, but it is limited to manufacturing because it lacks Silicon Valley's environment." Therefore, the task for TSMC, as Chang saw it, was to form close relationships with fabless design houses that worked closely with companies developing consumer electronic products. He wanted these design houses to treat TSMC as "their own fab. In order to realize this goal, both of our computer systems have to be interconnected so that [each fabless design house] operates just like it maintains its own fab."

In the first year of production, 1987, TSMC lost a little over 100 million NT$, but made 170 million NT$ the second year. In the third year, 1989, TSMC earned 400 million NT$, with revenues of about 2 billion NT$. "That made me happy," said Chang, "but the happiness did not last long." In 1990, the costs associated with building a second foundry in the Hsinchu Science Park and the lower revenues because of the reduced demand during the Asia-wide recession induced by the Plaza Accord hit TSMC's bottom line. The losses were substantial, but every year after that the production capacity increased and profits accumulated. TSMC had found its spot in the global semiconductor industry, a sweet spot that became central to the future of consumer electronics.

In the initial years, between 60 and 70 percent of TSMC customers came from Taiwan. Over forty design houses popped up in the first two years of operation. These were small operations, mostly startups by computer engineers who wanted to own their own firms. Silicon Integrated Systems (SIS) was one of these. SIS opened for business in December 1987 with ninety employees, fifty of whom were engineers, most of them from ERSO. Six months after SIS started business, its engineers had "come up with 20 products . . . consuming almost one-fifth of TSMC's output. 'Our strategy is to find niches, then develop products for them,' said Jeng Jong Guo, SIS's 34 year-old president." The first product SIS made was a game chip and the second a speech synthesizer. SIS also produced a "range of chips for imitating animal sounds—barks, bleats, meows, and roars—in toys."[64] A short time later, American fabless design houses, including Xilinx, the first design house ever established (in 1984),[65] began to test TSMC's capabilities with small orders, and then after "several tests with good results," Chang told us, "they continued with big orders. This took several years."

With this auspicious start, TSMC pioneered what initially appeared to be a niche market, but which later turned into being the mainstream. "Let me explain it to you," Chang said:

> I think small companies are the mainstream in the semiconductor industry. It is crystal clear that many people from big companies would like to start their own small companies. But to establish a fab now takes about one billion dollars. . . . Is it possible for them to get that kind of money? No way. However, if they just want to establish a design house, it only takes around 10 million dollars, which is much easier. . . . Therefore, like I emphasized, the trend is for

more and more design houses to be established. An OEM foundry followed from that fact.

Conclusion

We have recounted Morris Chang's remarks to us at some length for two reasons. First, many of the best scholars use Taiwan's semiconductor industry as a way to underscore the role of Taiwan's developmental state in creating Taiwan's industrialization. Looking back over the development of high technology industries in Taiwan, it is obvious that the government has been important. The export processing zones, science parks, specialized agencies to promote the development of products, advantageous tax policies, and private-public corporations—all these and many other measures were undertaken by Taiwan's government with the intention to promote economic growth. Some measures succeeded and some did not.[66] But whatever the government measure, it is equally obvious, that none of them actually caused Taiwan's industrialization. They were all attempts to buy into an ongoing rapidly transforming global economy—the rise of demand-led capitalism—that encompassed many countries and not just Taiwan. That Taiwan succeeded in the way that it did has to do more with a particular synergy developed, on the one hand, by big buyers from the United States, Japan, and Europe seeking their own self-interest by engaging Taiwanese firms to produce the goods they wanted to sell and, on the other hand, by the organization of interfirm networks that allowed Taiwanese firms to excel in producing those goods flexibly, quickly, and on demand. The causation works both ways: The more retailers and merchandisers succeed in the marketplace the more they need manufacturers that can produce on demand, and the more the manufacturers can produce on demand, the greater the success of these big buyers. Taiwan's specific integration into this new capitalist order is what drove Taiwan's industrialization forward.

The second reason we emphasize our interview with Morris Chang is that his vision of TSMC goes to the heart of demand-led capitalism. When he established TSMC as an OEM foundry, he could see that the success of a foundry would depend on the success of the products made with its chips. He also recognized that a manufacturer could not determine which chips would be successful; only final consumers could do that by buying the chip-bearing products they most desired. A foundry would open a new world of possibilities for designers and merchandisers to develop, at a reasonable cost, new products or to make old products better. Therefore, the best strategy would be to let final consumers determine the winners. Those companies selling the winning products would want to make more of them, which would produce a demand for chips of a particular kind. Chang saw that TSMC's success, then, would not come from picking winners, but rather from having winners pick TSMC as their fab. Accordingly, TSMC concentrated on two processes: first, standardizing chip design in order to streamline the process of OEM chip manufacturing and, second, fully integrating the fabless design houses with TSMC's production facility to make it profitable for them to make TSMC their fab.[67]

Both Chang's vision into the future of consumer electronics and his strategy for TSMC were correct. Fabless design houses opened up new semiconductor markets for all kinds of products.[68] ASIC chips are found in nearly everything—from toasters and toys and greeting cards to automobiles, airplanes, and spacecraft—and all are designed to accomplish some specialized task. From the start, one of the largest markets of all was for cell phones, bulky ones at first that grew more sophisticated with each generation of new, specialized semiconductors that allowed companies to miniaturize the phones even as they greatly increased their capabilities. We will analyze the role of Taiwanese manufacturers, including TSMC, in the cell phone industry in Chapter 9.

TSMC's foundry system proved to be the winning model for the production of semiconductors chips. Other than Intel, still the leading manufacturer for microprocessors, and the volume producer of DRAM chips, foundries dominate semiconductor manufacturing. Within a few years after TSMC started production, UMC gave up its design facilities and became a "pure play" foundry like TSMC. Other foundries also started operations in the 1990s, and by 2013, thirteen foundries claimed over 90 percent of the foundry business worldwide. Of the thirteen companies specializing in foundries, five are Taiwanese, three South Korean, two Chinese, two American, and one Israeli. In 2013, the revenues of TSMC's twelve fabs, including one in Taichung's Central Taiwan Science Park, were over four times larger than the revenues of the foundry manufacturer in second place.[69]

8

CONSOLIDATION IN CHINA

A New Age of Mass Production

As the twentieth century came to a close, many Asian economies were still reeling from the Asian financial crisis.[1] The crisis began in Thailand in July 1997, when the Thai government could not sustain the peg between the Thai *baht* and the US dollar. Currency speculators attacked the peg, forcing the Thai government to let the baht float against the US dollar. Within weeks, the baht had lost over 50 percent of its value against the US dollar. By November of that year, waves of speculation had hit the currencies of other Asian countries. The Philippines, Thailand, Indonesia, and South Korea were hit so hard that they invited the International Monetary Fund to bail them out. Most currencies throughout East and Southeast Asia fell, some precipitously, and many stock markets in the region lost between 30 and 50 percent of their value within those few months. The largest companies and business groups in the hardest hit countries were heavily indebted in US dollars, but had their balance sheets of expenses and revenues in local currencies. Now, unable to pay their loans, many of these firms declared bankruptcy. Over a third of the fifty largest *chaebol* in South Korea went out of business, including Daewoo, SsangYong, and Kia, all among the top ten business groups at the time.[2] Riding the surging demand in the United States and Europe for consumer electronics, Taiwanese industrialists, most of whose businesses were financed privately, fared well throughout the crisis, although Taiwan, too, adjusted its currency downward against the US dollar. Speculators attacked Hong Kong's fixed peg, but Hong Kong banks successfully fought them off, even as Hong Kong's property market collapsed.[3]

China's currency, however, remained unchanged and its economy continued to grow rapidly throughout this period. The renminbi, also called the *yuan*, was not traded in global currency markets and so was not a direct object of speculation. At the time of the Asian financial crisis, the Chinese government controlled China's banks and closely regulated its stock markets and currency. But in many other respects, China was moving rapidly toward a capitalist market economy.

The Chinese government had initially begun the shift from a command economy toward a privatized market economy after Deng Xiaoping's 1978 economic reforms. The reforms started with the rural sector and gradually opened the urban industrial sectors to market forces in the 1980s.[4] The reforms mainly focused on marketizing China's domestic economy. Throughout the first decade, the government placed restrictions on exports, but encouraged imports to modernize state-owned industries. Because China had limited foreign reserves, its need for imported goods required foreign exchange and loans from foreign banks based on China's credit trustworthiness, actions that in turn led to a series of additional reforms to combat inflation, to devalue Chinese currency, and ultimately to encourage exports. However, by mid-1989, at the time of the Tiananmen Square massacre, exports from China were still modest. Shocked by the political unrest, foreign businesspeople pulled back from China after the massacre.[5] For a short time, China's economic growth stalled. In 1992, in an effort to reignite development by promoting exports, Deng Xiaoping travelled to the export processing zones in Guangdong Province.[6] Deng's trip, widely touted as *nanxun*, "the southern inspection tour," coincided with, and gave reassurance to, the perception of many businesspeople in Taiwan and Hong Kong that if they were to remain competitive, now was the time to move some or all of their manufacturing facilities to China. After 1992, the growth in exports and in China's overall economy became linked, and both began to grow at extraordinary rates for the next twenty years.

As the exports began to flow after 1992, the Chinese government took several steps to make China even more attractive to foreigners who thought about locating their factories there. First, in 1994, the government again devalued the renminbi, setting the official exchange rate against the US dollar at 8.3 yuan and at the same time abolishing the secondary market for foreign exchange (one for foreigners and one for locals) that had been in place for the previous eight years. This monetary reform reduced the cost of land and labor for foreigners doing business in China and unified the exchange rate for all parties.[7]

Second, the Chinese government institutionalized its comparative advantage in cheap labor by strengthening the *hukou* system of household registration that fixed the rights and privileges of individuals to the birthplace of their mother, while at the same time encouraging temporary rural-to-urban migration of workers.[8] These migrants created a huge, constantly circulating pool of cheap labor consisting mostly of people from often distant, poor rural villages, who could live temporarily in the factory cities but had none of the rights of local residents. A large percentage of these temporary migrants were young, unmarried women.[9] Third, the government greatly increased the number of export processing zones throughout China's long coastal region and quickly built the roads, rails, and ports needed to support an export-oriented economy.[10] Fourth, although the central government maintained control of the core levers in the economy, it transferred the implementation of its economic policies to local government units, mainly district and metropolitan administrations, and selectively rewarded those local officials who were the most successful in economically developing their locales. This policy of decentralizing decision making created a competition among local governments in offering the best incentives to attract foreign firms to locate factories in their territory.[11] Finally, by the time of the Asian financial crisis, China was in negotiations to join the World Trade Organization (WTO), a move that would require China to adopt global standards of business.[12] Most businesspeople knew at the time that China would eventually gain membership, and that, they believed, would open the door to China's billion-plus consumers. Therefore, in contrast to the sea of financial chaos spawned by the Asian financial crisis, the Chinese economy appeared a calm, orderly, and low-risk environment for making money.

The disruptions and uncertainty surrounding other Asian economies and soon the opening of the China market to foreign firms made investments in China seem like a good idea. The financial troubles in Southeast Asia had come as an unintended consequence of the Plaza Accord.[13] As described in detail earlier, Japanese, South Korean, and Taiwanese investments in Southeast Asia had created an *emerging market* bubble. As East Asian money flowed into Southeast Asia, real estate prices soared. Stock markets for local firms opened and attracted increasing numbers of institutional investors from the United States and elsewhere interested in capitalizing on the booming Asian economies. Local economies were awash in capital seeking investment opportunities, and many local companies used the occasion to obtain loans to enlarge their business. When it all came suddenly to an end, Japanese and South Korean firms and business groups began to reevaluate their options, and many owners decided to relocate their investments to China, which was close to home and which seemed a much safer place to invest. In the decade between 1997 and the start of the Great Recession in 2007, a large portion of global consumer goods manufacturing consolidated in China.

In this chapter, we will examine two industries that Taiwanese manufacturers helped to consolidate in China in the twenty years after 1992: footwear and bicycles. In Chapter 10, we will continue this examination with two more industries: computers and smartphones. Taiwanese manufacturers, known collectively in China as *Taishang* (Taiwanese businesspeople), had transferred some of their manufacturing to China even before the Tiananmen massacre, but they, too, paused after the massacre and subsequent political unrest. But within a few years, firm after firm, in industry after industry, made the trek to China. Then around the time of the Asian financial crisis, clusters of firms in the supply chains manufacturing computers and mobile phones also made the move to the Mainland. Each of these industries reconstituted itself in new ways once it arrived. This chapter and the next look at the evolving organization of these industries in China, as well as their links to Taiwan, in the twenty-five years after Deng Xiaoping's southern tour.

Before doing that, however, we need to describe the extent and underlying dimensions of the global capitalist consolidation in China. As we will show, China's rapid industrialization came as an unintended consequence of the liberalization of the world's national economies that began with the Plaza Accord, consequences that greatly enlarged the effects and scope of demand-led capitalism.

The Consolidation of Manufacturing in China, 1992–2007

The global consolidation of export-oriented manufacturing in China is both extraordinary and easily misunderstood. It is extraordinary for several reasons. First, the value of China's imports and export rose by about tenfold between 1992 and 2006. Most of this growth came after 1999, when China's exports and imports grew at an astonishing annual rate of 25 percent[14] This rate of growth is less remarkable, however, when we understand the underlying causes of such a rapid increase. Most of the growth in exports came from foreign-owned firms that had built manufacturing facilities in China. In 1990, about 10 percent of

China's exports were from foreign-owned firms. That figure jumped to about 60 percent in 2004.[15] These investments are termed *foreign direct investments* (FDIs). Before 1985, FDIs in China were minor and focused on the domestic economy, mainly hotel construction and resource extraction. Starting from a low level, overall FDI grew modestly at around 14 percent a year between 1985 and 1991, but then ballooned in the years after 1992, growing at over 150 percent each year for the next three years and then leveling off after that.[16] By 2007, China had become the largest recipient of FDI in the developing world, and second only to the United States in the whole world. The key point is that a large portion of FDI in the two decades after 1992 was to establish manufacturing facilities in China for the principal purpose of exporting their products from China to the rest of the world.[17]

We get a clear sense of these export-only investments from the Chinese customs statistics, which divide exports and imports into two categories, *ordinary trade* and *processing trade*.[18] The processing trade classification applies to imports that are brought into China duty-free and are used exclusively in the assembly of products that are in turn exported. Goods produced with duty-free imports cannot legally be sold in China. By contrast, ordinary trade refers to imported goods (as well components thereof) destined to be marketed locally, and to exports of products manufactured in China with components made mainly in China. The distinction between the two categories is significant because in the first years of the new century, when exports were growing so rapidly, over 50 percent of Chinese exports were classified as processing trade. In other words, for over 50 percent of China's exports, China served primarily as an assembly site.[19]

Second, and more significantly, this consolidation represents not merely a change in location, but also a change in the absolute size of the factories producing the products. During the twenty years after 1992, fewer and fewer firms began to produce more and more goods for the entire world. This consolidation was a worldwide phenomenon, which occurred mainly but not exclusively in China.[20] This concentration of global production should be understood as a rationalization of demand-led capitalism. Starting in the early 1990s, retailers and brand-name merchandisers, using lean retailing techniques, began rapidly to systematize their global supply chains and to become huge global firms themselves. Their expansion created fierce competitions in consumer markets around the world. These are the decades in which US-based Walmart expanded globally to become the world's largest retailer; French-based Carrefour became the second largest; and Costco, Aldi (owner of Trader Joe's, among other retail firms), Metro, Target, and Tesco joined not only the ranks of the world's largest retail firms but also the ranks of the world's largest firms, period. A large portion of their growth in the decades after 1990s came from mergers and acquisitions.[21] These are also the years in which Apple and Samsung became the leading brands for smartphones and tablets; Zara, The Gap, H&M, and Forever 21 became the world's leading clothing retailers; and Nike, Adidas, and Reebok became the world's largest merchandisers for shoes. During these years, a few firms grew very large and successful in their respective sectors, and many other firms were absorbed into other companies or went out of business entirely.

The best illustration of this global transformation in retailing is Walmart, not only the world's largest retail firm but also for many of these years the world's largest firm and largest private sector employer.[22] Although Walmart began sourcing products from Asia in the 1970s, it did not start its international expansion of stores until 1991, when it began a joint venture in Mexico with Cifra. After growing rapidly in Mexico, Canada, and South America in the mid-1990s, Walmart aggressively targeted Europe and Asia in the decade after 1997. In order to rationalize its acquisition of goods and its distribution logistics for its far-flung stores, Walmart moved its global sourcing center to Shenzhen, China, in 2001. The Shenzhen office soon became Walmart's global purchasing headquarters, and in 2003, Walmart opened a second sourcing center in Tianjin. In 2004, Walmart bought over 18 billion US$ worth of goods from China, which represented 10 percent of all US imports and 30 percent of all big-buyer purchases from China for that year. Starting in the 1990s and continuing through 2016, Walmart was, by some margin, the leading importer of goods in shipping containers to the United States; most of these goods came from China.[23]

Despite its size, Walmart's actions are the rule and not the exception. Walmart and Carrefour represent the mass-market end of the consumer market continuum. Starting in the 1980s, for the big-box retailers, in-store or private label brands became more important, as the reputation and money-back guarantees of retailers stood as an assurance of quality to regular consumers. These retailers' ability to negotiate on price and their use of private labels squeezed the profits of brand-name manufacturers, forcing many of them to reassess how to deal with the changing cost structure of making goods themselves. Some brand-name manufacturers declared bankruptcy. Some turned to contract manufacturers to make their products. However, a great many of these companies with the best known brands sold the rights to their brand name to other companies. The latter became "brand-name holding companies." For example, Newell Brands, Fortune Brands, Nine West Holdings, Authentic Brand Group, and Hillshire Brands each hold dozens of well-known brands that have large market shares of their respective product niches.[24] A similar consolidation of brand names occurred in the upmarket segments as well. Even though most people might not recognize LVMH, Kering, Swatch Group, or Rembrandt Group (Richemont Group), they would recognize the dozens of exclusive brand names that each of these holding companies manages.[25] For non-food manufactured products, most of the brand-name holding companies used contract manufacturers to fill their inventories, and many of these contract manufacturers were in China.

This consolidation at the retail end matches the consolidation at the production end as well. The winners in global retail competitions, striving for profits and efficiency, concentrated their orders directly with the most reliable and cost-efficient contract manufacturers or indirectly by working through core intermediaries that specialized in sourcing goods from a variety of manufacturing firms. Working closely with these big buyers, contract manufacturers, as well as the large intermediaries, in turn developed their supply chains so that they could fill the full range of very large orders with high-quality, low-cost products. These supply chains (variously known in the literature as *global production networks*, *global value chains*, and *global commodity chains*), often led by their core assembly firms, were able to provide the big buyers with exactly the products the buyers had specified in their orders.[26] Many of these assemblers would have separate production lines for orders from different companies, each line with a firewall to prevent spillovers of proprietary information. We will defer our full discussion of these production clusters to the next chapter, but it is important to note here that in a considerable number of intermediate and final goods industries a small number of interfirm clusters attained a very high global market share for the products they manufactured.[27]

Third, between 1992 and 2007, FDI in China and exports from China were the most important factors driving China's rapid economic development. As a percentage of China's total economy, FDI represented only a small portion of the total capital investments made in China during those years, and, even at the high point in 2006, exports were only somewhat above 35 percent of China's GDP. However, if we add to these two items the imports of machine tools and components used in the manufacture of exported products; the extensive system of ports, rails, and roads in China's coastal provinces built to support the export economy; the huge number of workers hired for export production and the diffusion of the money they earned to other regions of China; the services in banking, housing, retailing, and local administration needed in exporting regions, as well as the rapidly rising value of property that enriched urban residents in coastal provinces; and just as important, the trade surplus in US dollars earned from preponderance of US-bound exports—then we see an economy that was significantly shaped by foreign-owned firms producing goods for export.

That China's exports grew spectacularly and that these exports were significant for China's economy are undeniable, but this rapid growth and global consolidation of manufacturing in China is often misconstrued. Much of the credit (and blame) for China's development has gone to the Chinese government's economic policies. Sometimes these policies have been labelled the China Model or the Beijing Consensus.[28] Without a doubt, and for the reasons given above, this assertion is certainly correct. The government played an important role, but global demand-led capitalism played an even more important role. Even though the United States was the largest recipient of Chinese exports, very few American manufacturing firms moved factories to China for the purpose of making products for the US market.[29] Most of the Chinese exports to the United States were produced by Taiwanese and Hong Kong contract manufacturers, who did move to China. Moreover, these investments came to China not because the Chinese government asked the owners of the investing firms to do so, but rather because these owners thought China was a place where they could stay competitive in response to big-buyers' demands. China represented a place where they could make money.

In the years after 1992, the Chinese government harnessed global capitalism as the driving force to develop the Chinese economy. This is the same tactic used by the governments of Japan, South Korea, and Taiwan in the previous decades. But there is also a large difference between the rapid export growth in China after 1992 and the growth in exports that had occurred earlier in Japan, South Korea, and Taiwan. In each of the latter countries, most of the growth in exports came from locally owned firms. Foreign firms were obviously not absent, but they were secondary to the firms owned by locals. As these economies developed in the period before 1985, export production became more internalized, more economically self-sufficient. By contrast, in China after 1992, export growth came predominately from firms owned by foreigners, and not just any foreigners but rather foreigners from other East and Southeast Asian countries. In the five years after 1992, the Chinese Statistical Yearbook shows that over 80 percent of foreign investments came from Hong Kong, Taiwan, South Korea, and Japan.[30] In the official statistics, the investments from Taiwan are understated because a great deal of the Taiwanese money invested in China came through Hong Kong (as well as the Cayman Islands, Bermuda, and the Virgin Islands), and partly for this reason, the FDI from Hong Kong totaled more than the FDI from all other countries combined.

It is also easy to misconstrue China's development as something that happened just in China, when in fact it is part of a regional system of production and global patterns of consumption. Trade statistics tell part of the story. Starting in the early 1990s, intermediate goods begin to flow into China from Taiwan and Japan. Leather and plastics for shoes, specialty metals and gear boxes for bicycles, flat screen panels and semiconductors for laptop computers—these and a vast array of other imports were needed in the assembly of finished products ready for export. The processed trade classification of imports and exports implies that, for over 50 percent of China's exports, most of the components came from sources outside of China. But many of those exports classified as ordinary trade also contained parts that were imported. So important were these imports of intermediate goods by the early 2000s that China became the largest trading partner for both Taiwan and Japan, a partnership based mostly in the level of those countries' exports to China. As time went on, more of the components were made in China, some by Chinese firms that began manufacturing the needed parts, and others by Taiwanese and Japanese firms that had moved their production of intermediate goods to China. However, the overall trade patterns continued, with many inputs for final products coming from Taiwan, Japan, and South Korea. In sum, China's extraordinary economic development in the first decade of the twenty-first century arose in large part from the increasing rationalization of demand-led capitalism throughout the world and from the regionalization of global manufacturing that occurred in East Asia. The Chinese economy was just one piece in a much larger picture.

Taiwanese Manufacturers in Taiwan and China, 1992–2007

After the Plaza Accord, Taiwanese manufacturers began, cautiously, to invest in export-oriented factories in China. These investments greatly accelerated after

1992, and within a decade, Taiwanese firms were among the leading exporters from China. By 2005, twenty-five of the top one hundred export companies in China were Taiwanese firms, and seven of the top ten.[31]

During the first decade of this movement, in contemplating their own moves to China, Taiwanese manufacturers recognized the risks. Experience told them that they could control most factors of production in Taiwan except the rising cost of labor and land, but those increases were crucial because with them their profits vanished. The Taiwanese had very limited leverage in negotiating the prices of the products they manufactured because the big buyers set those prices in the United States and Europe in relation to their competitors and their need for a certain level of profit. The big buyers wanted their contract manufacturers to be flexible in response to their requirements, and not the other way around. If the Taiwanese manufacturers were unable to be flexible, then the big buyers would find different manufacturers to make their goods, and in the late 1980s and early 1990s, there were many alternative manufacturers to choose from.

Acknowledging their dilemma, the Taiwanese bowed to the requests of the big buyers to move their assembly firms to China, where the cost of land and labor was much cheaper and where they could obtain, in the short term, tax breaks and other incentives for relocating there. Even so, moving their businesses to China meant taking on additional and often unknown risks. They did not know whether the Communist government would continue to support Taiwanese businesses in China. After all, the governments of Taiwan and China had no diplomatic relations, and China vowed eventually to take over Taiwan, through war if not in peace. Once ensconced in China, these Taiwanese businesses did not know whether they might be used for political purposes, perhaps as economic pawns to check Taiwanese resistance to merge with China. At the very least, the move of thousands of Taiwanese businesspeople to China would create an uneasy, unofficial, and unequal alliance between the various levels of Chinese government, on the one hand, and Taiwanese businesspeople, on the other hand.[32]

More urgently, however, moving the assembly plants to China created a set of problems that had to be solved right away. Despite ambiguous property rights throughout China, land for the factories had to be secured; factories had to be built, complete with the machine tools needed to manufacture the products; migrant workers had to be recruited, trained, fed, and housed; supply chains for the parts needed in the manufacture of products had to be created;

and local Chinese officials needed to be placated, sometimes by making them partners in joint ventures.[33] In the early 1990s, the risks were many, and the means to control the risks were relatively few and uncertain, even in the short run. Therefore, because they could not calculate the risks, as capitalists must, most Taiwanese businesspeople did not see the move to China as an all-or-nothing strategy. Rather, they hedged their bets.

Regardless of the industry they were in, most of them kept their headquarters, research and development departments, and trading companies in Taiwan and, initially, moved only the most labor-intensive parts of their business to China, usually just the assembly work. For those parts of their business remaining in Taiwan, many entrepreneurs targeted more expensive versions of the mass-market items made in China and searched for new products to make, often by transferring a core technology developed in one industry to another, entirely different industry.[34] For example, the owner of Thunder Tiger, Lai Chuan-lin, whose businesses we discussed in the introductory chapter, moved the production of his remote-controlled model airplanes to China in 1993, and used his plant in Taiwan to develop new, more expensive models, including a line of jet-propelled model planes. Later, he applied his expertise in making miniature turbines to making dental drills. Another person we interviewed began his business by manufacturing tennis rackets for US merchandisers. After moving his assembly plant to China, he used his factory in Taiwan to make very expensive carbon fiber tennis rackets, and then later, using his expertise in carbon fiber technology, he began making airplane components for Boeing and Airbus.

In China, as they had done in Taiwan, the Taiwanese entrepreneurs tried to mitigate some of their risks by sharing them. They clustered their factories in a limited number of districts in south and central China, primarily those in the Pearl River and Yangtze River Deltas. In each district where they located their factories, the Taiwanese organized associations of Taiwanese businesspeople (*Taishang xiehui*). The first of these associations was registered in 1990 in Shenzhen, the city next to the New Territories in Hong Kong. In 1996, there were forty-three associations of Taiwanese businesspeople, mostly in southern China, and by 2007, there were over one hundred, in districts spread throughout China's coastal provinces.[35] The businesspeople used these associations for a variety of purposes. The association officers would negotiate with local officials for the best set of incentives, for improvements in the local business environment, and for help in settling business disputes between members and locals.³⁶ The associations also provided a meeting place where members could share information on how to do business in the locale and where they could eat familiar food and drink, talk in the same dialect, and enjoy the company of their compatriots.

Although these associations helped to reduce some of the risks of moving, the more immediate task for the Taiwanese was reestablishing their businesses in a new location under very different conditions than existed in Taiwan. Different industries and different firms in the same industry solved these problems in their own distinctive ways. But across all industries, firms and clusters of firms greatly increased their output owing to the huge orders they were receiving.

Making Shoes in Taiwan and China

Footwear and apparel companies were among the first firms to move their factories to China.³⁷ In Taiwan, most of footwear firms were small or medium-sized and were able to manufacture large batches of shoes only by cooperating in interfirm networks using "round-table etiquette," as we described in Chapter 4.³⁸ After moving to China, however, the footwear manufacturers did not have the same system of local support. They did not have networks of relatives, neighbors, friends, and friends of friends who would invest in their firms or provide the needed labor. Nor were there networks of *laoban* whom they could call upon to join their satellite assembly systems. Moreover, the first of the firms to move to China were those with large orders from big buyers that had requested their move in the first place. They moved to China without their entire network of suppliers, because when asked to move, some suppliers chose not go. Up to a quarter of the 1200 footwear firms in Taiwan supplying the main assemblers simply decided to discontinue their involvement in the industry.³⁹ Therefore, most footwear firms moving to China had to solve problems in a way they had never faced before.

The companies mostly clustered in Dongguan, a district in southern China located between Hong Kong and Guangzhou. The first footwear firm to move there did so in 1987. By 1990, there were over 400, with many more soon to come in the next few years. Among these firms were those specializing in making "soles, insoles, packaging material, cutting dies, shanks, glue, decoration components, nails, simple tools, rubber rings, [and] paints." There were also "tanneries . . . printing services (for packaging boxes, price tags, and so on), machinery maintenance shops, as well as subcontractors of automated stitching and embroidery."⁴⁰ In addition, to the network of footwear suppliers moving to China, most assembly firms in the initial years still worked with their mother firm and with some of their suppliers in Taiwan to supplement the manufacturing process in China.[41]

We saw this division of labor directly when we visited Chairman Tony Lai at Top Star Shoe Company in Taiwan. The firm had moved all the assembly factories to China and Vietnam, but maintained its headquarters and the R&D department in Taiwan. At the time, Top Star was a supplier for several European brand-name merchandisers, including Fila, Diesel, and Puma. Each of these big buyers would design their shoes and fax a copy of the design to Top Star's R&D unit in Taiwan. There Top Star would turn the design, sometimes no more than a sketch, into a prototype. The first step in this transformation was to make a three-dimensional drawing of the picture using a computer-aided design (CAD) system. Then, in a small factory adjacent to the R&D unit, where the people had the same machine tools that the assembly firms used in assembling shoes, the headquarters unit would, step by step, make a prototype using the CAD dimensions. In less than a week, all the steps would be done quickly, in-house, including the cutting, stitching, and lamination. The finished prototype was then shipped by air to the European headquarters of the buyers, who would approve the shoe for production or call for changes. Once the buyer had issued a final approval, the headquarters in Taiwan would provide the network of upstream suppliers and the final assembly plant with exact instructions for production of the batch order. Within weeks after that, the order would be filled and shipped as instructed by the buyer. The shoes would bear the label Made in China or Made in Vietnam, depending on the location of the assembly plant.

Core Clusters (xieli gongchang)

For all the major footwear assemblers, the distance between the headquarters in Taiwan and their factories in China was more than just miles. Although the Taiwanese and Chinese both spoke Mandarin, they did not share the same cultural space. Round-table etiquette required mutual trust and predictability, but the Taiwanese soon learned that there was no trust and little predictability when working with Chinese factory owners and Chinese migrant labor. The Taiwanese felt like foreigners in a foreign land, and were usually treated as such.[42] Although large numbers of suppliers moved to China, not many of them succeeded. As larger orders came in, core assemblers worked with fewer suppliers than they had done in Taiwan, yet those suppliers had to provide larger quantities of the parts or services in which they specialized. The increasing size of the orders, the demand for higher quality, and the speed with which the product needed to be finished and shipped pushed companies toward tighter integration within each firm and within clusters of firms. These central clusters (*xieli gongchang*[43]) were centered on core assembly firms that received the orders and coordinated the production with the key suppliers. Less capitalized suppliers were unable to compete with other firms that could ramp up their production to match the needs of the core assemblers. Those suppliers able to increase their production at the required level of quality received yet more work from the main assemblers. And, in this way, tightly integrated interfirm clusters emerged, clusters that were able to handle very large orders for a variety of shoe designs from multiple buyers with very different demands.

During the two decades after 1992, seven main clusters of Taiwanese footwear manufacturers emerged. By 2015, these seven clusters accounted for nearly 70 percent of the world's footwear production.[44] Among the brand-name customers of these clusters are Clark, Timberland, Nike, New Balance, Nine West, Prada, Hugo Boss, Camper, Kenneth Cole, Cole Haan, Armani, Rockport, Columbia, Polo, Bass, Skechers, Liz Claiborne, Montrail, Walmart, North Face, and Under Armour. Most of these brand names are managed by brand-name holding companies that design and order the shoes. For instance, Nine West Holdings and VF Corporation each own an array of brand names for shoes along with brands for clothing and accessories. These brand-name holding companies order most of their shoes from the Taiwanese manufacturers and order the other products they handle from different contract manufacturers.

One of the seven clusters is centered on Company D. Preferring to remain in the background, the *laoban* of Company D, Chairman H, does not like publicity and asked that he and his firm remain anonymous. Given that stipulation, he was quite forthcoming about his firm and the footwear industry in general. In 1979, with fifty employees, his firm began making "uppers," the top parts of shoes. After building a good reputation, the company began assembling entire shoes in 1988 in Taiwan and, soon afterward, in its new factories in southern China and Vietnam, which it capitalized with a listing on the Hong Kong Stock Exchange. New Balance was the company's first American customer, followed by Asics, Nike, Under Armour, and many others in later years. Its big buyers had pushed the company to move to China to reduce the cost of production. Many of Company D's upstream suppliers followed its move to China and again to Vietnam.

After its move to China, Company D began building its cluster of upstream suppliers, most of whom were Taiwanese. Depending on the design, each model of shoe would require materials from thirty to forty suppliers. Working from their offices in Taiwan, the big buyers worked closely with the company to select the specific set of suppliers for each design. Chairman H said that the buyers had to sign off on all the suppliers because the buyers required not only quality in manufacturing but also compliance with the local regulations at the site of each factory. The necessity for these approvals started in the 1990s, after Nike was confronted with increasing consumer litigation about poor working conditions and environmental hazards in offshore factories making Nike shoes. In subsequent years, Nike and other shoe merchandisers began to insist on working with a list of approved suppliers. This approval process further decreased the overall number of suppliers and increased the cohesion among firms within the clusters and between the clusters themselves. Chairman H told us that, for each production run, the big buyers would set a unit price for the company to meet, and then he and the buyers would individually and collectively negotiate with the upstream suppliers to achieve that price. Sometimes the price set would be unrealistic, and then he would recommend changes in the design or a price increase. As trust between the big buyers and the manufacturing clusters increased over time, the relationship between buyers and manufacturers seemed more like a partnership, a complementary relationship in which each needed the other.

One Dragon (yitiao long)

Although these footwear clusters produce a large share of the world's shoes, the largest Taiwanese shoe manufacturer is not among them. That firm is Pou Chen, also known by its Chinese subsidiary, Yue Yuen, which is also listed on the Hong Kong Stock Exchange.[45] A business group with holdings in hotels, real estate, retailing, and electronics as well as shoes, Pou Chen is the world's largest single footwear manufacturer, making something approaching 20 percent of the world's athletic and casual wear shoes. As we described in Chapter 3, Pou Chen began in 1969 as a very small firm located in central Taiwan, not far from Taichung. With several large contracts in hand, Pou Chen established its first factory in China in 1988, in Gaobu, which is a small township in the northern part of the Dongguan district. It was the first footwear firm in Gaobu, and one of the first in the entire district. Unlike other Taiwanese footwear manufacturers, Tsai Chi-jui, Pou Chen's *laoban*, and his brothers decided not to rely on their network of Taiwanese suppliers. Instead, they decided to be "one dragon" (*yitiao long*), a euphemism for a vertically integrated company. They had already started the process of vertical integration in Taiwan in the mid-1980s, when the company set up a number of wholly owned subsidiaries to process its own specialized plastic fabrics and leather and to make other components used to manufacture shoes. However, moving to China well ahead of Pou Chen's Taiwanese suppliers, Tsai Chi-jui elected to further integrate by making most of the needed components in-house. To accomplish this task, Pou Chen bought out most of its suppliers.

Kao and his team visited Pou Chen's factory in Gaobu in 1992. A former graduate student of Kao's was working as the main administrator of the factory and invited Kao and his team to come for an interview. Excited to see the new facilities, they had to travel a crooked road to get to Gaobu, which was similar to road taken by many Taiwanese businesspeople at the time. First, because the Taiwanese government did not issue visas for travel in China, they instead got a visa to fly to Hong Kong. Then, once in Hong Kong, in order to get around the PRC travel restrictions, they applied for a special Chinese visa that allowed travelers to return to their ancestors' home town (*fanxiang zheng*). Receiving this visa, they then were able to enter China from Hong Kong and travel to Gaobu.

When they arrived at Yue Yuen, Pou Chen's Chinese subsidiary, they saw a city instead of a factory, a city surrounded by a rural countryside, a city that resembled a small kingdom more than anything else. Still in its early days in China, Yue Yuen already employed over 10,000 people at this site.[46] Besides a huge factory, there were also dormitories, athletic fields, a kindergarten, an elementary school, a hospital, and a huge cafeteria.[47] As Kao and his team looked down from an office on the second floor of the cafeteria building, they saw a river of people, flowing slowly, waiting for their turn to eat. It took four shifts for the 10,000 to finish one meal. Earlier, they had watched the employees on the athletic field doing morning exercises and then marching to work as if in an army. After years of visiting factories, they had seen nothing like this in Taiwan. The manager in charge, Kao's former student, explained the reason. Unlike their employees in Taiwan, the Chinese employees, mostly young unmarried women, were from poor villages in Jiangxi, Guizhou, and other faraway provinces. They were poorly educated and had limited skills. Their wages were less than 200 yuan (30 US$) per month, which was considerably more than they could earn in their home towns. They had to be trained to become good workers, trained first to be receptive to instruction and then trained task by task in the factory itself. On the whole, however, they were willing workers, eager to make money, eager to have a life away from their rural villages. Nonetheless, unlike the situation in Taiwan, there was a huge gap between the Taiwanese managers' expectations and the Chinese workers' dedication, a gap bridged by creating a military-like organization.

Yue Yuen expanded rapidly in the 1990s, adding separate factory lines for many of the top brands of athletic shoes, including Nike, Adidas, Reebok, and New Balance.[48] Yue Yuen guaranteed that the lines would be distinct, often in different locations, and each under separate management. The company guaranteed that no trade secrets or design innovations would leak across factory lines. Each brand-name buyer's lines responded to the buyer's directives. According to Leslie Chang, in the 1990s the brand-name buyers "gave factories ninety days from receiving an order to delivering a product; several years ago it was sixty days, and now [in 2008] it is thirty days. Orders are getting smaller, to allow for a rapid response when fashions change."[49] In the first decade in China, the employees worked very long hours, seven days a week to fill orders, but after the brand-name buyers complained, the company reduced the shifts to eleven hours and gave workers one day a week off.[50]

As Yue Yuen's footwear factories expanded, profits also grew, to the point that Yue Yuen opened its own retail outlets in China, and its parent company, Pou Chen, began to diversify into businesses unrelated to footwear. By 1997, the Pou Chen group had grown into the sixty-ninth largest business group in Taiwan by total sales, not counting its Yue Yuen assets and sales in China. In 2002, Pou Chen sold sixty-seven firms that made up its footwear supply chain to Yue Yuen, thus completing Yue Yuen's vertical integration. Shortly after that, although he remained the *laoban*, Tsai Chi-jui gave up his titles, stepped away from active management of the group, and appointed his brother's son, Tsai Nai-fung, also known as David Tsai, as the Tsai family's top manager. David Tsai simultaneously held the top positions in several of the group's firms. By 2013, however, as Pou Chen's revenues dipped and its electronics subsidiary faltered, Pou Chen's board of directors elevated Tsai Chi-jui's daughter, Tsai (Patty) Pei-chun, to the top positions. Tsai Pei-chun, who had completed an advanced degree at the Wharton School of Management, refocused the Pou Chen group on its core expertise, making and selling shoes. Two years later, in 2015, there was another shakeup, with the result that Chan Lu-min, who was not a family member, became the head of both Pou Chen and Yue Yuen.

Despite the apparent in-fighting among family factions (a common feature of Chinese business groups), *Forbes*'s 2015 ranking of the wealthiest people in Taiwan placed Tsai Chi-jui and his family at twenty-third, with an estimated fortune of 1.5 billion US$.

Making Bicycles in Taiwan and China

Taiwanese firms are the world's largest manufacturers of bicycles, and one Taiwanese firm, Giant, is the world's single largest producer of bicycles. Giant is also one of the world's leading brand names for bicycles, and Merida, another Taiwanese firm, is not far behind, as both a manufacturer and a leading brand name. Both firms started as contract manufacturers in the 1970s, but shortly before their move to China in the 1990s, they both began to build their brand names, as well as continuing as contract manufacturers. On the surface, these two firms would seem to be exceptions to the rule that Taiwanese contract manufacturers remain anonymous producers for merchandisers and retailers, and do not themselves develop well-known brand names. These exceptions, however, shed some light on the rule.

The reasons that Giant and Merida could develop their own well-known brand names and that large footwear manufacturers have generally chosen not to do so relate directly to the characteristics of the two industries in the context of global demand-led capitalism.[51] The consumer end of the footwear business is huge. Consumers buy many more shoes in their lifetime than they do bicycles, and they own different shoes for different occasions, shoes that vary in style, color, size, and quality and in the materials (leather, plastic, rubber, synthetic and natural cloth) with which they are made. Shoes are less a means of transportation than a statement about who you are as a person. The brand-name merchandisers (e.g., Nike and Under Armour) compete vigorously with one another to persuade consumers to buy their products. Footwear retailers are numerous and cover the gamut from big-box retailers (Walmart) and specialty retailers (Footlocker) to exclusive upmarket boutiques (Polo and Prada). The demand for shoes is continuous, but the fashion cycle—the time for what is "hot"—is not; it is short and often unpredictable. Wherever they are located in the hierarchy of shoe sellers, retailers need large inventories to match the varied desires of their customers, but they also need to cycle through those inventories quickly. In a world dominated by lean retailing, it is virtually impossible for either merchandisers or retailers to manufacture their own shoes and still be competitive; they both have to rely on contract manufacturers for constantly renewing inventories. Therefore, knowing the footwear business, contract manufacturers would much rather supply every merchandiser and retailers with shoes than design, merchandise, sell and compete with all the other companies that are already out there selling shoes.

By contrast, in demand-led capitalist economies, where nearly everyone buys multiple pairs of shoes, most people do not own bicycles. Automobiles and public transportation are the primary means of transportation; bicycles are secondary. The consumer market for bicycles is split between a broad spectrum of mass-produced, relatively inexpensive bicycles for children, adolescents, and adults and a narrower spectrum of much more expensive specialty bicycles for enthusiasts, a category that includes recreational bikers, racers, environmental advocates, and commuters who wish to dodge rush hour traffic on the way to work. Even mass-market bicycles are produced in smaller batches than are most runs of shoes. Despite the utilitarian aspect of using bicycles for transportation, our interviews show that, like shoes, bicycles are also a consumer product subject to fashion, but much less so than shoes.

The fashion component of selling bicycles relates directly to the emergence of Giant and Merida as brand-name manufacturers. In the first decades after World War II, most consumers bought bikes in specialty bicycle shops. Emerging in the 1950s, these specialty shops replaced a diverse set of retailers that included department stores, appliance stores, and mom-and-pop bicycle stores that doubled as bicycle repair shops. These retailers obtained their inventory from independent and wholesale distributors, who got the bicycles from manufacturers. In order to compete with European imports in the 1950s, Schwinn and other bicycle manufacturers in the United States developed a franchise system somewhat like the one we described for consumer electronics in Chapter 7, a system that restricted the number of retailers to those "authorized" to sell particular brands of bicycles. By the mid-1960s, America's best-selling brand, Schwinn, had reduced the number of dealer locations from tens of thousands (one distributor alone, in Madison, Wisconsin, sold Schwinn bikes to 1200 nearby dealers) to 1700. Of these dealers, around 75 percent sold only Schwinn products. The remaining dealers had to devote at least 50 percent of their floor space to Schwinn, that or lose Schwinn's authorization.[52] As the Schwinn Bicycle Company reduced the number of dealers, it also began to merchandise its brand heavily. Schwinn advertised on television, lined up movie stars to ride the bikes, sponsored bicycle racing teams, and ran sales promotions in the stores. Throughout this period, Schwinn's market share oscillated between 15 and 25 percent of the US market.

In the late 1960s and 1970s, however, Schwinn found itself losing its market share to the new lightweight bikes that Sears and other department stores, as well as specialty dealers, were beginning to sell. In 1967, Schwinn was forced to restructure its distribution system after the US Supreme Court ruled that it constituted an unfair restraint of trade.[53] Primarily sold in specialty bike shops, Schwinn bikes now had to compete head-to-head with foreign imports from Japan and Europe. By 1974, 75 percent of the US bicycle sales were for lightweights; Schwinn found itself falling behind the market.[54]

This is when Giant and Merida entered the picture. In late 1977, the Schwinn Bicycle Company placed a trial order with Giant for a multiple-speed bicycle that Schwinn planned to sell under another brand name. According to Michelle Fei-yu Hsieh's interview with a representative from Giant, Schwinn's management "did not want to take the risk of having our products carry Schwinn's brand name because they worried that it might ruin Schwinn's reputation."[55] At the time of this order, Giant was a small bicycle firm in Ta Chia, a small town near Taichung, and Schwinn was the largest brand-name manufacturer of bicycles in the United States.[56] The reason Schwinn placed this original order was that in the 1960s, the company did not have a model that competed directly with the increasingly popular European and Japanese imports, the three- and five-speed touring bikes and the ten-speed lightweight racing bikes. Schwinn specialized in product lines of sturdy single- and multiple-speed steel-framed bicycles for adults, as well as similar lines for children and adolescents, including the "wheelie" bikes with high handle bars and a banana seat. Rather than spend the money to retool its Chicago factory, Schwinn decided in 1973 to outsource the more fashionable models from several contract manufacturers in Asia, including two Japanese suppliers, Bridgestone and Panasonic, as well as Giant a few years later.[57]

When Giant received Schwinn's first order in 1977, it was using technology learned from Japanese companies that used Giant as one of their suppliers. As mentioned, Giant was a small bicycle assembler at this time, with fewer than thirty employees. It did not make its own parts but relied on an emerging network of bicycle parts suppliers located in or near Ta Chia. Using this cluster of parts suppliers and also sourcing some critical parts from Japan, especially the Shimano derailleurs,[58] allowed Giant to fill Schwinn's order. Satisfied with Giant's initial offering, and dissatisfied with the rising costs of production in Japan, Schwinn began to give Giant larger orders, this time for bicycles bearing the Schwinn brand name. By 1980, Schwinn "was buying about 100,000 models a year from Giant."[59] Then in 1979 and 1980, unionized workers in Schwinn's Chicago factory began negotiating for higher pay, and when Schwinn balked at the union's demand, the workers went out on strike. Recognizing that the company would be unable to supply dealers with an inventory of bicycles to sell, in late 1980, Schwinn abruptly asked Giant to supply a huge order of bicycles on quick delivery. Giant mobilized the Ta Chia network of suppliers, and shipped 80,000 bikes in the first five months after the order came in. Over the next two years, Schwinn shifted most of its orders to Giant and, in the fall of 1982, closed its Chicago factory.

One of the reasons that Schwinn closed its factory so quickly after the strike was that, in the early 1980s, the US market for bicycles had suddenly changed again. Mountain bikes became the rage in the United States, and to manufacture these bikes, Taiwanese manufacturers used lightweight chromium molybdenum alloy (chrome-moly) frames, which are stronger and much lighter than the steel frames used previously, but considerably more difficult to weld. To use the new material, which was mostly sourced from Japan, the Taiwanese pioneered a new technique called TIG (tungsten insert gas) welding. Developed in the aeronautical industry to weld parts of airplanes, TIG welding techniques were difficult to master, but once perfected, they allowed more flexible, customized production techniques. Wanting to sell into the new market for mountain bikes, Schwinn designed and Giant produced a line of chrome-moly mountain bikes, the Sierra and High Sierra, that instantly became popular. In 1984, Giant shipped an order of 500,000 of these mountain bikes to Schwinn and the next year nearly a million, which amounted to over two thirds of Schwinn's sales. In 1986, Giant manufactured about one million bicycles. The company supplied Schwinn with 80 percent of its inventory,[60] and "over 80 percent of (Giant's) total output went to supply Schwinn."[61] Schwinn's popularity among customers returned.

Both Schwinn and Giant recognized that each was dependent on the other, too much so. In 1985, Schwinn and Giant even discussed a joint brand, but Giant by this time had become Schwinn's indispensable partner, and the discussion went nowhere. Schwinn wanted a piece of Giant, but Giant would have none of that, and when Giant offered to buy a stake in Schwinn, Schwinn promptly rejected that idea.[62] Then in 1987, unbeknownst to Giant, a new leadership team at Schwinn decided to diversify. Schwinn secretly negotiated an agreement with the China Bicycle Company, a firm whose ownership was split between a Hong Kong entrepreneur and a local government agency in Shenzhen. Schwinn took a 33 percent equity stake in China Bicycle, and promised to shift most of its production to China in the coming years.

Giant's *laoban*, Tony Lo, not only felt betrayed but also desperate. Giant had an assembly factory and a network of suppliers capable of manufacturing a million bikes a year, but no other big buyer that needed that many bikes. Lo believed that Giant had no choice but to develop its own brand name.[63] In 1986, Giant had tentatively started exporting to Europe under its own brand name, and in 1987, Giant went full bore, exporting its own branded bikes to the United States and at the same time becoming a contract manufacturer for several high-end US bicycle brands, including Trek and Specialized. By 1991, Giant was selling 300,000 bicycles of its own brand to mass-market retailers and also specialty stores, and supplying several hundred thousand more bicycles of other brands to its big buyers. In 1992, after China Bicycle repeatedly failed to live up to its promises, Schwinn declared bankruptcy and after several attempts to revitalize the company, the rights to the Schwinn brand name were finally sold to Pacific Cycles, a brand-name holding company, which is in turn owned by Dorel Industries. Bill Austin, a former Vice President of Schwinn who later became the President and CEO of Giant's US marketing company, delivered the post mortem: the CEO, Ed Schwinn "couldn't cut the umbilical cord to manufacturing." He added: "Ed's sourcing strategy had been determined not by a quest for the best price, the best quality, or the best way to play off various vendors. Ed was driven by the premise that he needed to own a piece of his suppliers."[64]

Merida's story is much the same. In the 1970s, Bridgestone, a leading Japanese bicycle manufacturer, mentored Merida in order to make its small assembly plant a supplier for a line of bicycles to be exported to the United States.[65] After improving its production techniques, and using parts sourced from both Japan and Taiwan, the company began also to supply several US brand-name bicycle companies. Then in the late 1970s, Merida, working through Bridgestone, became a supplier of Raleigh bicycles. One of the oldest bicycle companies in the world, Raleigh built a vertically integrated manufacturing plant in central England after World War II and, in the 1950s, exported many of its roadster models to the United States. After the US government placed a tariff on bicycle imports in 1955, Raleigh established an American subsidiary, Raleigh USA, which began producing bicycles for the American market. However, in the 1970s, after the US government ended its tariffs on bicycles imports, the consumer shift to mountain bikes also caught Raleigh by surprise. Instead of obtaining bicycles from Raleigh's aging bicycle plant in England, Raleigh USA began to place some orders for mountain bikes from Japanese and Taiwanese contract manufacturers, among them Bridgestone and Merida. According to a top manager at Merida, "When mountain bikes were developing . . . I was in charge of production management. I never knew what a defect was, not to mention, product returns. What concerned our buyers was the delivery date. They only pushed us for an earlier and earlier delivery date."[66]

In 1982, Huffy Corporation, by this time the largest US manufacturer of bicycles, bought Raleigh USA, and with it the rights to use the Raleigh brand name. Huffy's market niche was the mass-market retailers. Using the Raleigh brand name, Huffy entered the specialty bike shops as well. However, Huffy did not use its US factories to manufacture the Raleigh lines, but instead sourced them from Merida, which could produce high-quality bikes more cheaply and efficiently than Bridgestone. Within a decade after that, both the specialty and mass-market bicycles merchandised by Huffy were produced exclusively by Taiwanese bicycle manufacturers. John Mariotti, the President and CEO of Huffy Bicycle Corporation for ten years during the 1980s and early 1990s, explained what had happened. During the 1980s, Huffy sold twenty different models to Walmart, all of which were manufactured in Huffy's US factories. One year, however, after Mariotti made a deal with Walmart to supply as many of the low-end bike as they wanted, the sales of that bike skyrocketed. "I woke up May 1," Mariotti recalled, "and I needed 900,000 bikes, [but] my factories could only run 450,000." Although Huffy's more expensive models were also selling well, Mariotti knew he had no option. He had to honor his commitment to Walmart or lose the contract for the future. "I made the deal up front with them. I knew how high was up. I was duty-bound to supply my customer." To solve the problem, Mariotti permitted rival manufacturers to make four of his higher-end, higher-margin products. "I conceded business to my competitors, because I just ran out of capacity . . . Wal-Mart didn't tell me what to do. They didn't have to. [Wal-Mart] is tough as nails. But they give you a chance to compete. If you can't compete, that's your problem."[67]

Huffy continued as a major Walmart supplier after Mariotti moved on to another job. After the above incident, Huffy began to source its lines of mass-market bicycles from Taiwanese suppliers, and "made its last bike in the United States in 1999."[68] In the same years, Walmart became the number one retailer of bicycles worldwide, Huffy the third largest bicycle merchandiser in the United States, and Raleigh Bicycles of England ceased manufacturing, and the rights to the Raleigh brand name ended up in the portfolio of Accell, Europe's leading brand-name holding company for bicycles. In the year 2000, firms in China, Taiwan, and Mexico manufactured 98 percent of the bicycles sold in the United States.[69] Most of those firms were owned by Taiwanese businesspeople.

Core Clusters (xieli gongchang)

As American, European, and then Japanese bicycle manufacturers fell victim, one after the other, to rising costs and old technologies, Taiwanese manufacturers took their place, this time as both contract and brand-name manufacturers. The cause of this displacement is rooted in the swings in the US and European consumer markets, a swing in the types of bikes that people wanted to buy and a swing in the locations where they bought them. These swings in demand are both a cause and a consequence of changes in how Taiwanese businesspeople were able to become the world's leading bicycle manufacturers.

In the 1970s and early 1980s, when Japanese and Taiwanese factories produced mostly specialty bicycles, the essential element of Taiwanese success was the round-table etiquette that allowed assemblers and parts suppliers to form cohesive, overlapping, yet constantly changing clusters. They were able to contain costs and still respond quickly to changing demands for upmarket bikes. Then, in the late 1980s and early 1990s, when the Taiwanese manufacturers began to produce for the big-box retailers, the essential part of their becoming the world's foremost bicycle producers was the flexibility of these clusters as they divided their production lines between upmarket and mass-market segments, moved the mass-market clusters to China, and focused the clusters remaining in Taiwan on producing expensive specialty bikes.

A 1990 survey of Taiwanese bicycle assemblers and parts suppliers gives us a summary of these clusters before the move to China. It was at this stage that the Taiwanese bicycle manufacturers developed their batch production techniques.

> The assemblers produced some parts in-house in the early period, but not in the later period. As for the present situation [1990], we find that, from a recent survey, over 90% of the bicycle assemblers produce no parts themselves, except for the frame. The same survey also shows the parts producers to be highly specialised, with over 90% producing only one type of bicycle part.... According to the survey... on average each bicycle producer has about sixty parts suppliers and each parts producer supplies up to twenty bicycle assem-

blers. Thus, the degree of dependence on a particular supplier or buyer is not particularly high.[70]

The same survey mentioned here also found that the parts suppliers were not exclusively tied to local assembly firms, but instead managed to export nearly 50 percent of their production.[71] This ability to export independently of the assemblers gave these parts suppliers incentives to achieve greater economies of scale and, more importantly, to upgrade and explore new markets for their core technologies.

In 1992, we got to see Taiwan's bicycle industry at the pre-China stage when, for the first time, we visited Lin Chun-shan, the *laoban* of A-PRO, whom we introduced in Chapter 3. Chairman Lin was one of the first frame manufacturer in Ta Chia to perfect TIG welding techniques. During our visit to his A-PRO factory before he moved part of his operation to China, we peered into the airtight, inert gas–filled welding chambers where the chrome-moly tubes were welded to make frames for mountain bikes. He had also begun using high-quality aluminum alloy tubing.[72] He had tested and retested the welding techniques for these materials, improving them beyond his Japanese competitors, because even one failure would destroy his reputation in the cluster of suppliers.[73] With Lin's persistence, A-PRO had become one of Merida's top-tier suppliers. He also supplied other assemblers with frames.

By 1992, Chairman Lin had already established five additional firms making bicycle parts and accessories. He explained that, by specializing in one product, each firm could constantly upgrade its product line to match changing conditions, and could position different variations of that product for different clusters and for the export OEM market. Chairman Lin regularly attended international trade fairs and had well-established global markets for his products, independent of the Taiwanese assemblers, especially for his A-PRO frames, which a number of European firms ordered to assemble their "made in Europe" bicycles. "A-PRO's frames are in great demand," he told us. "The secret of our success comes from the flexibility with which we can produce these frames." He explained that bicycle frames vary by the design of the bicycle; they cannot be stockpiled, but rather have to be manufactured, batch by batch, precisely according to the assemblers' specifications. "How big is a batch?" we asked. For the expensive, specialty bikes, he explained, "a batch could be fewer than one hundred frames, sometimes fewer than fifty." "How precise is precise?" was another question. "One small change on the bicycle," he replied, "requires a new blueprint. Consequently, blueprint and graph management becomes crucial as bicycle making becomes sophisticated and involves lots of variety in the final products."[74] The welding techniques Lin perfected made it easy for A-PRO to switch between designs. There was no need to retool the factory, no need to construct molds for lug-welding as Schwinn and Raleigh had done to manufacture their bicycles. A-PRO could produce any number of any type of frame for any customer quickly and on demand.[75]

The second stage of the Taiwan's bicycle industry began at about the time of our first interview with Chairman Lin. In this stage, Taiwanese manufacturers began to receive large orders for inexpensive bikes that the big-box retailers and brand-name merchandisers (some previously manufacturers) would sell to American and European consumers. The Taiwanese would make very little money on each bike, but orders were so large that they would make a lot of money from each batch. At this point, the main assemblers, led by Merida and Giant, made the move to China, and several clusters of parts suppliers followed. The first cluster of firms established themselves in Longhua, a small town just outside of Shenzhen in the Pearl River Delta. Lin and others expressed doubts about setting up the cluster in Longhua because the conditions were so primitive, but by 1992, the Longhua cluster was established, and Chairman Lin had decided to join the cluster. His factory came on line in 1993.

One of the bicycle parts suppliers that we visited before Lin's China factory opened was KMC Chain Industrial Company's factory in Longhua. KMC was, and still is, a top-tier supplier of bicycle chains that many assemblers use. KMC's Longhua factory was part of the Merida cluster of parts suppliers. The manager of KMC's China factory, Mr. Wu, called Longhua "the superstar of the bicycle industry." "The first comers here have built a good reputation, and so now our customers [the big buyers] know that they have to come to Longhua for quality products." We asked him about the advantages of building a plant in China. He told us that splitting production lines between Taiwan and China allowed KMC to put the labor-intensive assembly work for the mass-market bike chains in China and to keep the production of chains for specialty bikes and the "talent-intensive" work in Taiwan. Before KMC moved its main production lines to Longhua, the company seemed to be too wrapped up in filling the range of orders, which left little time for improving existing products and developing new ones. Now the Taiwan factories can do the R&D work necessary for the new products, with much of the production of bicycle chains being done in China.

KMC's rationale for splitting its line between Taiwan and China was true for the other firms as well. The bicycle firms kept their headquarters and smaller factories in Taiwan. Here they processed and received payment for all orders, did the necessary preparation to produce those orders, and manufactured small batches of many different brands and models of high-end bikes. Initially, the factories in China were strictly for long runs of one model of bike at a time. According to a Merida spokesperson, the factories in China "are too big, and so it is a lot of work to reorganize the production flow and assembly lines [because they are designed for a mass production of the same product].... For instance, on an assembly line of 100 people, if there is a mistake, it means that one would not find out until the end of the assembling process.... [I]n Taiwan, our factory is based on two people as a unit. If there is an error, we fix it immediately."[76]

KMC's manager, Mr. Wu, had a different complaint about his factory in Longhua, the same complaint we heard from most of the Taiwanese who maintained factories in China. He employed about 820 people, 107 of whom he had trained to be managers, mostly line supervisors. However, he told us, "the perspective of Chinese laborers coming from the interior is very limited." The turnover rate was very high. The migrant workers did not want to stay with the company even though KMC wanted local Chinese to manage the Longhua factory. They ended up with a "very strict" management style. Despite the high turnover, however, Manager Wu judged his factory in Longhua to be successful. He told us that the factory supplied about forty different customers, ten in Longhua, and the rest in other parts of China, including some Chinese-owned firms, but the factory in China did not send any bicycle chains back to Taiwan, because the factories in Taiwan supplied those. He told us that the "sales revenues [from the factory in Longhua] only come to about 15 percent of KMC's total revenues. Most of the KMC's revenues come from our factories in Taiwan. In 1992, we shipped about 20 million chains. I would guess that about one third of all the bikes in the world has KMC chains.... For bikes made in Taiwan, about 90 percent of them are assembled with KMC chains."

As they established their new cluster in China, the bicycle parts manufacturers expressed an additional concern about the risks of locating in China. There was an anxiety arising from the political differences between Taiwan and China. In our 1993 interview, Mr. Wu said he felt panic in a place that is not a free country. "We just have to wait and see. We just have to take a chance. It's like gambling; nobody wins all the time in gambling. We paid for the land here, but we don't own it.... When we talk with the Communist Party [in

China] and the KMT [in Taiwan], we talk in different ways.... We don't know what will happen. We are just small potatoes. We are in no position to see the future." But "for right now [1993]," he continued, "the development here [in Longhua] is really amazing. It has gone from a little town to a big city." In our 2002 interview, Chairman Lin made essentially the same points about China's political stability, but he also worried about government corruption and added that he saw a lot of inequality between China's coastal regions and its interior provinces, inequality that was sure to have repercussions in the future. He told us that, to be on the safe side, he had also bought some land in Vietnam.

Despite these misgivings about having their factories in China, the core bicycle assemblers and parts suppliers flourished during their first decade in China. However, after the 9/11 terrorist attack in New York City in 2001, the American economy entered a recession. With demand down in the United States, the Taiwanese economy also fell into a recession. When we visited Chairman Lin's A-PRO factory in Taiwan in 2002, he was justly worried about the Taiwanese economy and about his business. He was angry about Walmart's policy of taking ownership of the cluster's mass-market bicycles they sold only at the time of sale, thus forcing the Taiwanese manufacturers to pay for storage in Walmart's warehouses and to wait for payment after that. He was concerned about the growing retail consolidation in the United States, which resulted in increasing demand for low-margin standardized products. He was frustrated by the impersonal interactions that he had with US buyers. Not so many years ago, he had close personal relationships with his big-buyer customers. Now there was no trust and falling profits. In 2002, some of the other bicycle parts suppliers were going bankrupt or resorting to bank loans just to stay in business.

In the face of falling orders from the United States, Taiwanese manufacturers turned toward China as the next big market. Giant built a new assembly factory in Kunshan, a city a short distance from Shanghai, where it made bicycles for the Chinese domestic market. Lee Chi Enterprises built its brake factory there, a factory that Lee Chi's Chairman Lin (no relation to A-PRO's *laoban*) said at its maximum would employ 3000 people. Lee Chi's Taiwan factory had about 600 employees and around 200 subcontractors, but in China, Lee Chi's factory reduced its number of suppliers and made some of the needed parts in-house. In 2002, A-PRO's Chairman Lin had also joined the Kunshan cluster of part suppliers. He told us he liked Kunshan better than Longhua. Land was cheaper than in Hong Kong's hinterland; local officials bent over backward to help the Taiwanese businesses succeed, and were responsive to suggestions the

Taishang association made about how to improve the business environment; and the corruption, although still present, was less than in the Pearl River Delta.[77]

In late September 2006, a year before the global financial crisis, we interviewed Chairman Lin again at his A-PRO factory in Taiwan. The downturn in his business after the 9/11 attack was not as serious as he had feared it would be. The Green Movement in Europe was surging, and European governments were helping the local bicycle industries succeed, which was creating a huge market for specialty bikes. Seventy percent of Chairman Lin's revenues now came from Europe. Lin told us that he preferred working with his European buyers, who had lots of ideas for new products, especially for Yeh-Bao, the firm making bicycle accessories, which Lin's wife managed. He went to three different trade shows in Europe each year. The fashion for high-end bicycles was growing very complex. There were portable bikes, bikes that folded up, and electric bikes with electronic controls. Each model of each brand could be customized with special features. Moreover, many new brands of bikes were appearing in the European market, but unknown to most customers, most of the brands were managed by only a few companies. Still, each brand needed a distinctive niche, with an appearance and qualities that set each brand apart from the others.

Because of the growing complexity of the bike market, Chairman Lin was starting to use fewer suppliers and make more parts himself. In the previous four years, in Taiwan, A-PRO had perfected the manufacture of carbon fiber frames. A-PRO got the thin sheets of carbon fiber from three different producers in Japan, but Lin was hoping that there would soon be a supplier in Taiwan. In the factory, we watched the tedious, lengthy lamination process of turning the paper-like carbon fiber into unbelievably light, unbelievably strong frames. Chairman Lin also told us that the factories in China were doing well, but because the entire bicycle market was changing, his factories in China were also beginning to make parts for more expensive bikes. He told us that for the high-end frames, "I only have three competitors worldwide. Ten years ago, there were many, many more."

Conclusion

Starting with Deng Xiaoping's southern tour in 1992, the Chinese government used foreign firms as a way to develop its economy. From the first, this strategy denied these foreign firms open access to China's potentially huge domestic economy, but gave them incentives to locate themselves in China and to hire China's cheap labor to make products designed only for export to the rest of the world. Among other goals, the government's plan had a trickle-down component. Chinese firms, government officials believed, would benefit from the presence of foreign firms: the domestic firms would be able to acquire the technology and the industrial and managerial expertise to enter the ranks of world-class manufacturers, just as the Japanese, South Koreans, Hong Kongers, and Taiwanese had done before them.

Indeed, on the surface, the future looked rosy in 2006. After a detailed comparison of China's exports with those of other countries around the world, one of the leading development economists, Dani Rodrik, declared that "what is so special about China's exports is not that they are voluminous or that its large pool of labor gives it a huge labor cost advantage. What stands out is that China sells products that are associated with a productivity level that is much higher than a country at China's level of income."[78] Rodrik's concern was whether the Chinese government could sustain this level of "sophisticated" exports with the necessary incentives designed to create and maintain new industries with new products. Rodrik's analysis, however, did not poke below the surface. He did not recognize that around 60 percent of China's exports in 2006 came from firms partly or solely owned by foreigners, who had built state-of-the-art factories in China for the sole purpose of manufacturing sophisticated products for export.

In 2010, using the same export data for China that Rodrik used, but doing a more finely grained analysis over the period from 1997 to 2005, economists Bruce Blonigen and Alyson Ma asked "whether [China's sophisticated exports are] simply driven by the foreign firms in China or whether Chinese firms are also gaining greater sophistication from this foreign presence."[79] What they discovered "runs exactly counter to what one would expect if Chinese firms were catching up—foreign firms' share of exports by product category and foreign unit values relative to Chinese unit values is increasing over time, not decreasing. We see these patterns despite the fact that FDI into China as a percentage of GNP has not increased since before our sample."[80]

Our analysis agrees with Blonigen and Ma's conclusions: by 2007, Chinese firms were not catching up; if anything they were falling behind. Global demand for the sophisticated products coming out of Taiwanese firms in both China and Taiwan was rising. These Taiwanese-owned factories were producing more and more as their share of the market for their products grew larger and larger. As the production from the firms went up, the clusters of firms producing the products became smaller, more exclusive, and more cohesive. At the same time, the firms in the clusters grew larger, more efficient, and more vertically integrated.

The round-table etiquette practiced by the owners of the firms in the cluster required trust and cooperation. The Taiwanese manufacturers were reluctant to work with Chinese firms in China. The Taiwanese owners wanted to preserve their control of the industry they were in. One person from Lee Chi Enterprises, a supplier of brakes and seat posts, maintained that Lee Chi "cannot risk buying parts from Chinese producers because of the product liability issue." Chinese firms, he maintained, "do not have a concept of product liability." By contrast, Taiwanese firms have product liability insurance and will assume responsibility should anything happen.[81] An even more pressing issue was the fact that the Taiwanese manufacturers distrusted the Chinese because they knew that, if they let the Chinese manufacturers into the clusters, they would eventually lose control of the flow of orders, just as the Japanese had lost control in the previous decades. As Chairman Lin of A-PRO said, "The Japanese seized the opportunity in the '70s, and Taiwan seized it in the '80s. In the '90s, the Taiwanese continued to have control and did not let it go. It is like the Taiwanese have built a wall and contained it."[82] The spokesperson at Merida made the same point: "We set up a production base in China instead of subcontracting out to Chinese firms because we have learned the consequences. In fact, the bicycles industry is still in the hands of Taiwanese firms in China.... It is Taiwanese firms which deal with Taiwanese firms in China."[83]

Capitalism—the ability of people to make money methodically regardless of time and place and competition—is never a steady state or a continuous process. In 2007, the global financial crisis plunged the world economy into a prolonged recession, now known as the Great Recession, the most serious global economic decline since the Great Depression in the 1930s. Stock markets around the world sank, consumers in the United States and Europe started to save more than they spent, and the demand for products throughout much of the world subsided. As their orders deteriorated, Taiwanese manufacturers in both Taiwan and China wondered whether they would be able to survive. Rick Chen, the Executive Director of San Wu Textiles in Taiwan, said, "2008, that is when our troubles really started."

Worried that the Chinese economy would stop growing, the Chinese government pumped billions of yuan into an effort to keep the economy growing.

And the Chinese economy did continue to grow, and the Chinese consumers did continue to spend. Once again the capitalist game changed. In the final two chapters, we will examine the consequences of the Great Recession on the Chinese economy, on Taiwanese manufacturers, and on global capitalism in general.

9

CONSOLIDATION IN CHINA

Computers and Smartphones

The Great Recession arrived in the wake of the global financial crisis that started in the United States in 2007 but soon spread to Europe and beyond. The precipitating causes came from the bursting of a speculative bubble in the US housing market. The bubble arose when American financial companies consolidated subprime mortgage debt into various tradable products, called *derivatives*—mortgaged-backed securities, credit default swaps, collateralized debt obligations—which were then sold to institutional and private investors worldwide as a way for the financial companies to make money. When the US housing market began to fail in 2006 and 2007, these derivatives lost most and sometimes all of their value, causing a number of leading financial companies to go bankrupt, including Lehman Brothers, Bear Stearns, and Washington Mutual Saving and Loan. The breakdown in private debt from the bursting of the housing bubble and the collapse of institutional debt markets reverberated through the US and European economies, tipping both into prolonged recessions. Unlike the Asian financial crisis, which shook developing countries, the Great Recession struck at the financial heart of the world's most developed capitalist economies, those of the United States and Europe.

At the time, some analysts thought that global capitalism was teetering on the edge of total collapse. Nothing nearly so drastic as that happened. Feeling the pinch and hearing the warnings, consumers in the United States and Europe did reduce their spending, however, and with that reduction came a decline in demand for many consumer products. By 2008, exports for goods from China to the United States and Europe began to fall off, as did Taiwan's exports of intermediate goods to China. The newspapers reported that many foreign-owned factories in Guangdong were laying off workers and that some of them closed without compensating their employees. Worried that the effects of falling demand for exports would ripple through the Chinese economy, late in 2008, the Chinese government pumped 4 trillion yuan (586 billion US$) into infrastructure and housing projects designed to give the domestic economy a large boost. The stimulus package worked. China's economy dipped ever so slightly in 2009 to 9.2 percent GDP growth rate and then rebounded to over 10 percent in 2010.

However, in contrast to China's annual rate of growth before 2008, which averaged nearly 12 percent, this time China's economic expansion was different. Instead of concentrating its development strategy on China's coastal regions and its export sectors, the Chinese government began a concerted effort to develop the rest of the country and to shift its economy from an emphasis on exports to a focus on building domestic consumption. The new strategy had several moving parts. First, the government wanted to reduce the level of rural migration from the interior parts of China to its urbanized coastal regions. To accomplish this part of the plan, the government built high-speed freeways and airports in the interior provinces; constructed huge housing estates twenty, thirty, or more stories high in first-, second-, and third-tier cities; and began systematically to move the largely self-sustaining but very poor rural population into these urban and suburban apartments. Second, the government attempted to create jobs for this new urban population by moving factories from the coastal to the interior provinces. This relocation of industries included foreign-owned firms as well. Several Taiwanese factories owners that we interviewed in Kunshan told us that government officials had told them that a move to the interior would be "wise," and a number reluctantly agreed to do so. Third, the government instituted and began to enforce new rules that required foreign-owned firms to have domestic partners in order to sell products in China.[1]

These government measures began to drive a wedge between capitalism and economic development. China's previous strategy of growth had used production for global capitalist markets as the key driver of development, but with the new policies, state management began to replace foreign capitalist markets with domestic ones. The Chinese government had anticipated that a new domestic capitalism would emerge from its policies, new markets that the new urbanites would create from the money earned from their new wages. Speculative bubbles arose instead. In the seven years after 2008, urban land prices shot up, Chinese stock markets surged, corruption of government officials increased, and the upper- and upper-middle-class Chinese consumed foreign-branded luxury goods as if there would be no tomorrow. For many, China appeared to have discovered the state-supported path to unending wealth. But one by one, the bubbles burst. In 2014, the value of property, especially in second-tier cities and below started to decline. Many of the rapidly constructed housing estates remained mostly empty years after they were built. In 2015, China's stock markets lost nearly 50 percent of their value. By 2015, China's anticorruption drive had put some of the most prominent members of China's previous regime in jail for corruption and had thoroughly alarmed the rest of the bureaucracy. And once the other markets began to fade, the consumer desires of China's wealthiest people also started to subside.

To prevent further deterioration of the economy, the Chinese government in 2015, under President Xi Jinping's direction, doubled down on the state's management of the economy. State officials pumped billions of yuan into China's stock markets, directly prevented the wealthiest investors from selling stocks, and instituted other measures designed to prevent the markets' further declines. To sustain the property and job markets, the state also financed new construction projects, building more roads and more housing estates. Xi's government also promoted the development of China's economy beyond the borders of China with the One Belt, One Road initiative designed to connect China to Eurasia through building roads, rails, and ports internationally. The government also anticipated that this initiative would open up new markets that would absorb some of China's excess production in steel, cement, and other domestically made products. The government also planned that the construction projects spawned by this initiative would be financed by a new international bank that Xi's government proposed, the Asian Infrastructure Investment Bank, a multinational venture capitalized at 100 billion US$ that listed thirty-seven countries as co-signers, but not the United States or Japan. All these efforts to forestall further declines in China's economy also increased public and private debt and heightened the risk of even greater declines in the future.

In this chapter, we will examine China's leading exports—computers and smartphones—which form the core of what is, arguably, China's most important industry, consumer electronics. The shift from global markets to state management is a growing theme in this industry as well. As we described in Chapter 7, Taiwanese manufacturers became important players in this industry in the late 1980s and early 1990s, and grew to be a dominant force in the late 1990s, just as they were moving their assembly factories to China. They continued to consolidate their commanding position in the industry in the first decade of the twenty-first century with an array of products assembled in China for export and for China's domestic economy. In the past decade, however, a struggle over control of the industry has emerged, a struggle among three contending players: the core clusters centered on Taiwanese-owned assembly plants, a core cluster of predominantly Chinese-owned firms, and Samsung's vertically integrated *chaebol*. Here again, ever so subtly, China's government policies are driving a wedge between capitalism and economic development.

Reconsolidation of Consumer Electronics Manufacturing in Taiwan and China, 2001–2015

Before Taiwanese manufacturers started to move their assembly plants to China, China's production of consumer electronics was relatively small and globally insignificant. In 1995, just as Taiwanese high-tech manufacturers were starting to assemble goods in China, China's high technology exports were only 6.8 percent of China's total manufacturing exports. At 10.1 billion US$, these exports were only a little over 2 percent of the world's high-tech exports.[2] Fifteen years later, in 2010, high technology exports from China had soared to 492.4 billion US$, comprising over 30 percent of China's manufactured exports.[3] Forty-five percent of China's export growth between 2002 and 2007 came from the high technology sector, and only four products in this broad sector—cell phones, liquid crystal displays (LCDs), integrated circuits (ICs), and laptops—accounted for one third of the growth.[4] Having surpassed the United States in 2009, China now leads the world in the production and export of high technology products.

As with other categories of exports from China, the rapid rate of growth is less impressive when one examines trade statistics and the manufacturing census more closely. The rate is less impressive because China's exports in this broad sector are highly concentrated in only a few products, and the manufacture of those products is dominated by foreign-owned firms.[5] In the previous chapter, we showed that the processed trade category of imports and exports accounted for over 50 percent of China's exports. In the high-tech sector, however, the total is much higher than that. In 1993, when China exported only about 4 billion US$ worth of high-tech products, over 70 percent was processed trade. Even then, China served as an assembly site. By 2003, however, after Taiwan's high-tech firms had established themselves in China, as had some Japanese and South Korean firms, processed trade in the high-tech sector accounted to nearly 90 percent. By 2010, that figure had slipped to 80 percent, still an extraordinarily high percentage that shows China up to this point remained an assembly site for high-tech products. According to one analyst, China's high-tech exports are a "myth."

> When these assembled high-tech products are shipped abroad, Chinese Customs classifies them as high-tech exports, regardless of whether China's contribution is in labor or technology. The entire value of the assembled high-tech product is also credited to China, regardless of whether most of key parts and components are imported or domestically made. Therefore, the current trade statistics are misleading and greatly inflate the value of China's exports in high-tech products.[6]

Take, for example, Apple's iPhone. In 2014, Apple's self-reported supply chain contained a total of 748 suppliers, of which 47 percent were located in China and 5 percent in Taiwan. However, in terms of who owned these firms, Chinese owned only 5 percent, whereas Taiwanese owned 20 percent.[7] The production cost of the G3 iPhone was 179 US$, but only 6 US$ of that value was contributed by the Chinese. Despite the low value-added percentage from China, the iPhone is classified as an export from China, and the entire "US$ 179 is credited to China . . . [even though] most of the value associated with iPhone exports is actually attributed to imported parts and components from third countries and have nothing to do with China."[8]

What is specifically true for Apple products is broadly true for the entire sector of high technology products.[9] For the last two decades, when China's high technology exports have boomed, China has been mostly a site, and a source of cheap labor, for non-Chinese firms to assemble core components and final products that are made up of parts that companies have imported from other parts of the world.

Just as they did with Japan and other Asian countries in the previous decades, many pundits and politicians nowadays criticize China for undermining the US and European economies. But in doing so, they miss the most important features of the new global capitalist economy: in most industries, there has been a global rationalization of supply chains; aggressive, well-placed companies have captured key segments of these supply chains, a process that has led to new forms of oligopolization on a global scale. Calculable predictions of final demand have allowed (and almost forced) retailers, merchandisers, and manufacturers to reconsolidate around the probabilities of making money. This reconsolidation is global; it has become global because the barriers to global expansion have declined relative to the technological and organizational means to consolidate at a global level. Many companies fear, if they do not globalize in some calculated way, they will lose out to their globalizing competitors. They therefore try to lead the surge to capture those sections of supply chains that correspond best to their business; it's either that or sell out to those that do. Although the firms leading this reconsolidation recognize national borders, and take advantage of them when they can, their corporate strategies are global, as are the effects of their strategies.

Contract Manufacturing in the New Global Economy

One of the consequences of this global reconsolidation is the intensification of contract manufacturing. More accurately, contract manufacturing is both a consequence and a cause of these changes in the global economy. A term for this duality of consequence and cause is *co-evolution*.[10] Asian contract manufacturers and US and European retailers and merchandisers have, in a reciprocal dance, evolved over time. What began as tentative decisions on the part of retailers and merchandisers to have more leverage over products and prices by nurturing and supporting Asian manufacturers has led over time to increasingly close and sophisticated relations between the organization of demand and the organization of supply.

On the demand side, retailers and merchandisers have achieved, if you will, a freedom from production, a freedom from trying to match how to sell goods with how to make those goods in a specific factory. They specialize in selling products. This detachment from production leads to a focus on designing products in a way that encourages consumers to think of all goods as fashions, and to think of themselves as creations of their own sensibilities.[11] Consummate consumers, ranging from luxury-loving connoisseurs to environmentally friendly minimalists, become individually aware of the array of choices that are central to how they chose to live their lives. Their choices are recorded and tallied and made the substance of further calculations about what will sell to what sort of buyers. Retailers and merchandisers consciously organize their businesses around what they calculate, rightly or wrongly, to be the market for their consumers. Made in the midst of constant competition, these calculations lead them to contract manufacturing as the best way to acquire a stock of goods to sell, goods that they can clear from their shelves and still earn a profit. The specifics of the demand-side organization do vary according to the entrepreneurial dynamics of the industry, but these dynamics are variations on how to sell the goods the corporations order.

The supply side is equally organized and equally varied around the theme of how to make products that have been ordered by others. Sometimes contract manufacturers receive detailed, exacting specifications; at other times they do most of the design work themselves. They, too, have achieved a degree of freedom, freedom from having to be concerned about the vagaries of final consumers. They have specific customers, the big buyers, real people with whom they work out the specifications of the products being produced. Their focus is on the processes of production, on the coordination of all the parts needed to make the whole product, and on the harmonization among the cluster of suppliers.

This division of labor between supply and demand allows both demand and supply sides to rationalize, to become better—more efficient, more profitable, more competitive—at doing what they do best. In the previous chapters, we showed how Taiwanese industrialists have become the world's leading contract manufacturers by doing what they do best in various industries. As we will show in this chapter, their dominance is, if anything, even more striking in consumer electronics. Their ability to become so prominent as contract manufacturers is, in part, fortuitous; they happened to be in the right place at the right time. Their prominence, however, also goes beyond luck. They evolved. They adapted their social organization—the round-table etiquette—over time as a sophisticated, flexible way to organize overlapping clusters of firms to produce large quantities of very complex goods on demand.

We should not overstate our thesis, however. These changes in the organizations of supply are not just about the Taiwanese. Rather, they reveal the increasing consolidation of production worldwide, which is ongoing and has many players. The Taiwanese are a part of this mix. But many others are increasingly involved, too. However, the movement, everywhere, is in the direction of contract manufacturing, which gives Taiwanese manufacturers some advantages.

In this new era of demand-led capitalism, the process by which manufacturing consolidates differs in different industries, but the variations still reflect the division of labor between the process of selling goods, on the one side, and the process of making goods, on the other side. In the last chapter, we described these processes for footwear and bicycles, two industries in which Taiwanese manufacturers dominate. The huge variety in types of shoes, the proliferation of retailers, and the rapid product cycles encouraged manufacturers to consolidate their expertise in production, leaving the merchandising and retailing to others. Taiwanese bicycles manufacturers, however, needed more and different types of retailers, more variety in bicycles, and quicker product cycles to match their production capabilities. They filled that vacuum with their own brand names, which in turn forced their big buyers to specialize, some in brand-name holding companies and others in making expensive bikes using components made by Taiwanese parts suppliers. In both examples, the Taiwanese manufacturers were able to gradually consolidate their hold on supply, so that they now occupy an oligopolistic position vis-à-vis retailers and merchandisers, quite unlike their position before 1985.

These two examples sit between the apparel industry, on one side, and consumer electronics, on the other side. In the apparel industry, the variety of clothes, the variety of retailers selling clothes, and the amount of labor that goes into making the final goods dwarfs the issues of the footwear industry. The volume, variety, and hand labor inherent in the apparel industry makes consolidation difficult for those located at either end of the supply chain: the retailers and the manufacturers. In the past three decades, however, this industry has consolidated in the middle parts of the supply chain and around several products.

One product in the middle part of the apparel supply chain is the cloth used in garment manufacturing. Shortly before the global financial crisis in 2007, we interviewed R. C. Chen, Chairman of Nien Hsing Textiles. Nien Hsing was, and still is, the world's largest producer of denim cloth. Chairman Chen told us that the firm makes over 4000 different types of denim, each of which has a different item number. The company's textile mills in Taiwan, Mexico, Nicaragua, and Lesotho are vertically integrated cloth producers, starting with the spinning of the yarn and ending with up to seventy distinct steps in dying the fabric. He also told us that, at the time of our interview, the mills had been operating twenty-four hours a day, seven days a week, for the past four years. The company also used some of its denim to make clothing in its garment factories in Central America.[12] However, most of the denim is sold to merchandisers that use other third-party factories to make their clothes. Chairman Chen said that his factories produced only denim and clothes that have been ordered by their big buyers. They keep no stock on hand. The secret of Nien Hsing's success was its close relationship with its customers and the factories' very rapid turnaround time for the delivery of orders. "Some of our competitors," he said, "take up to five or six months to develop a new type of denim and to fill an order, but for us it takes two weeks." He added, "The closer our relationship is with our buyers, the more money everyone makes."

Another product in the middle of the apparel supply chain is service, meaning, in this case, the ability to match a customer's design with the exact suppliers needed to turn that design into a sellable product. For apparel, the widely acknowledged worldwide leader in providing this intermediary service is Li & Fung, a Hong Kong company that specializes in "managing supply chains for global brands, department stores, hypermarkets, specialty stores, catalogue-led companies, and e-commerce platforms." Li & Fung employs "25,000 people working in more than 300 locations in over 40 different markets ... [working with a] network of 15,000 global suppliers."[13] In an interview with the *Harvard Business Review*, the Chairman of Li & Fung, Victor Fung, succinctly explained his firm's role in the emerging supply-side organization of the apparel industry: "We're pulling apart the value chain and optimizing each step—and we're doing it globally."[14] He gave the following illustration of his firm's "capabilities ... to take an initial design idea all the way through to the finished product in the consumer's hands":[15]

> Say we get an order from a European retailer to produce 10,000 garments. It's not a simple matter of our Korean office sourcing Korean products or our Indonesian office sourcing Indonesian products. For this customer we might decide to buy yarn from a Korean producer but have it woven and dyed in Taiwan. So we pick the yarn and ship it to Taiwan. The Japanese have the best zippers and buttons, but manufacture them mostly in China. Okay, so we go to YKK, the big zipper manufacturer, and we order the right zipper from their Chinese plants. Then we determine that, because of quotas and labor conditions, the best place to make the garments is Thailand. So we ship everything there. And because the customer needs quick delivery, we may divide the order across five factories in Thailand ... 5 weeks after we received the order, 10,000 garments arrive on the shelves in Europe.[16]

Victor Fung's description captures the combination of fragmentation and consolidation that is the crucial element of contract manufacturing. Li & Fung's consolidation of its intermediary role allows it to separate and optimize each step of the value chain for apparel manufacturing. The exact combinations of consolidation and fragmentation vary by the competitive dynamics within and between industries, but the combinations are always variations on the capitalist theme of rationalizing production in order to make money.

Consumer Electronics in Taiwan and China
Making Computers

In the late 1990s, as Taiwanese computer manufacturers were just beginning to move some of their most labor-intensive factories to China, the computer industry was undergoing rationalizing changes at both ends of the supply chain. Before 1996, desktop computers dominated the PC market. There were many merchandisers and retailers, in large part because it was relatively easy for large retailers, such as Walmart, and merchandisers with well-known brand names, such as Gateway and Dell, to source desktop computers from a variety of Taiwanese PC assemblers.[17] In that year, the market share of the top five PC merchandisers was less than 35 percent of the market.[18]

However, by the late mid-1990s, the product mix was beginning to change. Laptops and notebook computers were converging into a single product, and their market share was growing at the expense of the larger desktop units. Unlike desktops, whose plug-and-play parts could be easily customized in the United States, notebook computers had closed cases and thus were finished products when they came out of the factory. The closed-unit concept soon extended to some PC desktop models as well. More powerful microprocessors, more DRAM, and more customized ASIC chips meant that every supplier had to redesign every component, and all the components had to fit seamlessly into a closed unit.[19] Moreover, this process of redesigning every component became an ongoing process. Advances in software and the ubiquity of the Internet greatly enlarged the number of consumers buying computers. To tap into the latest applications, consumers wanted the latest models; computers became fashion, with new generations of computers appearing several times a year. Some retailers operated on the basis of a new product every three months.[20]

The closed-unit construction meant that the assembly factories needed greater control over the design of the new computers. Everything had to fit into the case and everything had to work seamlessly. Without the assistance of the assemblers, the largest merchandisers of desktop computers in the United States, Dell and Compaq, did not have the capacity either to design the individual parts of the notebook computer or to fit these parts into the closed-unit cases. These tasks went to the clusters of computer assemblers and parts suppliers, who together worked out the process of modular assembly with continuous redesign capabilities. As notebook computers became the dominant PC, these clusters quickly gained market share within the industry, as did the main sellers and manufacturers of these computers. By 2006, 85 percent of the PC industry was controlled by the top five assembly firms, all Taiwanese owned (Compal, Quanta, Wistron, Inventec, and Asus).[21] In the same year, the top five merchandisers (Dell, HP, Lenovo, Acer, and Toshiba) sold over 50 percent of all PCs. Among the five merchandisers, only Acer manufactured its own computers, but even Acer sourced its notebook computers, initially from Quanta. So, too, did Lenovo, the Chinese-owned company that bought out IBM's PC computer business, and Toshiba, the only Japanese firm that remained a competitive brand name in the PC industry, both from Taiwanese manufacturers. By 2015, HP, Lenovo, and Dell remained among the top five merchandisers, with over 50 percent of the PC market divided more or less equally among them; these three had been joined by Asus and Apple, each with slightly over a 7 percent market share.[22] The five Taiwanese assemblers remained the same, producing over 90 percent of the world's personal computers.

The shift from desktop to notebook computers matched the movement of Taiwanese PC clusters in China from Dongguan to Kunshan and Suzhou.[23] When the desktop assemblers and parts suppliers first moved to China in the late 1990s, they located themselves in the Pearl River Delta, in and around Dongguan district. Many of their key Taiwanese suppliers either remained in Taiwan, as did the chip foundries TSMC and UMC, or moved just the most labor-intensive parts of their manufacturing to China. Most, if not all, of the businesses kept their headquarters and R&D units in Taiwan. Then in the opening years of the new century, as the more integrated PC notebook cluster was moving to China, government officials in Jiangsu Province in the Yangtze River Delta, especially those in Kunshan and Suzhou, offered these assemblers much better incentives than Dongguan presented. Led by its key assemblers, the notebook cluster decided to join the other Taiwanese manufacturers who had already settled in the region.[24] More than 50,000 Taiwanese settled in Kunshan alone, so many that it became known as Little Taipei.[25]

In 2010, we returned to Kunshan to check out the conditions of the Taiwanese manufacturers there. One of the people we talked with was Jerry Lin, one of the top managers in the Kunshan Gangyi Precision Technology Company. He gave us a tour of the factory he managed, a large factory, employing around 2000 people, that made only one product, hinges for the clamshell lids of notebook computers. He explained that this is a part that people don't think about; they just expect it to work flawlessly, to remain open in whatever position the lid is placed, and to open and close through the lifetime of the computer, through 100,000 openings and closings and more. The hinge had required a considerable amount of research and development and some reverse engineering, and Kunshan Gangyi was continuing to further refine the part for future generations of laptops. Most of the parts used for the hinge came from Taiwan. What we saw in the factory was the final assembly, consisting of thirty or more employees arranged in a horseshoe-shaped line, each performing a small step in the final assembly of the hinge. This line was one of many such in the factory, and in a year's time, the factory produced millions of hinges. The company Lin managed was one of four companies supplying this part to the Taiwanese notebook assemblers, all of whom were clustered in the vicinity. The company's market share was about 20 percent of the total production of around 120 million projected for that year. Manager Lin told us that a few years ago the company had received several US dollars for each hinge, but now it gets only around seventy cents.

Manager Lin voiced his concern about the future. He said that the notebook cluster of firms was part of what he called the "'strawberry generation' in China: apply a little pressure and we all get crushed." He explained that the labor shortage was getting very serious, wages were going up, and the owners were worried about how long the company could keep going. He further explained that a great many Taiwanese firms in China register in offshore locations because they want a registration separate from the mother firm in Taiwan, but they cannot register as Chinese firms, and so they pick Hong Kong or some Caribbean Island as the place to register their firms. Like the other firm owners and managers we interviewed, he, too, was worried about the politics between Taiwan and China, and how the Taiwanese working in China might become embroiled in the ongoing struggle.

We also followed up with an interview, in 2016, with Joe Hsieh, Corporate Vice President of Asus and General Manager of Asus's Motherboard Business Unit and New Product Planning Division.[26] Asus is the only notebook manufacturer that has successfully built a brand name. Four engineers left Acer to start Asustek in 1989. Working on the premise that companies should create their own supply chains instead of vertically integrating, Acer, through its Multitech Investment Fund, provided most of the capital to start the engineers' company. Shortly afterward, Asustek began supplying Acer and other companies with motherboards.[27] After the company became a going concern, Asustek's founders also decided to follow Acer's lead and to develop its own brand name, Asus, along with being a contract manufacturer. Owing to its award-winning motherboards, the company grew very quickly, and soon became a leading supplier of motherboards and graphic cards, as well as a producer of branded desktop computers. In the mid-1990s, starting first as a contract manufacturer and then as a brand-name manufacturer, the company began to make notebook computers, because the profit margins were so much better.

Joe Hsieh joined Asustek as its Vice President in 1992. He had worked previously in the company's American office in Silicon Valley for two years. After that, he returned to Taiwan, but a year later he rejoined Asustek and has been with the firm ever since. The 1990s, he explains, were the "golden decade." That was when the company's business was booming in the midst of fierce competition from other Taiwanese manufacturers. He told us that many of Asustek's Taiwanese competitors failed because their companies were not well managed; in order to get more and more orders, these competitors cut their prices and the quality of their products. "They had no long-term strategy." By contrast, Asustek worked on building relationships with both its own customers and its suppliers. "We valued the feeling of working with others, of building special relationships. We did this not because we wanted to make money, but because we were willing to work hard together. The feeling was important. The long-term relationships were important." Asustek frequently sent teams of engineers to collaborate with such customers as Apple Computer and Sony in order better to design the notebook computers.[28] Vice President Hsieh told us, "As an OEM, we were trained by our business partners especially those from Europe and the US, in terms of product design and management. We also learned something from Japanese companies as well." The company also worked with its suppliers to help them to continually redesign individual components. Hsieh called it a working culture of trust and cooperation.

When Asustek moved its assembly site to Suzhou in 2000, the company was one of first notebook manufacturers to move to China and was the biggest employer in the area, with about 60,000 people working in the factory at the time. The local government's incentives were extremely good, and the cost of land and labor was so much cheaper in China that the company had to move in order to remain competitive. Hsieh told us the cost of labor in Taiwan was about twice as much as it was in China. "The lower the labor cost is, the more competitive we become. And so after one or two companies moved to China, others followed quickly, either that or lose their business."

Asustek moved its assembly line to China without its Taiwanese supply chain. At first, the company tried vertical integration, but Vice President Hsieh noted that the company could not make "components as good as those from our original suppliers, and so vertical integration was not totally successful." The company also used some local suppliers for some of the less central components. Very soon, however, their main Taiwanese suppliers moved to China as well. "We did not ask them to move, but they had no choice. Either move with us or lose their market." By 2007, its cluster of suppliers intact, Asustek had entered multiple markets, including televisions and cell phones, in addition to computers and computer components. The management decided to clarify the organizational structure by separating into multiple companies. Now part of a business group, Asus became the name of the company making Asus-branded products, the company making electronic products contracted by big buyers became Pegatron, and the company making non-electronic parts for high-tech products became Unihan.[29]

Making Smartphones

In the fall of 2001, Apple Computer, which had been in the doldrums for over a decade, suddenly came out with some new products that transformed the consumer electronics industry and rapidly led to a convergence with the notebook PCs. The first item introduced was the Apple iPod, a device that combined computer functions (e.g., proprietary operating system, ASIC chips, internet connectability, and advanced digital audio processing) with the ability to download and listen to one's personal choices in music. Other merchandisers soon followed with their own devices (MP3 players) having the same functions with a more standardized platform. Earlier, in 1999, a Japanese company, NTT DoCoMo, had introduced the first mobile phone that was fully functional via wireless transmitters. The availability of such cell phones set in motion the spread of carriers offering high-speed wireless internet service. By 2001, responding to the third generation of wireless capabilities (3G), cell phones combined ASIC chips and high-speed data transmission with digital audio processing. In 2007, these two devices converged, first, in the form of the Apple's iPhone, which combined a wireless computer, a camera, a personal entertainment center, and a cell phone, all in one small package.[30] By the time Apple introduced the iPad in 2010, the iPhone had gone through four major updates (iPhone 4) and many minor revisions. The iPad started a new fashion for tablet computers that could do everything a smartphone could do, except the phone calls, in a slightly larger package. Apple's innovations in smartphones and tablets were matched by other merchandisers, such as HTC, a Taiwanese company managed by Cher Wang (the daughter of Wang Yung-ching, the *laoban* of Formosa Plastics) and two major brand-name producers from South Korean *chaebol*, Samsung and LG, all of whom offered smartphones using Android, an open, standardized operating system owned by Google.

As the sophistication of the overall products increased, the supply chains for these products also became increasingly specialized. Even though the Taiwanese desktop and notebook assemblers typically designed computers in conjunction with the big buyers, they always used a wide range of suppliers, many of whom were not Taiwanese owned. Japanese manufacturers made most of the LCD (liquid crystal display) screens; American firms (Intel and Applied Micro Devices, AMD) usually supplied the microprocessors, and many of the graphic chip sets were designed by Nvidia and other American fabless design houses. All of the major high-tech products were truly global products, each with hundreds, and some even with thousands, of parts that required sourcing. For instance, the HP notebook had 2196 parts, including software. Much as Li & Fung did in the apparel industry, Taiwanese PC assemblers choreographed the dance of suppliers. Taking the specifications from the merchandisers, they would turn the idea into a reality, into a product that could be mass-produced from components and services that they sourced worldwide. The difference, of course, was that they were both intermediary and assembler.

Smartphones and tablets required even more sophistication in every respect. Smartphones quickly became a global product, with a huge diversified market, in a way that computers had never achieved. By 2013, in a span of less than ten years, the number of smartphone users had gone beyond one billion. Smartphones allowed people in developing countries, without land lines and wired internet service, access to information, communication, and services comparable to those available in developed countries. For these markets, relatively inexpensive smartphones sold well. In developed countries, the largest sales went to the more expensive models, offering the best quality, service, and apps. And fashion was involved, too. New smartphones with new capabilities were constantly going on the market, which created very short product cycles, especially for those, such as Apple's iPhone and Samsung's Galaxy, that had more cachet than others. Competition among brand-name merchandisers was intense and had narrowed to only a few brand names.[31] Palm, Ericsson, Motorola, Nokia, Blackberry, and many other brand-name merchandisers dropped out. Similar to US television manufacturers in the 1970s, some smartphone firms, such as Nokia and Ericsson, began with their own manufacturing facilities, but in the face of competition changed to outsourcing their smartphones, before eventually selling their smartphone divisions to other companies. The smartphones of other firms, such as HTC, sold well for a short time, only to fall off later.[32] The shakeout has been ongoing, even as the sales dwarf those of any other consumer electronic product. In the first three months of 2016 alone, Samsung and Apple, the two leading smartphone brands, sold, respectively, 81.9 and 51.2 million of the 335 million smartphones sold to customers worldwide. In the last three years, these two have now been joined in the top five by three Chinese companies that are in the process of building global brand names: Huawei, Xiaomi, and Oppo.

The huge demand for smartphones is, of course, matched by the requirement to manufacture all those smartphones in the first place. As in selling, here, too, the global consolidation in manufacturing is striking. Since 2010, two types of supply chains for most of the world's smartphone businesses have dominated production. One type, represented by Samsung, consists of vertically integrated firms encased under a corporate umbrella. Practicing one-setism, Samsung owns most of the firms supplying the main components for its smartphones, including the firm that made the faulty batteries that caused the total failure of Samsung's Galaxy Note 7.[33] Samsung also sells some of these components to competitors as well. For example, for a time, Samsung was a major supplier of semiconductors for Apple's iPhone. Samsung's sunk cost in building and maintaining a state-of-the-art factory for each component part, as well as for the assembly site that is capable of producing over 300 million smartphones a year, is enormous. For Samsung, the stakes are very high to continue manufacturing at this level. Therefore, Samsung's largest expenses have been for advertising lavishly, a necessity for attracting customers to the company's phones. Although Samsung's smartphone has led the world in sales for several years, its profit level is not as high as Apple's, its top competitor. As one Taiwanese manufacturer told us wryly, "Samsung earns money with the right hand and burns it with the left."

The other *chaebol* producing smartphones, LG, has opted out of the vertically integrated production model, and is now a supplier, as well as a smartphone merchandiser, for the second type of smartphone supply chain. This supply chain is dominated by Taiwanese parts manufacturers and assemblers, and thus the *Nikkei Asian Review* has referred to this second type as "the Taiwan-centric way of making smartphones."[34] Many non-Taiwanese parts manufacturers, including LG, are also part of the Taiwanese-centered clusters. However, the main assemblers, Hon Hai Precision Industry Company (also called Foxconn) and Inventec are Taiwanese. Hon Hai/Foxconn employs over a million Chinese workers in its twelve factories in China. It also has factories in other countries, including Australia, the Czech Republic, Hungary, Mexico, Slovakia, Turkey, Brazil, and the United States. Analysts estimate that Hon Hai/Foxconn factories make up to 40 percent of the world's electronic products. One of its factories near Shenzhen, which in 2012 employed 230,000 people, assembled Apple's iPhone. At the behest of the Chinese government, Hon Hai/Foxconn has since moved Apple's iPhone production to a new site in China's interior, to Zhengzhou in Henan Province.[35] The Shenzhen factory now manufactures other products. In both locations, many of the top suppliers are also Taiwanese. Most of the central processing units (CPUs) are designed by two fabless design houses. An American firm, Qualcomm, designs the high-end CPUs, and the low-, medium-, and some high-end chips are designed by MediaTek, a Taiwanese owned firm. TSMC and UMC are the lead foundries for both of these chips, garnering the lion's share of the market. Until recently, Sharp, a Japanese high-tech firm, was the leading supplier of the LCD screens, but nudged by Apple, Hon Hai/Foxconn bought Sharp's LCD manufacturing facilities, and now supplies itself with the part.

Many other suppliers in the smartphone cluster are also Taiwanese. We recently interviewed some of them, principally the manufacturers of some of the core components. These firms are Apple suppliers and asked to remain anonymous because Apple does not like its exact supply chain for future products to be known, even though analysts in the United States are constantly speculating about which firm is supplying what part to the next generation of iPhones. Other big buyers require the same anonymity, in part because they wish to appear to their customers as manufacturers themselves and to hide their supply chain from competitors.

Without revealing names, we can summarize what we learned. One of the people we interviewed estimated that, until recently, Hon Hai/Foxconn assembled about 80 percent of all smartphones. Two other firms, Pegatron and Inventec split the rest with about 10 percent each. In terms of the core components, MediaTek's market share for smartphone CPUs is about 70 percent, with Qualcomm having much of the rest. TSMC is the main foundry and UMC the secondary foundry for both MediaTek and Qualcomm. Although, we could not independently confirm any of these figures, what is clear is that smartphone chip design and manufacturing, assembly, and core components are highly concentrated in very few firms, many of which are Taiwanese.

The reason that Huawei, Xiaomi, and Oppo were able to become such prominent brand names so quickly is that all of them started off using the Taiwanese-centered supply chain. At one of Xiaomi's product launches in 2014, the CEO of the company said, "Although we have business with 500 suppliers, I'd like to give special thanks to four companies."[36] The company logos appearing on the screen behind the CEO were for Qualcomm, Foxconn, Inventec, and Sharp. When it started selling smartphones, Huawei, too, used Foxconn as its main assembler, but it has since shifted to a Chinese-owned firm, BYD Electronics. The least expensive of the three Chinese brands, Oppo, uses MediaTek chips and a Taiwanese assembler.

Although all the top brands, except for Samsung, use the Taiwan-centered supply chain to make their smartphones, they all manage that supply chain in slightly different ways. Apple relies on merchandising innovations that no other company has at the time of its product introductions. To create these innovations, Apple relies on its own in-house engineers to develop new prototypes and to design the supply chains that will produce the mass-produced products. How much Apple relies on the guidance of the assemblers and the key component suppliers is an open question. However, we were told that Apple designs the machine tools that make some of the distinctive components for the new models. After the new product has been approved by Apple's management, the company calls the firms in the projected supply chain together to work out the details of production. The assembler then supervises the day-to-day manufacturing process to see that the parts come together as planned. Apple also develops a second supply chain for the new product as insurance that it will be delivered on time with the required specifications.

Apple is clearly a merchandiser that takes control of the actual process of contract manufacturing. That is, Apple takes on the role of lead firm in a global production network.[37] Most merchandisers, however, rely more heavily than Apple appears to do on the cluster of suppliers and assemblers to design and develop a product that meets the general specifications of the buyer. These specifications are often based on what the competition is doing, and the expectation is that the contract manufacturers will be able to come up with an approximation of the competitor's products without actually violating intellectual property rights. For this reason, Taiwanese contract manufacturers are sometimes called *fast followers*.[38]

All the recent interviews with electronics parts suppliers have emphasized that the supply-side organization for smartphones is changing. Since 2013, the Chinese government has developed a policy stance that the supply chains for consumer electronics (and other products, too) that are located in China should consist mainly of Chinese firms. Huawei, Xiaomi, and Oppo have all come under pressure to adopt the "red line," an all-Chinese supply chain for the component parts and the assembly of their products. So far there is no all-Chinese cluster that can adequately supply these brand-name companies with certain key components. The Chinese government has also encouraged Taiwanese firms to take Chinese partners. The several owners we interviewed have refused to do so. They estimated that they have maybe another five years in China before the red line is completed, and then they don't know what will happen. As we will discuss in Chapter 10, the future for Taiwanese firms in China and elsewhere is up in the air.

This change in supply-side organization is further complicated by the fact that at the low end of the supplier market, smartphones and their components have already become standardized commodities. It is now possible to make do-it-yourself smartphones and tablets from parts that are readily available in parts pavilions for next to nothing. The prices for the low-end products have fallen so much that Chinese firms are selling smartphones in India for less than 4 US$.[39] In Guangzhou, African merchants line up to buy cheap smartphones to take back to their countries to sell at rock-bottom prices. Smartphone merchandisers and manufacturers, especially Samsung but also Apple, find themselves squeezed at both ends of the market. Although Samsung Electronics sells relatively inexpensive smartphones in parts of South and Southeast Asia, Africa, and Latin American, the company cannot afford to reduce prices too far. For middle- and upper-range smartphones, the competition was increasingly fierce even before the debacle involving Samsung's Galaxy Note 7.

Although the limits of smartphone technology may be topping out, one of the component makers we interviewed remained optimistic. This *laoban* told us that he has been in business for forty years. His big break came when he got a large order to make a part for Sony's Walkman. To fill the order, he added over 200 employees, and all of his employees worked overtime every day. "The customer stood outside our doors and carried the [products] away as soon as they were made." After that first contract from Sony, many other contracts came in, from Nokia, Motorola, Ericsson, and others. What his company did was to narrow its focus to that part, and to perfect it, to make it the very best on the market. He told us, "We make a small business big." The buyers just "give us the specifications they want and we design and make it." But it is more complicated than just taking orders, he said. What is involved is that "you must catch the trend. R&D is really important. You have to be years ahead of the [product] that you have right now, and you have to guess where the market is going."

His guess was correct. When the laptop, smartphone, and tablet markets developed, this *laoban*'s business kept growing. The company established factories in both Shenzhen and Suzhou, each making different variations of the same product. The company now has over 6000 employees, most of whom are doing assembly work. However, the factories are highly automated, too. The parts for smartphones are so small that individuals cannot assemble the pieces properly. Therefore, he has had his factories automated. He told us that his R&D teams developed the machines. The company bought parts from Japan, and modified them. "When the Japanese come to service the machines, we will not let them see the machines because now the technology is proprietary." The part has become so specialized that he thinks his firm is safe from being displaced in the red line, at least for a while. In addition to his contract with Apple, he also has a contract with Huawei.

Conclusion

Capitalism and economic development often do not walk hand in hand. In the twenty-first century, capitalism is a global affair. Both ends of supply chains have become increasingly rationalized and made more systematic for making and selling products. These twin endeavors are ongoing, are compartmentalized, and operate at a global level. The trajectory of capitalism is to become ever more so—with making and selling ever more separated from each other, ever more global, and ever oriented to making money under the conditions that entrepreneurs, big and small, perceive and act upon. Whatever their size, wherever their location, these entrepreneurs measure their success in making money by calculating their profits.

By contrast, economic development is a national affair. Economists measure national economies by per capita income, by rates of growth, by rates of employment, by interest rates, by level of inflation, by the inward and outward flows of trade, and by any number of other measures, except profits. National economies have surpluses and deficits, but not profits. Economic development concerns national welfare, which is not always everyone's welfare. That is where the national debates arise, in arguments about whether economic policies of the government favor the rich or the middle class or the poor. Often politicians inveigh against the excesses of capitalism, and for good reason. Global capitalism in the twenty-first century has indeed changed national economies. Declining rates of manufacturing in the United States and Europe, as well as Japan, South Korea, and Taiwan, are directly linked to the increase of manufacturing in China and other parts of the world.

From 1992 on, China's economic development has been tied to the expansion of global capitalism, first in East Asia, and then in China itself. The economic expansion in China happened so rapidly and was so extraordinary in world history that many writers, including some Chinese officials, wrote about the unique formula for China's success. Over the thirty years that we have been following the transformation of East Asian economies, we have seen this national pride occur before. In the 1970s and 1980s, it seemed as if Japan had discovered the formula, so much so that American business schools taught courses on Japanese management style, quality circles, and just-in-time manufacturing systems. In the 1980s and 1990s, we heard people talk about Taiwan's and South Korea's economic invincibility. So much of what was perceived in these countries as national economic development was, in fact, an overlapping of capitalism and economic development. But when the capitalists moved on, when the profits shifted elsewhere, the economies moved through rough transitions.

Hubris moves on, too. It is now China's turn to confront the contradictions between capitalism, on the one hand, and economic development, on the other. It appears to us that the alliance between capitalism and economic development in China is beginning to unravel, with a future for both in China that is uncertain.[40] This is a topic we will address in more detail in our concluding chapter and in the epilogue.

10

GREATER TAIWAN, CIRCA 2016

The End of an Era?

A few people still ride the train from Taipei to Taichung and beyond, but not many. The train station, built in 1917 when Taiwan was a Japanese colony and refurbished a number of times since, needs another restoration. The downtown core around the old train station, which even as late as 1985 was the heart of the thriving city, is in even worse shape. Many buildings, long unpainted, are now shuttered. Near the train station and once a primary destination for shopping, the Far Eastern Department Store closed its doors in 2000. After several fires, the large building is mostly empty. The main bus terminal, connecting outlying areas to the city core, is still located next to the train station, but most people get off the bus before it gets there. On Sundays, however, when the foreign workers have their day off, the old core comes alive with people from Thailand, Vietnam, and Indonesia mingling with their compatriots in a place far from the better parts of the city, a place they have mainly to themselves.

After 1985, the center of Taichung City moved away from the old core. When the first expressway (Highway 1) was completed in the 1970s, the government determined that property prices were too expensive to allow the construction of a six-lane highway close to the city center. So the highway was routed through Taichung at the foot of Dadu Shan, the large hill where Tunghai University is located. The government reached the same conclusion when the second six-lane expressway was planned in the early 1990s and later completed in 2003. Although the two highways serve different parts of the Taiwan's western slope, they nearly converge in their passage through Taichung. Then, when the high-speed rail (called the Gaotie, the "High Iron") was completed in 2007, the track cut between the two freeways. The crowning touch in Taiwan's transportation infrastructure to date, the Gaotie makes Taichung only an hour away from Taipei to the north and Kaohsiung to the south, which is only slightly more time than it takes, during rush hour, to get from the ultramodern Gaotie station to the old downtown core.

The new center of Taichung has moved out to meet the two freeways and the Gaotie. In the early 1990s, the areas that would become Taichung's most exclusive areas today were still rice fields. The rice fields have now given way to wide streets lined with large Japanese and Taiwanese department stores (including the new Far Eastern Department Store), high-end hotels, exclusive condominiums costing over a million US dollars each, the new National Art Museum, and the just completed Taichung Opera House. Boutique retailers line the streets. Large foreign retailers, Costco and Carrefour, are nearby. None of Taichung's buildings rivals the 101-story skyscraper in Taipei, for a short time the tallest building in the world, but Taichung's newest buildings are still substantial. In 2016, Taichung City was in the process of constructing an overhead, urban light rail system to connect the different parts of the city. This light rail system starts in the far northeast corner of Taichung, then skirts the old city core in a wide semicircle that comes no closer than five kilometers to the old train station at any point, and ends up in southwest corner of the city, at the Gaotie.

Clearly, like the rest of Taiwan and the rest of East Asia, Taichung is no longer just a site for manufacturing but has increasingly become a site of consumption as well. Shopping is an activity; fads and fashions are important. The young often sport tattoos, and dress is varied and trendy. Most of the world's cuisines are represented by a number of restaurants. Cab drivers play Western and K-pop songs, and many, many women of all ages watch Korean soap operas. Nearly everyone most everywhere is looking into his or her smartphone. Singly and in groups, Taiwanese tourists travel the world. Even graduates fresh from high school regularly travel to Japan, South Korea, and other places in Asia. A few make it to Europe and the United States.

A new consumerism has diffused throughout Asia. However, the separation between the new and the old parts of Taichung is emblematic of a deeper division, both here and across Asia, between those who have the means and the desire to consume and those who have only the desire. As in so much of the rest of the world, the rising levels of inequality point to economies that force a gap to open between those who make more than enough to sustain a level of self-worth and those who do not or who barely make ends meet. As the middle class dwindles, people discover that poverty is never so onerous as it is when your life is permeated by lifestyles that you will never be able to experience, as if looking across a chasm that you will never be able to bridge.

In this chapter, we return to Taiwan, to the organizational center of Taiwanese industrialists who have extended their capitalist ethos beyond Taiwan and beyond China in search of the right conditions where their businesses will thrive. The search is elusive, as is their hold on contract manufacturing. In the second decade of the twenty-first century, we are entering, once again, into a new, even more intense phase of demand-led capitalism, a third phase that is mediated more by online retailers, such as Amazon and Alibaba, than by big-box retailers. Made possible by the spread of smartphones, computers, and cloud-based information systems, the new phase will have ramifications for contract manufacturing, but exactly what those ramifications are, it is too early to say. But for the present, contract manufacturing is still Taiwan's primary economic activity.

Manufacturing Is Still Paramount

In Taiwan

Despite the new consumerism and despite the presence of large numbers of Taiwanese manufacturers in other countries, manufacturing in Taiwan remains at the core of what has become Greater Taiwan. The twenty-first century is an age of modular industrialization on a global scale. Taiwanese industrialists came naturally to modularization, but the patterns before 1985 were local, made up of independent *laoban* sharing an ethic of cooperation as a preferred strategy for making money. The patterns of modularization in the twenty-first century are so different that they would have been unrecognizable in 1985.

Let us start in Hemei, the small town where we observed, in Chapter 1, the precocious beginnings of demand-led capitalism in Taiwan. The cotton textile industries in Hemei declined after 1985, falling victim to rising costs of land and labor and to inefficiencies in their response to big buyers. One firm, Nien Hsing, the vertically integrated textile and garment company we outlined in the last chapter, quickly took over the entire cotton denim business that was once the most important product of the small and medium-sized firms in Hemei. By the late 1990s, the apparel, textile, and footwear industries in the Hemei area had mostly disappeared. Some people had moved their businesses, successfully and unsuccessfully, to China. Some never left Taiwan; they just closed their shops and found other lines of work. The shuttered firms in the area gave it the aura of a ghost town.

By 2015, however, when we last visited Hemei, the area was coming back to life. Physically, the area looked much the same as it looked in the 1980s, with the same concrete two- and three-story block houses still scattered among rice fields. But some of the factories inside the block houses were churning again. Driving along the roads on the dikes of the irrigation canals that lined the rural countryside around Hemei, we arrived at the Taiwan Fu Da Precision Company, which is also the headquarters of the Mao Chuan Industrial Company, two small firms owned by the same people. There we interviewed the *laoban*, Frank Lai, and his sales representative, Patience Chen.[1] The company began in 1971 making metal parts for local satellite assembly systems. As the footwear boom started, the factory switched to manufacturing metal eyelets for shoes. In the early 1990s, when the footwear firms were moving to southern China, Lai's footwear assembler asked Lai to accompany him in the move, but he did not want to leave his family and, besides, the move seemed too risky. Without any customers, he began to look for the next opportunity. After nearly a decade of occasionally making small parts for local firms, he heard through some friends in Kaohsiung that some European automobile manufacturers needed small parts. He upgraded his metal stamping machines and, through contacts, got some orders for small metal parts. After his factory earned ISO 9001 certification for manufacturing excellence in 2003, he attended automobile parts trade shows in Taiwan and Europe, and began to obtain more orders for stamped metal parts directly from automobile manufacturers, including Volkswagen and Peugeot. He also began to make parts for appliance manufacturers, which ended up in products merchandised by Bosch, Stanley, Black and Decker, Alcoa, and many others. Every year, his two firms turn out millions of individual parts that go into products assembled in many areas around the world, and yet his firms remain modest in size.[2] He obtains the parts, and also some of the labor that goes into the parts that he makes, from the nearly 100 subcontractors that he works with in the Hemei area. Small firm owner Frank Lai runs a global business.

Frank Lai's firms are two of the 1,353,049 small and medium-sized firms found among a total of 1,386,128 firms of all sizes registered in Taiwan in 2014. That is, 97.6 percent of all registered firms in Taiwan are still small and medium-sized firms. With Taiwan's population of 23 million, that figures out to be one firm for every seventeen people— men, women, and children. The majority of these firms are not in the manufacturing sector, but nonetheless, the manufacturing sector remains Taiwan's source of strength. For instance, the Taichung Industrial Park, just south and down the hill from Tunghai University, is still completely full, and most of the firms in the park qualify as medium-sized firms. Still located in the industrial park, Chairman Lai's Thunder Tiger factory, which we outlined in the introductory chapter, would qualify as a medium-sized firm, in part because the thousands of workers that he employs in China making remote-controlled model cars and airplanes and small drones do not count in his total here. Nor do the employees in his new firm, TTBio, which is the firm manufacturing dental drills and other tools for dentists. TTBio is now part of Chairman Lai's business group, the Thunder Tiger Group of independent firms, and so someday, too, will be a newly minted firm that manufactures a line of garden tools he is developing.

Although Taiwan's economy continues to be characterized by modestly sized firms, many firms have become large, though not nearly as large as those in the South Korean *chaebol*. Unlike the vertically integrated *chaebol*, Taiwan's large firms are still interwoven with small and medium-sized firms that give large firms the flexibility to expand or contract as the orders dictate. The weight of the Taiwanese economy has shifted to these firms.

In 2015, we visited one of these large companies that is a harbinger of the future. Just beyond the Taichung Industrial Park is the new Taichung Precision Machinery Park. There we arrived at the headquarters of Hiwin and the site of its largest factory. Hiwin is one of the world's top companies specializing in manufacturing robotics and other machine tools for automating factories around the world and is listed among *Forbes*'s ranking of the "50 most innovative companies."[3] When we arrived at Hiwin, we were greeted by Enid Tsai, the President of Hiwin, and a coterie of high-level assistants and managers. President Tsai had just been listed among *Forbes*'s "50 Power Businesswomen in Asia," the only woman in Taiwan so honored.[4] Poised and in charge, President Tsai takes care of the merchandising and marketing for Hiwin. Eric Chuo, the founder and current Chairman of Hiwin, oversees the research and development and the overall operations of the factory.

This division of labor between Tsai and Chuo was established shortly after Hiwin started operations in 1989. After thoroughly investigating where new opportunities might exist in Taiwan's growing economy in the 1980s, Chairman Chuo bought a failing company making ball screws. Without any manufacturing experience, he learned everything he could about the machine tool industry in general and his niche in particular. Attending up to 200 trade shows a year, and listening closely to potential customers, Chuo and Tsai gradually began receiving orders for a range of machine tools. President Tsai described their business as demand driven: "50 percent of our ideas come from our customers. We run a service industry. We make new things all the time, things we design to fit into what the customers need to make the products that they sell." Making a wide range of products, everything from precision tools for semiconductor factories to robots for hospitals, Hiwin has grown into one of the most successful companies of its kind, a global business with R&D centers in Germany, Japan, and the United States, as well as Taiwan, and 150 distributors around the world. In Hiwin's showroom, we watched some of these machines in motion, and were amazed at what could be done by applying high technology to the timeless physics of simple machines: the lever, the screw, the inclined plane. Robotics, the mechanical mastery of small motions, forecasts a future (and even a present) when human labor in manufacturing will be, for better or worse, reduced to a minimum.

North across the road from Tunghai University is the Taichung Science Park. In contrast to the Taichung Industrial Park, which has 1037 firms,[5] the Science Park, although it covers a tract of land several times larger than the space Taichung Industrial Park occupies, contains fewer than 105 firms.[6] However, they are all large firms. TSMC has one large semiconductor foundry there, and is now building a second one. Corning has a factory there, which supplies glass to two large plants next door owned by AU Optronics, a company that makes thin-film transistor liquid crystal display panels, LCD screens that range in size from the ones used in smartphones to 65-inch television screens. AU Optronics is supposedly a supplier for many brand-name consumer electronics merchandisers, including Asus, Apple, LG, and Acer. Winbond Electronics has a DRAM factory there as well. Unlike Taichung Industrial Park, which is filled with independent businesses doing different things, Taichung Science Park has firms that are parts of interfirm clusters in overlapping supply chains.

One example of this is the supply chain for Vizio, one of the best-selling brands of flat screen LCD televisions in the United States. William Wang established Vizio in 2002, with 600,000 US$ raised from his family and friends, as well as from a mortgage on his house, to produce plasma and LCD televisions priced at around 4000 US$, far below his competitors' prices of 10,000 US$ or more.[7] Vizio's first and still one of its best big buyers is Costco, but Sam's Club and Best Buy are also key retailers. Wang credits their support for his success. Headquartered in southern California, Vizio started with only three employees. Within a few years, with very little advertising, Vizio became the largest selling LCD television in the United States. In 2012, Vizio still had only 417 employees, more than half of whom provided tech support from a call center in South Dakota. Big-buyer contracts in hand, CEO Wang relied almost entirely on Taiwanese contract manufacturers to design the televisions, organize a supply chain, and assemble and ship the televisions to US markets. To arrange the supply chain, Wang contacted former colleagues, Alpha Wu and Frank Wu, who had established a firm, AmTRAN Technology, that built televisions on contract. William Wang offered the Wu brothers a sizable stake in Vizio.

Wang and the Wu brothers started their collaboration just at the moment when televisions were starting to switch from analog to digital formats.[8] This switch allowed AmTRAN to take advantage of the clusters of firms making computers and computer parts. The supply chain that AmTRAN developed for Vizio includes Corning and AU Optronics, plus seventy other suppliers. Fifty-four (76 percent) of those suppliers are Taiwanese. In addition, fourteen Japanese and two South Korean firms are also part of Vizio's supply chain; all of these businesses have factories in Taiwan, and five of them have factories in Taichung Science Park. Although a large part of the supply chain thus resides in Taiwan, much of the assembly work is done in a plant near Suzhou, which is a joint venture between AmTRAN and LG, the South Korean *chaebol*. Most LG televisions are also assembled there.

Many other suppliers for Vizio are located in or near the Hsinchu Science Park. This park has continued to expand, now occupying six different areas in the vicinity and experiencing increasing numbers of firms and rising total sales.[9] The area just outside Taichung's industrial and science parks is filled with many businesses, large and small, as is the area to the north between Taipei and Hsinchu and to the south between Kaohsiung and Tainan. However, the pattern is consistent. High-end, capital intensive manufacturing is still done in Taiwan. Research and development is still done in Taiwan. Headquarters of companies are still located in Taiwan. However, much of the actual manufacturing, especially for the labor-intensive portions of assembly, has moved outside Taiwan. In one way or another, nearly every industry with which Taiwanese manufacturers are associated has consolidated on a global scale. With consolidation, just a few interfirm clusters in just a few locations can now produce and assemble enough components for enough televisions or smartphones or shoes, or whatever, to supply the world's population with that product.

As a consequence, Taiwan's wealthiest people are better off than ever; they have high-paying jobs in, or large holdings of stocks in, those companies that have succeeded. But those jobs that were once middle-income factory jobs are in the process of disappearing. For both men and women, factory work at which one can make a living wage or niches where the *laoban* of small, family-owned businesses can manufacture parts for a local satellite assembly system have become fewer and fewer. In place of these opportunities, young people now regularly obtain a level of education that was rare during the boom years before 1985. There are so many universities and colleges in Taiwan that these institutions must compete for students, and the numbers of young people obtaining higher degrees are going up much faster than the numbers of jobs open to these graduates are. The new reality of limited opportunities does not match the level of aspirations that education bestows.

Partly for these reasons, a new political awareness has set in, an awareness of a discord between Taiwan's political economy, on the one hand, and Taiwanese participation in global capitalism, on the other hand. People experience a Taiwanese economy that is no longer growing and that may be in the early stages of economic stagnation similar to what the Japanese have experienced for the last twenty-five years. People witness Taiwanese businesses moving out of Taiwan, to China and beyond, and see in those moves missed opportunities for themselves and for their children. They feel the mood swing from a welcome to a warning that Taiwanese should not rush headlong into China's embrace.

In China

The warning is real enough. In the past decade, Taiwanese manufacturers in China have been caught between changing retail landscapes for big buyers and changing conditions for manufacturing in China. For retailers and merchandisers, the competition in their home markets is no longer local. Rather, it is now truly global. Sitting in front of their computers or staring into their smartphones, consumers can see the prices for and can assess the quality of products that they have never physically seen or touched. The new demand-led reality in retailing is changing the ways people shop, the ways goods are sold, and the ways goods are manufactured. Shoppers' comparative pricing has ratcheted up retail competition to new levels. The competitive intensity has added incentives for retailers and merchandisers to find price points for the goods they sell where they can still earn a profit and stay in business. Big buyers, in turn, pressure their contract manufacturers to keep supplier prices low, even if that means requesting that their contract manufacturers move again to find new locations for their factories that have cheaper production costs in land and labor.

For Taiwanese manufacturers in China during the past decade, wages for workers have been rising steadily, the price of leasing land has skyrocketed, and the tax incentives have disappeared. Even worse, however, has been the changing relationship between Taiwanese manufacturers and the Chinese with whom they work. In our interviews, Taiwanese businesspeople uniformly expressed concern about having their manufacturing base in China. For fear of reprisals, they have all asked us not to identify them or their firms by name, but clearly their concern has grown, for some of them to the point of leaving China for other locations.

One person we interviewed in 2016 told us that Taiwanese firms in China now have to proceed very carefully. "Contracts in China mean nothing; they are even useless in court cases. . . . The government can change the rules at any time. . . . So things are very difficult for Taiwanese businesspeople in China. Chinese people are so oriented to their own benefit that they neglect the feeling of working with others. For Taiwanese people, we value good relationships, and look for harmony." However, in response to the question, "Then why not leave China?," this person replied, "My guess is that [our firm in a high technology cluster] will remain in China for another ten years . . . [even though] the labor costs are increasing. The supply chain is in China now and, most importantly, we speak the same language, which makes things easier. . . . The organization [of the industry] has been established, which makes moving to other places more difficult." Another person, the son of the owner of a firm supplying a component for other high technology firms, said simply, "We want to go back to Taiwan, but our clients are still here, and so we have to stay too."

A number of Taiwanese owners and managers of firms in China told us that even in China, the Taiwanese manufacturers still have some advantages that will not quickly go away. Repeating a comment that we had heard numerous times before, one person said, "Taiwanese businesspeople are better with global buyers. To be more specific, they trust us. When we develop products relating to security or health, buyers worldwide . . . trust us. Chinese, however, are not trusted by foreign buyers. Though they say 'no problem' to everything, buyers always think they are exaggerating or boasting." This lack of trust extends especially to the use of any type of personal data. In China, government policy is to scrutinize all internet traffic, and therefore, because "all products [made by Chinese manufacturers] must be consistent with government policies," there is a fear among many that systems designed by Chinese manufacturers will compromise the personal data of users.

These cautionary words apply especially to smartphones, an industry that the Chinese government is cultivating with particular vigor, but they also apply more broadly. One manufacturer told us that he is now building new factories outside China. He used to have a large factory in Kunshan, but in 2014, an explosion occurred in a factory making automobile parts, causing the death of 146 people.[10] The central government disciplined a large number of local government officials for failing to prevent the explosion. Ever since that incident, the rules about environmental protection have become very strict. The manufacturer's company was asked to improve its safety, and the company did so at considerable expense. However, he reported:

> No government official came to check us after we reported that we have finished the required changes. No matter how hard we complained or tried to negotiate, nothing happened. We want to follow the rules and laws, but they are too changeable, too hard to anticipate.... To be honest, we have lost a large amount of money in the Shanghai area for OEM and branded products. It was not until last year that we decided to withdraw from Kunshan and to move our factories to Shenzhen.... It is hard in China. The society is managed by people, but not by laws.

Taiwanese manufacturers in China universally recognize that it has become harder and harder to make money, given the changing conditions in China. However, this realization influences people in different industries in different ways. The clusters of firms in the high technology industries are so complex and capital intensive that the clusters are hard to move, even in the face of the advancing red line, the all Chinese-owned supply chain for smartphones and potentially for computers as well.

Acknowledging both the rootedness and the changing composition of supply chains, TSMC signed an agreement on March 28, 2016, with the local government in Nanjing to build a wholly owned foundry in the Pukou Economic Development Zone, which is in the vicinity of the overlapping notebook and smartphone clusters in the greater Shanghai region. In announcing the agreement, CEO Morris Chang said: "With our 12-inch fab and our design service center in Nanjing, we aim to provide closer support to customers as well as expand our business opportunities in China in step with the rapid growth of the Chinese semiconductor market over the last several years. We look forward to stronger collaboration with our customers to further expand our market share in China." According to the same announcement, TSMC currently holds "the largest foundry market segment share in China with more than 100 Chinese customers."[11]

Although high-tech clusters do not move easily, the same is not true for other industries. Although they still maintain factories in China, the clusters of firms making shoes are now centered in Vietnam. Taiwanese bicycle manufacturers are also moving some of their production out of China, also to Vietnam. In China, the Taiwanese are now facing price competition from Chinese bicycle manufacturers. One Taiwanese manufacturer told us that Chinese companies are "partly run by the government and when the government is involved, it is hard to judge by common sense." The key reason for Taiwanese manufacturers moving out of China, though, has to do with the new demand-led reality in retailing. In the words of the same Taiwanese manufacturer:

> For branded bike companies, like Giant and Merida, things are tough in China. . . . Basically, it is related to the growth of e-commerce. For the same product, you could find it on line with the price only half of that in bike shops. The traditional way of marketing, starting from wholesalers, dealers, retailers, and shops, is not working anymore. Now Giant, the role model in the bike industry, and Merida have to survive by trying to decrease the cost; they once used parts only made by Taiwanese manufacturers but now they are open to all part makers in China as long as they are cheaper. Generally speaking, the advantages we used to enjoy in China do not exist anymore for the bike industry as a whole.

Therefore, the cluster of bicycle assemblers and parts suppliers is starting to move where its firms can remain competitive.

In Vietnam

Between 1988 and 2014, Taiwanese firms invested over US$ 27 billion to establish firms in Vietnam. These investments were made in eleven different Vietnamese provinces, mostly in the south with Dong Nai, Ho Chi Ming City, and Binh Duong administrative units having the most direct foreign investments. Many different industries are now represented among the Taiwanese firms that have built factories in Vietnam.

Although Taiwanese footwear manufacturers still maintain a cluster of assemblers and parts suppliers in southern China, their primary manufacturing center is now in Vietnam.

Their movement from China to Vietnam was driven by a change of conditions in China. After nearly twenty years of manufacturing shoes in China, the Taiwanese shoe makers face problems similar to what they faced in Taiwan in the previous twenty years: a labor shortage and increasing costs in labor and land. Also, in Europe, antidumping laws against China forced some European merchandisers to ask their Taiwanese suppliers to move out of China. In looking for places to establish their factories, the Taiwanese manufacturers considered Indonesia, but most rejected sites there because they felt uncomfortable with Islam, the majority religion in Indonesia. They looked in other places as well, but settled on Vietnam, especially southern Vietnam where there were many overseas Chinese who had been living there for generations. Also, even though the languages are different, the Taiwanese and the Vietnamese still share a Confucian heritage, which makes the Taiwanese manufacturers somewhat more comfortable.

The Taiwanese initially split their assembly lines between those for low-end shoes, which were made in Vietnam, and those for high-end more expensive shoes, which they continued to make in China. Some of this division of labor still exists today. However, as Kao learned from a recent trip to their shoe factories in Vietnam, the Vietnamese factories have continually expanded production at the expense of the factories in China. Even after the 2014 anti-Chinese riots in Vietnam, during which many of the Taiwanese shoe factories were burned to the ground, the Taiwanese owners not only rebuilt their factories, but also expanded them. Despite the losses, not a single manufacturer left the country.[12]

More importantly, the footwear business for Taiwanese manufacturers is booming now because of the limited number of high-quality footwear manufacturers and the mutual trust that has been created over the years between the big buyers and the Taiwanese. Taiwanese manufacturers now design the shoes with their buyers, and they can even bargain with their buyers at some points. In interviews, they told Kao that they now "have more autonomy and more respect" than they had previously.

But in capitalism, conditions always change. Here is the calculation of the chairman of one of the leading footwear assemblers:

> When the cost of labor is over 25% of the total cost of production, then there would be no chance of making money.... Right now, we are ok in Vietnam

but we do not expect more for the future. After the French colonization, Vietnamese showed something weird. They learned something from Western societies, but didn't learn it well. For instance, they have unions and they protest sometimes. However, they don't fully realize how unions work in Western societies. They initiate protests without thinking seriously what they really want. For instance, in our factory, the dining package was good enough so that many people joined it. They still complained but didn't say what they wanted. It was hard to communicate or negotiate with them. It was really a big challenge for us, the same when talking with the government. But I think they basically welcome us because they hope to be rich.

Formosa Plastics found out how real these protests can be. To supply various industries in Vietnam, Formosa Plastics built a steel mill in Ha Tinh Province in north central Vietnam. In April and May 2016, after fishermen along the coast near the plant found huge numbers of dead fish along a 200-kilometer shoreline (estimated later at seventy tons of dead fish), people throughout Vietnam staged protests. After an extensive investigation, scientists concluded that industrial waste from the steel mill was the cause, which representatives of Formosa Plastics reluctantly admitted. The company will pay 500 million US$ in fines to help restore the coastline and provide compensations to fishermen who have lost their livelihood. However, the Vietnamese government gave permission for the construction of the new steel mill to continue.[13]

Despite the Vietnamese government's support for capitalist endeavors, Taiwanese manufacturers know the cost of production in Vietnam is going up. The chairman of a bicycle company told us that he is building a new factory in Pin Yang, in Bình Dương Province, where more than 1600 Taiwanese companies now have factories. He told us that before he committed to siting the factory in Pin Yang, he had "spent four months examining the environment there, basically visiting one province every month. The price of land kept increasing. The price we got is around three times more expensive than it was three months ago. And after another three months, the land price has increased another 25 percent." We asked the reasoning behind his decision to build a factory in Vietnam, despite the higher prices and despite the recent protests that caused many people to lose money. He replied, "We need another place where we could move to and stay if something wrong happened in China. Lives are really very, very hard for Taiwanese businesspeople right now. The investment environment as a whole is not beneficial to us anymore." He continued, "We guess, however, we can still work there for another five to eight years. In comparison with other places such as Indonesia, Philippines, Malaysia, or Cambodia, Vietnam is a better choice, though not perfect. In fact, the foreign direct investment in Vietnam has doubled in recent years. We are confident about the future, but dare not to expect too much."

Taiwanese footwear manufacturers have already started moving again. A number of them have built factories in Bangladesh, India, and Africa so that they can deliver low-cost shoes to their big buyers in America, Europe, as well as other areas around the world.

EPILOGUE

The Future of Demand-Led Capitalism

In a recently published book titled *The Rise and Fall of American Growth*, Robert Gordon argued that the most important innovations influencing the American economy occurred before World War II.[1] He singled out mass electrification, automobiles and mass transportation, indoor plumbing, refrigeration, telephones and mass communication, all of which were going concerns in the United States before World War II. The implication of the book, echoed by Paul Krugman, is that the American economy will never grow as fast or change as much as it did before World War II.[2] Going into the twenty-first century, Gordon and Krugman predict long periods of slow growth.

If we widen the frame of their observations to look at the world instead of just the American economy, then it is clear that the changes after World War II have been just as great as those before, and maybe even greater and in a shorter period of time. The United States has been integral to these changes. Before World War II, economic development and capitalism were intertwined, not the same, but still intimately connected. The companies driving industrialization in the century before that war were nation-based capitalist companies. For Great Britain, France, and Germany, nation-based companies often extended out into their respective colonies, but capitalism still remained largely a national affair, which colonial possessions helped sustain. Profit-seeking companies were usually circumscribed by the boundaries of the state, and only a few states had developed economies driven by such companies.

After 1945, the world economy changed from a capitalist few and an undeveloped many to a singular, ever-changing global economy. Some countries were more involved than others in this new global economy, but none was excluded. Capitalist acquisitiveness, empowered by technology, used consumption and the desire for goods to turn most of the world's population into consumers of one kind or another. In this new global economy, firms compete, countries do not, or at least not directly, not as they did in the first half of the twentieth century. Like the person who rides the tiger's back, countries today can ride capitalist trajectories, but these are hard to guide and harder still to dismount from. But following these trajectories does not lead to a "better" society, however better is defined. The contradictions between national welfare and capitalism are obvious, but the resolutions of the contradictions are not.

From an Asian vantage point in 2016, what we can say is that the world economy looks uncertain and unpredictable. When we began working on this book in the wake of the Asian financial crisis, around the time of the 9/11 attacks on the World Trade Center in New York in 2001, we had the same view, and so did the Taiwanese we interviewed. But shortly after that year, we recognized, as did they, that the Chinese economy was growing at an extraordinary rate and that a whole new era of capitalist expansion was beginning to open, with the center of manufacturing shifting to China. We did not know what to expect, even in the near term, and so we stopped writing and started watching. We resumed work on this book in 2010. After traveling to the World Trade Exposition in Shanghai in August of that year, we thought that Expo 2010 would be our concluding chapter. We would expound there on the theme of the recovery of the world economy from the Great Recession and the triumph of capitalism in China. However, we needed more interviews and did not write fast enough. The theme passed from view before we could use it, more a passing moment than a finale.

Unlike a book that needs a concluding chapter, the capitalist narrative in Asia has no easy or certain ending. We know that smartphones and computers cannot continue having a new cycle several times a year. Both smartphones and computers are becoming commodities that are valued more for their utility than their novelty, and the manufacture of both will be subject to lower prices and thinner margins. And so, we ask, what is the next big thing, that thing that will drive global capitalism forward?

Early in 2016, we asked Asus's Vice President Hsieh to reflect on the future of Asus. He wasn't sure. High technology industries are changing. He mused, "First we started in PCs, then in mobile phones, and now we're moving into cloud computing. I think we can do IOT [the Internet of Things], artificial intelligence, and maybe big data." He continued, "Whatever we do, we have to avoid labor-intensive businesses and cheap products.... We cannot compete with the Chinese." We asked him about the future of Taiwan. He was even less sure. "For the IT business from a national perspective, maybe we need somebody like K. T. Li, who had the vision for the future and was able to lead us to innovations. People in my generation were lucky, but how about the next generation? Maybe we should be like Korea; they have succeeded in the entertaining and gaming businesses, and are now enjoying considerable prosperity. We [the Taiwanese] really need a new mindset to find something which is suitable for Taiwan." The Taiwanese economy, more so than Taiwanese industrialists, has reached a point where the next big thing is not apparent.

Despite Vice President Hsieh's approving nod toward South Korea, the economic future there teeters on edge of a cliff. Unlike the Taiwanese economy, which is spread among firms of all sizes, the South Korean economy is skewed more than ever toward the top few *chaebol*. The economy rests heavily on the exports of these business groups. The total sales for Samsung, the largest *chaebol*, represent nearly 22 percent of South Korea's GDP. Samsung's role in the Korean economy is certainly very large, but when combined with the sales of the top ten *chaebol*, the total contribution to the national economy is huge. According to chaebol.com, an online financial data company, "the combined sales of the top 10 groups was 53.4 percent of the nation's gross domestic product in 2002 and 63.8 percent in 2008. In 2011, the proportion reached 76.5%."[3] The level of inequality in South Korea is high and rising, so much so that a global recession would have devastating effects on welfare of the entire society, and even a misstep by one of the large *chaebol*, such as the manufacturing flaw in Samsung's Galaxy Note 7 smartphone, has outsized consequences for the entire South Korean economy.

The Japanese economy, too, remains tentative, poised for decades on the runway with little chance of taking off any time soon. A substantial number of Japanese companies have been hugely successful in the global economy. Toyota, Honda, Nissan, and Subaru are global leaders, as are Canon, Nikon, and Fuji. Just as importantly, many of the upstream firms in the horizontal *keiretsu* are world-leading suppliers of primary and secondary components that go into final products made elsewhere. Many of these firms have production sites outside Japan, and so do not provide jobs for the working population that, with a declining birthrate, has gotten older and older. The aging population and the rising inequality between income groups have combined to keep consumption below what is needed to grow the economy.

Japanese, South Korean, and Taiwanese companies all looked to China as their source of salvation. Many of the owners and managers of these companies had hoped that China's one billion–plus consumers would buy what they were selling. That hope has seldom turned into reality, though, or if it did, then not for long. In the 1930s, Carl Crow, an American businessman in Shanghai selling American products to the Chinese, bemoaned the fact that "as soon as some foreign product which is easily manufactured builds up a good business in China, one or more Chinese manufacturers produce a product with packages and brands names which are similar." He illustrated this propensity with a story about selling hair cream. His agency had found a "sticky pomade" that developed a good sale, but as soon as the product was established on the market, "an average of one or more new imitations appeared every month. We finally began collecting them, like new issues of postage stamps. At one time we had twenty-one varieties."[4] The situation has not changed much even today; competition from Chinese manufacturers is fierce and imitative and usually successful in driving the price and the quality of products down. Foreign companies hoping to find their salvation in China may find it in a life hereafter, as did RCA and Schwinn and other companies, once so invincible, that ended up in a holding company's portfolio of brand names.

The question about China is, of course, will the policies driving internal economic development be enough to sustain a domestic capitalist economy of the sort that China is trying to develop.[5] China's economy is indeed huge and diverse, so that no genuine assessment is simple and short. However, withdrawing from the world economy at this point in time is not possible. The Chinese economy is so reliant on exports and inward foreign direct investment that any attempt to reduce those activities substantially will surely result in a decline, if not a collapse in the economy. However, the reverse course, for Chinese companies to compete with non-Chinese firms in the global capitalist pursuit of profits, is also risky. As Taiwanese industrialists have told us, the Chinese firms have to earn the trust of their buyers and have to be open to what have become global standards of doing business. Right now, the Chinese government restricts the free flow of capital and information. Many websites, including Google, Facebook, and most non-Chinese sources of news (such as the *New York Times*), are inaccessible in China.

Moreover, the steps taken by the Chinese government to privilege Chinese-owned firms and to develop China's own domestic capitalism are not an isolated trend. Other nations are now following suit. Economic nationalism is more alive in 2016 than it has been for generations. The Reagan policies that led to the Plaza Accord in 1985 were more about how to integrate the global economy around the most advanced capitalist economies than they were about closing the US economy off from other nations. Although many issues led to the "Brexit" vote in 2016, including the decline of manufacturing jobs, the effects of Great Britain's withdrawal from the European Union will certainly erect barriers to the free flow of capital, goods, and labor within Europe and probably beyond. Other European countries may follow Britain's lead, and thus the future of the European Union is another unknown. Just as ominously, the unexpected victory of Donald Trump in the 2016 US presidential election was partially fueled by the desire of many Americans to return the United States to its industrial past. Trump promised to restrict trade from China and Mexico and to bring manufacturing jobs back to the United States. As 2016 ended, the potential of global trade wars and the consequences thereof has made the future of global capitalism and of national development in the United States and elsewhere seem uncertain and unpredictable.

All this concluding speculation can be easily overturned. We should not project current trends into the future, especially when these trends seem to be turning yet again. However, those counting on a less global and more domestically focused capitalism cannot see into the cloudiness of the future either.

The analysis in this book suggests several trends that will certainly continue. The co-evolution of Western retailers and merchandisers and Asian manufacturers has shaped the global economy in the post–World War II era. This economy is demand led. The ubiquity of smartphones and computers only intensifies this trend. Continuing advances in information technology have allowed internet retailers and merchandisers to become the new intermediaries between manufacturers and consumers. Amazon and Alibaba, along with hundreds of other smaller but similar firms, are quickly changing the way people shop. The global marketplace presented through these online portals will certainly open niches for manufacturing new products and for manufacturing some current products in new ways. The variety of fashionable products will likely grow along with the variegation and diffusion of lifestyles, but the manufacture of these products in short product cycles and small batches will only increase, as will contract manufacturing. The growing dominance of online retailing will almost certainly lead to another restructuring of global retailing sectors, leading to the demise of some large, high-overhead, big-box retailers. Stock market analysts now watch former market leaders—Sears, Kmart (owned by Sears Holding Corporation), and Macy's—edge toward bankruptcy. As these retailers close some or all of their stores, service sector jobs will also decline, perhaps even drastically. These job losses will further exacerbate income inequality in the United States and elsewhere, because the very people who previously lost their manufacturing jobs will now be in danger of losing more recent service sector jobs, too. Every collapsing retailer and every economic decline turns consumers toward cheaper sources of the goods that they deem necessary for their lifestyles, which will lead to yet more buying through online retailers. The feedback loop between retailers and customers can be a vicious cycle.

Gordon and Krugman may be correct. A period of global economic stagnation may be in front of us. However, in trying to look forward into the twenty-first century, we are reminded that what Fernand Braudel wrote, in the concluding section of his three-volume study looking back at the history of capitalism from the fifteenth to eighteenth centuries, applies equally well today. Capitalism "is often ill but it never dies."[6]

NOTES

INTRODUCTION

1. Gary G. Hamilton and Cheng-shu Kao, "Max Weber and the Analysis of East Asian Industrialization," *International Sociology* 2 (1987): 289–300.

2. Lee Se, "Cheng-Shu Kao and His Thirteen Brothers," *Tianxia* (Commonwealth) 130 (1992): 84–89.

3. After moving to the University of Washington in 1993, Hamilton continued to collaborate with his colleagues at UC Davis.

4. Internal Revenue Code of 1954, section 167(a). Quoted from Thomas W. Hanchett, "U.S. Tax Policy and the Shopping-Center Boom of the 1950s and 1960s," *American Historical Review* 101, no. 4 (1996): 1094.

5. Ibid. A major shopping center is defined as one having a size of 300,000 square feet or more.

6. This term was first used by Gary Gereffi in his seminal chapter "The Organization of Buyer-Driven Global Commodity Chains: How U.S. Retailers Shape Overseas Production Networks," in *Commodity Chains and Global Capitalism*, ed. Gary Gereffi and Miguel Korzeniewicz, 95–122 (Westport, Conn.: Praeger, 1994). The term is particularly apt because it emphasizes intermediary demand created by retailers and merchandisers, who purchase the items they wish to sell. Intermediary demand creates markets among suppliers competing to sell goods to the big buyers. We call these *supplier markets*, in contrast to the markets among the retailers and merchandisers selling goods to final consumers, which we term *consumer markets*.

7. The following list (compiled from Ministry of Commerce of the People's Republic of China, *Top 500 Ranking of Chinese Enterprises of Import and Export in 2012*, June 19, 2013, http://tjxh.mofcom.gov.cn/article/n/201306/20130600167637.shtml) shows the ten Taiwanese companies among the top twenty exporters from China in 2013, and their relative rank:

No. 1. Foxconn Technology Group, Shenzhen (subsidiary of Hon Hai Precision Ind. Co., Ltd.)
No. 2. Tech-Front (Shanghai) Computer Co., Ltd. (subsidiary of Quanta Computer Inc.)
No. 3. Hongfujin Precision Electronics (Zhengzhou) Co., Ltd. (subsidiary of Hon Hai Precision Ind. Co., Ltd.)

No. 4. Pegatron Corporation (Shanghai) (subsidiary of ASUSTeK Computer Inc.)
No. 6. Hongfujin Precision Electronics (Chengdu) Co., Ltd. (subsidiary of Hon Hai Precision Ind. Co., Ltd.)
No. 9. Hongfujin Precision Electronics (Yantai) Co., Ltd. (subsidiary of Hon Hai Precision Ind. Co., Ltd.)
No. 10. Maintek Computer (Suzhou) Co., Ltd. (subsidiary of ASUSTeK Computer Inc.)
No. 11. Tech-Front (Chongqing) Computer Co., Ltd. (subsidiary of Quanta Computer Inc.)
No. 19. Compal Information (Kunshan) Co., Ltd. (subsidiary of Compal Electronics, Inc.)
No. 20. Compal Electronics Technology (Kunshan) Co., Ltd. (subsidiary of Compal Electronics, Inc.

8. "The MMI Top 50 EMS Providers in 2013," *Manufacturing Market Insider* 24, no. 3 (2014), http://mfgmkt.com/mmi-top-50.html

9. *ETtoday News*, June 19, 2013, http://www.ettoday.net/news/20140421/348682.htm, in Chinese.

10. Ministry of Commerce of the People's Republic of China, "Trade and Investment in Mainland China and Taiwan from January to April 2014," June 4, 2013, http://www.mofcom.gov.cn/article/tongjiziliao/fuwzn/diaoca/201406/20140600612561.shtml.

11. Robert C. Feenstra and Gary G. Hamilton, *Emergent Economies, Divergent Paths: Economic Organization and International Trade in South Korea and Taiwan*, Structural Analysis in the Social Sciences: 29 (New York: Cambridge University Press, 2006), 240–49.

12. These databases figure prominently in the following: ibid.; Gary G. Hamilton, *Commerce and Capitalism in Chinese Societies* (London: Routledge, 2006); Marco Orrú, Nicole Woolsey Biggart, and Gary G. Hamilton, *The Economic Organization of East Asian Capitalism* (Thousand Oaks, Calif.: Sage, 1997).

13. Tibor Scitovsky, "Economic Development in Taiwan and Korea, 1965–81," in *Models of Development: A Comparative Study of Economic Growth in South Korea and Taiwan*, ed. Lawrence J. Lau, 127–82 (San Francisco, Calif.: ICS Press, 1990).

14. Howard Becker, "The Power of Inertia," *Qualitative Sociology* 18, no. 3 (1995): 301–09.

15. Max Weber, "Prefatory Remarks to *Collected Essays in the Sociology of Religion*," in *The Protestant Ethic and the "Spirit" of Capitalism and Other Writings*, ed. Peter Baehr and Gordon C. Wells (New York: Penguin Books, 2002 [1920]), 359.

CHAPTER 1

1. In 2014, in recognition of a new bus transit system, the Taichung City government officially changed the name of Taichung Harbor Road to Taiwan Boulevard. The locals still refer to the road as Harbor Road.

2. Construction of the Port of Taichung Harbor started in 1969, and the port officially commenced operation in 1976. In 2013, the traffic to and from China constituted over 27% of both the imports and exports from the port. Hong Kong is the second most common source and destination, with 14% of the imports and over 19% of the

exports. The main items exported to China are plastic goods (26.61%) and metal goods (22.78%). Both of types of goods are primarily intermediate inputs for products that will later be exported from China. See Port of Taichung, Taiwan International Ports Corporations Ltd., *2014 Annual Statistical Report of the Port of Taichung Harbor*, http://tc.twport.com.tw/en/cp.aspx?n=3157F8B1AF143094, 6/22/2014. The data are from the Excel file attached to the report.

3. Based on data updated in 2015: Taichung Industrial Park Service Center, http://www.moeaidb.gov.tw/iphw/taichung/, accessed September 24, 2016.

4. See David Hackett Fischer, *Historians' Fallacies: Toward a Logic of Historical Thought* (New York: Harper & Row, 1970).

5. *Annual Report on Taiwan's Economy, 1965* (Taipei: Council for International Economic Cooperation and Development, 1966), 43–44, 59.

6. John F. Kennedy Presidential Library and Museum, "Chiang Ching-Kuo, Written Statement, 1964" (JFK #1, 1964), http://www.jfklibrary.org/Asset-Viewer/Archives/JFKOH-CCK-01.aspx.

7. For instance, Robert Wade, in what is arguably the best political economy analysis of state-led industrialization in Taiwan, makes this statement: "If parts of Taiwan's industry continued to be substantially protected during the 1970s to the mid-1980s, how then did manufactured exports grow so fast? A large part of the answer lies with export incentives. The export incentive schemes of the 1960s continued through the 1970s, but were slowly scaled back as foreign exchange reserves mounted." See *Governing the Market: Economic Theory and the Role of Government in East Asian Industrialization* (Princeton, N.J.: Princeton University Press, 1990), 139.

8. For Park's exhortations, see Alice H. Amsden, *Asia's Next Giant: South Korea and Late Industrialization* (New York: Oxford University Press, 1989), 64–70. Like Taiwan, South Korea needed foreign exchange to maintain its huge standing army ready to defend South Korea from its North Korean enemy, whose border was only a few miles north of Seoul.

9. Shirley W. Y. Kuo, "Government Policy in the Taiwanese Development Process: The Past 50 Years," in *Taiwan's Development Experience: Lessons on Roles of Government and Market*, ed. Erik Thorbecke and Henry Y. Wan (Boston: Kluwer Academic, 1999), 60.

10. Ibid.

11. Dani Rodrik has also noted the absence of a jump in exports as a consequence of these government measures, in "Getting Interventions Right: How South Korea and Taiwan Grew Rich," *Economic Policy*, no. 20 (1995): 64–66. Also see the discussion in Chapter 5 of this volume on the change in exports before and after the mid-1960s.

12. K. T. (Guoding) Li, *The Evolution of Policy Behind Taiwan's Development Success*, ed. Gustav Ranis and John C. H. Fei (New Haven, Conn.: Yale University Press, 1988), 94.

13. Ibid., 97–99.

14. The Japanese had built electrical generation plants, railways, roads, petroleum refineries, and ports—all this in addition to the sugar and fertilizer plants. State theorists incorrectly conflate the basic infrastructure taken over by the KMT with the state's first step in industrialization. In addition, the KMT directly owned and tightly controlled

a number of businesses that operated in the public sphere. These businesses included important assets in the mass media, such as radio and TV stations and newspapers, all strategic holdings for manipulating public opinion.

15. Tsu-Tan Fu and Chun-yi Shei, "Agriculture as the Foundation for Development: The Taiwanese Story," in *Taiwan's Development Experience: Lessons on Roles of Government and Market*, ed. Erik Thorbecke and Henry Y. Wan, 207–30 (Boston: Kluwer Academic, 1999).

16. Samuel P. S. Ho, *Economic Development of Taiwan, 1860–1970* (New Haven, Conn.: Yale University Press, 1978), 147.

17. *Taiwan Statistical Data Book* (Taipei: Council for International Economic Cooperation and Development, 1994), 194.

18. Qiao Duan, *Determinants of Financial Savings in Taiwan Farmers' Associations, 1960 to 1970* (Nankang, Taiwan: Institute of Three Principles of the People, Academia Sinica, 1976), 15.

19. Ibid., 16.

20. Ibid., 21.

21. Erik Thorbecke and Henry Y. Wan, eds., *Taiwan's Development Experience: Lessons on Roles of Government and Market* (Boston: Kluwer Academic, 1999).

22. Fu and Shei, "Agriculture as the Foundation for Development."

23. Takao Taniura, "Management in Taiwan: The Case of the Formosa Plastics Group," *East Asian Cultural Studies* 28, no. 1–4 (1989): 72.

24. Ibid.

25. "Commanding heights" is a phrase used to characterize the role of state enterprises in Taiwan's development. See Wade, *Governing the Market*, 178. Also see Thomas B. Gold, *State and Society in the Taiwan Miracle* (Armonk, N.Y.: M. E. Sharpe, 1986), 75.

26. Ichiro Numazaki, "The Role of Personal Networks in the Making of Taiwan's Guanxiqiye (Related Enterprises)," in *Business Networks and Economic Development in East and Southeast Asia*, ed. Gary G. Hamilton (Hong Kong: Centre of Asian Studies, University of Hong Kong, 1991).

27. Feenstra and Hamilton, *Emergent Economies*, 279–80.

28. China (Republic), Zhu ji chu, *Zhonghua Min Guo Qi Shi Nian Tai Min Di Qu Gong Shang Ye Pu Cha Bao Gao* (Report on 1981 Industrial and Commercial Census Taiwan-Fukien Area, the Republic of China), 32 vols. (Taibei Shi: Xing zheng yuan, 1983), 220–23.

29. National Statistics: Republic of China (Taiwan), July 30, 2010, http://www.stat.gov.tw/ct.asp?xItem=14616&CtNode=3564&mp=4.

CHAPTER 2

1. Economists like to illustrate this abstractness with a curved, all-purpose graph indicating this shifting price-point equilibrium between supply and demand, assuming that all other things beside price are equal and that buyers are ready to substitute one good for another good if the price in any one good gets too high.

2. For a full description of the meaning of *market maker*, see Gary G. Hamilton,

Benjamin Senauer, and Misha Petrovic, *The Market Makers: How Retailers Are Reshaping the Global Economy* (Oxford: Oxford University Press, 2011).

3. Barry Bluestone et al., *The Retail Revolution: Market Transformation, Investment, and Labor in the Modern Department Store* (Boston: Auburn House, 1981). When Bluestone and his colleagues used the term *retail revolution* to describe the transformation in US retailing after World War II, they were referring to the growing dominance of three type of retailers: large department store chains, discount stores, and national retail holding companies. At the time of their research in the late 1970s, Sears and J. C. Penney were the two largest department store chains, Kmart the largest discount store, and Federated Department Stores the largest holding company.

4. The changes in the sector are nicely described by Bluestone et al., *Retail Revolution*, 1981.

5. For example, shopping centers have spread across the most affluent parts of Africa, where the local middle classes are spending more on a per capita basis on consumer goods than people are in other parts of the world (Nicholas Kulish, "Africans Open Fuller Wallets to the Future," *New York Times*, July 20, 2014, A-1).

6. The migration had started earlier, but picked up stream in the post-war years. See Neil Fligstein, *Going North: Migration of Blacks and Whites from the South, 1900–1950* (New York: Academic Press, 1981).

7. Both Sears and Montgomery Ward began business in the late 19th century as catalog stores, but after World War I, when rural populations began to decline and urban populations began to grow, both firms began to establish chain stores across the United States. For more detail, see Misha Petrovic, "U.S. Retailing and Its Global Diffusion," in *The Market Makers: How Retailers Are Reshaping the Global Economy*, ed. Gary G. Hamilton, Benjamin Senauer, and Misha Petrovic 79–116 (Oxford: Oxford University Press, 2011).

8. For more information on the Consumer Goods Pricing Act, H.R. 6971 (94th), see https://www.govtrack.us/congress/bills/94/hr6971.

9. One of the very first discounters, Toys "R" Us, started discount operations in 1957.

10. Some of these discount retailers started as specialty stores, and adopted big box retailing sometime after the original store opened. The store dates given in the following sentence are the dates discount retailing began.

11. As a rule of thumb, merchandised goods made by contract manufacturers outcompete those made by brand-name manufacturers. In computers, the success of Dell and Apple as merchandisers eventually forced Compaq and IBM to abandon manufacturing and instead to rely on contract manufacturing themselves.

12. In the case of Apple Computer, however, the alliance between Apple and its contract manufacturers has given Apple an advantage in new product introduction for the past two decades.

13. Feenstra and Hamilton, *Emergent Economies*, 230.

14. Marc Levinson, *The Box: How the Shipping Container Made the World Smaller and the World Economy Bigger* (Princeton, N.J.: Princeton University Press, 2006), 52.

15. Ibid., 149.

16. Most containers in use are forty feet long, and thus measure two TEUs. In 2008, Walmart alone accounted for one out of every twenty-four containers imported into the United States, or 720,000 TEUs ("Top 100 Importers in 2008," *Journal of Commerce* 10, no. 21 [2009]: 21A–28A).

17. Levinson, *The Box*, 183.

18. Ibid., 171–88.

19. Ibid., 188.

20. Ibid.

21. Ibid., 74.

22. Frederick H. Abernathy et al., *A Stitch in Time: Lean Retailing and the Transformation of Manufacturing—Lessons from the Apparel and Textile Industries* (New York: Oxford University Press, 1999), 52.

23. Computer History Museum, "Timeline of Computer History," http://www.computerhistory.org/timeline/computers/.

24. See Stephen A. Brown, *Revolution at the Checkout Counter* (Cambridge, Mass.: Harvard University Press, 1997). The Grocery Industry Ad Hoc Committee on Universal Product Coding was "manned by top executives of firms such as Heinz, General Mills, Bristol Myers, General Foods and retail executives from Kroger, A&P Tea Company, Wegman's, First National Stores, and Super Value Stores." These people represented "six grocery trade associations, one representing manufacturers and five representing retailers" (ibid., 5).

25. The ad hoc committee established the Uniform Code Council as an unbiased, nonprofit organization dedicated to allocating UPC numbers for products. For the story of the creation of the UPC, scanning devices, and barcodes, see Brown, *Revolution at the Checkout Counter*, 1997.

26. Quoted by Bob L. Martin, "From Vision to Reality," in *Twenty-Five Years Behind Bars: The Proceedings of the Twenty-Fifth Anniversary of the U.P.C. At the Smithsonian Institution, September 30, 1999*, ed. Alan L. Haberman (Cambridge, Mass.: Harvard University Press, 2002), 39. For a more detailed account of Walmart's use of information technology in fostering its rise to prominence, see Misha Petrovic and Gary G. Hamilton, "Making Global Markets: Wal-Mart and Its Suppliers," in *Wal-Mart: The Face of Twenty-First-Century Capitalism*, ed. Nelson Lichtenstein, 107–41 (New York: The New Press, 2006).

27. Edna Bonacich and David V. Waller, "The Role of US Apparel Manufacturers in the Globalization of the Industry in the Pacific Rim," in *Global Production: The Apparel Industry in the Pacific Rim*, ed. Edna Bonacich et al. (Philadelphia: Temple University Press, 1994), 81–82.

28. Ibid.

29. Siu-lun Wong, *Emigrant Entrepreneurs: Shanghai Industrialists in Hong Kong* (Hong Kong: Oxford University Press, 1988).

30. Lee C. Nehrt, Gano S. Evans, and Lamp Li, "Hong Kong Textiles, Ltd.," in *Managerial Policy, Strategy and Planning for Southeast Asia*, 273–81 (Hong Kong: Chinese University of Hong Kong, 1974).

31. Bulk cargo consists of items that cannot be split apart, such as oil or grains. Break-bulk cargo consists of individual items that can be separated, such as automobiles. Both types of cargo are loaded directly into the cargo holds designed for those products.

32. Nehrt, Evans, and Li, "Hong Kong Textiles, Ltd.," 278.

33. Kresge, "Annual Report" (Troy, Mich.: Kresge, 1969), 6. In 1976, Kresge officially changed its name to Kmart.

34. Gary Gereffi and Mei-lin Pan, "The Globalization of Taiwan's Garment Industry," in *Global Production: The Apparel Industry in the Pacific Rim*, ed. Edna Bonacich (Philadelphia: Temple University Press, 1994), 137.

35. Brian Levy, "Transactions Costs, the Size of Firms and Industrial Policy: Lessons from a Comparative Case Study of the Footwear Industry in Korea and Taiwan," *Journal of Development Economics* 34, no. 1 (1990): 151–78.

36. Feenstra and Hamilton, *Emergent Economies*, 238.

37. These databases can be found at the website for the National Bureau of Economic Research (http://www.nber.org/data/) and the website for the Center for International Data (http://www.robertfeenstra.info/data/).

38. Feenstra and Hamilton, *Emergent Economies*, 244–49.

39. W. Brian Arthur, Preface, in *Increasing Returns and Path Dependence in the Economy* (Ann Arbor: University of Michigan Press, 1994).

CHAPTER 3

An earlier version of this chapter appeared as Chapter 6 in Gary G. Hamilton, Benjamin Senauer, and Misha Petrovic, *The Market Makers: How Retailers Are Reshaping the Global Economy* (Oxford: Oxford University Press, 2011).

1. Chiang Ching-kuo had been active in the KMT government for some time before becoming president, serving first in a succession of positions and then in 1972 as prime minister. Whereas his father had politicized most aspects of government, making everything serve his political goal of returning to the Mainland, Chiang Ching-kuo tried to separate politics from administration. In 1972, he obtained a reputation of being above politics. In that year, in a show trial designed to "kill the chicken to scare the monkeys," Chiang Ching-kuo allowed his second cousin, via his father's mother's relatives, to be sentenced to life in prison for accepting a bribe from a businessman. In 1973, he made an appeal to the National Assembly that the Ten Great Construction Projects be completed in the next five years. Although some of these projects, such as the freeway, had been started, most others had not.

2. Samuel Ho was among the first to analyze the importance of small and medium-sized firms in Taiwan's industrialization, in "Economic Development and Rural Industry in South Korea and Taiwan," *World Development* 10, no. 11 (1982): 973–90. However, his first major work on the topic of Taiwan's industrialization, *Economic Development of Taiwan, 1860–1970*, makes no mention of the topic.

3. Customs data on Taiwan's exports to the United States in 1972 indicate that con-

sumer electronics, namely televisions and radios, accounted for nearly 50% of those exports.

4. During the decades after the American occupation of Japan ended, Japanese business groups grew at a pace much faster than Japan's rapidly growing economy. In addition to selling finished products, the general trading companies for the main business groups imported intermediate goods needed by firms within the group. However, in the 1960s, as the main *keiretsu* firms grew more proficient in securing their own inputs and marketing their own products, many in Japan began to worry that the trading companies would lose their central role. This decline in local business "led to a belief that the trading companies would gradually become less and less useful and would eventually die out, a belief popularized in the so-called 'demise theory.'" This belief prompted most trading companies to internationalize their operations. See Terutomo Ozawa and Kiyoshi Kojima, *Japan's General Trading Companies: Merchants of Economic Development* (Washington, D.C.: OECD, 1984), 13.

5. Ibid.

6. Feenstra and Hamilton, *Emergent Economies*, 262–64.

7. For example, see Gold, *State and Society in the Taiwan Miracle*, and also Wade, *Governing the Market*. Constance Lever-Tracy ("The Irrelevance of Japan," in *Chinese Business and the Asian Crisis*, ed. David Fu-Keung Ip, Noel Tracy, and Constance Lever-Tracy [Burlington, Vt.: Gower, 2000]) argues that Japanese trading companies had only a limited role in the development of East Asian economies outside Japan. However, her argument misses the important contribution that the Japanese trading companies made to creating competent suppliers in Taiwan and South Korea.

8. The Kuomintang government, however, did not help in this matter. It had banned speaking Japanese in public, a law that was in force after 1947. The Mainland migrants to Taiwan, of course, viewed the Japanese with dislike and distrust. After all, they had fought a war against Japan. Taiwanese residents, however, had not experienced World War II in the same way. Although they were not without hard feelings toward the former colonizers, local Taiwanese could deal with the Japanese without animosity.

9. These data are from "The Monthly Salary of Workers in Textile Factories of Taiwan, Japan, and the U.S.," in Chengpu Duan and Qinghai Han, *Taiwan Zhan Hou Jing Ji* (Taibei Shi: Ren jian chu ban she 台北市：人間出版社, 1992), ch. 7, tbl. 3.

10. Felicity Marsh, *Japanese Overseas Investment: The New Challenge* (London: Economist Intelligence Unit, 1983).

11. Duan and Han, *Taiwan Zhan Hou Jing Ji*, 236.

12. Alice H. Amsden and Wan-wen Chu, *Beyond Late Development: Taiwan's Upgrading Policies* (Cambridge, Mass.: MIT Press, 2003), 21.

13. Karl J. Fields, *Enterprise and the State in Korea and Taiwan* (Ithaca, N.Y.: Cornell University Press, 1995); Lawrence Olson, *Japan in Postwar Asia* (New York: Council on Foreign Relations/Praeger, 1970); and Wade, *Governing the Market*. Also see the discussion of this issue in Feenstra and Hamilton, *Emergent Economies*, 261–65.

14. "Taiwan Statistical Data Book," 1997, 194.

15. Gereffi and Pan, "Globalization of Taiwan's Garment Industry."

16. Feenstra and Hamilton, *Emergent Economies*, 242–50.

17. Among the top ten exports were two types of TVs, one type of radio, one type of integrated circuit for an unspecified final product, one type of Christmas tree lights, and one type of mahogany plywood, as well as three types of clothing (acrylic sweaters, knit shirts, and trousers made from synthetic material) and one category of footwear (vinyl shoes), all for women and girls. The consumer electronic products and clothing were likely made in factories wholly or partially owned by Americans or Japanese, but the other two products likely came from factories owned by Taiwanese.

18. For more detail on these product categories, see Feenstra and Hamilton, *Emergent Economies*, ch. 6.

19. It was not until 1990, however, that most multinational manufacturers had withdrawn from Taiwan. See the discussion in Amsden and Chu, *Beyond Late Development*, 19–28.

20. This number in itself is, of course, sizable, especially as compared to Korea in the same period (Feenstra and Hamilton, *Emergent Economies*, 268–72).

21. Lu-lin Cheng and Yukihito Sato, *The Bicycle Industries in Taiwan and Japan: A Preliminary Study Toward Comparison Between Taiwanese and Japanese Industrial Development*, Joint Research Program Series (Tokyo: Institute of Developing Economies, 1998), 8.

22. Ibid.

23. For more detail, see Chapter 8 in this volume.

24. It is almost certain that the Tsai brothers owned other shoe companies in the region. At the time, the general pattern was to own multiple companies and thereby to be a part of multiple networks, instead of creating one big firm to vertically integrate the operations.

25. Nike's agreement with Pou Chen came after Nike had made a near-disastrous attempt to contract production from Chinese firms in China. In the 1980s, Nike had located a manufacturer in China to make a large portion of its shoes, but the effort failed due to poor quality manufacturing and the lack of supporting suppliers. Nike returned its operation to Taiwan, and started to work with Pou Chen.

26. Among the most recent of the writers who say that Taiwan's mode of production is inferior to that of South Korea is Joe Studwell, *How Asia Works: Success and Failure in the World's Most Dynamic Region* (New York: Grove Press, 2014), 98–100.

CHAPTER 4

An earlier version of this chapter was published in Gary G. Hamilton and Kao Cheng-Shu, "The Round Table: A Reconsideration of Chinese Business Networks," in *Rethinking Hong Kong: New Paradigms*, ed. Elizabeth Sinn, Siu-lun Wong, and Wing-hoi Chan, 175–200 (Hong Kong: Centre of Asian Studies, University of Hong Kong, 2009).

1. See in particular Walter W. Powell, "Neither Market nor Hierarchy: Network Forms of Organization," *Research in Organizational Behavior* 12 (1990): 295–336. The growing use of the term *network* points to a shift in theory more than to a qualitative change in business practices. For *network* to be a useful term to describe economic

phenomena, there needed to be a move away from neoclassical economics both within and outside economics. Within economics, the most prominent movers were the "new institutionalists." Inspired by an early provocative essay by Nobel laureate Ronald Coase ("The Nature of the Firm," *Economica* 4, no. 16 [1937]), Oliver Williamson, also a Nobel Prize winner, among others, argued that market transactions are not costless, and that on many occasions entrepreneurs are economically better off internalizing some of the more costly market activities inside the firm, where they are subject to the entrepreneur's authority, rather than working through market transactions. This theoretical observation concerning the "agency" of economic actors led to Williamson's famous distinction between markets and hierarchies, a distinction that opened a wide theoretical space between authoritative actions within firms and impersonal, arm's-length transactions in the marketplace. See Oliver E. Williamson, *Markets and Hierarchies, Analysis and Antitrust Implications: A Study in the Economics of Internal Organization* (New York: Free Press, 1975). Williamson soon filled this space with a notion of hybrid firms, by which he meant various types of business networks. See his article, "Transaction Cost Economics and Organization Theory," in *Handbook of Economic Sociology*, ed. Neil Smelser and Richard Swedberg, 77–107 (Princeton, N.J.: Princeton University Press).

Williamson was encouraged to create a theoretical space for business networks by suggestions and critiques from sociologists, as well as from his fellow economists. One of the most spirited and influential critiques came from sociologist Mark Granovetter, who persuasively argued that market activities are founded on trust, and trust is "embedded" in social networks. Granovetter's observation came out of his association with a methodological/theoretical tradition known as *network theory*, and his critique of Williamson was his attempt to move networks into a theoretically central position in the analysis of economic activities. He wildly succeeded. His 1985 article, "Economic Action and Social Structure: The Problem of Embeddedness" (*American Journal of Sociology* 91, no. 3, 481–510), became the seminal document in the founding of the field of economic sociology. Suddenly, networks became the way for sociologists to analyze economies in a way that economists seemed unable to do. As Walter Powell argued, "network forms of organization" were "neither market nor hierarchy."

2. Katherine Faust and Stanley Wasserman, *Social Network Analysis: Methods and Applications* (New York: Cambridge University Press, 1994).

3. I think it is fair to say that we played a role in creating this linkage between sociological theory and the empirical reality of Chinese economic activities. We plead guilty, but in our own defense, we have always maintained that social relationships in modern Chinese society are diverse and complex, that a calculus of relationships forms the framework for social action in Chinese societies, and that these diverse and changing relationships should be understood in a historical, comparative context. See Gary Hamilton and Kao Cheng-Shu, "The Institutional Foundations of Chinese Business: The Family Firm in Taiwan," *Comparative Social Research* 12 (1990): 135–51; Gary G. Hamilton and Nicole Woolsey Biggart, "Market, Culture, and Authority: A Comparative Analysis of Management and Organization in the Far East," *American Journal of Sociology* 94, no.

S1 (1988): S52; and Cheng-shu Kao, "Personal Trust in the Large Businesses in Taiwan: A Traditional Foundation for Contemporary Economic Activities," in *Business Networks and Economic Development in East and Southeast Asia*, ed. Gary G. Hamilton (Hong Kong: Centre of Asian Studies, University of Hong Kong, 1991).

4. Hamilton, *Business Networks*; Nicole Biggart and Gary G. Hamilton, "On the Limits of a Firm-Based Theory to Explain Business Networks: The Western Bias of Neoclassical Economics," in *Networks and Organizations: Structure, Form, and Action*, ed. Nitin Nohria and Robert G. Eccles, 471–90 (Boston: Harvard Business School Press, 1992).

5. For this comparison see Fei Xiaotong, *From the Soil, the Foundations of Chinese Society: A Translation of Fei Xiaotong's Xiangtu Zhongguo, with an Introduction and Epilogue*, trans. Gary G. Hamilton and Wang Zheng (Berkeley: University of California Press, 1992), ch. 4.

6. Ibid.

7. Max Weber, *Economy and Society* (Berkeley: University of California Press, 1978), 67.

8. Kao Cheng-shu, *Toujia Niang (the Boss's Wife)* (Taipei: Lien Chin, 1999).

9. However, with the economic slowdown and rising unemployment that occurred in the 1990s, independent entrepreneurial opportunities declined, employment stabilized, and firms consolidated their economic position and grew larger accordingly.

10. Although we have no special knowledge about the origin and longevity of the round table in Chinese societies, we do know that the Asian neighbors of the Chinese, the Japanese and the Koreans, do not prefer round tables and normally eat at rectangular ones, as do most Europeans and Americans. The round-table etiquette of Chinese societies is probably not unique, but it is certainly distinctive and speaks to a mode of everyday interaction that provides a social underpinning to many institutionalized forms of activity, including economic activity.

11. Gary G. Hamilton and Wei-an Chang, "The Influence of Commercial Organization on Commodity Production: Cotton Textiles in 19th and Early 20th Century China," in *The Resurgence of East Asia: 500, 150 and 50 Year Perspectives*, ed. Giovanni Arrighi, Takeshi Hamashita, and Mark Selden, 173–213 (London: Routledge, 2003).

12. Gary G. Hamilton, "Why No Capitalism in China? Negative Questions in Historical, Comparative Research," *Journal of Developing Societies* 1, no. 2 (1985): 187–211. See also Hamilton, *Commerce and Capitalism in Chinese Societies*.

13. Wai-keung Chung, "The Emergence of Corporate Forms in China, 1872–1949: An Analysis on Institutional Transformation" (PhD thesis, University of Washington, 2004); W. K. Chung and G. G. Hamilton, "Getting Rich and Staying Connected: The Organizational Medium of Chinese Capitalists," *Journal of Contemporary China* 18, no. 58 (2009): 47–67.

CHAPTER 5

1. Tyler S. Biggs, "Financing the Emergence of Small and Medium Enterprise in Taiwan: Heterogeneous Firm Size and Efficient Intermediation," EEPA Discussion Paper (Washington, D.C.: Employment and Enterprise Policy Analysis Project, 1988). Also see Scitovsky, "Economic Development in Taiwan and Korea."

2. See Alfred D. Chandler, *Scale and Scope: The Dynamics of Industrial Capitalism* (Cambridge, Mass.: Belknap Press, 1990) for a general analysis of this phenomenon, and Amsden, *Asia's Next Giant*, for an application to Asia.

3. Cecilia Chang, "Everyone Wants to Be the 'Boss,'" *Free China Review* 38, no. 11 (1988): 10–13.

4. Ibid.

5. Hui-lin Wu, "A Future for Small & Medium Enterprises?," *Free China Review* 38, no. 11 (1988): 6–9.

6. Tyler S. Biggs, "Financing the Emergence of Small and Medium Enterprises in Taiwan: Financial Mobilization and the Flow of Domestic Credit to the Private Sector," EEPA Discussion Paper (Washington, D.C.: Employment and Enterprise Policy Analysis Project, 1988), 3–4. For more detail on Taiwan's industrial structure, see Gary G. Hamilton, "Organization and Market Processes in Taiwan's Capitalist Economy," in *The Economic Organization of East Asian Capitalism*, ed. Marco Orrù, Nicole Woolsey Biggart, and Gary G. Hamilton (Thousand Oaks, Calif.: Sage, 1997).

7. T. C. Chou, *Industrial Organization in the Process of Economic Development: The Case of Taiwan, 1950–1980* (Louvain-la-Neuve, Belgium: Ciaso, 1985).

8. Feenstra and Hamilton, *Emergent Economies*, 120–65.

9. For more detail, see Hamilton, "Organization and Market Processes in Taiwan's Capitalist Economy."

10. In 1985, China had just initiated elementary market reforms a few years earlier, in 1978, and was at the time a domestically oriented, inwardly developing socialist economy. Except for Singapore, Southeast Asian countries were exporting mainly agricultural goods and natural resources, such as oil from Indonesia and palm oil from Malaysia, but were not manufacturing consumer goods.

11. The six horizontal groups in 1985 were Mitsubishi, Mitsui, Sumitomo, Fuyo, DKB, and Sanwa. The ten independent groups in the same year were Tokay Bank, Industrial Bank of Japan, Nippon Steel, Hitachi, Nissan, Toyota, Matsushita, Toshibe-OHI. Tokyu, and Seibu.

12. See Michael L. Gerlach, *Alliance Capitalism: The Social Organization of Japanese Business* (Berkeley: University of California Press, 1992). Also see Orrù, Biggart, and Hamilton, *Economic Organization of East Asian Capitalism*.

13. Orrù, Biggart, and Hamilton, *Economic Organization of East Asian Capitalism*. The data come from Dodwell Marketing, *Industrial Groupings in Japan*, Rev. ed. (Tokyo: Dodwell Marketing Consultants, 1984).

14. For details, see Gerlach, *Alliance Capitalism*, 85.

15. For details see Feenstra and Hamilton, *Emergent Economies*. Hyundai and Samsung chaebol linked together, respectively, 26 and 24 firms.

16. Ibid., 269, also 55.

17. In 1982, the 16 largest *keiretsu* had over 33% of all manufacturing sales in Japan (ibid., 55.)

18. *Taiwan Statistical Data Book*, 1972, 70–76.

19. Ibid., 137–46.

20. "Economic Development," *Free China Review* 13, no. 9 (1963): 57–59; S. C. Chen, "More and Better Textiles," *Free China Review* 14, no. 8 (1964): 31–34; Yen-pin Teng, "Cotton, King of Textiles," *Free China Review* 15, no. 2 (1965): 22–24.

21. "Cement Export," *Free China Review* 14, no. 10 (1964): 57.

22. For information about Tatung in the 1960s, see Shih-hong Liu, "Free Enterprise Provides the Key," *Free China Review* 13, no. 2 (1963): 37–42.

23. "Precision Machinery," *Free China Review* 13, no. 1 (1963): 43.

24. Kao remembers buying his first car from Yulon in 1979: a light yellow sedan, yellow because that is what they had at the time. Its engine came from Japan, made by Nissan; the rest of the car was made and assembled by Yulon subsidiaries. He ordered the car and waited three months for it to be delivered. When it arrived with some paint defects, the salesman said it was not too bad. Kao drove it for four years, and sold it because it leaked. "When it rained," he recalled, "it rained inside."

25. "Economic Milestones," *Free China Review* 15, no. 7 (1965): 49.

26. "Economic Development," *Free China Review* 13, no. 9 (1963): 59.

27. This argument is made by Wade, *Governing the Market*; Gold, *State and Society in the Taiwan Miracle*; Studwell, *How Asia Works*; and others.

28. *Taiwan Statistical Data Book*, 1983, 189, 204.

29. Ibid., 191.

30. Ibid., 81–83.

31. Liu, "Free Enterprise Provides the Key," 40.

32. For the number and size of firms making automobile parts, see Directorate-General on Budget, Accounting, and Statistics, Executive Yuan, *The Report on 1986 Industrial and Commercial Census, Taiwan-Fukien Area, The Republic of China* (Taipei: Directorate-General on Budget, Accounting, and Statistics, Executive Yuan, 1988), 204–05. For a good summary of the automobile industry in Taiwan, see Chu Yun-han, "The State and the Development of the Automobile Industry in South Korea and Taiwan," in *The Role of the State in Taiwan's Development*, ed. Joel D. Aberbach, David Dollar, and Kenneth Lee Sokoloff, 125–69 (Armonk, N.Y.: M. E. Sharpe, 1994). For US imports of automobile parts from Taiwan, see Feenstra and Hamilton, *Emergent Economies*, 249.

33. Lindy Li Mark, "Taiwanese Lineage Enterprises: A Study of Familial Entrepreneurship" (PhD dissertation, University of California, Berkeley, 1972), 28. This swarming behavior is not a solely Taiwanese trait but has been a noted characteristic of Chinese businesses for a long time, a sort of race to the bottom.

34. Tai-li Hu, *My Mother-in-Law's Village: Rural Industrialization and Change in Taiwan* (Taipei: Institute of Ethnology, Academia Sinica, 1984), 78–79.

35. Stevan Harrell, "Effects of Economic Change on Two Taiwanese Villages," *Modern China* 7, no. 1 (1981): 35.

36. Bernard Gallin and Rita S. Gallin, "Socioeconomic Life in Rural Taiwan: Twenty Years of Development and Change," *Modern China* 8, no. 2 (1982): 211–15.

37. For details on South Korean and Taiwanese business groups, see Feenstra and Hamilton, *Emergent Economies*, ch. 2–4.

38. Hamilton, "Organization and Market Processes in Taiwan's Capitalist Economy."

39. Feenstra and Hamilton, *Emergent Economies*, 241; 1972 is the first year of the TSUSA data

40. The best examination of this phenomenon can be found in Guoxiong Xie, *"Boss" Island: The Subcontracting Network and Micro-Entrepreneurship in Taiwan's Development* (New York: P. Lang, 1992).

41. China Credit Information Service, "Business Groups in Taiwan" (Taipei: CCIS, 1990–1991): 12. In the same year, Formosa Plastics was Taiwan's largest business group in sales, assets, revenues, and every other measure, and it remained so for the entire period from 1970 to 1990.

42. Toyota, "Company History," http://corporatenews.pressroom.toyota.com/corporate/company+history, accessed December 5, 2014.

43. Feenstra and Hamilton, *Emergent Economies*, 91–92, app. B.

44. See ibid., 86–93.

45. For the list of the world's fifty largest container ports in 2013, see World Shipping Council, "Top 50 World Container Ports," http://www.worldshipping.org/about-the-industry/global-trade/top-50-world-container-ports.

PART TWO

1. In Japan's vertically integrated business groups, the upstream firms producing intermediate components are more profitable if they operate at full capacity. Firms within the business groups use some, but typically not all, of this production. The remainder is sold to other firms worldwide at market prices.

CHAPTER 6

1. Yeh Chi-tien, who made this song popular, became so well-known that he was elected to Taiwan's congress in 1992.

2. According to the Maddison historical GDP data, Taiwan's per capita GDP in 1965 was equivalent to 1810 US$, and by 1985, the figure had jumped to 6762 US$ (http://www.worldeconomics.com/Data/MadisonHistoricalGDP/Madison%20Historical%20GDP%20Data.efp).

3. The Maddison historical GDP data for 1985 also show Taiwan's per capita income was over 15% higher than South Korea's, but still 47% lower than Hong Kong's, and 55% lower than Japan's.

4. See Ming-ching Luoh, 台灣總生育率下降的表象與實際 (The appearance and reality of declining total fertility rates in Taiwan), *Journal of Taiwan Studies* (December 2007).

5. The Employment Service Act, passed in 1992, allowed low-skilled foreign workers to be employed in Taiwanese factories. Before that time, up to 40,000 foreign workers had already entered Taiwan. See Joseph S. Lee, "The Role of Low-Skilled Foreign Workers in the Process of Taiwan's Economic Development," *Asia Pacific Business Review* 8, no. 4 (2002), 41–66.

6. Abernathy, *Stitch in Time*, 55–70. This landmark study was the first to spell out

the essential features, or what it calls the "building blocks," of lean retailing and to demonstrate the effects of retailing on manufacturing.

7. The concept of a standardized package and its implications were spelled out earlier, in the Introduction.

8. The prevalence for "supply chains" and "supply chain management" was determined with Google's N-gram.

9. Feenstra and Hamilton, *Emergent Economies*, 233.

10. According to the website for Logicbroker, "Nearly 12,000 companies in the United States were using EDI by 1991. In 1996, The Uniform Code Council started EDI over the internet (EDIINT) to standardize the communications of EDI data over the internet" ("EDI History," 2013, http://www.logicbroker.com/edi-history/).

11. For a list of defunct stores, see Wikipedia, "List of Defunct Retailers of the United States," http://en.wikipedia.org/wiki/List_of_defunct_retailers_of_the_United_States#Department_and_discount_stores.

12. For the internationalization of European retailing, see Michael Wortmann, "Globalization of European Retailing"; and Misha Petrovic and Gary G. Hamilton, "Retailers as Market Makers," in *The Market Makers: How Retailers Are Reshaping the Global Economy*, ed. Misha Petrovic Gary G. Hamilton, and Benjamin Senauer, 117–54, 31–49 (Oxford: Oxford University Press, 2011). For the internationalization of American retailing, see Misha Petrovic, "U.S. Retailing and Its Global Diffusion."

13. For instance, the leading specialty retailer in the United States for women's clothing in the late 1980s was The Limited, which through its exclusive buyer, Mast Industries, ordered 100% of its inventory from Taiwan. See Gereffi and Pan, "Globalization of Taiwan's Garment Industry," for detailed information on big-buyer apparel orders in Taiwan during this period.

14. The logic of an inevitable balance between imports and exports derives from David Ricardo's discussion of comparative advantage, which is found in his classic book *On the Principles of Political Economy and Taxation* (1817). In 1994, Frankel called this interpretation an "old-fashioned view of exchange rate determination," namely "that the supply and demand for foreign exchange are dominated by exports and imports (respectively) so that under floating rates the exchange rate adjusts so as to clear the trade balance." He added, "What makes this view old-fashioned is that foreign exchange markets today are dominated by financial transactions, rather than by trade, and have been ever since the major industrialized countries removed their major controls on the international flow of capital" (Jeffrey A. Frankel, "Exchange Rate Policy," in *American Economic Policy in the 1980s*, ed. Martin S. Feldstein [Chicago: University of Chicago Press, 1994], 313). As Frankel acknowledged, this old-fashioned view still had some advocates in 1985.

15. Peter T. Kilborn, "How the Big Six Steer the Economy," *New York Times*, November 17, 1985.

16. Ibid.

17. Peter B. Kenen, "The Coordination of Macroeconomic Policies," in *International Policy Coordination and Exchange Rate Fluctuations*, ed. William H. Branson, Jacob A. Frenkel, and Morris Goldstein (Chicago: University of Chicago Press, 1990), 69.

18. As Paul Krugman noted in reference to the Plaza Accord, "For better or for worse, it is now taken as a matter of course that the G5 countries will at any given time form a collective view about the appropriate levels of nominal exchange rates, and make at least some effort to stabilize actual rates in the vicinity of those appropriate rates" (Paul Krugman, "Equilibrium Exchange Rates," in *International Policy Coordination and Exchange Rate Fluctuations*, ed. William H. Branson, Jacob A. Frenkel, and Morris Goldstein [Chicago: University of Chicago Press, 1990], 159).

19. In considering nations trying to match nominal exchange rates with real exchanges, Krugman laments that "the current situation is one in which an intelligent appreciation of what we know about equilibrium exchange rates leads to a definite 'don't know' in response to questions about where to go from here" ("Equilibrium Exchange Rates," 186).

20. Yōichi Funabashi, *Managing the Dollar: From the Plaza to the Louvre* (Washington, DC: Institute for International Economics, 1988), 283. In the US Treasury report to Congress in 1988, both Taiwan and South Korea were labeled as countries that "manipulate the rate of exchange between their currency and the US dollar for purposes of preventing effective balance of payments adjustments or gaining unfair competitive advantage in international trade." Quoted from Ramon Moreno, "Exchange Rates and Trade Adjustment in Taiwan and Korea," *Economic Review—Federal Reserve Bank of San Francisco*, no. 2 (1989): 30.

21. The Taiwanese government relaxed foreign exchange controls in 1987. This measure allowed Taiwanese citizens to hold foreign exchange. Then in 1989, the government moved from a managed foreign exchange rate to a floating rate. Since that time, Taiwan's Central Bank buys or sells currencies to maintain Taiwan's nominal exchange rate relative to foreign currencies. See John C. H. Fei and Yun-Peng Chu, "Liberalization Promotes Development: Evidence from Taiwan," in *Taiwan's Development Experience: Lessons on Roles of Government and Market*, ed. Erik Thorbecke and Henry Y. Wan, 177–206 (Boston: Kluwer Academic, 1999); Paul C. H. Chiu and Teh-Chian Hou, "Prices, Money and Monetary Policy Implementation Under Financial Liberalization: The Case of Taiwan," in *Financial Opening: Policy Issues and Experiences in Developing Countries*, ed. Helmut Reisen and Bernhard Fischer, 173–200 (Paris: Organisation for Economic Co-operation and Development, 1993).

22. This turn toward US-directed global economic coordination led to what has loosely been called the "Washington Consensus," a term introduced by John Williamson in his book *Latin American Adjustment: How Much Has Happened?* (Washington, D.C.: Institute for International Economics, 1990).

23. Department of the Treasury, Office of International Affairs, *Report to Congress on International Economic and Exchange Rate Policies* (Washington, D.C.: U.S. Department of the Treasury, Office of International Affairs, 1989), 7.

24. American Apparel and Footwear Association, *ShoeStats 2001*, https://www.wewear.org/assets/1/7/ShoeStats2001.pdf.

25. "Japan's stock market experienced an unprecedented boom and bust in the late 1980s through the early 1990s. The Nikkei 225 Stock Average (the Nikkei Average) stood at 13,113 on the last trading day of 1985 and climbed almost uninterruptedly, in spite

of Black Monday in 1987, to 38,915 on the last trading day of 1989—virtually tripled the level of exactly four years earlier. This was against a background of easy money conditions after the Plaza Agreement in 1985 and increasingly diversified and aggressive financial activities of Japanese firms under the rapid progress of financial liberalization" (Yasuhiro Maehara, "Japan's Stock Market: Lesson from the Recent Boom and Slump," *Journal of Asian Economics* 6, no. 1 [1995]: 119).

26. "While the large increase in stock prices in the second half of the 1980s served as one factor which stimulated the shift of Japanese firms to *zai-tech*, such a shift in turn exacerbated the stock price spiral. Shares have increasingly become 'a financial commodity,' not as an ownership interest in a firm. In this way, the rise in stock prices and more active *zai-tech* were mutually reinforcing in the second half of the 1980s. This seems to have led to the proliferation of the so-called 'herd mentality' without much corporate accountability" (ibid., 123).

27. See for instance, Steven R. Weisman, "Japanese Are Concerned About Rockefeller Deal," *New York Times*, November 1, 1989.

28. Walter Hatch and Kozo Yamamura, *Asia in Japan's Embrace: Building a Regional Production Alliance* (New York: Cambridge University Press, 1996), 163.

29. Ibid., 24–25.

30. Andrew Mair, Richard Florida, and Martin Kenney, "The New Geography of Automobile Production: Japanese Transplants in North America," *Economic Geography* 64, no. 4 (1988): 352–73.

31. See Richard F. Doner, *Driving a Bargain: Automobile Industrialization and Japanese Firms in Southeast Asia* (Berkeley: University of California Press, 1991). Also see Hatch and Yamamura, *Asia in Japan's Embrace*.

32. Nan-Kuang Chen, "Asset Price Fluctuations in Taiwan: Evidence from Stock and Real Estate Prices 1973 to 1992," *Journal of Asian Economics* 12, no. 2 (2001): 215. Ya-Hwei Yang and Jia-Dong Shea comment: "Although there are no official data on the value of real estate transactions, [market information] shows that the total trading value of listed stocks increased drastically from NT$195.2 billion in 1985 to NT$25,408 billion in 1989" ("Money and Prices in Taiwan in the 1980s," in *Financial Deregulation and Integration in East Asia*, ed. Takatoshi Ito and Anne O. Krueger, 227–46 [Chicago: University of Chicago Press, 1996], 231).

33. See Robert Weller's description of how *dajia le* was played, in "Capitalism, Community and the Rise of Amoral Cults in Taiwan," in *Asian Visions of Authority: Religion and the Modern States of East and Southeast Asia*, ed. Charles F. Keyes, Laurel Kendall, and Helen Hardacre (Honolulu: University of Hawaii Press, 1994), 151–53.

34. Yang and Shea, "Money and Prices in Taiwan in the 1980s," 231.

35. Chen, "Asset Price Fluctuations in Taiwan," 215.

36. The largest movement of capital was to the United States, where Taiwanese purchased mainly property. The second largest amount went to Malaysia.

37. Schive Chi and Regina Y. S. Chyn, "Global Logistics: A New Way of Doing Business in Taiwan," *Industry of Free China* 91, no. 7 (2001): 92. Forty-five percent of the total investment went to Malaysia.

38. Recognizing the jump-or-die dilemma faced by Taiwanese businesspeople, Lee Teng-hui, who became Taiwan's president in 1988 after Chiang Ching-kuo died, started the Go South Campaign in 1993. This campaign encouraged Taiwanese businesspeople to establish factories in Southeast Asia. However, by this time, Mainland China was the key site for Taiwanese investments. For Taiwanese investments in Southeast Asia, see Tain-Jy Chen, *Taiwan's Small- and Medium-Sized Firms' Direct Investment in Southeast Asia* (Taipei: Chung-Hua Institution for Economic Research, 1995).

39. A couple of articles appear somewhat later in English language newspapers as well: Joyce Huang, "Two Lives and Two Wives for Some Taiwanese," *Taipei Times*, January 29, 2001, http://www.taipeitimes.com/News/local/archives/2001/01/29/0000071462; Xing Bao, "Gambling on Youth, Beauty," *Shanghai Star*, July 3, 2002, http://app1.chinadaily.com.cn/star/2002/0703/fo6-1.html.

40. I. M. Destler and C. Randall Henning, *Dollar Politics: Exchange Rate Policymaking in the United States* (Washington, DC: Institute for International Economics, 1989), 46.

CHAPTER 7

1. A pioneer of color televisions, RCA sold its color picture tubes to other firms as well. See Alfred D. Chandler, *Inventing the Electronic Century: The Epic Story of the Consumer Electronics and Computer Industries* (New York: Free Press, 2001), 29–34.

2. In 1958, these seven firms "accounted for 86 percent of market share" for their black-and-white televisions (ibid., 28, 32–33). The recording industry was quite different. Phonographs and related products, including records, were made by both large and small companies.

3. Michael E. Porter, *Cases in Competitive Strategy* (New York: Free Press, 1983), 451.

4. Alfred Chandler's most insightful books are *The Visible Hand: The Managerial Revolution in American Business* (Cambridge, Mass.: Belknap Press, 1977), and *Scale and Scope: The Dynamics of Industrial Capitalism*. Chandler's last book, *Inventing the Electronic Century*, extended his thesis, made in the two earlier books, that vertically integrated manufacturing firms would dominate these industries as they did in previous decades. Chandler, however, did not anticipate the changes that would come from demand-led industrialization, when specialized contract manufacturing would challenge and mostly replace vertically integrated brand-name manufacturers.

5. Paul Vitello, "Jack Wayman, 92; Loved Selling Electronics," *New York Times*, September 20, 2014, A-21.

6. RCA was originally spun off from General Electric in 1919. Jointly funded by Westinghouse and AT&T, RCA was to be the radio production arm of these firms, but following an antitrust suit, RCA became an independent company in competition with GE and Westinghouse. At that time, RCA also started to manufacture a broad range of appliances, including refrigerators and stoves. RCA sold its large appliance division to Whirlpool in 1955.

7. Porter, *Cases in Competitive Strategy*, 451–52, 84. One of the reasons buying from an authorized dealer was important was that these retailers also provided service. The

early televisions often required repairs, because picture tubes and other components would frequently need to be replaced.

8. Ibid., 508.

9. Ibid., 467–68.

10. Japanese electronics manufacturers had entered the US market earlier in a small way with transistor radios, which were "first imported into the United States by a group of general merchandise (e.g., cigarette lighters, toys) importers working through Japanese trading companies" (ibid., 465.). These radios were sold mostly in "five and dime" stores.

11. Ibid. Porter, *Cases in Competitive Strategy*, adds that "Sony products were expensive, provided high dealer margins, and were not discounted. Sony also handled its own distribution almost from the very beginning."

12. RCA was the inventor and patent holder for color television technology, which allowed RCA to make more money selling components and licensing technology than actually selling TVs (Chandler, *Inventing the Electronic Century*, 31–32).

13. Jefferson Cowie, *Capital Moves: RCA's Seventy-Year Quest for Cheap Labor* (Ithaca, N.Y.: Cornell University Press, 1999).

14. Victor Chen, "Showcase of Industry," *Free China Review* 21, no. 10 (1971): 31.

15. "Economic Milestones," *Free China Review* 20, no. 9 (1970): 50–51.

16. Kao-tang Chen, "Electronics Explosion," *Free China Review* 17, no. 3 (1967): 34–37.

17. In 1970, Chinese-owned factories (both Taiwanese and Overseas Chinese) comprised over 55% of the total number of registered electronic firms. Japanese firms owned nearly 27%, American firms 16%, and the Dutch firm 2%. Most of the Chinese-owned factories were small and were located in northern Taiwan. American firms, however, invested the most (58%); the Chinese invested 20%, the Dutch 15.5%, and the Japanese 7%. Investments in the sector totaled nearly 150 million US$. See W. J. Lee, "Electronic Escalation," *Free China Review* 20, no. 1 (1970): 22–23.

18. Chen, "Electronics Explosion." Also see "Export Zones Offer Incentives," *Free China Review* 20, no. 6 (1970): 47.

19. Office of Technology Assessment, *International Competitiveness in Electronics* (Washington, D.C.: Congress of the United States, 1983), 128.

20. Ibid., 126; Porter, *Cases in Competitive Strategy*, 485.

21. Wade, *Governing the Market*, 149. Also see Amsden and Chu, *Beyond Late Development*, 19–28.

22. *Taiwan Statistical Data Book*, 1982, 84.

23. Porter, *Cases in Competitive Strategy*, 486.

24. Office of Technology Assessment, *International Competitiveness*, 116. The import figure includes televisions from those American manufacturers in Taiwan. Japanese firms by this time were assembling televisions in the United States. These televisions made by Japanese firms in the United States are not included in the total.

25. Porter, *Cases in Competitive Strategy*, 508.

26. Office of Technology Assessment, *International Competitiveness*, 116–17.

27. Tatung started a plant in Long Beach, California, and Sampo established its factory in Atlanta, Georgia (Office of Technology Assessment, *International Competitiveness*, 114).

28. Office of Technology Assessment, *International Competitiveness*, 112.

29. *The 1981 Industrial & Commercial Censuses of Taiwan and Fukien Area, Republic of China* (Taipei: Xing Zheng Yuan Tai Min Di Qu Gong Shang Ye Pu Cha Wei Yuan Hui, 1983), 38, shows firm size skewed toward large firms of 500 or more employees. Fifty-four percent of the total number of employees in the sector worked in factories having 500 or more employees. Of that total working in large factories, 62% were women. These large factories were likely assembling televisions and other mass-produced products. The second largest group of firms (28%) consisted of those having between 30 and 299 employees. Of the total number of employees working in this groups, women constituted 61% of the employees. The third largest group of firms (9%) employed 29 or fewer employees, of which 44% were women.

30. *Taiwan Statistical Data Book*, 1982, 84.

31. Office of Technology Assessment, *International Competitiveness*, 158–59.

32. Office of Technology Assessment, *International Competitiveness*, 148.

33. AnnaLee Saxenian, *The New Argonauts: Regional Advantage in a Global Economy* (Cambridge, Mass.: Harvard University Press, 2006), 39.

34. Core PC components include a motherboard containing a central processing unit (CPU), random access memory (e.g., DRAM), read only memory (ROM), and disk drives and a power unit. Peripherals include pointing devices (mouse or joystick), keyboards, printers, monitors, and other *plug-ins*.

35. Mei-Lin Pan, *Local Ties and Global Linkages: Restructuring Taiwan-Based Production Networks in the Apparel and Computer Industries* (Ann Arbor, Mich.: ProQuest Dissertations Publishing, 1998), 88.

36. Honghong Tinn, "From DIY Computers to Illegal Copies: The Controversy Over Tinkering with Microcomputers in Taiwan, 1980–1984," *IEEE Annals of the History of Computing* 33, no. 2 (2011). Tinn reports that "in Taiwan today, computer-industry workers I interviewed all agreed that this ban [on video gaming machines] contributed to the rise of Apple II–compatible manufacturers and that the ban, in this way, merits an important page in the history of computer manufacturing in Taiwan."

37. Wu Chen-xiu, "Acer Succeeded in Reforming; Barry Lam Called Stanley Shih 'Big Brother,'" *Business Weekly*, January 16, 2003.

38. Tinn, *From DIY Computers to Illegal Copies*.

39. Ibid.

40. In the United States, at the same time, Radio Shack was one of the stores that sold do-it-yourself kits for making home computers.

41. Tinn, *From DIY Computers to Illegal Copies*, 78–79. Tinn reports that many of those she "interviewed had never seen an authentic Apple II computer" and did not initially realize they were making illegal copies. Many thought "that tinkering with microcomputers was an extension of the preceding practice of buying kits to make radios and audio systems."

42. The owners of the eight firms had their prison sentences commuted to fines. See Tinn, *From DIY Computers to Illegal Copies*, 80–81, for a more complete description of Apple's legal actions and their outcome.

43. IBM also took legal action to prevent the manufacture of IBM PC clones, but these lawsuits occurred in the US courts and were uniformly unsuccessful.

44. China Credit Information Service, "Business Groups in Taiwan," 1990–1991.

45. Jason Dedrick and Kenneth L. Kraemer, "Market Making in the Personal Computer Industry," in *The Market Makers: How Retailers Are Reshaping the Global Economy*, ed. Gary G. Hamilton, Misha Petrovic, and Benjamin Senauer (Oxford: Oxford University Press, 2011), 293.

46. See Wikipedia, "List of Computer System Manufacturers," https://en.wikipedia.org/wiki/List_of_computer_system_manufacturers, for some indication of the computer firms that went bankrupt and those bought out by other firms.

47. Saxenian, *The New Argonauts*.

48. Jason Dedrick and Kenneth L. Kraemer, *Asia's Computer Challenge: Threat or Opportunity for the United States & the World?* (New York: Oxford University Press, 1998), is the best single source on the differences in the PC industry among the East Asian countries.

49. Ibid., 76–115. Dedrick and Kraemer's conclusion is right on target: "Japan's large, vertically integrated firms were well suited to high-volume, capital intensive components production. They also did quite well in the relatively stable mainframe, because they could marshal the necessary resources with their *keiretsu* groups and count on the members of those groups as captive customers. However, in the industry segments such as PCs and hard disk drives, where product cycles are short and timing critical, the Japanese industry structure was a liability. Unable to make decisions quickly, Japan's computer makers had limited success in such businesses" (113).

50. Ibid., 138.

51. Ibid.

52. Eun Mee Kim, *Big Business, Strong State: Collusion and Conflict in South Korean Development, 1960–1990* (Albany: State University of New York Press, 1997), 145.

53. Office of Technology Assessment, *International Competitiveness*, 132.

54. Ibid.

55. Ibid., 137–38.

56. One of the products of ERSO was a reverse engineered, "clean room," IBM PC–compatible BIOS that many firms making IBM PC clones used.

57. For a good account of this agreement and subsequent transfer, see Saxenian, *The New Argonauts*, 140.

58. Ibid., 149.

59. Ibid., 140.

60. Ibid., 139.

61. Ibid, 144–45. AT&T was an exception, but its facility came only as a "prerequisite for winning a government telecommunication contract."

62. Some analysts argue that Philips was brought in to transfer technology, but our

interview and those by Constance Squires Meaney ("State Policy and the Development of Taiwan's Semiconductor Industry," in *The Role of the State in Taiwan's Development*, ed. Joel D. Aberbach, David Dollar, and Kenneth Lee Sokoloff, 170–92 [Armonk, N.Y.: M. E. Sharpe, 1994], 182), suggest otherwise. There was probably no technology to transfer, because TSMC invented the process of functioning as an OEM foundry.

63. Ibid., 183.

64. Bob Johnstone, "Taiwan Has Designs on Booming Niche Markets," *Far Eastern Economic Review*, August 18, 1988, 84.

65. Xilinx, "Leveraging the Industry's Leading Process Technology to Remain a Generation Ahead," http://www.xilinx.com/about/all-programmable-leadership.html.

66. For examples, see Gary G. Hamilton and Nicole Woolsey Biggart, "The Organization of Business in Taiwan: Reply to Numazaki," *American Journal of Sociology* 96, no. 4 (1991): 999.

67. Xilinx, "Leveraging the Industry's Leading Process Technology," the earliest and one of the largest design houses, has said much the same thing: "When we embarked upon the design of our current generation UltraScale™ architecture, we continued our close collaboration with TSMC to ensure we derived the maximum advantages of TSMC's leading edge 20nm SoC and 16nm FinFET processes. Through our collaboration we are able to extend our current industry leadership delivering industry breakthroughs in system performance, power, and integration that address the performance, power, and integration needs of the industry's most demanding applications."

68. For a discussion of the fabless design houses currently in Taiwan, see Jenn-hwan Wang, Jun-ming Chen, and Sheng-wen Tseng, "Fast Follower's Innovation and the Organizational Structure of the Taiwanese IT Industry," paper presented at the Annual Conference of the Association for Asian Studies, Hawaii Convention Center, Honolulu, 2011. According to these authors: "Taiwan has 261 IC design firms that together have amassed a 26.5% world market share, and whose combined revenue exceeds US$10 billion. The scale of the Taiwanese fabless IC design industry is second only to that of the United States. . . . Taiwan's IC design firms are particularly specialized in ASIC . . . areas that are related to PCs, memory, graphics, the Internet, communications, LCD drivers and other products related to consumer electronics products."

69. Data from IC Insights, *Research Bulletin*, January 28, 2014, http://www.icinsights.com/data/articles/documents/640.pdf. For information about TSMC's twelve fabrication facilities in 2013, see TSMC, Company Profile, http://www.tsmc.com/english/aboutTSMC/company_profile.htm.

CHAPTER 8

1. For summaries of the events leading up to the crisis, as well as the debate about the causes, see Stephan Haggard, *The Political Economy of the Asian Financial Crisis* (Washington, D.C.: Institute for International Economics, 2000); and T. J. Pempel, *The Politics of the Asian Economic Crisis*, Cornell Studies in Political Economy (Ithaca, N.Y.: Cornell University Press, 1999).

2. Robert C. Feenstra, Gary G. Hamilton, and Eun Mie Lim, "Chaebol and Catastro-

phe: A New View of the Korean Business Groups and Their Role in the Financial Crisis," *Asian Economic Papers* 1, no. 2 (2002): 1–45.

3. Hong Kong's main banks (namely HSBC, Standard Chartered Bank [Hong Kong] Ltd., and Bank of China [Hong Kong] Limited) act, on behalf of the Hong Kong Monetary Authority, as a de facto main bank for Hong Kong and are able to issue Hong Kong currency.

4. Because this chapter and the next focus on Taiwanese industrialists in China, this is not the occasion for a comprehensive analysis of China's political economy. Those interested in a more detailed analysis of China's economy during the past fifty years should see the following excellent studies: Barry Naughton, *Growing Out of the Plan: Chinese Economic Reform, 1978–1993* (New York: Cambridge University Press, 1995); and *The Chinese Economy: Transitions and Growth* (Cambridge, Mass.: MIT Press, 2007); Yasheng Huang, *Capitalism with Chinese Characteristics: Entrepreneurship and the State* (Cambridge: Cambridge University Press, 2008); and Ho-fung Hung, *China and the Transformation of Global Capitalism*, Themes in Global Social Change (Baltimore: Johns Hopkins University Press, 2009); and *The China Boom: Why China Will Not Rule the World*, Contemporary Asia in the World (New York: Columbia University Press, 2016).

5. According to David Autor, David Dorn, and Gordon Hanson, "Between 1984 and 1990, China's share of world manufacturing exports ticked up only modestly, from 1.2% to 1.9%" ("The China Shock: Learning from Labor Market Adjustment to Large Changes in Trade," NBER Working Paper [Cambridge, Mass.: National Bureau of Economic Research, 2016], 6).

6. During Deng's month-long trip to Guangdong Province, he visited the special economic zones in Shenzhen and Zhuhai. These zones were set up to attract foreign-owned firms that would assemble products in China that would later be exported to other countries around the world.

7. For more details on currency reforms, see Naughton, *The Chinese Economy: Transitions and Growth*.

8. In the 1980s, government officials debated whether rural-to-urban migration should be permitted. By the 1990s, the debate ended as "central-level politicians as a group modified their prereform exclusionary stance somewhat. This they did as they eventually decided—perhaps rather quixotically—that using officially engineered labor markets to bring in migrants could make for an all-around positive outcome. For such guidance could check any potential chaos coming from farmers in town, while the peasants' presence would stimulate economic growth" (Dorothy J. Solinger, *Contesting Citizenship in Urban China: Peasant Migrants, the State, and the Logic of the Market*, Studies of the East Asian Institute, Columbia University [Berkeley: University of California Press, 1999], 54).

9. For a description of the lives of these young women, see Leslie T. Chang, *Factory Girls: From Village to City in a Changing China* (New York: Spiegel & Grau, 2008).

10. There were many types of locations where foreigners could site their China-based facilities. For one of the first and still one of the best studies of foreign direct in-

vestment (FDI), see Yasheng Huang, *Selling China: Foreign Direct Investment During the Reform Era*, Cambridge Modern China Series (New York: Cambridge University Press, 2003). By 2007, the Chinese government has established five special economic zones (SEZ), fourteen coast open cities (COC), fifty-four economic and technological development zones (ETDZ), fifteen free trade zones, fifty-three high technology industrial development zones, and thirty-eight export processing zones, all of which were created to attract foreign direct investments. For details see Shalendra Sharma, Miao Wang, and M. C. Sunny Wong, "FDI Location and the Relevance of Spatial Linkages: Evidence from Provincial and Industry FDI in China," *Review of International Economics* 22, no. 1 (2014).

11. One of the best analyses of this decentralized implementation of the central government's economic policies appears in Chenggang Xu, "The Fundamental Institutions of China's Reforms and Development," *Journal of Economic Literature* 49, no. 4 (2011): 1076–151. Xu calls this system a "regionally decentralized authoritarian (RDA) regime." He describes the RDA regime "as a combination of political centralization and economic regional decentralization. On the one hand, the national government's control is substantial in that the Chinese political and personnel governance structure has been highly centralized. Subnational government officials are appointed from above, and the appointment and promotion of subnational government officials serve as powerful instruments for the national government to induce regional to follow the central government's policies.... Regional economies (provinces, municipalities, and counties) are relatively self-contained, and subnational governments have overall responsibility for initiating and coordinating reforms, providing public services, and making and enforcing laws within their jurisdictions" (1078).

12. See Naughton, *The Chinese Economy*, 389–91, for a summary of China's WTO negotiations.

13. Gary G. Hamilton, "Asian Business Networks in Transition: or, What Alan Greenspan Does Not Know About the Asian Business Crisis," in *The Politics of the Asian Economic Crisis*, ed. T. J. Pempel, 45–61 (Ithaca, N.Y.: Cornell University Press, 1999).

14. Robert C. Feenstra and Shang-Jin Wei, eds., *China's Growing Role in World Trade* (Chicago: University of Chicago Press, 2010).

15. Bruce A. Blonigen and Alyson C. Ma, "Please Pass the Catch-Up: The Relative Performance of Chinese and Foreign Firms in Chinese Exports," in *China's Growing Role in World Trade*, ed. Robert Feenstra and Shang-Jin Wei (Chicago: University of Chicago Press, 2010).

16. John Whalley and Xian Xin, *China's FDI and Non-FDI Economies and the Sustainability of Future High Chinese Growth*, NBER Working Paper No. 12249 (Cambridge, Mass.: National Bureau of Economic Research, 2006), 2.

17. The FDI channeled to the United States had a very different purpose. Foreign firms invested in the United States to gain unimpeded access to the American consumer market. Also, a large portion of these investments went to buy property, some for firms and a lot for private individuals making speculative investments in real estate.

18. For a description of these statistics, see Feenstra and Wei, *China's Growing Role in World Trade*.

19. The distinction between ordinary and processing trade does not, however, define the boundaries of contract manufacturing in China. Most exports coming from processing trade came from foreign-owned firms, either wholly owned or in a joint venture with a Chinese firm, and most of these foreign-owned firms were contract manufacturers relocated from Hong Kong and Taiwan. However, contract manufacturing also includes many of the exports classified as ordinary trade. It is probable that a sizable portion, if not most, of Walmart's exports from China were classified as ordinary trade.

20. For a summary of this global consolidation, see Timothy Sturgeon, John Humphrey, and Gary Gereffi, "Making the Global Supply Base," in *The Market Makers: How Retailers Are Reshaping the Global Economy*, ed. Misha Petrovic Gary G. Hamilton, and Benjamin Senauer, ch. 8 (Oxford: Oxford University Press, 2011).

21. For an account of these mergers and acquisitions among the leading retailers in Europe, see Wortmann, "Globalization of European Retailing."

22. For details about Walmart's international expansion and global buying, see Petrovic and Hamilton, "Making Global Markets: Wal-Mart and Its Suppliers." See also Nelson Lichtenstein, *The Retail Revolution: How Wal-Mart Created a Brave New World of Business* (New York: Metropolitan Books, 2009). For Walmart operations in China, see Anita Chan, ed., *Walmart in China* (Ithaca, N.Y.: ILR Press, 2011).

23. About 80% of US non-oil imports arrive by sea in container ships. The yearly statistics on the largest importers and exporters in terms of containerized shipping are published in the *Journal of Commerce*, and are archived at http://www.joc.com/. Also see Edna Bonacich and Jake B. Wilson, *Getting the Goods: Ports, Labor, and the Logistics Revolution* (Ithaca, N.Y.: Cornell University Press, 2008).

24. Newell Brands has fifteen categories of consumer products, which include such brand names as Sunbeam, Calphalon, Oster, Rubbermaid, Sharpie, Paper Mate, Coleman, Baby Jogger, Waterman, Parker, Rawlings, Bicycle (playing cards), and First Alert. Fortune Brands has four categories of consumer products, which include KitchenCraft, WoodCrafters, Moen, Rohl, and Master Lock. Nine West Holdings' brands include Anne Klein, Easy Spirit, Nine West, Givenchy Jewelry, Gloria Vanderbilt, and Bandolino, among many others. Authentic Brand Group lists twenty-eight brands, including Jones of New York, Hind, Bobby Jones, Vision Street Wear, Prince, Tapout, Thalia, and Tretorn.

25. A French brand-name holding company, LVMH, has four major categories of consumer products. The brand names in the fashions and leather goods category include Berluti, Céline, Dior, Fendi, Emilio Pucci, Marc Jacobs, Loewe, and Louis Vuitton, among others. The watches and jewelry category includes Bulgari, De Beers Diamond Jewellers, TAG Heuer, Zenith, among others. Kering is also a French brand-name holding company. Kering is divided into two divisions, luxury goods, on the one hand, and sports and lifestyle, on the other. Kering's brands include Gucci, Saint Laurent Paris, Bottega Veneta, Alexander McQueen, Puma, Cobra Golf, and Volcom, among others. The Swatch Group is a Swiss brand-name holding company specializing in watches. The

group's 19 brands of watches range between such luxury brands as Breguet, Omega, and Jaquet Droz, to such low-end watches as Swatch and Flik Flak. In between these two ends are such brands as Rado, Hamilton, Longines, Mido, and Tissot. The Richemont Group is a South African–owned brand name holding company whose 20-plus brands include Cartier, Chloé, Dunhill, Jaeger-LeCoultre, Montblanc, Piaget, Shanghai Tang, Van Cleef & Arpels.

26. For analyses of global value chains and global production networks, see Neil M. Coe and Henry Wai-chung Yeung, *Global Production Networks: Theorizing Economic Development in an Interconnected World* (Oxford: Oxford University Press, 2015). Also see Sturgeon, Humphrey, and Gereffi, "Making the Global Supply Base."

27. See Richard P. Appelbaum, "Transnational Contractors in East Asia," in *The Market Makers: How Retailers Are Reshaping the Global Economy*, ed. Misha Petrovic Gary G. Hamilton, and Benjamin Senauer, 255–70 (Oxford: Oxford University Press, 2011); and Sturgeon, Humphrey, and Gereffi, "Making the Global Supply Base."

28. Stefan A. Halper, *The Beijing Consensus: How China's Authoritarian Model Will Dominate the Twenty-First Century* (New York: Basic Books, 2010). Also see Suisheng Zhao, "The China Model: Can It Replace the Western Model of Modernization?," *Journal of Contemporary China* 19, no. 65 (2010): 419–36. For an update on this discussion, see Suisheng Zhao, "Whither the Chinese Model: Revisiting the Debate," *Journal of Contemporary China* 26, no. 103 (2017).

29. Lee Branstetter and C. Fritz Foley, "Facts and Fallacies About US FDI in China," in *China's Growing Role in World Trade*, ed. Robert C. Feenstra and Shang-Jin Wei, 513–39 (Chicago: University of Chicago Press, 2010).

30. On this point, see the discussion in Branstetter and Foley, *China's Growing Role in World Trade*.

31. These seven firms are "Foxconn (Shenzhen), Dafang (Shanghai), Asus (Suzhou), Dakong (Shanghai), Compal (Kunshan), Acer Peripheral (Suzhou), and AOC (Fujian), all of which are in IT-related industries and five of which are in the Yangtze River Delta" (Shiuh-Shen Chien and Litao Zhao, "Local Economic Transition in China: A Perspective on Taiwan Investment," in *China's Reform in Global Perspective*, ed. John Wong and Zhiyue Bo [Hackensack, N.J.: World Scientific, 2010], 234–35).

32. For an excellent discussion of the uneasy relationship between Taiwanese businesspeople and Chinese officials, see Chun-yi Lee, "Between Dependency and Autonomy—Taiwanese Entrepreneurs and Local Chinese Governments," *Journal of Current Chinese Affairs*, 39, no. 1 (2010).

33. See David Wank's superb study of the relations between Taiwanese businesspeople and local officials in Xiamen: *Commodifying Communism: Business, Trust, and Politics in a Chinese City* (New York,: Cambridge University Press, 1999). Also see Chien and Zhao, "Local Economic Transition in China," 253.

34. We should note that as time went on, Taiwanese firms began to differentiate their operations in Taiwan more sharply from those in China. According to surveys of companies in 2001 and 2007, "First in 2007, Taiwan firms in Taiwan specialized in order management issues (49%), marketing (48%), and R&D (44%), while Taiwan firms in

China are mainly in charge of production (74%) and exports (58%). On top of that, Taiwan firms in China are upgrading their business functions from pure production into more complicated operation centers, with more activity in financial management (from 12% in 2001 to 23% in 2007) and in documentation (*ya hui*) (18% in 2007, similar to that in Taiwan 20%). Third, Taiwan is certainly losing its position for production-related functions, as there are less and less Taiwan firms doing order, production, and export activities in Taiwan" (Chien and Zhao, "Local Economic Transition in China," 244).

35. Ibid., 253–56. According to the official website listing Taiwanese business associations in China, in 2016, there were 102 Taiwanese business associations scattered in 25 provinces and metropolitan administrative areas, including 19 in districts in Guangdong Province, 17 in districts in Jiangsu Province, and 9 districts in Fujian Province. See "List of Mainland China Businessmen Associations in 2008," Taiwan Businessmen, http://tbm.cna.com.hk/links/tbm_listpage.php.

36. For one of the most revealing studies of a Taiwanese business association in action, see Chun Yang and Chen-wei Chen, "Farewell to the Developmental State? Local Government and Taiwanese Businesses in the Kunshan Miracle," *Zhongguo Zhengzhi Xuebao* (*Chinese Political Science Review*), no. 37 (June 2005).

37. The most important study of Taiwanese footwear manufacturers in China: You-tien Hsing's *Making Capitalism in China: The Taiwan Connection* (New York: Oxford University Press, 1998).

38. Nearly 60% of the 874 footwear factories registered in Taiwan in 1986 had 100 or fewer employees, and over 90% had fewer than 300 employees (ibid., 44–45).

39. Ibid. One group of former footwear suppliers that we interviewed decided to regroup as a satellite assembly system making helicopters. Unfortunately, there was very little demand for helicopters, and so after a few years, this group of firms disbanded.

40. Ibid., 70.

41. According to a 1993 survey by Charles Kao and his colleagues of 140 Taiwanese firms with operations in both Taiwan and China, over 90% received orders in Taiwan and over 80% developed and tested products in Taiwan, but about 70% did all their production in China. See Charles Kao et al., *Taishang Jingyan* (The Taiwan investment experience in Mainland China), (Taipei: Commonwealth, 1995).

42. For an excellent survey of the research literature on Taiwanese businesspeople in China, including their sense of being foreigners in China, see Gunter Schubert, Lin Rui-Hua, and Tseng Yu-Chen, "Taishang Studies: A Rising or Declining Research Field?," *China Perspectives*, no. 1 (2016): 29–36. Also see Gunter Schubert, ed., *Taiwan and the "China Impact": Challenges and Opportunities* (London: Routledge/Taylor & Francis Group, 2016).

43. *Xieli gongchan* means "firms joined in a common effort." See Chapter 4 for a discussion of this term as applied to Taiwan's economic way of life.

44. Liang Ren-wei and Cai Yao-lian, "The Maker of Invisible Rich," *Business Today*, http://www.businesstoday.com.tw/article-content-92751-115260.

45. Pou Chen is listed on the Taiwan Stock Exchange.

46. A decade later, Yue Yuen's Gaobu factory employed over 70,000 people (Chang, *Factory Girls*, 99). By 2015, the number of employees totaled 80,000.

47. See Chang, *Factory Girls*, for a description of the services provided by Yue Yuen in the mid-2000s.

48. See Appelbaum, "Transnational Contractors in East Asia."

49. Chang, *Factory Girls*, 115.

50. Ibid., 113–15.

51. We should note that Pou Chen has opened its own retail outlets in China, where the company sells not only branded shoes but also shoes of its own brands. See Li Xusheng, "Breaking Through OEM Enterprises by Creating Brands," http://channel.megaport.tw/2011/06/blog-post.html.

52. Judith Crown and Glenn Coleman, *No Hands: The Rise and Fall of the Schwinn Bicycle Company: An American Institution* (New York: H. Holt, 1996), 54–69.

53. Crown and Coleman, *No Hands* (60–61, 79–80), give a good summary of the antitrust case.

54. Ibid., 95. The market for bicycles, as well as for a great many other consumer items, changed in the same period of time in large part because of the new lineup of retail stores crowding the aisles of newly built shopping malls. The new discount stores, Kmart, Walmart, and others, were just beginning operations, and just beginning to carry mass-market bicycles.

55. Michelle Hsieh, "The East Asian Miracle Revisited: The Taiwan–South Korea Comparison Based on a Case Study of the Bicycle Industry," PhD dissertation, Department of Sociology, McGill University 2005 (Ann Arbor, Mich.: ProQuest Dissertations Publishing, 2006), 202. This dissertation is the best source for the early development of Taiwan's bicycle industry. Also see Wan-Wen Chu, "Causes of Growth: A Study of Taiwan's Bicycle Industry," *Cambridge Journal of Economics* 21, no. 1 (1997): 55–72; and Cheng and Sato, *Bicycle Industries in Taiwan and Japan*.

56. Ibid., 21.

57. Crown and Coleman, *No Hands*, 101.

58. A *derailleur* is a variable-ratio transmission used on bicycles to change gears. The world's leading brand, Shimano, has become the Intel of the bicycle world, making a component part that is essential to the operation of the whole.

59. Crown and Coleman, *No Hands*, 159.

60. Ibid.

61. Hsieh, "The East Asian Miracle Revisited," 204.

62. Crown and Coleman, *No Hands*, 183.

63. During Hsieh's interview with Giant, Mr. Hsu, a spokesman for the company, said, Schwinn "did not notify us in advance, and as we learned about this news, our company's survival was at stake. The joint venture [between Schwinn and the China Bicycle Company, CBC] would imply that they would shift their production to China soon. Consequently, it accelerated our efforts and speed in brand name manufacturing and marketing. . . . In our case it forced us to start OBM [original brand manufacturing]. Should Schwinn have chosen to work with us and did not go on to invest in CBC,

maybe today we would have slowed down our pace on OBM or probably you would not have heard of Giant. We would still be their OEM supplier" (Hsieh, "The East Asian Miracle Revisited," 240).

64. Ibid., 209.

65. Hsieh's interview with a top manager at Merida recounts the painful process that Merida went through to become a competent supplier to Bridgestone. The first bicycles that Merida produced for Bridgestone were rejected. "We were forced to take all the bicycles apart and reassemble them. That was a big loss for our company. Then, the company made the decision to send us, the chief executives, to Bridgestone's Japanese headquarters for a study tour to see their whole production process, how they run the production lines, and to get a sense of how developed Japan was at the time.... After our trip to Japan, Bridgestone sent their technicians to our company to supervise the production. They checked on every single production process. If there was a problem, the line stopped and production was gone over again. This has forced us to learn and develop" (Hsieh, "The East Asian Miracle Revisited," 201–02).

66. Ibid., 213.

67. Charles Fishman, "The Wal-Mart You Don't Know," *Fast Company*, no. 77 (2003).

68. Ibid.

69. Ibid.

70. Chu, "Causes of Growth," 63–64.

71. Ibid.

72. Chairman Lin complained to us about the one Japanese firm that controlled the technology for, and was the sole supplier of, chrome-moly tubing. Lin often had trouble getting the tubing when he needed it, and when he did, it was too expensive. Instead, he began experimenting with aluminum-alloy tubing, which was much less expensive, nearly as strong, and much easier to work with. This tubing was used exclusively in mass-market bicycles.

73. See Cheng and Sato, *Bicycle Industries in Taiwan and Japan*, for Sato's description of the failure of Japanese bicycle manufacturers to adopt TIG welding techniques (44–48).

74. This latter question was one asked by Hsieh, "The East Asian Miracle Revisited," 237.

75. Hsieh observes that "many interviewees express the view that the crucial factor that accounts for Taiwan's dominance in the field of [mountain bikes], and in sustaining the development of the bicycle industry, is its dominance in frame making" (ibid., 232).

76. Ibid., 236.

77. See the very interesting discussion of the relationship between Kunshan's local officials and Taiwanese businesspeople in Yang and Chen, "Farewell to the Developmental State?"

78. Dani Rodrik, "What's So Special About China's Exports?," *China & World Economy* 14, no. 5 (2006): 17.

79. Blonigen and Ma, "Please Pass the Catch-Up," 506.

80. Ibid.
81. Hsieh, "The East Asian Miracle Revisited," 253.
82. Ibid., 255.
83. Ibid.

CHAPTER 9

1. Huang Qian-min, "Introduction and Analysis of Investment Law of the People's Republic of China," *Taiwanese Businessmen*, no. 193 (2015), http://www.chinabiz.org.tw/News/GetJournalShow?pid=162&cat_id=174&gid=195&id=2866.

2. Yuqing Xing, "China's High-Tech Exports: The Myth and Reality," *Asian Economic Papers* 13, no. 1 (2014): 117.

3. Ibid., 114.

4. Brett Berger and Robert F. Martin, "The Chinese Export Boom: An Examination of the Detailed Trade Data," *China & World Economy* 21, no. 1 (2013): 71.

5. Ibid.

6. Xing, "China's High-Tech Exports," 116.

7. Xu Kai-Ling, "Report of Apple's Suppliers," *Business Next*, http://www.bnext.com.tw/article/view/id/26580.

8. Xing, "China's High-Tech Exports," 117.

9. For an earlier and more complete analysis of the profit distribution in electronic supply chains, see Jason Dedrick, Kenneth L. Kraemer, and Greg Linden, "Who Profits from Innovation in Global Value Chains: A Study of the iPod and Notebook PCs," *Industrial and Corporate Change* 19, no. 1 (2010): 81–116.

10. For a discussion of the concept of co-evolution as applied to contract manufacturers in Taiwan, see Timothy J. Sturgeon and Ji-Ren Lee, "Industry Co-Evolution: A Comparison of Taiwan and North American Electronics Contract Manufacturers," in *Global Taiwan: Building Competitive Strengths in a New International Economy*, ed. Suzanne Berger and Richard K. Lester, 33–75 (Armonk, N.Y.: M. E. Sharpe, 2005).

11. For an excellent study of the role of design in making products desirable to consumers, see Harvey Luskin Molotch, *Where Stuff Comes From: How Toasters, Toilets, Cars, Computers, and Many Others Things Come to Be as They Are* (New York: Routledge, 2003).

12. These factories have now been closed, and new garment factories started in Cambodia and Vietnam.

13. This description is taken from the Li & Fung website, http://www.lifung.com/.

14. Joan Magretta, "Fast, Global, and Entrepreneurial: Supply Chain Management, Hong Kong Style," An Interview with Victor Fung, *Harvard Business Review* 76, no. 5 (1998): 106.

15. Ibid.

16. Ibid.

17. For an excellent analysis of PC retailers, see Dedrick and Kraemer, "Market Making in the Personal Computer Industry."

18. "Compaq and IBM Winners in 1996 Market Share," *PC World*, January 27, 1997, https://en.wikipedia.org/wiki/Market_share_of_personal_computer_vendors.

19. For a cogent argument about the link between the very rapid expansion of memory capabilities (in accord with Moore's law) and the equally rapid product cycles for high-tech products, see An-chi Tung and Henry Wan, "Chinese Electronics Export: Taiwanese Contract Manufacturing—the Win-Win Outcome Along the Evolving Global Value Chain," *World Economy* 36, no. 7 (2013): 827–42.

20. Dedrick and Kraemer, "Market Making in the Personal Computer Industry," 295.

21. See Wikipedia, "List of Laptop Brands and Manufacturers," https://en.wikipedia.org/wiki/List_of_laptop_brands_and_manufacturers#cite_ref-4.

22. Gartner, "Gartner Says Worldwide PC Shipments Declined 8.3 Percent in Fourth Quarter of 2015," Press release, http://www.gartner.com/newsroom/id/3185224.

23. For one of the best studies of Taiwanese PC clusters in China, see Chun Yang, "Strategic Coupling of Regional Development in Global Production Networks: Redistribution of Taiwanese Personal Computer Investment from the Pearl River Delta to the Yangtze River Delta, China," *Regional Studies* 43, no. 3 (2009): 385–407.

24. Many of the assemblers and parts suppliers that had first moved to the Dongguan region kept their factories in Dongguan, but opened a second factory in the Yangtze River Delta as well.

25. Yang, "Strategic Coupling of Regional Development in Global Production Networks," 401.

26. AnnaLee Saxenian also interviewed Joe Hsieh, at least ten years before we did. Information from this interview can be found in Saxenian, *The New Argonauts*, 181–82.

27. Ibid., 160.

28. Ibid., 181.

29. In 2008, Unihan Company became a wholly owned subsidiary of Pegatron.

30. Nokia introduced what is recognized as the first smartphone in 2006, but it was Apple's iPhone that changed the industry.

31. The market share among smartphone brands is determined not only by consumers but also by the wireless transmission carriers. These carriers provide plans giving access to certain smartphone merchandisers and not others. The US has five large carriers (Verizon, T-Mobile, AT&T, Sprint, and US Cellular); China has three (China Mobile, China Unicom, and China Telecom). The governments of both the US and China license and regulate the carriers; carriers, however, decide which phones to stock, at least in principle.

32. HTC is also a contract manufacturer and has had many top brand-name customers, including Apple and Google.

33. Samsung was forced to recall the entire production run of Galaxy Note 7 smartphones because, in some instances, the lithium ion battery inside the phone burst into flame.

34. Shuhei Yamada and Kentaro Ogura, "The Taiwan-Centric Way of Making Smartphones," *Nikkei Asian Review*, August 7, 2014.

35. For an excellent description of Hon Hai/Foxconn's new factory in Zhengzhou,

see David Barboza, "China's 'iPhone City,' Built on Billions in Perks," *New York Times*, December 29, 2016, A1, B6–7.

36. Yamada and Ogura, "The Taiwan-Centric Way of Making Smartphones."

37. For the most recent attempt to theorize about global supply chains, see Coe and Yeung, *Global Production Networks*.

38. For a discussion of the fast follower phenomenon, see Jenn-Hwan Wang, *The Limits of Fast Followers: Taiwan's Economic Transition and Innovation* (Taipei: Jyu-liu Books, 2010), in Chinese.

39. Jessica Hartogs, "World's 'Cheapest' Smartphone Released in India," CNBC, February 17, 2016, http://www.cnbc.com/2016/02/17/worlds-cheapest-smartphone-released-in-india.html.

40. For a detailed and provocative discussion of the fragility of the Chinese economy, see the excellent discussion in Hung, *The China Boom: Why China Will Not Rule the World*.

CHAPTER 10

1. Patience Chen once worked in the footwear business, until those firms moved to China. She would not leave her children, and so she did not move to China with the firm. Like many of her contemporaries, she had to start all over again. Poised and speaking English well, she now makes the case for Frank Lai's companies to his buyers.

2. To see the array of metal parts that Lai's companies make, see the company's website at http://www.maochuan.com.tw/index.php.

3. Hiwin is ranked first in Taiwan in the machine tool industry, and second in the world for "linear motion control technology" as applied to robotics.

4. "Asia's Power Businesswomen 2015," http://www.hiwin.tw/user_hotnews.aspx?newsID=3688.

5. See Taichung Industrial Park Service Center, https://www.moeaidb.gov.tw/iphw/taichung/index.do?id=133.

6. See Central Taiwan Science Park, http://www.ctsp.gov.tw/chinese/01news/10statistics_view.aspx?v=1&fr=529&no=538&sn=1850.

7. Nilay Patel, "Vizio Reboots the PC: A Quiet American Success Story Takes on Sleeping Giants," *The Verge*, June 15 2012.

8. Willy Shih, Jyun-Cheng Wang, and Karen E. Robinson, "Amtran Technology Ltd.," Harvard Business School Case 613-069 (Revised March 2015).

9. See Hsinchu Science Park, http://www.sipa.gov.tw/english/index.jsp.

10. Wikipedia, "2014 Kunshan Explosion," https://en.wikipedia.org/wiki/2014_Kunshan_explosion.

11. "TSMC and Nanjing Sign 12-inch Fab Investment Agreement," March 28, 2016, http://www.tsmc.com/tsmcdotcom/PRListingNewsArchivesAction.do?language=E.

12. These riots came about as a protest over China's incursion into the South China Sea, where China's military has built runways and buildings on several artificially created islands.

13. Gary Sands, "The Company Behind Vietnam's Largest Environmental Disaster,"

Foreign Policy Association, July 14, 2016, http://foreignpolicyblogs.com/2016/07/14/company-vietnam-environmental-disaster/.

EPILOGUE

1. Robert J. Gordon, *The Rise and Fall of American Growth: The U.S. Standard of Living Since the Civil War* (Princeton, N.J.: Princeton University Press, 2016).

2. Paul Krugman, "The Powers That Were," *New York Times Book Review*, January 31, 2016.

3. "The sales of Samsung, the largest chaebol, [were] 21.9% of GDP, followed by Hyundai Motor (12.6%), SK (11.7%), LG (9%), GS (5.4%), Hyundai Heavy Industries (5%), Lotte (4.5%), Hanwha (2.8%), Hanjin (1.9%) and Doosan (1.7%)," (Wang Hwi Lee, "Is Good Governance Really Good for Company? Corporate Governance Reform of the Korean Chaebol after the Asian Financial Crisis," Paper presented in the Korea studies colloquia series at the Center for Korean Studies, Jackson School of International Studies, University of Washington, 2013, 23–24). We want to acknowledge Professor Yong-Chool Ha for bringing this paper to our attention.

4. Carl Crow, *Four Hundred Million Customers* (New York: Armed Services Editions, 1944), 271.

5. For an excellent discussion of the effects of China's one-child policy on China's economy, see Karen Eggleston et al., "Will Demographic Change Slow China's Rise?," *Journal of Asian Studies* 72, no. 3 (2013): 505–18.

6. Fernand Braudel, *The Perspective of the World* (New York: Harper & Row, 1984), 623.

INDEX

Accell, 203
Acer, 165–66, 222, 223–24, 238
Adidas, 78, 80, 185, 196
Admiral, 154–55, 157–59
Africa, 246
Agriculture, 25–26, 29, 33–34, 111
A-I, 114
"Ai-biahnh Jah-eh Eah" (song), 132, 266n1
Alcoa, 236
Aldi, 136, 152, 185
Alibaba, 235, 251
Alpert, Irving, 52
Amazon, 235, 251
Amsden, Alice, 122
AmTRAN Technology, 239
Android, 226
Animal feed, 72–74
Anne Klein, 46
Antidumping laws, 244
Apparel industry, 219–20
Apple, 2, 41, 47, 50, 122, 124, 129, 159, 161, 165, 185, 216, 222, 224–31, 238, 257n12
Apple II clones, 163–67, 272n41
Apple iPad, 226
Apple iPhone, 216, 225–28, 283n30
Apple iPod, 225
Application-specific integrated circuits (ASICs), 173, 179
A-PRO, 148, 204–5, 207–8, 210
Armani, 193
Arthur, W. Brian, 56
Asia Cement Corporation, 109
Asian capitalism: dynamic character of, 15; explanations of, 13–16; US economic influence on, 41–57. *See also* New Asian Economy
Asian financial crisis, 180–83
Asian Infrastructure Investment Bank, 214
Asian miracle, 57
ASICs. *See* Application-specific integrated circuits
Asics, 193
Asics Tiger, 79
Associated Electrics, 6
Associated Merchandising Corporation, 65
Associations, of Taiwanese businesspeople in China, 190–91, 279n35
Asus, 222, 223–25, 238, 248
Athletic shoes, 78–80
AU Optronics, 238, 239
Austin, Bill, 201
Authentic Brand Group, 186, 277n24
Authorized dealers, 154, 198, 270n7

Baker, James A., III, 138–39
Bandi (boss's personal staff), 92–94
Bangladesh, 246
Bao Chaoyun, 91
Barnes and Noble, 46
Baseballs, 70–71
Basic input-output system (BIOS), 161–62
Bass, 193
Batch production, 203–5
Bear Stearns, 212
Becker, Howard, 17
Bed, Bath, and Beyond, 46
Beijing Consensus, 187
Benetton, 46

Best Buy, 45, 136, 158, 239
Bicycles, 74–76, 197–208, 243, 280n54
Big buyers: Americans as, 65–68; anonymity required by, 228; defined, 3; impact of, 57, 115–16, 189; Japanese trading companies as, 61–65; as market makers, 42; price setting by, 117–18, 145; and supplier markets, 253n6; and US retail revolution, 41–42
Big Push, 170
BIOS. *See* Basic input-output system
Black and Decker, 8, 236
Blackberry, 227
Blonigen, Bruce, 209
Bloomingdale's, 43
Blue Ribbon Sports, 79
Borders, 46
Bosch, 236
Brand-name holding companies, 186, 193, 277n24, 277n25
Brand-name products, 46, 185–86, 197–98, 201
Braudel, Fernand, 252
Brexit, 251
Bridgestone, 199, 201–2, 281n65
Business failures, 15, 16
Business groups: domestic focus of, 101–2; export focus of, 102–6; integration patterns of, 102, 103; of Japan, 62–63, 102–6; of South Korea, 104–6
BYD Electronics, 229

Calculators, 163
Calvin Klein, 46
Camper, 193
Canon, 249
Capitalism: central tenet of, 16; economic development in relation to, 2, 213, 215, 231–32; national character of, 232, 245–46; nature of, x–xi, 210, 231; role of, in global economy transformation, 2–3. *See also* Asian capitalism; Demand-led capitalism
Carrefour, 136, 152, 184–85, 234
Casio, 64, 163
Category killers, 45, 136
CBS (manufacturer), 52

Cell phones, 179, 225
Central Taiwan Science Park, 27, 179
Chaebol, 104–6, 123, 128, 158, 169, 180, 249
Chain stores: computerization of, 50–51; discounters and specialty retailers, 45; logistics of, 47–50; standardization in, 51; and US retail revolution, 43
Chairman T, 9–12, 14, 68, 142
Chandler, Alfred, 154, 270n4
Chang, Leslie, 196
Chang, Morris, 173–79, 242–43
Chang Yung-fa, 40, 124
Chan Lu-min, 196
Chen, Patience, 236, 284n1
Chen, R. C., 219–20
Chen, Rick, 120, 210
Chen Chieh-Hsi, 120–21
Cheng-shu Kao, 262n3
Chen Hsian-chen, 60
Chiajang (family head), 89
Chiang Ching-kuo, 30, 36, 59, 133, 259n1
Chiang Kai-shek, 22, 28–30, 32, 36, 59, 106, 133
Chiayi, Taiwan, 71–73
China: business networks in, 85; business organization in, 97; consolidation of manufacturing in, 181–88, 215–21; eating practices in, 84–89; economy and economic policies of, 181–82, 187, 208–9, 213–14, 232, 250, 275n8, 276n11; exports of, 183–84, 187–89, 215–16; family firms in, 89–92; family in, 88; FDI in, 184, 186, 188, 275n10; government interference in, 241–42, 250; international recognition of, 58; Taiwanese contract manufacturers in, 3–4, 21, 26, 71, 73, 143–51, 183, 188–232, 240–43; Taiwan's relations with, 4, 30, 189, 206–7, 223
China Bicycle Company, 200–201
China Credit Information Service, 124
China External Trade Development Council, 67
China Model, 187
China Steel, 36, 37, 73
China Trust Group, 35
Chinglu, 78
Chou Jai-hua, 149

Chou Yinxi, 91
Christian Dior, 46
Chuan Nao, 162–63
Chung-Hua Arcade, 164
Chungkang Export Processing Zone, 27
Chung-shing business group, 37, 109
Chuo, Eric, 237–38
Cifra, 185
Circuit City, 45, 136, 158
CITC, 78
Civil rights movement (US), 44
Clark (company), 193
Clark, Jack, 52
Clean room design, 162
Coach, 46
Coase, Ronald, 262n1
Co-evolution, in global economy, 217
Cold War, 27–28
Cole Haan, 193
Columbia, 193
Columbia Pictures, 140
Commanding heights, 36–37, 256n25
Committee on Fiscal, Economic, and Financial Affairs, 36
Commodore, 161
Compal, 163, 222
Compaq, 161, 221
Computerization, 50–51, 134–36
Computer language protocols, 135
Computer malls, 164
Computers, 160–70, 221–25
Confucian culture, 13, 244
Consumer choice, 217–18
Consumer electronics: as capital intensive industry, 153–55, 170; contract manufacturing of, 46–47; discounting of, 158; export of, 157; reconsolidation of (2001–2015), 221–32; in US retail revolution, 45. *See also* Computers; High technology industries; Semiconductors; Smartphones; Televisions
Consumer Electronics Association, 154
Consumer Goods Pricing Act (US, 1975), 45
Consumer markets, 253n6
Containerized shipping, 48–50, 124–25, 258n16
Contract manufacturing: Big Five of, 52;

brand-name goods produced by, 46; of computers, 166–68; cost effectiveness of, 257n11; currency revaluation's effect on, 142; defined, 3; limitations of, 98; maintenance of Taiwan presence by, 190, 192, 205–6, 222, 239, 278n34; in new global economy, 217–21; origins of, 8–9, 22, 52; price setting effects on, 117–18, 145, 194; principles of, 81, 220; for private label products, 3, 8–9, 52; products of, 3; of semiconductors, 174–77; shoes vs. bicycles as products of, 197–98; specialization in, 55–56; Taiwanese-owned, in China, 3–4, 21, 26, 71, 73, 143–51, 183, 188–232, 240–43; Taiwanese-owned, in Vietnam, 243–46; Taiwanese prominence in, 2–4, 122–25, 129, 218, 253n7; of televisions, 160; types of trade involved in, 277n19. *See also* Original equipment manufacturing (OEM); Small and medium-sized firms
Core clusters (*xieli gongchang*), 94–95, 192–94, 203–8. *See also* Networks
Corning, 238, 239
Costco, 3, 46, 185, 234, 239
Crate and Barrel, 46
Crow, Carl, 250
Currency, 11, 21, 31, 127, 137, 139, 142
CVS, 45, 136

Daewoo, 104, 106, 170, 171, 180
Dajia le (everybody's happy) lottery, 142
Data General, 50, 169
Dayton Hudson, 65
DEC, 169
Dedrick, Jason, 169, 273n49
Dell (company), 164, 167, 221, 222
Dell, Michael, 167
Demand-led capitalism: China's economic growth sparked by, 187; concentration of global production resulting from, 184–88; consumer choice as basis of, 178–79, 217–18; defined, 2; feedback loop in, 252; online retail and, 235, 243, 251–52; shoes vs. bicycles as products in, 197–98; and US retail revolution, 41–42
Demand-led industrialization, 58–83;

American buyers and, 65–68; case studies in, 70–80; demand-responsive manufacturing, 80–83; dynamic character of, 69–70; imitation and innovation in, 68–69; Japanese trading companies and, 61–65; origins of, 61
Demand-responsive economies, 56–57, 60
Demise theory, 260n4
Democratic Progressive Party, 133
Deng Xiaoping, 148, 181, 208, 275n6
Denim cloth, 219–20
Dental drills, 7–8
Department stores, 43
Derivatives, 212
Design houses. *See* Fabless design houses
Destler, I. M., 152
Developmental state theory, 13, 31, 35, 36
Diesel, 192
Digital Equipment Corporation, 50
Direct sales business model, 167–68
Discount retailers, 45–46, 158, 257n10
Dorel Industries, 201
Downstream firms, 36, 110, 121
DRAM. *See* Dynamic random access memory
DTK, 163
Dynamic random access memory (DRAM), 169, 171, 173, 179

East Asia, map of, 126
Eating practices, 84–89
E-commerce, 235, 243, 251–52
Economic development, 2, 13, 15, 186, 188, 213, 215, 231–32
Economic nationalism, 251
Economic sociology, 262n1
Economic theory, 137, 261n1
Eddie Bauer, 46, 123
Education, 133, 157, 240
Eileen Fisher, 46
Eisenhower, Dwight, 44
Electronic Data Interchange (EDI), 135
Electronic gaming machines, 162–63
Electronics & Radio-TV Technical Monthly (magazine), 164
Electronics Research and Services Organization (ERSO), 172–73, 177

Employees. *See* Workers
Endaka (rising value of yen), 141
EPZs. *See* Export processing zones
Ericsson, 227, 231
ERSO. *See* Electronics Research and Services Organization
European Union, 251
Evergreen Group, 40, 124
Ever Trust (freighter), 40
Exchange rates, 137–39, 267n14, 268n18, 268n19, 268n21
Export orientation, 2
Export processing zones (EPZs), 32. *See also* Chungkang Export Processing Zone; Kaohsiung Export Processing Zone
Exports: agricultural, 111; Asian, 53–54; of China, 183–84, 187–89, 215–16; consumer electronics as, 157; incentives for, 255n7; of Japan, 64, 102–6; of KMT-governed Taiwan, 31–32, 34; product types of, 65–66; small and medium-sized firms engaged in, 101; of South Korea, 104–6; of Taiwan, 54–55, 65–66, 101, 111, 117, 145–46, 157, 259n3, 261n17

Fabless design houses, 174–77, 179, 228
Failures, business. *See* Business failures
Fair trade laws, 45
Family, 88, 132, 151
Family firms: bosses of, 89–93; core personnel of, 92–94; lineage of, 97; numbers of, 101; spirit of, 86–89; tensions in, 93
Far Eastern business group, 109
Far Eastern Department Store, 233, 234
Fashion, in consumer goods, 76, 153, 166, 196–99, 217, 221, 226, 234
Fast followers, 230
FDIs. *See* Foreign direct investments (FDIs)
Federal Trade Commission (FTC), 157
Federated Department Stores, 43, 65
Feenstra, Robert, 55
Feminist movement (US), 44
Fila, 192
Filene's, 43

Firm failure. *See* Business failures
Firm registration, 223
Flip-flops, 77
Footwear. *See* Shoes
Foreign direct investments (FDIs), 63–64, 184, 186, 188, 275n10, 276n17
Forever 21, 46, 185
Formosa Chemical and Fibers, 116
Formosa Plastics, 10, 35–36, 40, 108, 112, 116–17, 120–21, 124, 176, 245
Fortune Brands, 186, 277n24
Foundries (semiconductor factories), 174, 178–79
Foxconn, 148, 228–29
France, 138
Frankel, Jeffrey A., 267n14
Fuji, 249
Fujitsu, 156, 171
Fung, Victor, 220
Fung-Tai, 79

Gallin, Bernard and Rita, 115
Gaotie, 234
The Gap, 45, 185
Gateway, 164, 168, 221
General Electric, 153–55
General Instruments, 155, 157, 174
Germany, 138–39
Giant (bicycle company), 74, 197–201, 205, 207, 243, 280n63
Global commodity chains, 186
Global economy transformation: capitalism's role in, 2–3; concentration of production and, 184–88; consumer-driven nature of, 217–18; contract manufacturing and, 217–21; economic development affected by, 232; future of, 251; Great Recession and, 210–11, 212–13; national boundaries superseded by, 248; New Asian Economy and, 152–53; origins of, 1–2, 60, 139–40, 152; persistence of, 12–13; price competition in, 240–41; supply chains in, 216–17; Taiwan's role in, 22; Washington Consensus and, 268n22
Global production networks, 186
Global value chains, 186
Gold rush effect, 113–14

Google, 226
Gordon, Robert, 247
Government role: in computer industry, 169–72; in economic growth, 14; in economic policy, 30–34; Mainlanders' impact on, 107–8; state-owned and -subsidized businesses, 35–37, 106–12
Granovetter, Mark, 262n1
Grant, W. T., 53
Great Recession (2007), 144, 183, 210, 212–13, 248
Groupe Bull, 166
G7, 139
Gu (Koo) family, 35, 109
Guangdong. *See* Pearl River Delta, China
Guanxi (relationships), 14, 85
Gucci, 46
Guess, 46
Gulf of Tonkin incident, 27–28

Hamilton, Gary G., 262n3
H&M, 185
Harmonized Tariff Schedule, 55
Harrell, Stevan, 114–15
Hatch, Walter, 141
Hemei, Taiwan, 37–40, 120, 146, 235–36
Henning, C. Randall, 152
Heshen Textile Company, 38
Hewlett-Packard (HP), 124, 222
High technology industries, 153–79; in China, 215–16, 230; computers, 160–70; semiconductors, 170–78; televisions, 154–60
Highway system (US), 44, 47–48
Hillshire Brands, 186
Hitachi, 32, 64, 103, 155, 156, 171
Hiwin, 237–38, 284n3
Home Depot, 3, 46, 136
Honda, 141, 249
Honeywell, 169
Hong Kong, 52–54, 97–98, 124, 144, 147–48, 180
Hon Hai. *See* Foxconn
Horizontal integration, 103
Household appliances, 154
Hsieh, Joe, 223–25, 248–49
Hsieh Tsai-yun, 5–6, 9

Hsinchu Science Park, 173, 176–77, 239
Hsinfu, 72–73
Hsiyouchi (*The Journey to the West*), 146
Hsueh Jenhwa, 149–50
HTC, 226, 227, 283n32
Huawei, 227, 229, 230, 231
Huffy, 202
Hugo Boss, 46, 193
Huiguan (regional associations), 97
Hu Tai-li, 114
Hwagang, 78, 80
Hyundai, 4, 104, 106, 122, 170, 171

IBM, 50–51, 155, 159–62, 167–69, 171, 222, 273n43
IBM clones, 161–65, 273n43
I. Magnin, 43
Imitation, 68–69, 164
Import substitution, 110–11
Income inequalities, 234–35, 240, 252
Increasing returns, 56
India, 246
Indonesia, 180, 244
Industrialization. *See* Demand-led industrialization; Taiwan's economy: industrialization in
Industrial Technology Research Institute (ITRI), 160, 171–75
Innovation, 68–69, 229, 237
Integrated circuits, 172. *See also* Application-specific integrated circuits
Integration: of business groups, 102, 103; demand-responsive, 115–22; horizontal, 103; vertical, 76, 98–99, 102, 103, 105, 116, 195–96, 225, 227
Intel, 161–63, 167, 175–76, 179, 226
Intellectual property rights, 230
Intermediate demand, 57, 253n6
International Monetary Fund, 180
Inventec, 222, 228–29
Inventory tracking, 134
Islam, 244
ITRI. *See* Industrial Technology Research Institute
I wo feng ("swarm of bees" model of competition), 113

Jacks, 71–73, 86

Japan: business groups of, 62–63, 102–6, 273n49; colonialism of, in Taiwan, 33, 255n14; competitive advantage of, 128; and computer manufacturing, 168–69, 222; consumer electronics produced by, 158, 271n10; consumer goods produced by, 49; contract manufacturing by, 22; economic boom and bust in, 21, 122, 143, 268n25; economic future of, 249–50; exports of, 53–54, 102–6; foreign investments by, 140–41; investment by, in Taiwan, 63–64; labor costs in, 63; and Plaza Accord, 138–41; and price setting, 123; production methods learned from, 22, 39, 69, 70, 75, 78, 83, 94, 199, 201, 281n65; semiconductor manufacturing in, 175; and Taiwanese textiles, 38–39; Taiwan's relations with, 33, 260n8; trading companies of, 52–53, 61, 260n4, 260n7
J. C. Penney, 10, 43, 52, 65, 155
Jeng Jong Guo, 177
Jobs, Steve, 50
Johnson, Lyndon, 27–28, 49
Jungxing Textile Group, 91
Jun-ye, 74, 76
Just-in-time delivery, 83, 134–35
JVC, 159

Kai Hsiang, 71–73
Kaohsiung Export Processing Zone, 70, 113, 155–57, 162
Kaohsiung Port, 26, 125
Katz, Hy, 52
Keiretsu (business groups), 63, 102–5, 123, 140–41, 168–71
Kennedy, John F., 30
Kenneth Cole, 193
Kering, 186, 277n25
Kia, 180
Kihachiro Onitsuka, 79
Kinmen Island, 28
Kinpo Electronics, 163
Kmart, 10, 45–46, 51, 54, 65, 68, 77, 123, 134, 136, 158, 252
KMC Chain Industrial Company, 205–6
KMT. *See* Kuomintang
Knight, Philip, 79

Kohl's, 45
Korea, 28. *See also* South Korea
Korea Fair Trade Commission, 123
Kraemer, Kenneth, 169, 273n49
Kresge, 54
Kroger, 43
Krugman, Paul, 247, 268n18, 268n19
Kuang-Hua Public Market, 164
Kudoka (hollowing out of domestic economy), 141
Kunshan, China, 207–8, 222–23
Kunshan Gangyi Precision Technology Company, 222–23
Kuomintang (KMT), 22, 28–32, 38, 106–7, 144, 147, 162, 255n14

Labor. *See* Workers
Labor Standards Act, 133
Lai, Frank, 236
Lai, Tony, 192
Lai Chuan-lin, 5–9, 14, 68, 149, 190, 237
Lam, Barry (Lin Baili), 163
Language, 62, 147–48
Laoban (boss), 86, 89–93, 101, 146, 150–51
Laobanniang (boss's wife), 90–91, 150–51
Large business groups: in 1960s, 36; in service and capital intensive sectors, 116, 123; small firms in relation to, 112–13, 116, 121, 237
Laura Ashley, 46
Lean retailing, 134–36, 197
Lee Chi Enterprises, 207, 210
Lee Teng-hui, 133
Lehman Brothers, 212
Lenovo, 222
Leung, C. C., 163
Lever-Tracy, Constance, 260n7
Levinson, Marc, 50
LG. *See* Lucky-Goldstar
Li, K. T. *See* Li Kuo-ting
Li & Fung, 124, 220
Li Ka-shing, 90
Li Kuo-ting (K. T. Li), 32, 111, 171–72, 174, 249
Lin Kuo-ying, 111
The Limited, 45, 65, 123, 267n13
Limited liability companies, 97

Lin Chun-shan, 74–76, 148, 204–5, 207–8, 210
Lin, Jerry, 222–23
Ling Suen-yi, 72
Ling Wen-chuen, 71–73, 142–43
Liu Ts'o, Taiwan, 114
Liz Clairborne, 46, 193
Lo, Tony, 201
Local trading companies, 66–68
Logistics, 47–50, 134–35
Longhua, China, 205–7
Lowes, 46
Lucky-Goldstar (LG), 4, 104, 106, 158, 170, 171, 226, 227–28, 238, 239
Lukang, Taiwan, 144, 146
LVMH, 186, 277n25

Ma, Alyson, 209
Macy's, 43, 252
Magnavox, 154, 157–58
Mainframe computers, 160–61
Making money: agriculture-to-industry transition motivated by, 40; for the buyer, 81–82; as chief motivation of Taiwanese businesspeople, 16–17; as chief principle of contract manufacturing, 81–82; sociology of, 17–19; for yourself, 82
Malaysia, 144
Mandarin, 147
Mao Chuan Industrial Company, 236
Mao Zedong, 58
Mariners (baseball team), 140
Mariotti, John, 202
Market makers, 42
Marlene, 52
Mast Industries, 65
Matsushita, 103, 156, 158, 171, 175
Matsushita (Panasonic), 64, 155, 159
Mattel, 46
McLean, Malcom, 48–50
MediaTek, 228–29
Merida, 197–99, 201–2, 204–6, 210, 243, 281n65
Metro, 136, 152, 185
Microcomputers, 161
Microsoft, 161–62, 167

Middle class, 43–45, 235
Midstream firms, 119–21
Minicomputers, 161
Ministry of Economic Affairs, 171
Mitsubishi, 64, 78, 103
Mitsui, 49–50, 52, 103
Mizuno, 78
Modularization, 19, 80–82, 235. *See also* Standardization
Monopsony, 118
Montgomery Ward, 45, 155, 257n7
Montrail, 193
Motorola, 154–55, 158, 171, 227, 231
Multitech, 165

Nanxun (southern inspection tour, in China), 181, 208, 275n6
Nan Ya Plastics, 36, 77, 116, 120–21
National Broadcasting Company (NBC), 153
National Interstate and Defense Highways Act (US, 1956), 44
Nationalism, 251
Networks: case example of, 86–89; Chinese business networks as archetypal, 85; concept of, 85, 261n1; cooperative ethos of, 95, 142–43; in economic theory, 261n1; of family firms, 94–96; flexibility of, 76, 82, 87, 119, 203; impermanent nature of, 96; Japanese business groups as, 103–4; in lean retailing, 135; modeled on networks in everyday life, 84–89; participating in, 82; shared knowledge in, 69, 72–73. *See also* Core clusters
Network theory, 262n1
New Asian Economy: bursting of bubble in, 143–46; China as site for businesses in, 146–51; future of, 248–52; geographic moves in, 128; global nature of, 152–53; money and profits in, 140–43; Plaza Accord's role in, 127, 136–40, 151–52
New Balance, 80, 193
Newell Brands, 186, 277n24
New institutionalism, 262n1
Nichols, J. C., 53
Nien Hsing Textiles, 219–20, 235
Nike, 2, 27, 41, 46, 54–55, 79–80, 140, 185, 193, 194, 196, 261n25

Nikon, 249
9/11 terrorist attacks (New York City), 207, 248
19-point Economic and Financial Reform (1959), 31
Nine West, 140, 193
Nine West Holdings, 186, 193, 277n24
Nintendo, 162
Nippon Electric, 171
Nissan, 103, 110, 249
Nixon, Richard, 58
Nokia, 227, 231, 283n30
Nominal exchange rates, 137–38, 268n18, 268n19
North Face, 193
Notebook computers, 221–22
NTT DoCoMo, 225
Nvidia, 226

O Cheng-ming, 164
OEM. *See* Original equipment manufacturing
Office Depot, 46
Office of Technology Assessment (US), 160
Oligopsony, 118
One dragon (*yitiao long*), 195
One-setism, 104, 170, 227
Oppo, 227, 229, 230
Orderly Market Agreement, 158
Ordinary trade, 184, 188, 277n19
Original brand manufacturing (OBM), 280n63
Original design manufacturing (ODM), 81
Original equipment manufacturing (OEM), 8–9, 68–69, 81, 145, 174–76, 224. *See also* Contract manufacturing
Outdoor furniture, 9–12
Outsourcing, 161

Pacific Cycles, 201
Palm, 227
Pan-Asian economy. *See* New Asian Economy
Panasonic, 199
Park Chung Hee, 31, 105, 170
PCs. *See* Personal computers
Pearl River Delta, China, 147–48

INDEX   295

Pebble Beach golf course, 140
Pegatron, 225, 228
Personal computers (PCs), 159, 161–70, 221–22
Peugeot, 236
Philco, 154–55, 158
Philippines, 180
Philips, 32, 64, 155–58, 176
Pierre Cardin, 46
Plaza Accord, 11, 14, 21, 61, 127, 136–41, 147, 151–52, 177, 182, 251
Point-of-sales (POS) inventory systems, 51, 134–35
Polo, 193
Pottery Barn, 46
Pou Chen (Yue Yuen), 27, 76–80, 144, 194–96, 261n25, 280n51
Powell, Walter, 262n2
Prada, 193
Price maintenance laws, 45, 157
Price setting, 117–18, 123, 145, 194, 240–41
Private label products, 3, 8–9, 52, 155, 185
Processing trade, 184, 188, 277n19
Production networks. *See* Networks
Product liability, 210
Prototypes, 68–69, 192
Pukou Economic Development Zone, 242
Puma, 192

Qualcomm, 228–29
Quanta, 163–64, 222

Radio Shack, 161
Raleigh, 201–3, 205
Ralph Lauren, 46
R&D. *See* Research and development (R&D)
RCA (Radio Corporation of America), 32, 153–55, 157, 172, 250, 270n6, 271n12
Reagan, Ronald, 127, 138–39, 251
Real exchange rates, 137, 139
Reciprocity (*huxiang*), 95
Red line (all-Chinese supply chain), 230, 242
Reebok, 78, 80, 140, 185, 196
Regal Accessories, 52
Relationships, business, 2, 18, 152, 166, 176, 194, 207, 220, 224, 241. *See also* Round-table etiquette; Trust
Rembrandt Group. *See* Richemont Group
Remote-controlled vehicles, 5–9
Republic Cellini, 52
Research and development (R&D), 10, 80, 123, 164, 190, 192, 205, 222, 231
Retail entrepreneurs, 43–47
Retail revolution: chain store logistics in, 47–51; defined, 257n3; diversity of intermediate demand in, 54–56; feedback loop in, 43–47; global factors in, 52–54; origins of, 42–43; second phase of (1985–2007), 134–36; third phase of (2007 to present), 235; US phase of (post–WWII), 41–57, 111
Reverse engineering, 68, 162
Ricardo, David, 267n14
Richemont Group (Rembrandt Group), 186, 278n25
Ricoh, 64
Rite Aid, 45, 136
Robotics, 237–38
Rockefeller Center, New York City, 140
Rockport, 140, 193
Rodrik, Dani, 209
Round-table etiquette, 87–88, 95–97, 191, 192, 203, 210, 218, 263n10
Rural areas, small-firm growth rooted in, 113–15

Safeway, 43
Sakura, 70–71
Sampo, 158, 159
Sam's Club, 46, 239
Samsung, 4, 104, 106, 122, 129, 158, 170, 171, 185, 215, 226, 227, 229, 230, 249
Samsung Galaxy, 226
Samsung Galaxy Note 7, 227, 230, 249, 283n33
Santron, 163
San Wu, 119–21, 210
Sanyo, 32, 64, 155, 156
Satellite assembly systems, 94, 128, 151
Saxenian, AnnaLee, 168, 172–73
Schwinn (company), 46, 123, 198–201, 205, 250

Schwinn, Ed, 201
Science parks. *See* Central Taiwan Science Park; Hsinchu Science Park; Taichung Science Park
Seagate Technology, 124
Sea-Land, 48–50
Sears, 43, 45, 52, 65, 77, 154, 158, 199, 252, 257n7
Semiconductors, 170–78
Shanghai, China, 148–49
Sharp, 155, 228–29
Shih, Stanley, 165
Shimano, 75, 199, 280n58
Shoes, 76–80, 144–46, 191–98, 243–46
Shopping centers, 2, 43
Silicon Integrated Systems, 177
Silicon Valley, 168, 176
Silvertone, 154
Singapore, 124
Skechers, 193
SKUs. *See* Stock keeping units
Small and medium-sized firms: anonymity of, 122–23; competition for large firms provided by, 112–13; demand-responsive integration of, 115–22; growth of, 60, 100–101, 112–15; large firms in relation to, 112–13, 116, 121, 237; prevalence of, 236–37; product types of, 115–16; in semiconductor industry, 177; state-supported firms in relation to, 111; success of, 98–99. *See also* Contract manufacturing; Family firms
Smartphones, 170, 225–31, 242, 283n30, 283n31. *See also* Cell phones
Sneakers, 78
Social movement (US), 44
Sogoshosha (general trading companies), 63
Sony, 47, 103, 122, 155, 158, 159, 224, 271n11
Sony Walkman, 159, 230
Southeast Asia, Taiwanese investment in, 144
South Korea: army of, 255n8; and Asian financial crisis, 180; business groups of, 104–6; competitive advantage of, 128; and computer manufacturing, 168–69; consumer electronics industry in, 170–71; economic boom in, 21, 122; economic future of, 249; exports of, 4, 31, 54–55, 104–6, 255n8; industrial growth pattern in, 100, 105; Japanese trading companies and, 62; Plaza Accord's impact on, 139; and price setting, 123; shoe manufacturing in, 79; television manufacturing by, 158
Spartan Mayro, 52
Specialization, 55–56, 204
Specialized (company), 201
SsangYong, 180
Standardization, 48, 51, 82, 166–68. *See also* Modularization
Stanley, 236
Staples, 46
State-owned and -subsidized firms, 35–37, 106–12
Statute for Encouragement of Investment (1960), 31
Stock keeping units (SKUs), 51
Student movement (US), 44
Subaru, 249
Subcontractors, 87, 94–95, 142–43
Suitcase companies, 67
Suitcase manufacturing, 72–73
Sunkyong, 104
Sun Yat-sen, 107
Sun Yun-suan, 171
Supermarket chains, 51
Supplier markets, 253n6
Supply chain management, 135
Supply chains, 135, 186
Suzhou, China, 222, 224
Swatch Group, 186, 277n25
Sylvania, 154, 174
Sylvania-Philco, 157
Syngman Rhee, 105

Tablet computers, 226
Ta Chia, Taiwan, 74–75, 145
Tah Hsin Plastics, 25–26
Taichung, Taiwan, 25–27, 59, 131, 233–35
Taichung Industrial Park, 26, 237
Taichung Precision Machinery Park, 27, 237
Taichung Science Park, 238, 239

INDEX   297

Tainan business group, 37
Taipei World Trade Center, 67
Taiwan: China's relations with, 4, 30, 189, 206–7, 223; competitive advantage of, 128; currency in, 11, 21, 31, 127, 137, 139, 142, 268n21; current manufacturing in, 235–40; exports of, 31–32, 34, 54–55, 65–66, 101, 111, 117, 145–46, 157, 259n3, 261n17; features of, 4; foreign investments by, 144, 269n36; Japan's relations with, 33, 260n8; KMT in, 28–32, 38, 106–7, 147, 162, 255n14; Mainlanders' impact on, 107–8; maintenance of presence in, by firms manufacturing chiefly in China, 190, 192, 205–6, 222, 239, 278n34; map of, 20; martial law in, 31, 106–7, 143; post-KMT government of, 133; transformations in (1965–85), 132–34; travel restrictions lifted in, 143, 147; US relations with, 30, 58–59. *See also* Taiwan's economy
Taiwan Cement Corporation, 35, 108–9
Taiwanese businesspeople: associations of, 190–91, 279n35; capitalism as core commitment of, 16–17; case examples of, 5–12; Chinese future of, 230; common elements in stories of, 12; in contract manufacturing, 2–4; educational backgrounds of, 8, 10, 68, 74; maintenance of Taiwan presence by, 190, 192, 205–6, 222, 239, 278n34; risks for, in moving production to China, 189–91, 206–7; self-reliance of, 169; sources of capital of, 66, 71, 75, 77; sources of knowledge of, 68–69; sources of orders for, 66–69. *See also* Taiwan's economy
Taiwan Fu Da Precision Company, 236
Taiwan's economy: agricultural basis of, 25–26, 29, 33–34, 111; anonymity of, 122–23; boom and bust in, 11, 142–43, 207; demand-responsive character of, 56, 60, 80–83, 98; economic way of life in, 19, 84–99; government policies on, 30–34; growth of, 59–60, 142; industrialization in, 37–40, 58–83, 100–101, 108, 124; Japanese trading companies and, 61–65; pre-1965, 21–22, 25–40; state-owned and -subsidized businesses in, 35–37; US retail revolution's impact on, 41–57, 111; watershed in (1965), 27–31. *See also* Taiwanese businesspeople
Taiwan Semiconductor Manufacturing Company (TSMC), 173, 175–79, 222, 228–29, 238, 242–43
Taiyuan business group, 37
Target, 2, 3, 45–46, 65, 136, 185
Tariff Schedule of the United States Annotated (TSUSA), 55, 117
Tatung, 62, 102, 109, 112, 158, 159, 162
Taxes: on business property, 1–2, 42–43; exemptions for foreign firms, 157; vertical integration discouraged by, 76
Ta Yang, 70–71
Tayao, 39
Televisions, 154–60, 162
Ten Great Construction Projects, 36, 40, 59, 259n1
Tennis shoes, 78
Tesco, 136, 152, 185
Texas Instruments, 155, 157, 171, 174
Textile manufacturing, 37–39, 120, 235–36
Thailand, 180
Three Principles of the People, 107
Thunder Tiger, 5–9, 26, 68, 149, 190, 237
Tiananmen Square massacre (1989), 145, 147, 181
Tiansha wu bu san de yanxi (In this world, there are no unending banquets), 96
TIG welding. *See* Tungsten insert gas (TIG) welding
Timberland, 140, 145, 193
Tinkerers, 164
Titles, business, 90
TJX, 45
Tongxin xieli (working together with the same spirit), 94
Top Star Shoe Company, 192
Toshiba, 62, 103, 109, 154, 155, 168–71, 171, 222
Toyota, 103, 122, 141, 249
Toys "R" Us, 257n9
Trade balance, 138–40, 152, 267n14
Trader Joe's, 185
Trading companies. *See* Japan: trading companies of; Local trading companies
Trek, 201

Truck transportation, 47–48, 134–35
Trump, Donald, 251
Trust, 92, 192, 194, 207, 210, 224, 241, 244, 250, 262n1
TRW, 155
Tsai (Patty) Pei-chun, 196
Tsai, Enid, 237–38
Tsai Chi-jui, 77–79, 144–45, 194–97
Tsai Nai-fung (David Tsai), 196
TSMC. *See* Taiwan Semiconductor Manufacturing Company
TSUSA. *See* Tariff Schedule of the United States Annotated
TT Bio, 8, 237
Tunghai University, 25
Tungsten insert gas (TIG) welding, 200, 204–5
Twenty-foot equivalent unit (TEU), 48, 258n16
Two-part pricing, 123

UMC. *See* United Microelectronics Company
Under Armour, 193
Unihan, 225
United Board for Christian Higher Education, 25
United Kingdom, 138
United Microelectronics Company (UMC), 173, 179, 222, 228–29
United Nations, 4, 28, 58, 105, 133
United States: big buyers from, 65–68; consumer electronics in, 154–60; decline of manufacturing in, 1–2; economy of, 122–23, 207, 212, 247; FDI in, 276n17; imports of, 47, 158; investment by, in Taiwan, 63–64; Plaza Accord's impact on, 137–40; retail competition in, 158; retail revolution in, 41–57, 111, 257n3; Taiwan's relations with, 30, 58–59; trade deficit of, 138–40, 152
United States Agency for International Development (USAID), 35
Universal Microelectronic, 164
Universal product codes (UPCs), 51, 134, 258n24, 258n25
Upstream firms, 36, 108–10, 112–13, 116, 119, 121

US Congress, 1–2, 42, 45, 160
US Department of Justice, 161
US Federal Reserve Board, 138
US Supreme Court, 199
US Treasury Department, 139–40, 158

Vendors, 135
Vertical integration, 76, 98–99, 102, 103, 105, 116, 195–96, 225, 227
VF Corporation, 193
Victoria's Secret, 46
Videocassette recorders (VCRs), 159
Video game parlors, 162
Vietnam, 27–28, 33, 243–46
Vietnam War, 44, 48–49, 58, 111
Viven Wu Yen, 110
Vizio, 238–39
Vogel, Ezra, 122
Volkswagen, 236
Voluntary Interindustry Commerce Standards (VICS), 135

Wade, Robert, 255n7
Wages, 157, 195, 224–25
Walgreens, 136
Walmart, 2, 3, 10, 45–46, 51, 54, 68, 77–78, 123, 134, 136, 152, 158, 184, 193, 202, 207, 221, 258n16
Wang, Cher, 226
Wang, William, 238–39
Wang Laboratories, 169
Wang Yung-ching, 35–36, 40, 91, 108–9, 112, 121, 124, 175, 176, 226
Washington Consensus, 268n22
Washington Mutual Saving and Loan, 212
Wayman, Jack, 154
Weber, Max, ix, 16
Weixing gongchang. See Satellite assembly systems
Weiya banquet, 86–89
Western Electric, 171
Westinghouse, 153–54
Westinghouse Electric, 109
Williamson, John, 268n22
Williamson, Oliver, 262n1
Williams Sonoma, 46
Willys Motor Company, 110

Winbond Electronics, 238
Windows, 167
Wintel, 167
Wireless transmission carriers, 283n31
Wistron, 222
Wives, second, 151
Women: and business relocation to China, 149–50; as workers in China, 195–96
Workers: Chinese, 182, 195–96, 206; Japanese, 175; Taiwanese, 157, 175; in Taiwanese-owned Chinese factories, 150; US, 155, 175
Working conditions, 196
World Trade Organization, 182
Wozniak, Steve, 50
Wu, Alpha, 239
Wu, Frank, 239
Wu Kuan-hsiung, 67

Xiaomi, 227, 229, 230
Xieli gongchang. See Core clusters
Xijing (going west), 146–47
Xi Jinping, 214
Xilinx, 177
Xingfu, 86–89, 88
Xin Xing, Taiwan, 115
Xu, Chenggang, 276n11

Yamamura, Kozo, 141
Yeh-Bao, 74–76, 208
Yeh Chi-tien, 266n1
Yen Tjing-ling, 110
Yitiao long (one dragon), 195
Yuanlin, Taiwan, 77
Yue Yuen. *See* Pou Chen
Yu Kuo-hua, 175
Yulon, 101–2, 109, 110, 112
Yves Saint Laurent, 46

Zaibatsu (business groups), 62–63, 102–3
Zaitech (speculation) boom, 140, 269n26
Zara, 185
Zenith, 153–55, 157

The authorized representative in the EU for product safety and compliance is:
Mare Nostrum Group
B.V Doelen 72
4831 GR Breda
The Netherlands

www.ingramcontent.com/pod-product-compliance
Lightning Source LLC
Chambersburg PA
CBHW030608230426
43661CB00053B/1888